Seymour Martin Lipset has just joined the Sociology Department of the University of California. Previously, he was an Associate Professor in the Graduate Department of Sociology of Columbia University, and Assistant Director of the Bureau of Applied Social Research. He is co-editor of *Class, Status and Power* published by the Free Press, and author of *Agrarian Socialism,* and three monographic essays: "The Political Process in Trade Unions," in Morroe Berger, *et al.,* eds.; *Freedom and Control in Modern Society;* "The Sources of the 'Radical Right' " in Dan Bell, ed., *The New American Right;* and (co-author) "The Psychology of Voting," in Gardner Lindzey, ed., *Handbook of Social Psychology.* Martin Trow teaches sociology at Bennington College, and is presently completing a study of political beliefs in a New England community. James S. Coleman, a Research Associate in the Bureau of Applied Social Research during this study, is with the Sociology Department of the University of Chicago, and one of the authors of *Mathematical Thinking in the Social Sciences* published by the Free Press. During 1955-1956, Lipset and Coleman have been Fellows of the Center for Advanced Study in the Behavioral Sciences at Stanford, California.

Union Democracy

A REPORT OF THE BUREAU OF APPLIED SOCIAL RESEARCH
COLUMBIA UNIVERSITY

Seymour Martin Lipset

COLUMBIA UNIVERSITY

Martin A. Trow

BENNINGTON COLLEGE

James S. Coleman

BUREAU OF APPLIED SOCIAL RESEARCH

Union Democracy

THE INTERNAL POLITICS OF THE INTERNATIONAL TYPOGRAPHICAL UNION

WITH A FOREWORD BY CLARK KERR

THE FREE PRESS, GLENCOE, ILLINOIS

To Elsie, Joy, and Lu

Foreword

CONCERN OVER THE DISTRIBUTION of power must be as ancient as the first social groupings of men. In recent times, however, this perennial concern was partially obscured by the overriding preoccupation with the distribution of the new wealth. The rapid growth of wealth certainly had something to do with this shift of emphasis, as did the controversy over the several socialist and neo-socialist views concerning the distribution of income. But a resurgence of interest in the more basic issue of the location of power has marked the past decade.

This interest has spread also from power relations between the state on the one hand and private associations and individuals on the other, to those between private associations and the individuals who belong to them—and particularly the trade unions and their members. Good reasons lie behind this change of emphasis. The private governments of the corporation and the trade union exercise increasing discipline over the employee and member, with more rules to regulate him and more strength to make these rules effective. While industrialization is not the invention of the twentieth century, it is assuredly its greatest innovation affecting the daily affairs of men; and as industrialization proceeds on its course, this issue of power distribution can only become more acute.

This is the problem on which Lipset, Trow and Coleman have focussed their attention. They discuss it not in terms of society at large, but rather in terms of a single trade union. Their study is certainly the classic work to date in the general area of the internal processes of a union and the definitive study, perhaps for all foreseeable time, of the particular union under scrutiny, the International Typographical Union. This union was chosen because it is an exception to Michels' famous "Iron Law of Oligarchy." One might almost say it is the one permanently deviant case among American unions, at the level of the national officers. The ITU is a rare, even unique, phenomenon—a union with a recognized and long-continued two-party system. Lipset and his colleagues analyze the origins of this system, the environmental forces which aided its development and support its continuation, and the operational components which comprise it. Facts there are, and very carefully marshalled too. But the essence of the book is the general hypotheses it sets forth about the conditions which favor the wide distribution of power in democratic institutions, and the connections it establishes between the internal political behavior of one trade union and the basic thoughts on power in society and in private associations—from Aristotle to Arendt.

This study raises many fundamental questions on which scholars will disagree, for the facts are as yet far from fully known, the definitions still open to question, and the value judgments and the prescriptions for action hotly contested. But Lipset, Trow and Coleman solve, to my satisfaction at least, the famous puzzle of the two-party system in the ITU in this careful, thoughtful, definitive analysis. They do much more than that, however. They illuminate the whole question of the prospects for democratic conduct within the private governments of an advanced industrial society. And they whet one's appetite for more such case studies so that even further progress can be made in relating the alternative forms of private government to the environmental and historical factors which lie behind them. This is a fascinating and provocative book which will contribute alike to understanding and to controversy.

CLARK KERR
University of California

Preface

THIS BOOK IS A DETAILED STUDY of democracy in a single trade union, the International Typographical Union. This union, alone among North American labor organizations has maintained a two-party political system, much like that existing in national politics, for over half a century. The study deals with many aspects of the political life of the ITU: the history of the unique two-party system; the behavior of the union members, in and out of the shop; the way in which leaders are recruited; the reasons why their power over the union does not become absolute; the way members become interested in union politics, and the reasons why they are sufficiently concerned about the government of their union to keep it democratic. Basically this book is designed to explain why the ITU has managed to maintain a system of democratic self-government for generations.

But an understanding of the democracy of the ITU is only the proximate aim of the study. The workings of democracy in a union, in other voluntary organizations, or even in the state itself are not so dissimilar that the understanding of democracy in one situation will not help us to understand it (or its absence) in another. A larger objective of this book, therefore, is to illuminate the processes that help maintain democracy in the great society by studying the processes of democracy in the small society of the ITU.

§ History of the Study: Research as Process

THE STUDY IS BASED on data gathered over a long period of time, by diverse methods, and from many sources. Chronologically, it has moved through four phases, each marked by different concerns and characterized by different methods of collection and treatment of data.

(*ix*)

PHASE I: DEFINITION OF THE PROBLEM
AND INITIAL EXPLORATIONS

The study first began to take shape in 1949 and early 1950. The senior author for various personal and professional reasons had for some years been interested in the ITU's unique two-party system and internal democracy. As early as 1943, while still a graduate student, he had written a term paper on the subject, and in 1949, while a member of the faculty of the University of California at Berkeley, he began to study the union in greater detail and more systematically.

His preliminary investigations involved an examination of the literature on printing unionism, together with an inspection of the publications and voting records of the ITU itself. He also held some exploratory interviews with informed members of the ITU locals in the San Francisco area. It was in this period that the basic problems of the study crystallized: on the one hand, to explain the unique characteristics of the ITU's internal politics, as they appeared in sharp contrast to the internal politics of other trade unions here and abroad; and on the other hand, to consider these democratic internal processes in the ITU as a crucial deviant case challenging the powerful body of organizational theory stemming from Michels' development of his "iron law of oligarchy" in private organizations.

During this period, a critical review of various hypotheses which had been put forward by students of trade-unionism to "explain" the ITU's unique internal political arrangements indicated that no one of the factors so far cited was adequate to account for the phenomenon. At the same time certain other factors in the union, occupation, and industry emerged which had been ignored, up to that time, but which appeared to better explain the persistence of the union's internal democracy than many of the factors cited earlier. Among these new elements was the large and important role played by the printers' "occupational community." The preliminary formulation of hypotheses which might account for the ITU's internal political system—hypotheses based on a qualitative analysis of union documents and exploratory interviews—was particularly reported in an article written at the time.[1]

PHASE II: ELABORATION AND RESPECIFICATION
OF THE PROBLEM THROUGH QUALITATIVE ANALYSIS

In the second phase, extending from the fall of 1950, when the senior author came to Columbia University, through the fall of 1951, the exploratory work begun at Berkeley was extended and deepened. During

---

1. S. M. Lipset: "Democracy in Private Government," *British Journal of Sociology*, 3:47-63 (March 1952).

this period a systematic study of the history, and especially the political history, of the ITU was undertaken, based largely on primary sources. This work was facilitated by the existence in the library of Columbia University of a special collection of primary materials on printing and printing unionism. In addition, the fact that New York City is the center of the printing industry in the United States and home of the ITU's largest local, Big Six, which has had a long and lively political life of its own, made available large numbers of active and informed union members for exploratory interviews.

Aside from long exploratory interviews with key informants in the union, members of the research team that was organized around the study familiarized themselves in every way possible with the actual political life of the union, attending union meetings, party caucuses, and chapel meetings, while paying particular attention to the events preceding the local union election held in May 1951.

The additional knowledge and insight gained during this period led to a sharpening and respecifying of hypotheses. This thinking was reported in an article dealing with the historical origins and the contemporary structural supports of the union's political system.[2] These ideas formed the study design that was carried out in the next phase.

At this point it seemed that certain crucial aspects of the internal political process of the ITU could best be studied through survey research methods, and moreover, that such a study could be practically carried out among the members of the New York local. A proposal to that effect was written, setting forth the problems that such an effort would focus on together with the outlines of a study design, and financial support was gained for this additional major effort of field research.

PHASE III: DESIGN OF THE STUDY AND THE FIELD PROBLEM

During the fall of 1951 the vitally important task of gaining the consent and at least tacit support of both political parties active in the New York local was accomplished. Simultaneously an interview schedule embodying the major theoretical and substantive ideas that had emerged to date was constructed, tested among members of Big Six, revised, tested again, again revised, and finally administered to a sample of Big Six members. Sample design and other methodological problems, together with a copy of the interview schedule, are presented in an appendix.

---

2. S. M. Lipset and Martin Trow: "Trade Unionism in the Printing Trades," in J. B. S. Hardman, *Towards an Understanding of Trade Unions.* Forthcoming. (University of Chicago Press.) This article was written in 1951.

This schedule had built into it questions designed to produce quantitative data bearing on most of the factors and variables which the preceding years of preliminary and exploratory work had suggested might be relevant to an understanding of the nature and processes of the union's unique political system. Thus we asked questions not only about the respondent's sentiments and loyalties in union politics but also about his attitudes toward a variety of extraunion social and political issues. We asked questions not only about his activities and participation in union political affairs but also about his involvement in all other kinds of union-connected activities and his relations with other printers' organizations. And we asked about his relations with other printers in his shop as well as whether he spent time with them during his leisure hours away from work.

At the time the schedule was designed we did not by any means anticipate all of the implications and findings that would and did flow from the data we were aiming to collect. Nevertheless the inclusion of many questions bearing on the printer's informal relations with other printers, both at work and in his leisure time, was not a happenstance. Besides our previous sensitization to the importance of the union's "occupational community" for its politics, several lines of theory and research in sociology and social psychology had already given clear evidence that knowledge of men's informal social relations is a prerequisite to any clear or adequate understanding of their behavior in any of the formal organizations to which they belong or in which they are employed. The classic studies by Roethlisberger and Dickson in the Hawthorne plant of Western Electric had been followed by many other studies in industrial sociology which also emphasized the importance of primary-group relations and the "informal organization" to the workings of a formal organization. In other traditions the work of Moreno and his followers and of Kurt Lewin and the "group dynamics" school he fathered had produced much evidence on the crucial importance of small primary-group relations to an understanding of the actual processes that go on within formal organizations. And just about the time we were considering the relevance of these factors for our study, George Homans' *The Human Group* summarized and reanalyzed a number of studies bearing on the same general problem.[3]

So far as we knew, a systematic concern for small-group processes

---

3. For a fuller review of the development of ideas and concepts in the study of the small group, see Elihu Katz and P. F. Lazarsfeld: *Personal Influence*, Glencoe, Ill., Free Press, 1955. Cf. also: Edward A. Shils: *"The Study of the Primary Group,"* in Daniel Lerner and Harold D. Lasswell (eds.), *The Policy Sciences*, Stanford, Calif., Stanford University Press, 1951; David Truman: *The Governmental Process*, New York, Alfred A. Knopf, Inc., 1951, Chap. 20.

and informal social relations had not been incorporated into any studies of trade-union organization or behavior. But at the time we designed our study the small group and informal social relations as special areas of focus were clearly prescribed by the considerable body of recent solid empirical work done in neighboring areas, and they became integral parts of our research design and analysis. And if the directive of contemporary research and theory in other fields had not been enough, our own preliminary explorations, and especially the identification of the printers' "occupational community" as a crucial element in the union's political life, were additional reasons for incorporating questions in the schedule bearing on these areas.

While the interview schedule was being constructed, we decided on a stratified random sampling method, with shop size defining the several strata, as the best way of choosing an accurate representative sample of Big Six members. At the same time it was decided to interview an additional sample of shop chairmen, in order to have for analysis comparative data on a larger number of these especially important men than would be included in a wholly representative sample. Interviewing of these shop chairmen also provided better information on the structure of the union as a whole than would a simple random sample. A total of 500 interviews was projected, of which 434 constituted the representative sample, and sixty-six the added sample of chapel (shop) chairmen.

During the winter of 1951-52 the interviews were collected with the aid of the facilities and technical assistance of Columbia's Bureau of Applied Social Research. In addition, it was decided at that time to carry through a separate and independent series of intensive, "focused" interviews with substantially all of the active political leaders in Big Six. These included both party and nonparty men, in and out of office. An interview guide for this series was constructed, and these interviews, some thirty-five in number, each taking from two to five hours, were conducted during the winter and spring of 1952.

PHASE IV: FOLLOW-UP STUDIES, THE ANALYSIS OF DATA, AND THE WRITING OF THE REPORT

With the bulk of the field work completed, the interview data were coded and transferred to IBM cards, and preliminary analysis of the quantitative data began in the spring of 1952. At about that time the forthcoming election of ITU international officers in May suggested the possibility of the conversion of our sample into a "panel" for the collection of data bearing on certain crucial aspects of the union's political process. Reinterviewing of the whole sample was out of the question for many reasons, but a short mail questionnaire with two follow-ups, aimed particularly at learning how our respondents voted in that international election, elicited a response of over 70% of the original sample. These data were also transferred to IBM cards in the summer of 1952 while preliminary analysis of the interview data proceeded. Finally the national presidential election in November 1952 suggested an effort to gain additional comparative data on the voting behavior of our sample (or panel members) in a national election. Three mailings of a post-card questionnaire elicited a 55% response.

The period from the fall of 1952 through the spring of 1954 was devoted to the intensive analysis of a great part of the qualitative and quantitative data gathered in earlier phases, and to the writing of this report. During this period, special problems arising in the course of analysis and writing required the collection of certain additional data —as for example, a detailed breakdown of voting in past ITU elections by locals. But the only adequate summary of this final phase of the work is this book itself.

§ Plan of the Book

VERY BRIEFLY, the plan of the book is as follows:

An introductory chapter lays out some of the major theoretical assumptions upon which the book is based. In Chapter 2 we sketch rapidly some of the salient characteristics of printing unionism, as it has developed over the past several hundred years here and abroad. In Chapter 3 we present a short history of the ITU's political system, there setting forth material and suggesting problems to which we return in later analytic chapters.

The following section, Part II, is devoted to an analysis and assessment of the role of the "printers' community"—the clubs, teams, organizations, and the patterns of informal association which bring printers together in their leisure hours. In the first chapter of this section, Chapter 4, we discuss certain ideas and hypotheses, most notably the theory of the "state of the masses," which as developed by political scientists and sociologists point to the possible relevance of the printers' occupational community for the political life of their union. In that same chapter, we document the existence, and explore the extent and nature, of the printers' occupational community. Chapter 5 turns to the consequences of the occupational community on the union's political system, and analyzes in some detail some of the ways in which the patterns that make up the occupational community work, often in unintended fashions, to sustain the union's unique party system. Chapters 6 and 7 address themselves to the question: how can we account for the existence of the occupational community among printers—what are its determinants and continuing supports—and we find some of these in specific characteristics of the occupation, the industry, and the men who work at the trade.

In Chapters 8 and 9, our focus shifts from the extra-work life of the printers to their relations with one another, with management, and with their union in their shops. In these chapters we explore in some detail the political significance of the economic organization of the industry, and especially of the size distribution of print shops, as this affects a printer's relations with all of the important elements in his work life —shopmates, boss, and union.

In the four chapters of Part III we back off from the detailed analyses of the preceding six chapters, and attempt to develop a "structural-functional" analysis of specific elements in the union-occupation taken as a social system. The first two of these chapters, 10 and 11, take as their point of focus the normative system which legitimates the union's two-party system, while the latter two, 12 and 13, center on the patterns of leadership—their recruitment, their relations with the rank and file and with each other, their turnover—which characterize the union's political institutions. These four chapters, taken together, address themselves to the central question: how can we account for the existence and persistence of an institutionalized two-party system in the ITU.

If Part III asks: how can we account for the existence and persistence of the two-party system in the ITU, Section IV deals with the question: how can we account for the specific forms and patterns it takes in the printers' union? More precisely, it asks: what are the bases of political diversity, and through what processes are they maintained? With this focus, this section describes and analyzes the nature of the persistent cleavages of interest and orientation that have provided the actual content of internal ITU politics. These cleavages are examined on the level of the international as a whole, as they occur within and between local unions, as they are affected by the political climate within the shop, and as they affect the political behaviors of individual printers. Part of this section is an analysis, based in part on ITU and local union vote records, of the factors affecting the voting behavior of ITU members in union elections.

Finally, a concluding chapter attempts to recapitulate what we see as the major findings of the study, and attempts also to speculatively appraise the significance of our findings for a theory of trade unions and for political sociology more generally.

Acknowledgments

TO LIST ALL THE INDIVIDUALS who contributed to this study in some fashion would take more space than can be justifiably alloted to a preface. It is a fact, however, that hundreds of individuals were involved in the research, and it is necessary to acknowledge their role.

Clearly the most important group is composed of the members and leaders of the ITU who gave willingly of their time to help us in this work. We were repeatedly astonished at the warm reception which we received from these men and the extent to which they were willing to give us information. It is our earnest hope that they will find this book a sufficient reward for their cooperation. Among the officers and leaders of the two ITU parties who contributed most are William Talbot, Lawrence Victory, Tom Bishop, Abraham Wisotsky, James Mooney, Alfred Whittle, John Landy, John Fahey, Valentine Crawford, John O'Neill, Dan Glass, Andrew Ohmberger, Louis Rubin, Thomas Kopeck, and John Farrell.

While the ITU members and leaders contributed most to our substantive knowledge, the staff of the Bureau of Applied Social Research of Columbia University aided immeasurably in the actual research operation. The Bureau, which is the research arm of the Columbia Sociology Department, has over the past two decades been involved in hundreds of studies in the areas of communications behavior, politics, mental health, opinion leadership, morale, community organization, and many others. While the substantive fields covered in such research vary widely, it is an interesting fact that most of these studies have contributed to an accumulation of methodological and theoretical acumen, which is transferable from one area to another. It would be impossible to separate out the various ideas and techniques which we secured from our knowledge of previous Bureau studies or from discussions with members of the staff who are working in fields seemingly far removed from the subject of trade-union political organization. There are, however, some individuals who did play a direct and important role in this project. Among

(*xvii*)

them are Elihu Katz, Eric Meyerhoff, Joseph Greenblum, Babette Kass, Sally Fyne, and Charles Y. Glock.

A large number of our academic colleagues gave freely of their time in advising us on various phases of the work. These include Robert K. Merton, William Goode, Richard Hofstadter, Herbert Hyman, Daniel Bell, and Bernard Barber of Columbia University; Jack London, Reinhard Bendix, William Kornhauser, Robert Raschen, Grant McConnell and the late Lloyd Fisher of the University of California; Oliver Garceau of Bennington College; and David Riesman of the University of Chicago.

Nathan Glazer played a major role in bringing the book to its final stage by giving us the benefit of his editorial experience. Two men who were never directly involved in the study nevertheless deserve mention for having counseled us, out of their extensive knowledge of the operation of the labor movement, that we were on the right track—Selig Perlman of the University of Wisconsin, and J. B. S. Hardman, formerly editor of *Advance*, the organ of the Amalgamated Clothing Workers Union.

We are especially grateful to Clark Kerr, chancellor of the University of California at Berkeley, for the encouragement which he gave the study while head of the Berkeley Institute of Industrial Relations, and for the foreword he has contributed to this book.

Last, but obviously far from least, are the organizations which contributed financially to making this study possible. These groups include the Rockefeller Foundation, the Council on Research in the Social Sciences of Columbia University, the Social Science Research Council, the American Philosophical Society, the Publications Fund of the Bureau of Applied Social Research, the Institute of Industrial Relations of the University of California, and the Center for Advanced Study in the Behavioral Sciences.[1]

1. The total amount contributed by these agencies was about 17,000 dollars.

Contents

Figures

(*xxiii*)

Tables

Section *I*

Introduction and History

CHAPTER *1*

Democracy and Oligarchy

in Trade Unions

IN RECENT YEARS political democracy has proved so vulnerable to changes in social structure that the better understanding of these processes has become one of the major tasks of social science. Few still believe (as the American negotiators in Paris in 1919 seemed to believe) that formal guarantees and written constitutions can insure democracy. The most carefully worded guarantees have been swept aside, and the most intelligent of constitutions ignored, until now men seem liable to the opposite error of considering guarantees and constitutions worthless.

In few areas of political life is the discrepancy between the formal juridical guarantees of democratic procedure and the actual practice of oligarchic rule so marked as in private or voluntary organizations such as trade unions, professional and business associations, veterans' groups, and cooperatives. In fact, as many observers have noted, almost all such organizations are characterized internally by the rule of a one-party oligarchy. That is, one group, which controls the administration, usually retains power indefinitely, rarely faces organized opposition, and when faced with such opposition often resorts to undemocratic procedures to eliminate it. This is especially true for national organizations.

There is, however, one trade union—the International Typographical Union (ITU), the organization of the men who set type in the print shops of North America—which does not fit this pattern. It is the only American trade union in which organized parties regularly oppose each other for election to the chief union posts, and in which a two-party system has been institutionalized. Since the beginning of this century, the officers of the international union and of most of the larger locals have been chosen in biennial elections, in which two or more political parties have offered a complete slate of candidates for all offices. The two major parties of the union operate much as do the Democratic and Republican Parties in American politics, though they have no connection with any group or party outside the union. The parties have been of roughly equal strength in the international since 1920, so that turnover in office occurs at least as frequently as in national politics. In the thirty-five years since 1920, five incumbent presidents of the international have been defeated for re-election. In the New York local of the union, the largest local of the ITU, containing 10% of the membership, seven out of the last fourteen elections have resulted in defeat for the incumbent president. Probably nothing like this has happened in any other trade union or other of the private governments (as we may call voluntary organizations) anywhere in the world.

§ The Theory of Oligarchy

THE PATTERN WHICH CHARACTERIZES almost all voluntary organizations was generalized over forty years ago by the German sociologist, Robert Michels, when he laid down his famous "iron law of oligarchy" in the following terms: "It is organization which gives birth to the dominion of the elected over the electors, of the mandataries over the mandators, of the delegates over the delegators. Who says organization says oligarchy."[1]

The experience of most people as well as the studies of social scientists concerned with the problem of organization would tend to confirm Michels' generalization. In their trade unions, professional societies, business associations, and cooperatives—in the myriad nominally democratic voluntary organizations—men have learned, and learn again every day, that the clauses in the constitutions which set forth the machinery for translating membership interests and sentiments into organizational purpose and action bear little relationship to the actual political processes which determine what their organizations do. At the head of most private organizations stands a small group of men most of whom have held high office in the organization's government for a long time, and whose tenure and control is rarely threatened by a serious organized internal opposition. In such organizations, regardless of whether the membership has a nominal right to control through regular elections or

1. Robert Michels: *Political Parties*, Glencoe, Ill., Free Press, 1949, p. 401. This book was first published in Germany in 1911.

conventions, the real and often permanent power rests with the men who hold the highest positions.

Since Michels first wrote, many books and articles have been written about oligarchy in voluntary organizations, but almost invariably they have documented the operation of his iron law in another set of circumstances. They have shown how control of the organizational machinery, combined with membership passivity, operates to perpetuate oligarchic control. From these studies it is clear that unions and other voluntary organizations more closely resemble one-party states in their internal organization than they do democratic societies with organized legitimate opposition and turnover in office. Indeed, the pattern of one-party oligarchy is so common in the labor movement that one defender of the Soviet Union has pointed to it as a justification of the one-party regime in that country:

> What is totalitarianism? A country that has a totalitarian government operates like our union operates. There are no political parties. People are elected to govern the country based upon their records. . . . That is totalitarianism. If we started to divide up and run a Republican set of officers, a Democratic set, a Communist set and something else we would have one hell of a time.[2]

Oligarchy becomes a problem only in organizations which assume as part of their public value system the absence of oligarchy, that is, democracy. In societies or organizations in which the self-perpetuation of the governing elite is the norm few people will raise questions regarding the determinants or consequences of oligarchy. In such organizations oligarchy is a thing given, not a phenomenon to be explained. However, when one finds an organization ostensibly devoted to the extension of democracy which is nevertheless itself undemocratically governed, some explanation seems demanded. Thus in his *Political Parties* Michels, himself a socialist at the time he was writing, raised the question of why the German Social-Democratic Party and the German labor movement, though ideologically committed to a completely democratic society and actively engaged in fighting for democratic rights within Germany, were themselves oligarchic in their internal structures. To Michels, oligarchy within the democratic socialist movement was significant because it was an "unintended consequence" of organization. For him, the fact that the conservative German political parties or other organizations were also oligarchic was not a problem, since they did not believe in democracy to the same degree as the socialists, and in fact often upheld the principle of oligarchy for the larger society. In the same way and at about the same time the oligarchic structure of Ameri-

---

2. Harry Bridges, in *Proceedings of the Seventh Biennial Convention I.L.W.U.*, *April 7-11, 1947* (San Francisco, 1947) p. 178.

can political parties attracted the interest of some observers such as Moise Ostrogorski, who were struck by the apparent contradiction between American democratic ideals and the reality of the boss and the machine.[3]

The problem had been recognized earlier, of course, but until Michels, European socialists took a generally optimistic view of the problem of machine domination of workers' organizations. Marx and Engels themselves viewed oligarchy as part of the early stage of the political emergence of the working class. They believed that the workers could come to control their institutions as soon as large numbers of them acquired class consciousness and political sophistication. Clique domination of socialist groups could not survive when workers really understood the facts of political life.[4]

American political scientists, with their generally liberal and optimistic outlook, took a similar point of view. They saw the boss and the machine as social problems which would gradually be solved as democracy advanced, the immigrant was assimilated, and education was extended. They viewed the American political party as progressively moving out of close control of a small group of leaders, first to the caucus, then to open conventions, and finally to the ultimate stage of the preferential primary. During the first period of this century, this point of view found expression in a movement to extend formal popular control through the direct primary, initiative, referendum, and recall.

In Europe where the idea of a popular democracy did not actually come to fulfillment in terms of universal adult or male suffrage without class restrictions until after World War I, few efforts were made to formally democratize the structure of political parties. But the left and labor groups, which were concerned with achieving a more complete democracy, invariably set up formal blueprints which provided for a high degree of popular control over the selection of leaders and formation of policy by way of regular conventions, discussion periods, and elections.

Despite the optimistic hopes of early socialist bodies and the institu-

---

3. Moise Ostrogorski: *Democracy and the Organization of Political Parties*, New York, The Macmillan Company, 1902. Bryce, examining the oligarchy endemic to political organizations, considers boss control normal. Cf. James Bryce: *Modern Democracies*, New York, The Macmillan Company, 1921, Vol. 2, Chap. 75.

4. "The fact that here too [in the British Independent Labour Party] people like Keir Hardy, Shaw Maxwell, and others are pursuing all sorts of secondary aims of personal ambition is, of course, obvious. But the danger arising from this becomes less as the Party itself becomes stronger and gets more of a mass character."—Engels to Sorge, in Karl Marx and Frederick Engels: *Selected Correspondence*, New York, International Publishers Co., Inc., 1942, p. 507. Cf. also Nicolai Bukharin: *Historical Materialism*, New York, International Publishers Co., Inc., 1925, Chap. 8.

tion of formal democratic control, the problem remained. As the trade-union and the socialist movement grew in size and power, members who came to disagree with the policies of incumbent leaders found, with rare exceptions, that it was impossible to dislodge those leaders from office. They discovered that offices whose authority originally and formally derived from the consent of the members gave officials power over the members. In most cases, however, the opponents of an existing oligarchy did not generalize from their own experience, nor did they raise the question, is there something in the nature of large-scale organizations which engenders oligarchic control?[5] Rather, like Karl Marx they tended to view the problem in terms of evil or weak men who were corrupted by power, and to place the democratic solution in a change of personnel.

By itself the existence of oligarchy in voluntary organizations rarely leads to great concern even in democratic societies and organizations. In most cases where men have forcefully and articulately opposed oligarchy, their concern has usually arisen from disagreement with the policies of a specific oligarchy. Thus the critics of the American party machine were not basically incensed by boss control *per se*, but rather by the fact that the machine was linked to corruption and inefficient government or refused to support the various social and economic reforms favored by the critics. In the pre-World War I socialist movement Lenin, for example, attacked the leadership of the German Social Democratic Party, not primarily for being oligarchic, but for having betrayed "Marxism." The CIO critics of AFL leadership in the mid-1930's in the United States were obviously not concerned with the lack of democracy within the AFL, but with the fact that the AFL was not organizing the mass production industries. Two American books which first brought Michels' analysis to the attention of the American labor movement were written by supporters of left-wing labor groups, and they objected more to the fact that many union leaders were restraining the post-World War I strike wave than to the fact that they were dictatorial.[6]

Occasionally the criticism of oligarchic control within the labor movement led to successful attempts to further democratize the constitutional structure of unions so as to reduce the power of the officials. A favored remedy introduced in some unions before World War I was to replace convention election of officers by a direct vote of the membership and to require referenda for constitutional changes, as well as

---

5. Bukharin, *op. cit.*, pp. 306-7, explicitly notes this fact that critics of oligarchy are concerned only with policy, not with oligarchy.

6. Sylvia Kopald: *Rebellion in Labor Unions*, New York, Boni & Liveright, 1924; William Z. Foster: *Misleaders of Labor*, Chicago, Trade Union Educational League, 1927.

to make it possible for members to directly initiate referenda. The Industrial Workers of the World (IWW) tried to insure turnover in office by limiting the number of years that a man might hold office and requiring that he return to the shop after his term as an official.

With very few significant exceptions all the efforts to reduce oligarchic control by formal mechanisms have failed. In those cases where an entrenched oligarchy was finally dislodged, the new leaders soon reverted to the same tactics as they had denounced in the old in order to guarantee their own permanent tenure in office and reduce or eliminate opposition. Even anarchist political and labor groups, whom we might expect to be highly sensitive to the dangers of oligarchy on the basis of their ideology, have succumbed to the blight. In pre-Franco Spain and in other countries where the anarchists had large organizations, a small semipermanent group of leaders maintained itself in power and selected its own replacements through a process of cooptation (selection by the leaders themselves). There is no more persuasive illustration of the unanticipated consequences of men's purposeful social actions than the recurrent transformations of nominally democratic private organizations into oligarchies more concerned with preserving and enhancing their own power and status than in satisfying the demands and interests of the members.[7]

What are the factors that account for the lack of democracy in labor unions? Why do opposition groups find it so difficult to survive? Michels and others who have dealt with the problem have summed it up in broad generalizations: The nature of large-scale organizations is such as to give the incumbent officials overwhelming power as compared with that of the opposition; the situation of the leaders of most unions is such that they wish to stay in office and will adopt dictatorial tactics to do so; and the relationship of the members to their union results in a low level of participation by the members. These factors have been discussed in considerable detail in another publication by the senior author.[8] Some of these generalizations are deserving of treatment here.

---

7. It is, of course, true that the leaders' objectives of personal power and permanent tenure need not conflict with the needs of the members. Most voluntary organizations do in fact represent their members' interests in conflicts with other groups. But there may arise a situation in which the needs and goals of the leaders or simply their desire for peace and quiet as they remain in office lead them to oppose or not fight for membership objectives. In an organization in which the members cannot vote on alternative procedures or courses of action, it is impossible to know whether a leadership decision is in fact something that the members desire.

8. "The Political Process in Trade Unions: A Theoretical Statement," in Monroe Berger *et al.*, *Freedom and Social Control in Modern Society*, New York, D. Van Nostrand Company, Inc., 1954, pp. 82-124; cf. also Philip Selznick: "An Approach to the Theory of Bureaucracy," *American Sociological Review*, 8:47-54 (1943).

Large-scale organizations give union officials a near monopoly of power

(a) Unions, like all other large-scale organizations, tend to develop a bureaucratic structure, that is, a system of rational (predictable) organization which is hierarchically organized. Bureaucracy is inherent in the sheer problem of administration, in the requirement that unions be "responsible" in their dealings with management (and responsible for their subordinate units),[9] in the need to parallel the structures of business and government, in the desire of workers to eliminate management arbitrariness and caprice, and in the desire of the leaders of unions to reduce the hazards to their permanent tenure of office.

The price of increased union bureaucracy is increased power at the top, decreased power among the ordinary members. With the increase in the power of the top officials over local units and members, the sources of organized opposition are controlled or reduced. Most unions have given their executive boards the right to suspend local officials for violating policies of the central bodies. Whether they follow a conciliatory tone (as when they call for intraunion discipline and responsibility) or a militant one (as when they call for union solidarity in a dispute with management) union leaders strengthen their own hands and justify their monopolization of internal power in the course of articulating organizational needs and purposes.

(b) Control over the formal means of communication within the organization is almost exclusively in the hands of the officials. The individual member's right of free speech is not an effective check on administrative power if the union leaders control all public statements made by members of the administrative or field staff and the union newspaper. Since the only viewpoints about union matters that are widely available to the members are those of the administration, even widespread discontent which might result in organized opposition cannot be effectively expressed.[10]

(c) In most unions, one of the chief factors perpetuating the power of the incumbents is the administration's almost complete monopoly of political skills and the absence of those skills among the rank and file.[11] Within a trade union the principal source of leadership training is the

---

9. Cf. Joseph Shister: "The Laws of Union Control in Collective Bargaining," *Quarterly Journal of Economics*, 60:513-545 (August 1946).

10. Cf. in this connection P. F. Lazarsfeld and R. K. Merton: "Mass Communication, Popular Taste and Organized Social Action," in Lyman Bryson (ed.), *The Communication of Ideas*, New York, Harper & Brothers, 1948, pp. 95-118.

11. Cf. Max Weber: "Politics as a Vocation," in H. Gerth and C. W. Mills (eds.), *From Max Weber: Essays in Sociology*, New York, Oxford University Press, 1946, pp. 77-128.

union administrative and political structure itself. The union official, to maintain his position, must become adept in political skills. The average worker, on the other hand, has little opportunity or need to acquire them. Rarely if ever is he called upon to make a speech before a large group, put his thoughts down in writing, or organize a group's activities.[12] To the extent that union officers possess a monopoly of political skills, they inhibit the rise of an effective opposition.

The leaders want to stay in office.

There is a basic strain between the values inherent in society's stratification system and the democratic values of the trade-union movement. With few significant exceptions, every trade-union official has moved up in the status hierarchy by becoming an official. The leader of a large local or national union has the income and prestige of a member of the upper-middle class,[13] and often wields more power than the average upper-middle class person. Most high-status positions carry with them some security of tenure. Democracy, on the other hand, implies permanent insecurity for those in governing positions: the more truly democratic the governing system, the greater the insecurity. Thus every incumbent of a high-status position of power within a democratic system must of necessity anticipate a loss of position.

It is hard for the persons in such positions to accept this insecurity with equanimity. Once high status is secured, there is usually a pressing need to at least retain and protect it.[14] This is particularly true if the discrepancy between the status and the position to which one must return on losing the status is very great. In other words, if the social distance between the trade-union leader's position as an official and his position as a regular worker is great, his need to retain the former will be correlatively great.[15]

---

12. The history of the British labor movements testifies to the value of such training. Many of its early leaders were men who first served as officers or Sunday-school teachers in the Methodist or other nonconformist churches. Cf. A. P. Belden: *George Whitefield the Awakener*, London, S. Low, Marston & Co., Ltd., 1930, pp. 247 ff.

13. Cf. Cecil C. North and Paul K. Hatt: "Jobs and Occupations: A Popular Evaluation," in Logan Wilson and William A. Kolb (eds.), *Sociological Analysis*, New York, Harcourt, Brace and Company, Inc., 1949, pp. 464-73.

14. Furthermore, as Shepard points out, "The demands on leadership are heavy and their positions precarious. . . . To survive, leaders must be extraordinarily able, and able leaders are capable of consolidating their positions." Cf. Herbert A. Shepard: "Democratic Control in a Labor Union," *American Journal of Sociology*, 54:311-316 (1949).

15. Public officials in a democratic society are also faced with this problem. Most of them, however, come from occupational positions or social strata which permit them to return to private life without a sharp decline in income.

The strenuous efforts on the part of many trade-union leaders to eliminate democracy (the possibility of their defeat) from their unions are, for them, necessary adaptive mechanisms. The insecurity of leadership status endemic in democracy, the pressures on leaders to retain their achieved high status, and the fact that by their control over the organizational structure and the use of their special skills they can often maintain their office, all help in the creation of dictatorial oligarchies.

The members do not participate in union politics.

Although high participation is not necessarily a sign of democracy (dictatorships also find participation useful), the maintenance of effective opposition to incumbent leaders requires membership participation and interest. Ordinarily, however, few members show much interest in the day-to-day political process within the union; apathy of the members is the normal state of affairs. There are good reasons for this. Most union members, like other people, must spend most of their time at work or with their families. Their remaining free time is generally taken up by their friends, commercial entertainment, and other personally rewarding recreational activities.[16]

Most trade unions in addition are concerned with technical administrative matters, which cannot be of deep interest to the average member. The typical union appears to its members as an administrative agency doing a specific technical job for them. Union leaders will often attempt to sustain this image to prevent "interference" with their conduct of their job. Consequently only a small minority finds the rewards for participation in union affairs great enough to sustain a high level of interest and activity.

The leaders of the trade unions and other formally democratic organizations must in some way explain and justify the suppression, and to do so they make two points: that trade unions are organized for political or industrial conflicts; and that their membership is more homogeneous in background and interests than the citizens of a nation or some other civic political unit. Officials of trade unions have argued that since the group is engaged in perpetual conflict with management, internal opponents only serve the objective interests of the external enemy. They argue further that there is no basis for factionalism in their organization (other than the illegitimate selfish desire for office of ambitious individuals, or the outside interference of Communists)

---

16. Cf. Bernard Barber: "Participation and Mass Apathy in Associations," in A. W. Gouldner, *Studies in Leadership*, New York, Harper & Brothers, 1950, pp. 477-504.

since all the members are workers and have common interests and objectives. According to this thesis, organized political conflict should take place only among classes, not within them. These same two arguments are, of course, used by the Communists to justify the contradiction between the one-party state and democratic values in the Soviet Union. They explain that since the Soviet Union is surrounded by the capitalist enemy, any domestic opposition is in effect treason; and that in any case in a one-class workers' state there is no legitimate basis for disagreement.

Strengthening the force of these arguments is the fact that the political decisions of trade unions and of other groups which are totally or in part political pressure groups, such as the American Legion or the American Medical Association, often fall into the realm of "foreign policy": that is, they involve the tactics and relations that these groups should adopt towards outside groups or the state. And just as in national politics there are many pressures toward a unified bipartisan foreign policy, so in trade unions and other voluntary groups we find similar pressures. Potential oppositionists are consequently faced with the likelihood that if they exercise their constitutional democratic rights, they will be denounced for harming the organization and helping the enemy.

The fact remains, however, that the democratic political system of the International Typographical Union does exist. It is obviously no temporary exception, for the party system of the union has lasted for half a century, and regular political conflict in North American printing unions can be dated back to 1815. As we shall note in later sections of this book, there are also a few other unions which deviate from the iron law of oligarchy. Up to now almost all analysts of the political systems of private governments have devoted their energies to documenting further examples of oligarchy. Rather than do this we have undertaken an analysis of the major deviant cases. From the point of view of the further development of social research in the area of organizational structure, and indeed, the general expansion of our understanding of society, these deviant cases—cases which operate in ways not anticipated by theory—supply the most fruitful subjects for study. Kendall and Wolf have noted that the analysis of deviant cases

can by refining the theoretical structure of empirical studies, increase the predictive value of their findings. In other words, deviant case analysis can and should play a *positive* role in empirical research, rather than being merely the "tidying up" process through which exceptions to the empirical rule are given some plausibility and thus disposed of.[17]

---

17. Patricia Kendall and Katherine Wolf: "The Analysis of Deviant Cases in Communications Research 1948-1949," in Paul F. Lazarsfeld and Frank Stanton

In the course of our analysis of the ITU we have systematically looked for the various *oligarchic mechanisms*—the elements and processes which Michels and others found operative in the organizations which they studied. Many of these mechanisms—for example, the monopolies of power, status, funds, and communications channels which the officials of most unions ordinarily possess—are not found in the ITU, or if present their effects are greatly mitigated by other elements in the system. A large part of our analysis is directed at specifying those elements in the structure of the ITU and the printing industry which work against oligarchic mechanisms, and at spelling out the processes by which they contribute to the maintenance of the union democracy. And as we look for those attributes and patterns in the ITU which work to nullify the oligarchic tendencies present in large organizations, we are implicitly or explicitly setting forth the conditions necessary for the maintenance of democratic politics within private organizations. In this our purpose is not, of course, to "refute" Michels or other previous workers in this area, but rather to refine and build on their insights and findings, paying them the respect of using them more often than we quote them.

§ A Theory of Democracy

THE PROBLEM OF DEMOCRATIC or oligarchic political institutions may be approached from two vantage points. We may ask, as we have asked in the previous section, what are the conditions which are responsible for the development and institutionalization of oligarchy, or alternatively we may ask under what conditions democracy arises and becomes institutionalized. All the literature that deals with political institutions in private governments deals with the determinants of oligarchy. We have found only one article that raises the question of under what conditions democracy, the institutionalization of opposition, can exist in voluntary organizations.[18] There is of course a voluminous literature discussing democracy as a system of civil government, but we must ask ourselves whether a variable which seems related to the existence of democracy in states is relevant to the existence of democracy in organizations.

Aristotle, for example, suggested that democracy can exist only in

(eds.), *Communications Research, 1948-1949,* New York, Harper & Brothers, 1949, p. 153.

18. Philip Selznick, "The Iron Law of Bureaucracy," *Modern Review,* January, 1950 pp. 157-165.

a society which is predominantly middle class.[19] In essence he and later theorists argued that only in a wealthy society with a roughly equal distribution of income could one get a situation in which the mass of the population would intelligently participate in politics and develop the self-restraint necessary to avoid succumbing to the appeals of irresponsible demagogues. A society divided between a large impoverished mass and a small favored elite would result either in a dictatorship of the elite or a dictatorship of demagogues who would appeal to the masses against the elite. This proposition still appears to be valid. Political democracy has had a stable existence only in the wealthier countries, which have large middle classes and comparatively well-paid and well-educated working classes. Applying this proposition to trade-union government, we would expect to find democracy in organizations whose members have a relatively high income and more than average security, and in which the gap between the organizational elite and the membership is not great.

A second proposition which has been advanced about democracy is that it works best in relatively small units, in which a large proportion of the citizenry can directly observe the operation of their governments:[20] for example, the small Greek city-states, the New England town meetings, and the Swiss cantons. While historical research has indicated that much of the popular mythology about the democratic character of these societies is untrue, it is probably true that the smaller a political unit, the greater the possibility of democratic control. Increased size necessarily involves the delegation of political power to professional rulers and the growth of bureaucratic institutions. The translation of this proposition of the level of private government is clear: The smaller the association or unit, the greater membership control. There can be little doubt that this is true in the trade-union movement.[21]

Both of these approaches to democracy, that in terms of internal stratification, and that in terms of size, however, are somewhat unsatis-

---

19. Aristotle: *Politics*, IV, 11.

20. Thomas Jefferson advocated "general political organization on the basis of small units, small enough so that all members could have direct communication with one another and take care of all community affairs."—John Dewey: *Freedom and Culture*, New York, G. P. Putnam's Sons, 1939, p. 159. Cf. also Gunnar Myrdal: *An American Dilemma*, New York, Harper & Brothers, 1944, pp. 716-19; John Dewey: *The Public and Its Problems*, New York, Henry Holt and Company, Inc., 1927, Chap. 5; "The Federalist, No. 10," in *The Federalist*, New York, Modern Library, Inc., 1937.

21. It has been pointed out as well that in small homogeneous societies a political democracy often succumbs to the danger of extreme democracy: intolerance of the minority by the majority. The authors of the *Federalist Papers* were well aware of this and pointed out the dangers of a small "pure" democracy. See *The Federalist*, pp. 57-59.

factory as solutions to the problem of democracy in complex societies or large private organizations. Clearly democratic political institutions do exist in large, complex, and bureaucratically run societies and in societies which have wide variations in the distribution of income, status, and power. There is a third proposition about the conditions that favor democracy that seems to be of greater value for our understanding of democracy in large private organizations. We know it under two names, the theory of political pluralism, and the theory of the mass society. Writers in English-speaking countries, trying to explain why democracy exists in these countries, have developed the theory of political pluralism. European writers, trying to explain why democracy seems so weak in Germany and other countries, have developed the theory of the mass society. Both theories say in essence the same thing. They argue that in a large complex society the body of the citizenry is unable to affect the policies of the state. If citizens do not belong to politically relevant *groups*, if they are "atomized," the controllers of the central power apparatus will completely dominate the society. Translated to the realm of the internal politics of private organizations, this theory suggests that democracy is most likely to become institutionalized in organizations whose members form organized or structured subgroups which while maintaining a basic loyalty to the larger organization constitute relatively independent and autonomous centers of power within the organization. Or to put it in another way, democracy is strengthened when members are not only related to the larger organization but are also affiliated with or loyal to subgroups within the organization.[22] Since it is this approach which we have found most useful in understanding the internal political system of the ITU, we will briefly characterize it here.

Democratic rights have developed in societies largely through the struggles of various groups—class, religious, sectional, economic, professional, and so on—against one another and against the group which controls the state. Each interest group may desire to carry out its own will, but if no one group is strong enough to gain complete power, the result is the development of tolerance. In large measure the development of the concept of tolerance, of recognition of the rights of groups with whom one disagrees to compete for adherents or power, arose out of conflicts among strong and indestructible groups in different societies. There were a number of processes through which tolerance became legitimate. In some situations groups such as the Catholic and the Prot-

---

22. "The stability of any democracy depends not on imposing a single unitary loyalty and viewpoint but on maintaining conflicting loyalties and viewpoints in a state of tension."—R. H. S. Crossman: "On Political Neuroses," *Encounter*, 2:66 (May 1954).

estant churches attempted to destroy the opposing faction, but finally recognized that the complete victory of one group was impossible or could occur only at the risk of destroying the very fabric of society. In these conflicts minority or opposition groups developed a democratic ideology, an insistence on specific minority rights, as a means of legitimating their own right to exist. These groups might then force the dominant power group to grant these rights in order to prevent a revolutionary upsurge or achieve power themselves. For them to reject their own program may then mean a considerable loss of support from adherents who have come to hold the democratic values.

Once democracy is established in a society, private organizations continue to play a positive role. These organizations serve as channels of communication among different groups in the population, crystallizing and organizing conflicting interests and opinions. Their existence makes more difficult the triumph of such movements as Communism and Fascism, for a variety of groups lay claim to the allegiance of the population, reinforcing diversity of belief and helping mobilize such diversity in the political arena.[23] This brief discussion of theories of political pluralism and of mass society does not pretend to be an adequate summary. A fuller discussion of these concepts as applied to voluntary organizations will be found in Chapter 4 and other parts of this book. We have discussed them here to sensitize the reader to the type of factors which we were looking for in our analysis of the political system of the ITU.

---

23. Calhoun thought these factors so important he wanted to institutionalize faction by means of the concept *concurrent majority*. Cf. John C. Calhoun: *A Disquisition on Government*, New York, Political Science Classics, 1947.

CHAPTER 2

The Social and Historical Background of the ITU

SOCIOLOGICAL STUDIES of contemporary groups and institutions have been notoriously deficient in historical background. This ahistoricism stems in part from sociological theory and in part from developments in methods of social research. Sociology has largely taken over from functional anthropology its tendency to account for the existence and persistence of institutions or patterns of behavior by the way in which they are related to other parts of a functioning social system. In the eyes of the functional analyst the historical explanation, which takes the form of a description of the origins and development of an institution or social pattern, cannot account for its persistence. All social patterns have histories, but some patterns persist while others disappear. The sociologist directs himself rather to the question of why given patterns persist than to the question of how they come to be in the first place, a problem he leaves to the historian.

Nor do the methods of contemporary sociology favor historical explanation. Sociologists increasingly prefer data collected from living persons through interviews, questionnaires, and direct observation. Since there are more than enough problems and hypotheses that can be explored by the favored methods, those that require the use of the necessarily less reliable and valid documentary and historical sources of information tend to be neglected.

In this study we will be dealing primarily with data relating to the current behavior of men and institutions. It is clear, however, that any analysis of such a unique set of social forces and relationships as is represented by the two-party system in the ITU requires interpretation on two levels—the historical and the functional. We must consider both the historical conditions which gave rise to this social structure and the factors which support and maintain it as a going system.

§ The History of the ITU

IN MOST COUNTRIES in the Western world, printers were among the first workers to form permanent labor unions. American printers were no exception. An organized printers' strike occurred in New York City as early as 1776. Printing trade-union organization as such began in the United States in 1795 with the formation of a New York local. Until 1848, however, most local unions of printers which were organized either disappeared after a few years or became benevolent societies. Starting in that year, however, printing unionism in the United States began to build a stable base, with the establishment in the succeeeding decades of local unions in most of the large cities. By 1860, 34 local unions of printers were in existence; in 1873 there were 103. In 1850 the printers' locals joined together to form a national trade union. This organization, now known as the International Typographical Union, has been in continuous existence since that time, and is the oldest national union in the United States.

The formation of a national and later an international organization did not mean the immediate establishment of a powerful central office with power over the local affiliates. For a long time the union was a loose confederation of cooperating but wholly autonomous locals, with two major functions, neither of which was seen by the membership as requiring a central national office or field staff. The first, common to all unions, was, and is, the provision of mutual aid to locals in distress, especially during strikes. The second function of the national organization during this period, and one of crucial importance in the printing trades, was to prevent the importation of strikebreakers into cities in which printers were on strike. During the nineteenth century most printing was done for the local market. There was little competition between printing firms in different cities, but there was always "the possibility that in any disagreement with employers, workmen from other cities might be imported to take their places."[1] This latter danger was especially grave since many nineteenth-century printers were "tramp printers" who wandered from city to city.[2]

---

1. George Ernest Barnett: "The Printers, A Study in American Trade Unionism," *American Economic Association Quarterly*, 10:39 (October 1909).

2. About 13% of the members of the union took traveling cards in 1859. In 1885, when the union had grown considerably, over 40% moved from one city to another.—*Ibid.*, p. 31.

No full-time officials were employed during the first thirty-two years of the ITU's existence. Each local operated more or less as an independent entity, with international cooperation secured through correspondence and annual conventions. The president of the international continued to work at the trade and received only a small honorarium for his services. With few exceptions, presidents stepped down after one-year terms. Organization of new locals was left largely in the hands of existing locals, which were assigned responsibility for neighboring areas.

Beginning in 1884, however, the character of the national union changed drastically. Many members regarded the extreme decentralization of the union as a distinct liability, since as a consequence the organization of new locals and the distribution of strike aid to existing locals was being done on a haphazard basis. Other trade unions had grown much stronger than the ITU and seemed to bear witness to the virtues of a strong national organization. The convention of 1884, therefore, voted to hire a full-time national organizer, and in 1888 the president and secretary-treasurer were made full-time national officers, with the former placed in charge of organization work. In the same year the union also established an international defense fund and provided that grants could be made to locals only when a strike had the approval of the international officers. This latter change was decisive in modifying the character of the union, for it involved international officers more deeply in local affairs and correlatively increased the concern of local leaders and members with the nature of the leadership of the international union.

The official functions and revenues of the international increased rapidly, since the international officers continually sought greater control over organizing and strikes. By the first decade of the twentieth century, the international Executive Council had the right to appoint an ever-growing number of international organizers (now known as representatives) and could suspend or otherwise penalize locals which struck without international sanction. The international officers and representatives were also authorized to take part in collective-bargaining negotiations on local levels, if the local concerned requested their assistance. Since strikes could be called only with the permission of the international, it gradually became common practice to invite international assistance in negotiations whenever employers proved difficult.

The growth in the organizing and collective-bargaining functions of the international was paralleled by the development during the same period of a number of important beneficiary activities. These included the establishment of a Union Printer's Home (for the sick) in Colorado, an old-age pension, and a mortuary benefit. While the development of these activities did not immediately and directly increase the power of the international officers over the locals, they did greatly increase the number of persons on the ITU payroll, and probably contributed indirectly to the increase in power and prestige of the international officers.

The increased centralization of the ITU was followed by the withdrawal from the international of a number of crafts which felt that the compositors, who comprised the majority of the membership, were neglecting their interests. Thirteen pressmen's locals seceded in 1889 and formed the International Printing Pressmen and Assistants' Union. The pressmen were followed out in the next two decades by the bookbinders, the stereotypers and electrotypers, the type founders, and the photoengravers. By 1910 the ITU was a craft union of composing-room workers plus a small minority of newspaper mailers and an even smaller group of journalists. Jurisdiction over the journalists was dropped in the thirties, when the CIO American Newspaper Guild was formed.

Despite the development of an ITU bureaucracy the locals remained in almost complete control of the most important function of a labor union, collective bargaining. A large part of the printing industry—almost all the newspapers together with a considerable segment of the commercial book and job shops—is not competitive with plants in other cities or parts of the country. The ITU has never attempted to establish regional or national collective bargaining on issues such as wages and working conditions; there have been and continue to be large discrepancies in wages received and hours worked by ITU members in different cities. Even today there are small locals in the metropolitan New York area, but outside the jurisdiction of the New York local, whose wage scale is 15% to 20% below that of New York. Locals have remained in control of those matters which most affect the lives of their members. Unless a strike or serious breakdown in negotiation occurs, the international need never enter the local scene. Day-to-day grievance procedures, administration of apprenticeship regulations, disputes over the operation of seniority rules, discharge cases, and many other similar activities are largely handled by the locals. An individual who feels that his local's action in his case is unfair may appeal the local's decision to the international Executive Board and even to the international convention, but this right is exercised in only a small minority of grievance cases.

A major distinction must be made, however, between the large and small locals. The small locals, those with less than a hundred members, are highly dependent on the international for continual assistance. Their officers work at the trade and must administer the union after work, whereas some of the large metropolitan locals employ ten or more full-time officials. Small unions, therefore, are more likely to call on the international for assistance in their local negotiations and problems. The research and statistical bureaus of the international are of considerable importance to them. The officers of the large locals, on the other hand, are jealous of their prerogatives and powers. The full-time local officials in the large locals must make a record of their own to justify re-election and are reluctant to permit the international to share credit for achievements. In general, therefore, the ITU is composed of two distinct types of locals: the large, relatively autonomous locals, such as New York, Chicago, Boston, Washington, St. Louis, San Francisco, Los Angeles; and the hundreds of small, dependent locals whose strength and bargaining power is tied to that of the international. As might be expected, the smaller locals tend to be supporters of a strong international union, while the large locals have fought for the maintenance of local autonomy.[3]

§ Collective Bargaining and the Job Situation

THE HISTORY OF COLLECTIVE BARGAINING in the ITU is similar to that of other craft unions of skilled labor, with the exception that the ITU has generally been more militant, more prone to use the strike weapon, and since 1922 less inclined to submit to conciliation and arbitration proceedings. After winning recognition, which in most cities occurred in the middle or late years of the nineteenth century, the local printing unions fought for higher wages, standardized methods of payment, abolition of piece work, shorter hours, and better sanitary and working conditions. Almost from their origin they also attempted to secure some version of a closed or union shop.

While the absence of a national or regional bargaining pattern in the industry has meant that locals are on their own in making demands, there have been a number of major nation-wide struggles conducted by the ITU to force employers to accept certain minimum standards throughout the country. The first and most important union struggle

---

3. This insistence on decentralization is not unique to American typographers. In France the Paris local of the French Typographers' Union has constantly been at odds with the National Typographical Union and continually fought for local autonomy. In Great Britain the largest local union, the London Society of Compositors, has remained outside the national union because of its desire to protect its special rights and privileges. In Belgium the typographical union was for many decades the only union in the country to maintain local bargaining practices and resist the trend to centralization.

requiring a consistent national policy was fought over control of the linotype machines, which when introduced in the 1890's threatened to displace many printers. The employers initially insisted that the level of skill required to operate the new machines was less than that required to set type by hand and on these grounds attempted to introduce new, lower-paid workers. The union responded to this threat by establishing schools to train its members in linotype work and then demanding that only competent printers who knew every skill of the trade and had served a regular apprenticeship should be employed on the linotype machine. A series of strikes were fought over this issue, but ultimately the employers accepted the union's conditions. The ability of the machine to increase individual productivity was utilized by the union to decrease the hours of labor and to eliminate piece-rate payments.

A similar problem was presented to the ITU by the use of matrices, by which a single advertisement or column could be reproduced in scores of newspapers or magazines without the need to set type. The ITU insisted successfully that every paper using matrices, usually for advertisements, reset them in its own shop and later destroy the reset work, since the matrices are used in the actual printing. This has meant that an advertisement used in 500 publications is reset and destroyed 500 times. As other new technological devices have entered the trade, the ITU has safeguarded the positions of its members by claiming jurisdiction over each new machine.[4]

Over the years, the union has continued to win economic gains for its members. Most of these have accrued gradually through the victories of particular locals around the country. After a sizable number of the locals have been able to win a certain point, the international union will pass a union law providing that after a certain date, no local may sign a contract without that specific provision in its contract. This practice of establishing and extending minimum standards throughout the country has involved the ITU in three major nation-wide strike waves. In 1906 the union attempted to establish the eight-hour day as standard through the industry, and called strikes in many cities which did not yet have these hours. A number of these strikes were lost and the membership declined temporarily, but within a few years the eight-hour day became the rule in union print shops. In the early 1920's the union waged strikes

---

4. A. R. Porter, Jr.: *Job Property Rights: A Study of the Job Controls of the International Typographical Union*, New York, King's Crown Press, 1954, pp. 56-57. A case in point is the union's current reaction to the new teletypesetter, which operates much like a typewriter; it has set up schools to train its members to operate the new machine at the union scale.

in many cities to enforce the forty-four-hour week, and gradually made this the maximum work week.[5]

In the last decade there has been a new outburst of militancy. In the last year of World War II the ITU repudiated the wartime no-strike pledge because it felt that the War Labor Board's policies were drastically reducing the real wages of ITU members while employers were making increased profits. Since the war the union has been involved in a large number of strikes fought to retain past gains (such as the closed shop and rigid seniority practices) which it felt were threatened by the Taft-Hartley law. The ITU has probably resisted the impact of that law more strenuously than any other trade union in America.

Today the ITU continues to be one of the most powerful unions for its size in the nation. In most large cities its members earn over $5,000 a year, work less than forty hours, and are members of company-supported pension plans. It has also been successful in winning "the most complete control over job conditions of any union in the world."[6] The union has insisted on the closed shop, guaranteed either through written contract or verbal agreement, even though the closed shop is illegal under the Taft-Hartley law. Every worker in the composing room, including the foreman, must be a member of the ITU. The inclusion of the foreman as a member of the union, which dates back to the nineteenth century, has meant that foremen are subject to union sanctions if they violate union laws at the behest of the employer.[7] There have been many cases in the history of the union in which foremen were fined for violating union laws. Union laws which must be accepted by union publishers in every contract prescribe that employees must be hired or discharged under the regulations of the union's priority (seniority) system. All vacancies must be filled from among the irregularly employed men who are on the substitute list of a given plant, and the substitute who has been longest on the list must be given the first vacancy regardless of the employer's or foreman's opinion of the relative capabilities of available men.[8] Similarly, reductions in the size of the work force must follow the priority order of employment in the shop.

---

5. During the 1930's a forty-hour week or less became common. Today printers in most large cities work less than forty hours a week.

6. Selig Perlman and Philip Taft: *History of Labor in the United States*, New York, The Macmillan Company, 1935, p. 51; see Porter, *op. cit.*, for a detailed description of the ITU's job controls.

7. Elizabeth Baker: "The Printing Foreman—Union Man: A Historical Sketch," *Industrial and Labor Relations Review*, January 1951, pp. 223-35.

8. The foreman can reject a man before he becomes a substitute, for being below minimum standards of competency. But any man so rejected can appeal this decision to the union.

ITU laws which determine conditions of employment, maximum length of work week or work day, priority, closed shop, use of reproduced material, control over all composing-room work, and other work conditions, are nonnegotiable in local contracts. All union employers must accept all provisions of the ITU law. Any dispute about an interpretation of such laws between an employer and his employees can be appealed only within the political structure of the union. For example, if an employer wishes to discharge a man with priority standing and the local union objects, the employer can appeal the decision of the local union to the international Executive Council of the ITU and to its annual convention if the issue in dispute involves a point of union law. The ITU's position regarding union law is that workers have a right to set the conditions under which they will work, and employers must accept these conditions or face sanctions.[9] These rigid provisions have led to many disputes with newspaper publishers and other printing employers, but in general the ITU has been able to enforce union law.

The nature of the job control exercised by the ITU has meant that to a considerable extent the workers run the composing room. The employers' main rights concern the way in which work shall be done. The job, however, belongs to the man rather than to the foreman or the shop. So strong is the workers' proprietary right to their jobs that a printer with a regular situation designates the substitute who shall take his place if he decides to take a day off or is obliged to take one off because of the need to cancel overtime. This rule that a man may designate his temporary replacement has been in existence since the turn of the century.

Even more indicative of the strength of the union is the rule that no person not a member of the union—including employers—may be on the floor of the composing room during working hours. In practice, of course, this rule is rarely enforced by the workers in the shops, and its

---

9. The union's position on this matter can be seen most explicitly in its reaction to the provisions of the Taft-Hartley law which outlawed certain union laws, particularly those sections which prohibit closed-shop contracts under which a union has full control over the supply of labor. The ITU responded to this threat by changing the union law on contracts to include the observation:

"Even the Taft-Hartley law provides that: Nothing in this Act shall be so construed as to require an individual employee to render labor or service without his consent, nor shall anything in this Act be construed to make the quitting of his labor by an individual employee an illegal act.

"Upon the expiration of existing contracts, and until the laws above referred to are amended and free collective bargaining is again recognized, our members may accept employment only from employers who are willing to employ them under the 'Conditions of Employment' which the several unions adopt, after approval by the Executive Council of the ITU."—*Book of Laws of the International Typographical Union*, Indianapolis, 1950, p. 103.

enforcement would probably play havoc with the operations of many shops and newspapers. Yet its existence is a reminder of a power relationship, and it may be invoked when the workers in a given shop have a grievance. In one New York newspaper some time ago the men stopped working when a well-known anti-labor columnist who had written articles attacking the ITU walked into the composing room to deliver his copy.

The position of the foreman as a union member subjected to union discipline has already been mentioned. In some of the larger shops the employers follow the practice of clearing all foremanship appointments with the chapel (union shop) chairman. In the larger plants the chapel chairman rather than the foreman is the most powerful man in the composing room. He can make life difficult for a noncooperative foreman by insisting on the rigid application of the numerous union and chapel rules. In the course of the interviewing portion of this study the interviewers, who conducted most of the interviews in the shops during working hours, would be told by the employer or his representative that the man to see for permission to interview in the shop was the chapel chairman. Significantly, in some of the shops after the chapel chairman agreed to the interviews, the foreman of the shop entered into "negotiations" with the interviewers, asking that they arrange the interviews in ways that would least interfere with his work schedule.

It is indicative of our own almost unconscious early recognition of the power relationship in the industry that we never even thought it necessary to consult the employers' organizations for their permission to conduct a study within the shops of their members. About halfway through the interviewing period a representative of one of the printing employers' associations called us for information concerning the study. He said that a number of his members had asked him to find out what it was all about, who the men were who were interviewing printers during work hours. This was not a demand that we curtail our interviewing, but rather simply a request for information. Our failure to consult the employers was undoubtedly bad research procedure, but it did contribute another example of the nature of union-management relations in the printing trade.

§ The Social Organization of Printers

THUS FAR we have focused on formal organizational aspects of the development of the printers' union in North America. The various histories and studies of printers' organizations in different parts of the world point to certain distinguishing characteristics of printing as an occupation which have set it off at many different times and places from other manual trades.

Printers have differed from other members of the manual working class in a singular manner. By the very nature of his trade the printer was required to be literate at a time when even the middle and upper classes were not wholly so. Impressionistic evidence from various labor histories suggests that this combination of literacy plus knowledge of a skilled, highly paid trade meant that the printers were the status elite of the workers; so much so that nineteenth-century histories of the labor movement written by socialists complain of the snobbishness and caste-like behavior of printers. A number of French books about labor quote the words of the Communard poet Lamartine: "Printing is the most intellectual of the manual trades," and the goal of printers is "to remain the elite of the working class." Perhaps as a result of this combination of skill, literacy, and high status, printers appear to have been the first group of workers to develop economic self-defense organizations and trade unions in almost every country of the Western world.

In France and England printers were negotiating with and sometimes striking against their employers as early as the sixteenth century.[10] And there is clear evidence that printers were either the first or among the first two or three crafts to organize into unions in Belgium, Germany, Sweden, Norway, Italy, Switzerland, Spain, Ireland, Russia, Austria, Australia, Canada, Chile, Argentina, and Mexico.[11]

---

10. A French economic historian describes the great strike in 1539 of the printers of Lyons in the following terms: "Nothing was lacking in this crisis that might be lacking in a modern strike, neither the demand for salary increases, nor the protests against the conscious efforts of the employers to reduce the skill level required in the trade, nor the recourse to employer organization . . . or the intervention, first of the municipal, and later of the central authorities."—Henri Hauser: *Les origines historiques des problèmes économiques actuels*, Paris, Vuibert, 1930, p. 178.

In Britain as early as 1587 the employers agreed to regulations limiting the number of copies which could be run off from one set of type. Editions of books were limited to 1500 copies with the exception of devotional and school books. See Ellic Howe: *The London Compositor, 1785-1900*, London, The Bibliographic Society, 1947, p. 15.

11. Emile Vandervelde: *Enquête sur les associations professionelles d'artisans et ouvriers en Belgique*, Brussels, Imprimerie des Travaux Publiques, 1891, p. 66; Peter Gay: *The Dilemma of Democratic Socalism*, New York, Columbia University Press, 1952, pp. 121-122; Rudolph Heberle: *Zur Geschichte der Arbeiterbewegung in Schweden* (Schriften des Instituts für Weltwirtschaft und Seeverkehr an der Universität Kiel, No. 39), Jena, Gustav Fischer Verlagsbuchhandlung, 1925, p. 19; Humbert L. Gualtieri: *The Labor Movement in Italy*, New York, S. F. Vanni, 1946, p. 8; Otto Bechtle: *Die Gewerkvereine in der Schweiz*, Jena, Gustav Fischer Verlagsbuchhandlung, 1887, p. 8. Antonio Billesteros y Beretta: *Historia de España*, Barcelona, P. Salvat, 1936, Vol. 85, p. 700; A. Witte: *Die*

While it is difficult to answer satisfactorily the question of why printers were better able than members of other occupations to organize in the face of the tremendous obstacles facing early union organization, certain aspects of the occupation's social organization seem to be relevant. Before they had trade unions, printers in various countries met formally or informally with one another for social or benevolent purposes. The King of France issued a number of edicts during the sixteenth century forbidding printers "to have banquets as a group . . . to assemble together . . . to form an occupational religious association."[12] The ability of printers in various countries repeatedly to organize secretly, and to plan successful strikes in periods when union organization was illegal also indicates a high degree of previously existing craft solidarity and informal intracraft social relationships. It was probably not difficult for printers to convert their informally organized occupational community into a formal trade union.[13] As we shall see in a later chapter, a high level of leisure-time social relations among printers has been characteristic of the social organization of printing down to the present time.

Literacy undoubtedly contributed to the early development of printers' organizations, apart from its relationship to the high-status position of the craft. As a literate group, printers knew how to draw up documents and present grievances and had knowledge of the ways in which other organized groups operated. As early as the middle of the sixteenth century, printers in England and France were in communication with each other. Shop rules drawn up by workers in the two countries often were similarly worded, and the same organizational structure in the shops was adopted by French and English printers.

Gewerkschaftsbewegung in Russland (Volkswirtschaftsliche Abhandlung der Badischen Hochschulen, Vol. 10, Karlsruhe, 1909, Appendix 3, Vienna, 1908, p. 13; J. T. Sutliffe: *A History of Trade Unionism in Australia,* Melbourne: The Macmillan Company, 1921, p. 18; Harold A. Logan: *The History of Trade-Union Organization in Canada,* University of Chicago Press, Chicago, 1928, pp. 7-8; Tulia Lagos Valenzuela: *Bosquejo histórico del movimiento obrero en Chile,* Santiago de Chile, El Esfuerzo, 1941, p. 16; Marjorie Ruth Clark: *Organized Labor in Mexico,* Chapel Hill, University of North Carolina Press, 1934, p. 18; Robert J. Alexander: *Reseña del movimiento obrero en la América latina,* Washington, D.C., Union Pan Americana, 1950, p. 19.

12. Hippolyte-Gaston Cavaignac: *Le Mouvement syndical dans la typographie française,* Paris, Jouve et Cie., 1932, pp. 9-10.

13. "If we examine the evidence of the rise of combination in various trades, we see the Trade Union springing, not from any particular institution, but from every opportunity for the meeting together of wage-earners of the same occupation. Adam Smith remarked that 'people of the same trade seldom meet together even for merriment and diversion, but the conversation ends in a conspiracy against the public, or in some contrivance to raise prices.' "—Sydney and Beatrice Webb: *The History of Trade Unionism,* London, Longmans Green and Co., Ltd., 1950, pp. 22-23. The words of Adam Smith are to be found in *The Wealth of Nations,* Book I, p. 59 of McCullough's edition, 1863.

The diffusion of organizational forms and ideas both within and between countries was due not only to the fact that printers could exchange written communications, but also to the fact that printers were geographically highly mobile. The possession of a needed skill together with a high sense of status and occupational solidarity made it possible for printers to travel from one part of a country to another or to different countries and obtain employment. Young journeymen, especially, would travel around after completing their apprenticeship and in the process would carry news of printers' activities from place to place. Given their strong sense of craft solidarity and the personal and written channels of communication among them, it is not surprising that the printers of a number of countries attempted to form national bodies of printers' benevolent organizations even before they had trade unions. Indeed, the printers of Italy had a national benevolent and social organization in the early eighteenth century long before the national unification of that country was anything more than a dream.

Not only were printers the first group to organize on a national scale in many countries, but they were also the first craft to form an international group, the International Association of Typographers. This body formalized the traditional practice of accepting alien printers on a basis of equality with natives. Membership cards in typographical unions around the world are still interchangeable; a member of a foreign printers' union can automatically transfer to the ITU. Following the rise of Hitler, printers who fled from Germany were made members of the French Typographical Union and had a much easier time securing employment in that country than any other comparable group of German refugees. The norm of international printer solidarity withstood even the pressures toward the restriction of employment opportunities flowing from the serious unemployment of the depression of the thirties.

Given their strong pride of craft and sense of craft solidarity, the printers were able at an early date to discipline by ostracism those of their workmates who violated the norms of the group. Reports of printer shop organization in the seventeenth century in England indicate that violators of work norms were placed "in Coventry." No one would speak to them, and their life in the shop would be made impossible. "The spirit of the chapel" would disappear with their tools or drop heavy weights on their feet.[14] With the coming of trade unionism those men

---

14. George A. Stevens: *New York Typographical Union No. 6* (New York, N. Y. State Department of Labor, 1912) gives documents on early practices of English printers. See especially pp. 114-30. Similar procedures are employed today to discipline non-union printers in the Government Printing Office in Washington, D.C. While the government will not sign a contract giving the ITU a closed or union shop, one is maintained there informally. Men who refuse to join the

who violated the most important norm of the union, not to work ("scab") during a strike, were officially designated "rats." As early as 1807 the Philadelphia Typographical Society sent the names of expelled members to other local unions.[15] In 1809, members of the New York Typographical Society refused to work with a printer who, they discovered, had worked at a previous time for wages below the wage scale.

Another characteristic of printers which has persisted down through the centuries is their insistence on controlling the conditions of work within the print shops, a control now formalized in the ITU law. In large measure printers have demanded and won the right to be treated as independent craftsmen who control their own work and maintain and enforce their own standards of workmanship. As early as the middle of the seventeenth century, English printers controlled shop discipline. Many of the early chapel rules concerned the deportment of men in the shop, some being designated to protect the shop against fire or unsanitary conditions. Men who violated the rules were fined by their fellow workers and forced to contribute to a shop benevolent fund. The pride in craft of early American printers may be seen in the fact that a member was expelled from the New York Typographical Society in 1817 and "his name was sent to all known societies because he had 'turned wrong a half sheet of 24's, and without mentioning the fact to his employers left the city, even neglecting to note down the signature letter in his bill—conduct highly derogatory to the New York Typographical Society and disgraceful to himself as a member.' "[16]

A further characteristic of early printers which is important for an understanding of their behavior was the linkage between printing and journalism. Many of the early publishers, newspaper journalists, and editors began as printers. Benjamin Franklin, Horace Greeley, and Henry George are perhaps the three outstanding examples in American history, but there are thousands of others. In the nineteenth century and to some extent today local small-town weeklies were and are often written and printed by the same men. Until World War I and in some cases afterward some newspaper compositors also practiced journalism as a side line. A number of them eventually became reporters. It is significant to note that many of this latter group remained members of the ITU, and some even served as leaders of the union after changing occupational roles.

union or who have a past history of antiunion activity, are placed "in Coventry," in much the same fashion as in seventeenth-century London.

15. Ethelbert Stewart: *A Documentary History of the Early Organizations of Printers*, Indianapolis, International Typographical Union, 1907, pp. 14-15.

16. *Ibid.*, p. 25.

Another connection between printing and journalism in many parts of the world has been the labor press. Printers started many labor papers and then edited them. Before the organization of the American Newspaper Guild in the mid-thirties, many of the editors of local and international union papers in the United States were printers. Even today a large number of AFL editors are men who began work as compositors and still retain membership cards in the ITU. The close connection between printing and writing probably had considerable effect, especially among the printers themselves, in enabling them to sustain their high-status image as the elite of the working class.

Printers not only stand out as one of the first organized occupations but also have contributed greatly to the organization of the labor and socialist movement in many countries in the world. A cursory examination of the occupational origins of the first leaders of such movements reveals a high proportion of printers in the Russian, German, Danish, Spanish, and Norwegian labor movements, among others. In the United States printers played a major role in forming the American Federation of Labor. At the early AFL conventions a large number of the delegates representing local city and state bodies were members of the ITU. Frank Morrison, who served as secretary-treasure of the AFL for over forty years, was an active ITU member.

The printers could furnish leadership to the labor and socialist movement partly because they were organized before most other unions and thus were frequently able to render assistance to younger and struggling groups of workers in other occupations. In addition (and this in the long run was more important) the printers' union included a disproportionately large number of men who had had the kinds of formal and informal education which enabled them to organize and present their ideas effectively in the ways required of organizational leadership. In a real sense the printers were the intellectuals of the working class.

It is difficult to estimate to what extent these past elite patterns continue to operate today. With the introduction of the linotype and other printing machines the degree of skill required in the trade has declined. Union printers must still serve a six-year apprenticeship, but this regulation is as much a product of the union's power as of the actual skill requirements of the trade. A minority of printers, especially those in the large newspapers, spend much of their work careers at what is essentially an elaborate typing machine. It is doubtful that this work gives them the same sense of craftsmanship that the old hand printer had. Of course the day of the printer craftsman is far from dead. Most of the workers in the book and job shops and many in the newspapers still do hand work. The elaborate and complex color and advertising plates on which some printers work probably require greater skill than most of the printing jobs of the nineteenth century. Moreover the long apprenticeship, which requires every printer to learn all the skills of printing, still enables printers to regard themselves as highly skilled artisans even though many of them rarely use most of their skills.

The increase in the general educational level has also helped reduce the differences between printers and other workers, although fairly recent studies still suggest that printers are on the average better educated than other groups of skilled workers. But while there can be little doubt that the general social status and craftsman aspect of printing have declined, the average printer still believes, rightly or wrongly, that his occupation commands considerable respect from others; and unlike many manual workers, he likes his job. Over 60% of the members of our random sample of the members of the New York union stated that they thought the general prestige of printing was "excellent"; about two-thirds said that if they had their choice of jobs today, they would choose printing; about three-quarters stated that they liked printing "extremely well"; and when asked why they like the trade, the overwhelming majority gave what might be called craftsman reasons, such as "it is creative," "challenging," "educational," and other similar responses.

The discussion of some of the social characteristics of printers as an occupational group should not be allowed to obscure the fact that the basic power of the printers' union lies in their control of a relatively scarce skill, together with their high sense of group solidarity. Not the least part of their power comes from the fact that many of their employers produce a highly perishable commodity for a local market. Newspaper publishers have always been extremely vulnerable to strikes, and since they operate within a local market, they are able to pass on the increased costs to the readers or advertisers. Printers' unions, therefore, have always been stronger in the newspapers than in the rest of the industry.

One of our basic assumptions in analyzing contemporary printing is that many of the elements inherent in printing as an occupation from the sixteenth through the nineteenth centuries still persist. Despite the spread of rational capitalism, printing has retained more aspects of the old guild patterns of economic organization than have most other occupations. For example, as we shall see in Chapter 4, many printers today spend much of their leisure time in the company of other printers, thus continuing an old craft pattern. Nevertheless, as suggested above, there has been a steady narrowing of the traditional differences between printers and other workers. To some extent the strength of the printers' union has served to maintain some of the characteristics of the trade, such as its high pay and long apprenticeship, after the economic and technological factors which gave rise to and supported them have vanished. And the high wage scale and long apprenticeship in turn continue to serve as indicators (now perhaps spurious) of the high skill and status apparently inherent in the occupation. Whether this condition can persist indefinitely is questionable; but that it exists today is certain.

CHAPTER 3

The History of Internal Conflict in the ITU

INTERNAL CONFLICT between factions and parties in the printing unions is almost as old as the unions themselves. And while over the past 150 years the factions and parties in printing unions have had many different names and fought over many different issues, one basic cleavage has divided printers throughout this period and has underlain most of the specific issues which printers have fought about inside their own unions. In the printing unions, as in the society at large, there have always been some men who favored an aggressive policy while others urged moderation and conciliation in relations with employers and the governments. The fight between militants and moderates, which frequently has also been a fight between men who are more liberal (or radical) and men who are more conservative on larger social issues, has been continuous throughout the history of the ITU and its predecessors, and the end of this fight is not in sight.

One of the early manifestations of this left-right cleavage in American printing unionism occurred in the Columbia Typographical Society, organized in Washington, D.C., the oldest printing union in this country. This union from its founding in 1815 until at least 1842 was the arena for a conflict between two internal factions, the *alimoners* and the *industrialists*.[1] The alimoners, the union conservatives of their day, desired

---

1. Stewart, in his history of early printing unions, reports constant conflicts and shifts in majority control in the Washington union up until 1842. (This date does not represent the end of factionalism in the Washington union, but is simply the last date mentioned by Stewart in connection with factionalism in the Washington local.) See E. Stewart, *Documentary History*, pp. 70-73.

to limit the activities of the embryo union largely to welfare and benevolent functions, while the industrialists pressed for a greater concern with
wages and working conditions. Similar conflicts occurred within the
Philadelphia and New York Typographical Societies in the late 1820's.

The militants and conservatives also divided during this period over
the question of the control and regulation of apprentices. During the
1820's and 1830's, the employers attempted to break down the young
unions' rules governing the employment of apprentices by employing
as journeymen printers' boys who had not served a regular apprenticeship. The militant faction in a number of cities responded to this challenge by proposing that these newer, less well-trained printers be
brought into the union, *after* which the apprenticeship rules could again
be enforced. The conservatives on the other hand, insisted that only
men who had served an apprenticeship should be allowed into the typographical societies. Moreover, the "radicals" also wanted to restrict the
number of apprentices that an employer could have in one shop, while
the "conservative" elements were willing to accept more apprentices.[2]

Conflict over these two issues, the stringency of the rules governing
apprentices and the even more basic question of the proper functions of
a typographical society—benevolent as opposed to "trade-union" activities—continued during the 1840's.[3] On both of these issues a liberal-
conservative conflict is apparent.

§ The Keepers of the Union

THE CONTEMPORARY two-party system of the ITU rests on the same
basic cleavage that divided printers before the national body was formed
in 1852. The international and its locals are still divided into two factions
which can be described in much the same left-right terms used to describe the factions existing in the early nineteenth century, although

2. In reporting the first convention of the National Typographical Society in
1836, Tracy states: "There had for years been two factions in the societies—one,
seeing that the apprenticeship requirements were creating an army of printers
sufficiently large to do all the work, outside of the societies, because of ineligibility,
wanted temporarily to let down the bars and organize the trade, and then increase the
requirements; the other faction, sticking to the old traditions, sought to remedy
the evil by increasing the severity of the apprenticeship."—George A. Tracy:
History of the Typographical Union, Indianapolis, International Typographical
Union, 1913, pp. 87-88.

3. E. Stewart, *op. cit.*, p. 77. The last-reported early flare-up over benevolent
activities occurred in 1853 when a group of book-and-job printers seceded from
the New York union because of their opposition to combining benevolent and
trade-union activities. The two groups reunited in 1857. See George A. Stevens:
New York Typographical Union No. 6, pp. 258-75.

there is no direct connection between these earlier groupings and the present-day union parties.

The present political system had its origins in the response of union printers to recurrent organizational crises in the second half of the nineteenth century. The union, though stronger than most other labor organizations of that time, faced the problem common to all unions of retaining its members during depressions. Employers who signed contracts with the union in periods of labor scarcity often attempted to reduce wages or even to break the union during depressions; their principal antiunion tactic was to fire and black-list active unionists. Faced with a situation in which the employer held great power while unions were not yet accepted as legitimate, printers responded by forming secret organizations of the most active union members. These secret societies were designed to conceal from the employer and his spies within the shop or union the plans of the active militant unionists and to create within the union a cadre or caucus of loyal members which would work as an organized group in two directions: first, to sustain the militancy of the union against the more conservative or fearful members, and second, to engage in activities within the print shop which would force the employer to accept the terms of the union.

The earliest mention of such a secret printers' society occurs in 1843. The Franklin Typographical Society, the New York printers' union of the time, collapsed in the depression of that year, while other local printing unions were also adversely affected. In order to preserve printing unionism, Stewart notes, "an attempt was made to found a national secret society, to be composed of picked men from the local associations in all cities, and to be called 'The Order of Faust.' The move was started in New York City, and it is said that such of the leaders as were approached in Albany, Washington, Cincinnati, Boston and Philadelphia were ready to join and to found coordinate branches. Only rumors of it ever reached the surface."[4]

There is no further record of the activities of the Order of Faust. Its principal significance lies in the fact that it set a pattern which was subsequently followed by a succession of printers' secret societies created to meet the problem of employer power and union weakness. In 1857, a year of large-scale unemployment among printers, a group of members of the New York local met in Albany and formed a secret society of loyal union members within the seven-year-old ITU to help preserve the larger organization in that period of crisis. The young union was still highly vulnerable to attack. Known and active unionists

---

4. E. Stewart, *op. cit.*, pp. 76-77.

were being fired, while betrayal of a fellow worker as a member of the union often enabled a man to keep a steady job.[5]

The Brotherhood of 1857, like its predecessor, the Order of Faust, left no written records behind it, and it is impossible to tell what effect it had on the union, except that subsequent secret orders knew of its existence and claimed lineal descent from it.

The final establishment of a secret society (and this one was to have continuous existence down to the 1930's) occurred at some time in the 1870's. The depression of 1873-1878 again severely weakened the ITU. It lost close to half its affiliated locals and membership, and most of the remaining locals were forced to accept severe cuts in wages. Once again the existence of a large reservoir of unemployed and the absence of strong union contracts made it dangerous to be an active unionist. As a result printers in different parts of the country organized or revived the Brotherhood of the Union (of Printers) of North America as a secret society which operated both to protect active union members from discrimination by the employers and to keep union policy control in the hands of men who were willing to sacrifice to further the cause of the union.

To carry out its objectives the Brotherhood found it necessary to get control of the international and many of its locals, and to control the hiring polices of printing plants. The first task was apparently carried out by operating as a secret caucus or faction within the union. The various lodges of the Brotherhood caucused before union meetings. At that time policies were adopted which would be pushed through the larger body, and speakers were designated to move and speak for these policies on the floor of the meeting. The group also ran slates of candi-

---

5. A pamphlet put out by the Administration Party of the ITU in 1927 gives a picture of conditions in those days.

"A financial and industrial panic struck the United States in 1857. Business went to smash. Unemployment became virtually universal. The then recently organized Typographical Union No. 6, in common with all unions, was hard hit. It was compelled to reduce its already low scale. . . . Disorganization and dissolution threatened to wreck the very structure of trade union organization. Hunger and want caused many deserters. To betray a fellow-worker as a member of the union often meant preference and a steady job. . . . No man knew whom he could trust. . . .

"Realizing that utter annihilation impended, a few stalwart union patriots met in Albany in the fall of 1857. It is true that they met in secret. They had to. Their conference was held to devise means to preserve from destruction the remnants of the Typographical Union. Had the facts regarding their efforts been known, these men would not have been employed by any boss printer or publisher. Hence, the drawn blinds. They held the union together in those old cruel, hard days, and they came to be known as the Brotherhood, to the company of which no man was admitted if he had ever been guilty of dishonorable conduct."
—*Administration Party Was Born in Panic of 1857*, New York, 1927.

dates for office in many locals. In order to prevent discrimination against union men in hiring, the Brotherhood attempted to recruit foremen, who then had control over hiring. It is difficult to understand why foremen should have been willing to join this secret conspiratorial organization, though there is evidence that the Brotherhood was successful in recruiting many foremen. It may be that foremen in printing who themselves had come from the ranks were sympathetic to the union and were willing to work with a secret group which would protect their jobs. It is also possible that one of the principal factors related to the creation and perpetuation of the secret society was the need to provide a protective device for the large number of foremen who were supporters of the ITU.

The economic crisis which had given rise to the Brotherhood ended, and in the late seventies and early eighties the union regained many of its old members and much of its old strength. However, the Brotherhood did not disband with this upturn in the union's fortunes, but continued to function as a secret society on the grounds that it had to prevent the union from falling into the hands of the "whitewashed rats" —the printers who had abandoned the union in times of strikes or depressions but returned in periods of prosperity and union strength. Such men constituted a large proportion of the union's membership when it regained its strength. But from the point of view of those ITU members who were not members of the Brotherhood, its role in the union, after the conditions which had brought it into existence had passed, was wholly illegitimate. They came to see it as a powerful political machine, having the support of many union officers and shop foremen, whose principal function was to keep its members in union office and in the best jobs in the trade.

Documentary evidence of open conflict between the members of the Brotherhood and their opponents dates from the year 1879, though some of the discussion which took place then suggests that a fight had been going on earlier in some locals. In that year the St. Louis section of the Brotherhood apparently tried to expel a large number of its opponents from the union. Its opponents, who claimed to be the majority of the local union, printed a leaflet or pamphlet, *Typographical Union vs. The Brotherhood of the Union of North America*. On the title page of this pamphlet was the Latin phrase, *Quis custodiet custodies?*" —"Who shall keep the keepers?" This phrase clearly indicates part of the objection of rank-and-file printers to the self-proclaimed role of the Brotherhood as the safeguarders of the purity of the union.[6]

---

6. Unfortunately we do not have a copy of this document and have had to rely on portions reprinted in a party newspaper in 1912. The reprinted portion of

Between 1880 and 1896 the role of the Brotherhood in the ITU was a hotly debated issue at many of the international conventions and in local meetings all over the country. Oppositionists attempted to pass union laws outlawing membership in any secret society, while the members of the Brotherhood usually denied that any such organizations existed, and opposed restrictive legislation on the grounds that it might be used to penalize good union members. If the votes on anti-secret-society legislation are any index of the comparative political strengths of the two groups, then it would appear that the union was evenly divided. Control appears to have shifted back and forth between the two factions during this period.[7]

At the convention of 1896 the matter of secret societies was again brought to a head when a New York delegate presented a document containing the initiation ritual of the Brotherhood, which the delegate indicated had been in his possession for almost twenty years. This delegate implied that he had been a member of the order and could attest to the accuracy of the document from his personal knowledge. The document, which was later printed in the convention supplement, left little doubt of the existence and operation of the secret society.[8]

The convention of that year was definitely in the hands of the opponents of the secret societies and passed the following union law:

It shall be unlawful for any member . . . to belong to any secret organization, oath-bound or otherwise, the intent or purpose of which shall be to influence or control the legislation or the business of such local union or of the International Typographical Union, the selection or election of officers of such local or international union, or the preferred or other situations under their jurisdiction.[9]

In an attempt to eliminate what appeared to many opponents of the secret societies to be the source of minority control of the union by a secret group, the convention voted to abolish annual conventions and

the exposé refers to tactics pursued by members of the Brotherhood within the St. Louis local. The most interesting section of the report was not reprinted in the 1912 paper, but was summarized there as follows: "Then [in the original pamphlet] follows a long statement embracing confessions by former members [of the Brotherhood], showing how conventions were controlled and legislation enacted for the benefit of the secret membership; how those who opposed the plotters were denied employment."—*The Progressive*, Denver, 1:1 (April 1912).

7. In addition to advocating and securing passage of laws outlawing secret societies the opponents of the Brotherhood also succeeded in getting the convention of 1885 to condemn the practice of foremen's giving jobs to fellow members of organizations other than the union.

8. See "Convention Supplement," *Typographical Journal,* November 1896.

9. *Ibid.,* p. 80.

changed the system of electing international officers from an election by convention delegates to direct referendum election in the print shops. This convention also initiated a system of direct membership government by referendum. Every union law and policy had to be voted on by the entire membership, and five local unions could initiate a referendum on any subject which they desired. The somewhat utopian assumption of those opposed to caucuses and secret societies was that direct government would prevent a minority of the union from using the union's machinery to control it.

The system of direct self-government broke down within three years under the pressure of frequent referenda. Many members became tired of being polled on referenda every few weeks, and 1898 the membership voted by an overwhelming majority to re-establish annual conventions and to do away with the necessity for frequent referenda. In the same vote, however, they decided to retain the practice of direct election of international officers.[10]

Because of varying demand for printing and variations in the size of newspapers on different days of the week and in different seasons of the year, the printing industry requires that many more workers be available for work than it is possible to employ regularly. To regularize job placement the practice developed in the nineteenth century of establishing lists of men available for work in a given shop, known as substitute lists. Early in the history of the union efforts were made to have union foremen limit such lists to union members only, and one of the principal functions of the secret societies was to protect such pro-union foremen. Once the union was accepted in the industry, however, the incidence of foremen membership in the secret order meant that preference in hiring and firing became an asset of a union faction rather than of the union as a whole.

Beginning in the early 1880's the oppositionists therefore attempted to limit the power of the foremen. This first took the form of outlawing the substitute lists, and later of establishing rigid seniority, or as it is known in the printing trade, priority. From 1890 to 1930 various union conventions and referenda were concerned with the question of extending or weakening the priority system. In general the secret-society faction opposed rigid priority, while their opponents fought for fixed rules

---

10. *Typographical Journal*, January, 1899, p. 95. Efforts to restrict the absolute power of union conventions actually began some years before 1896. In 1889 the constitution was amended to provide that any future constitutional amendments must be submitted to referendum (George A. Tracy, *op. cit.*, p. 432). In 1892 the constitution was further changed to specify that any proposed constitutional amendment or union law must be sent to referendum (*Ibid.*, pp. 480-81).

which limited the discretionary powers of foremen. A priority law has existed since 1892, with the exception of a brief period during World War I.

§ The Emergence of the Party System

IT IS IMPOSSIBLE to trace with great precision the emergence of the party system in the ITU out of the struggles over the secret societies. In spite of the passage of legislation outlawing secret societies in the eighties and nineties, there can be no doubt that they continued to operate under different names. In the late eighties or early nineties the Brotherhood, following repeated exposures, either dissolved into or changed its name to the Caxton League. The League in turn simply dropped its name to prevent exposure. From some time in the nineties a secret society operated in the union without using any formal name. From then on, the society is referred to as the No Name Society, or more popularly, the Wahnetas. The origin of the latter name is unknown.

Before 1898, the year of the first direct membership election of ITU officers, the principal arenas for struggle over control of the ITU were the local meetings and international conventions. While oppositionist groups existed in many locals, there is no evidence of any national opposition organization as long as the convention was the final governing and electing body of the international union. With the coming of direct elections, however, the situation changed. Any opposition was now faced with the problem of nominating a slate for a large number of international offices and then of winning membership support all over the country. In this first election Samuel Donnelly, a former Wahneta and past president of the New York local, was elected international president. Donnelly was defeated for re-election in 1900 by James Lynch, a Wahneta leader.

With the exception of the election of 1906, Lynch and the incumbent Wahneta international officers were opposed for re-election by an opposition slate in every election from 1902 to 1910. But this opposition to the incumbent Wahneta administration was not formally organized as a national political party and apparently did not maintain any organization between the biennial ITU elections. During these years opposition delegates to ITU conventions came together at these meetings and designated a list of candidates. Campaign clubs would then be established in various locals to carry on election campaigns.

While the opposition remained an informal and loosely organized group, the Wahnetas, in control of the International administration, operated as an efficient union political machine. They had a formal organization, known as the Grand Lodge, which was headed by L. C. Shepard, whose role was similar to that of party boss in national politics. He remained party chief until he died in 1920, although he never held a major union office. Shepard corresponded with local "circles" of Wahnetas, which were organized in most of the larger locals. Before every international election the Wahnetas held a regular primary election, using printed ballots, at which candidates for party nomination were voted on by all members of the society.[11]

It is somewhat difficult to understand why the Wahnetas maintained a secret organization from the 1890's until sometime around 1928 or 1930. In practice it was the inner circle of a political machine or party having branches throughout the country. Yet despite the fact that other union groups existed openly, while secret societies were illegal under the union's constitution, the Wahnetas continued the rigmarole of a secret lodge with handshakes, passwords, oaths of secrecy, and so forth. As one might expect, it was impossible to keep such an organization secret for long. Disgruntled former members occasionally revealed its secrets, or the opposition sent spies into it.[12]

The most comprehensive report on the activities of the Wahnetas is

---

11. "The October meeting was the one at which the nominations were made for International officers, and the following month the ticket was sent to all lodges to be voted on, and then later on, perhaps about January, Shepard notified all the local lodges of the results of the referendum vote, sending to each local the slate thus made out for the guidance of the Inside men throughout the jurisdiction of the International Typographical Union."–From the stenographic report of "Investigating Committee vs. Supposed Secret Society Known as 'Wahneta' or 'Inner Circle,'" Herman Greenblatt, stenographer, minutes of January 3, 1911, p. 7.

12. The character of the secrecy rituals within the Wahnetas may be seen from the following sections from the book of instructions of the group. A new member was told the following:

"You have been invited here to join a secret organization of . . . composed of men of good character, and competent workmen, whose object is to encourage all . . . men; to purify our trade of incompetent and unworthy persons; to calmly and dispassionately discuss and decide upon all vital questions affecting our trade, and after having so decided, to go into the . . . and endeavor to carry out such decisions."

After having sworn the secrecy oath, the new member was to be told the following:

"Brother, you are now a member of the . . . Unlike most secret societies, the existence of this Order is not to be known outside of its membership. You will, therefore, see the necessity of speaking of the Order only at its meetings, and avoid all conversations outside in regard to its business and objectives. Never approach anyone in regard to the Order until he has been duly elected, and then in the most guarded manner. A knowledge of how you were approached will doubtless aid you in proceeding secretly."–Quoted in a document circulated by the Denver local, dated November 1, 1911. (The blank spaces are in the original document.)

contained in the more than three hundred pages of stenographic minutes of hearings conducted by the New York local between December 1911 and May 1912. An investigatory committee was established following a raid on a New York meeting of the Wahnetas. At the hearing a number of former members who testified under oath made it clear that the Wahneta organization operated primarily as a political machine within the union. For example, the New York circle was limited to about thirty-five members, but many of these men had been officers in the New York local. These former members who testified before the investigatory committee described the operation of a disciplined union caucus, which existed throughout the country and met secretly before all union meetings to plan strategy and coordinate efforts.[13] While the members of the Wahnetas never admitted the existence of the Order, they obviously required some sort of public group for electoral purposes. This took the form of Administration Clubs or Parties in different locals in the country. These front organizations included many men who were not members of the secret group. In some cities the Administration Party actually developed considerable independence with respect to the Wahnetas. For example, in New York City two formal political parties, the Administration and the Anti-Administration Parties, existed from the late 1880's to about 1910. Both of these groups were formally organized, published or were supported by weekly newspapers, and held regular primary elections to nominate local candidates. The Wahnetas operated within the Administration Party and for the most part were able to nominate their own men. But on at least one occasion the Wahnetas lost control of the New York Administration Party, and anti-Wahnetas were nominated.[14]

Basically, the issues between the Administration and Anti-Administration Parties in New York City, and between the Wahnetas and their opponents on the international level, centered on conservative versus militant trade-union action. The differences in the ideological positions of the two groups may have been set by the fact that the Administration-Wahneta group, as its public name suggests, was the historic "in" party, while the Antis were the "outs." The Administration Party, as the "responsible" party, advocated conciliation and arbitration rather than

13. "All members of the lodge were instructed by a majority vote to vote at the union meeting as a body on certain specific propositions . . . and certain men were selected to take the floor and speak in favor of the . . . policy."—New York Investigating Committee Report, p. 9.

14. See the files of *The Unionist* (New York) *circa* 1880-1910 for Administration Party activities, and the *New York Union Printer* for the Anti-Administration Party.

strikes as the best means of securing concessions from employers, while the Antis attacked arbitration and argued that printers could make gains only through demonstrating their economic strength. When discussing the priority issue, for example, an Administration Party president of the New York local argued that a rigid seniority system would work to the disadvantage of the most capable men and would help the inefficient, while the Antis' spokesman argued that union printers must protect each other as a collective group.

§ The Formalization of the Two-Party System

THE ANTIS on both local and international levels were initially hampered by the fact that though a union faction they were in principle opposed to the existence of factions and parties in the union as part of their general attack on the Wahnetas. This prevented them from forming an active permanent international opposition group and reduced the effectiveness of their campaign organization. In New York, for example, the Anti party in 1907 succeeded in passing a law outlawing party caucuses. In 1908 the election was fought between a previous Anti leader, who ran as an independent opponent of factionalism, and a former Administration leader, who appealed in an election leaflet for the support of "the members of the Union constituting what was known as the Administration Party before the abolition of the officially recognized caucuses."

After ten years of unsuccessfully fighting international elections with loose informal organization, the opposition delegates to the 1911 convention of the ITU decided to form an international union political party, which they called the Progressive Party. This party, the first open international party in the union, absorbed various local anti-Wahneta groups throughout the country and began the task of setting up regular permanent party clubs in the locals. To stress the differences between themselves and the Wahnetas the Progressives proclaimed the policy, which is still followed, that any member of the ITU may attend any meeting of the Progressive Party, regardless of whether he is a member of the party.

In the campaign of 1912 the Progressives charged that a secret society was in control of the union and that the administration which had been in power for twelve years had become conservative and timid in its dealings with employers. They also attacked it for attempting to centralize too much power in the national office. The Administration forces, in turn, denied the charges that they belonged to a secret society and pointed to the great increase in the size of the union and to the economic benefits that had been gained under their admittedly conservative leadership.[15]

The Wahneta-Administration slate was re-elected in 1912, but since that election two international parties have continued to exist and contest elections within the union. Between 1912 and 1928 the two parties were known as the Progressive and Administration Parties, with the old Wahneta organization the controlling group within the Administration Party. The latter group won every international office until 1920, though the opposition Progressives succeeded in capturing the administrations of a number of important locals and were also powerful enough to force through legislation by referendum. For example, in 1917 a referendum proposal initiated by Progressive locals revived the priority law which had been repealed by a Wahneta-controlled international convention in 1915.

The turning point in the development of the international political system occurred in 1919-1920. In 1919 the New York locals of the ITU and of the Printing Pressmen attempted to win the forty-four-hour week in the book and job shops and decided to strike when the publishers refused this demand and proposed arbitration. The international officers of both unions refused to sanction a strike in New York, on the grounds that the national employing printers' association had agreed to recommend to its members that they sign a forty-four-hour agreement as of May 1, 1921. On October 1, 1919, the New York locals of both unions launched strikes which were immediately branded illegal by their respective international unions. Since the strike was illegal under the ITU constitution, it was described by the strikers and the local as a voluntary vacation rather than a strike, and the strike movement became known as the "vacationist movement." Marsden Scott, the Wahneta President of the ITU, did everything possible to get the men to return to work, including publicly supporting the position of the employers. The pressure for a strike in New York had largely come from the opposition Progressives, but rank-and-file support for it was so strong that many of the local Wahnetas and the president of the New York local, Leon Rouse, who previously had been elected with Wahneta support against Progressive opposition, supported the vacation. The vacationist strike was ultimately lost, but it had the effect of bringing into

---

15. It is interesting to note that the Administration Party always used the word *conservative* as a positive virtue, thus: "it was necessary to put forward the most able and *conservative* men in the party." At the Anti-caucus, however, "conservatism had no place."—*The Unionist*, 31:No. 8, p. 1 (May 10, 1906).

the Progressive ranks many men, such as New York's President Rouse, who had been opponents of the party.[16]

The campaign of 1920 was perhaps the bitterest ever fought in the history of the ITU. The Wahnetas recognized that adverse reaction to their handling of the New York strike and to their general policy of avoiding strikes while relying on conciliation and arbitration threatened their twenty-year domination of the ITU. In a desperate effort to retain power, they devoted much of their campaign literature to the argument that the Progressive Party was under the control of Bolsheviks and Wobblies, while the Administration Party was presented as the "American party." Their principal piece of campaign literature was headed THIS IS AMERICA—NOT RUSSIA. The Wahnetas even went so far as to charge in a letter sent out by the head of the Grand Lodge that the Progressive candidate for ITU president had committed adultery with the wife of a sick member and had abandoned the woman after she had become pregnant.

The Progressives in turn charged that the Wahneta leaders were reactionaries who preferred the good will of the employers to that of the members. They attempted to prove that the Administration Party was supported and even financially aided by employers. They blamed Scott and his fellow officers for the loss of the 1919 forty-four-hour strike, and asserted that under Wahneta control the ITU had fallen behind other unions in the struggle for economic gains. The Progressives also were not above using personal arguments and charged that the Administration secretary-treasurer was an alcoholic and unable to properly perform his duties as a union officer.

This election witnessed the first defeat of the Wahneta-Administration Party. Marsden Scott was defeated for re-election by the Progressive candidate John McPharland, a leader of the 1919 New York vacationist strike. The Administration Party, however, retained control of the international Executive Council, as the secretary-treasurer and the two vice-presidents elected were candidates of that party. In large measure, Scott's defeat could be attributed to the fact that the New York membership turned overwhelmingly against him in the election.

In the four elections between 1920 and 1926 the ITU membership was almost evenly divided between the two parties. Winning candidates for international office usually secured only slightly over 50% of the total vote (see Table 1). Given the closeness of the race, it is not sur-

16. See *The New York Situation*, a pamphlet issued by New York Typographical Union No. 6, for copies of many relevant documents on the 1919 strike. See the *Typographical Journal*, issues from July 1919 to May 1920, for the position of the ITU administration; see also Sylvia Kopald, *Rebellion in Labor Unions*.

Table 1—Election Returns in the ITU from 1898 to 1954, with Proportion of Members Voting

Year	FOR PRESIDENT, %			FOR 1st VICE-PRES., %			FOR 2nd VICE-PRES., %			FOR SEC.-TREAS., %			MEMBERS VOTING FOR PRESIDENT, %
	P	W-I	O	P	W-I	O	P	W-I	O	P	W-I	O	
1898	58.7	34.8								24.7	75.3		66.6
1900	41.4	59.6								(Unopposed)			73.8
1902	25.7	74.3								(Unopposed)			72.4
1904	39.1	60.9								15.4	84.6		74.3
1906	(Unopposed)									(Unopposed)			(Unopposed)
1908	38.2	61.2		40.7	59.3					38.0	62.0		78.8
1910	41.8	58.2		44.5	55.5					37.0	63.0		79.1
1912	44.2	55.8		51.0	49.0					44.4	55.6		80.2
1914	(Unopposed)			27.4	62.1					(Unopposed)			67.8
1916	(Unopposed)			(Unopposed)						35.3	64.7		70.1
1918	35.9	64.1		36.9	63.1					35.7	64.3		67.0
1920	51.3	48.7		48.0	52.0		46.7	53.3		45.4	54.6		77.8†
1922	54.3	45.7		52.0	48.0		50.1	49.9		47.6	52.4		77.1†
1924	47.7	52.3		48.5	51.5		46.8	53.2		44.7	55.3		81.4
1926	51.7	48.3		47.4	49.1	3.9	50.0	50.0		48.3	51.7		80.5†
1928	63.9	36.1		63.4	36.6		61.4	38.6		56.5	43.5		76.6
1930	59.1	23.1	18.8	58.9	25.7	15.4	62.9	21.0	16.1	61.9	38.1		74.7
1931				49.4	50.6								64.1*†
1932	54.6	45.4		58.7	25.7	8.8	51.2	40.0	8.8	63.5	36.5		72.0
1934	57.0	43.0		64.1	35.9		59.2	25.5	15.3	65.5	34.5		69.1
1936	58.8	41.2		63.7	36.3		57.4	31.1	11.5	66.5	33.5		69.1
1938	38.8	61.2		51.2	48.8		47.2	52.8		51.8	48.2		71.5†
1940	47.8	52.2		50.9	49.1		43.3	43.8	12.8	50.2	49.8		74.8†
1942	48.2	51.8		46.3	53.7		45.3	54.7		51.0	49.0		71.4†
1944	51.7	32.6	15.7	57.0	43.0		50.3	39.3	10.5	48.5	34.7	16.8	62.1
1945										63.1	36.9		69.2*
1946	71.7	28.9		69.4	30.6		69.0	31.0		65.3	34.7		76.0
1948	57.5	42.5		61.4	38.6		59.2	40.8		63.1	36.9		74.4
1950	55.4	44.6		53.7	46.3		58.2	41.8		57.5	43.5		79.6
1952	56.6	43.4		55.1	44.9		55.7	44.6		58.8	41.2		80.0
1954	50.4	49.6		50.8	49.2		54.4	45.6		55.0	45.0		79.9

* Special election: incumbent died in office.
† No party had complete control of the Executive Council

P Progressive W-I Wahneta-Independent O Other

Source: Calculated from election returns in Typographical Journal.

prising that in three out of the four elections in this period neither party won complete control of the four major offices—president, two vice-presidents, and secretary-treasurer. In 1920, as was indicated above, the Administration Party won three out of the four posts; in 1922 the parties divided the four positions, the Progressives taking the presidency and the first vice-presidency. John McPharland, the Progressive president, died shortly after re-election and was succeeded by Charles Howard, the Progressive first vice-president, who was to remain the national standard-bearer of the Progressives until his death in 1938. In 1924 James Lynch, who had been President of the ITU from 1900 to 1912 and had retired to take a New York State political job, was elected as ITU president over Howard. He carried the entire Administration slate with him, though the majorities were small. In 1926 Lynch was beaten by Howard, but the Administration Party still retained control of the other three executive positions. The first complete triumph of the Progressives occurred in 1928, when Howard and the entire slate of Progressive candidates were elected by majorities, in most cases, of over 60%. The Progressives succeeded in retaining complete control of the Executive Council (with the exception of a temporary one-year loss of the first vice-presidency) from 1928 to 1938.

The years 1920 to 1928 were important in the extension and legitimation of the party system in the ITU. Between 1900 and 1920, few persons, if any, thought that the anti-Administration group had much chance of winning. While the governing party had contact through its control of the union apparatus with almost every local in the international, the opposition had limited resources and could not reach many of the smaller locals with its arguments. Moreover, the officers of these smaller locals were in large part dependent on the good will of the international administration for the successful conduct of local affairs. Negotiations with employers were often handled by international representatives, who were also political organizers for the Administration party. The small locals, therefore, usually gave large majorities to the Administration candidates. And Wahnetas often made efforts to recruit the local leaders to their organization. Membership in the Wahneta organization both helped a local leader to fill his local leadership role and gave him a sense of participating in an elite group which made the real policy of the union. As a "Wah," he was on the inside.

Effective opposition to the national administration could develop only within the larger locals. They were relatively independent of the international. They had been strong organizations long before the international actually had any power, and, jealous of their autonomy, they often came into conflict with the international administration. Many of them had their own cleavages, based on local issues but involving on one side or another the Wahneta organization. The Progressive Party was in large measure organized by men from the large locals and gained its first electoral triumphs there.

This was changed in the years between 1920 and 1928, when the party divisions penetrated all but the smallest locals. Progressive and Administration Party clubs were founded everywhere; both parties created state organizations and published many local and regional papers. During this period the parties also published national monthly magazines which went out to members and locals all over the country. All of this political activity cost both parties tens of thousands of dollars, which were raised from party members and supporters. The uncertainty of the outcome of future elections, plus the fact that each party held some international offices throughout this period, broke the domination of the Administration group over the smaller locals. Since the union organ, the *Typographical Journal,* publishes articles by every officer each month, the division of international offices in these years meant that both parties were able to reach every man in the union through the columns of the official *Journal.* While the Administration group retained control of every international convention in this period, these conventions became arenas for parliamentary debates between the two parties over every conceivable issue. In addition, many issues were submitted to referendum, and partisan political activity continued between elections. Local elections, which were usually held annually, often became contests between the local Administration conservatives and the opposing Progressives. It is obvious from reading the documents of the day that thousands of printers throughout the country were involved in the party struggle during these years and spent a great part of their time, both at work and at leisure, debating issues or more actively engaged in the party fights.

§ The Progressive Period

THE YEAR 1920 was the turning point in the history of the Administration-Wahneta group. Not only did it lose the presidency of the ITU for the first time, but L. C. Shepard, who had directed the Wahnetas from the turn of the century, died shortly before the election. These events confronted the organization with the problem of succession of leadership as different groups within it struggled for control of the party machinery and for the nomination for ITU president. The factional struggle within the Administration Party ended in a public split in 1928, and it is possible that this was the decisive factor behind the Progressives' sweep of international offices in the election of 1928.

Having lost control over the international offices, the Wahnetas had no further use for the name Administration Party. The dominant section of the party reconstituted itself as the Conservative Party, while an opposition faction merged with a group of disgruntled Progressives and became the Unionist Party. In 1930 the Progressives under Howard again swept the election, while the two new parties divided the opposition vote. The Conservative presidential candidate received 23% of the vote as compared with 19% for the Unionist.

The 1930 election results clearly indicated that the two opposition parties would be politically impotent unless they reunited. Impetus for such reunity was created by a special election held in the latter part of 1931 to fill the vacant office of first vice-president. Leon Rouse, who had been president of Big Six, the New York local, from 1915 to his defeat in 1931, attempted to get the Progressive nomination for the vacant vice-presidency. He was refused the nomination, broke with his party, ran as an independent candidate with the backing of both opposition parties, and was elected. Following this victory the Conservatives formally joined with Rouse to form a new party, the Independent Movement (later the Independent Party). The Unionists refused at first to join this new group, but were unable to maintain significant electoral strength in subsequent elections and ultimately dissolved.

From 1932 on, the political scene in the ITU was clear-cut. The union again had a two-party system: the incumbent Progressives and the opposition Independents. While a few leaders and undoubtedly many supporters had changed allegiance, these were essentially the same two factions which had contended for union office since 1900. The Progressives remained the militant party of the union, while the Independents succeeded to the role of the conservatives.

The change in status, with the conservatives in opposition and the militants in office, plus the problems faced by the union as a consequence of the Great Depression, made it difficult if not impossible for the two parties to be consistent in their ideological positions. The Progressives, for example, though traditionally advocates of administrative decentralization and local autonomy, found it necessary to resist the pressures from the larger locals to cut down on the work week or increase the local dues levied on the employed members for the benefit of the unemployed. In the elections of 1934 and 1936 the opposition Independents attacked the incumbent Progressives for not rigidly enforcing the five-day week, for being lax in organizing non-union plants, and for increased centralization of authority in the international office.

The Progressives, however, were able to carry their slate into office from 1932 to 1936 in spite of the depression situation, though their vote underwent a secular decline. Factionalism developed within the party as many of the more militant or radical Progressives in the larger cities attempted to make the party more aggressive. Efforts were made in 1934 and 1936 by factions within the Progressives to defeat Charles Howard for renomination as party candidate for ITU president. The large locals were turning against Howard, in part for the same reasons that had turned them against the Wahnetas in the twenties. Howard, who had earlier favored local autonomy and aggressive action, was now weakening on both these points. One of the major issues of this period concerned autonomy of the locals in handling the unemployment problem. Howard and the Progressive Party opposed this and steadily lost the support of the large locals. Howard's policies became increasingly centralist and conservative.

The ability of the Progressives to retain office in the early and middle thirties may be attributed in part to the fact that while the depression strengthened membership sentiments favorable to more militant action, this shift could not be expressed electorally because the opposition on the national level was conservative. Evidence for this interpretation may be found in the great growth in electoral strength of third parties, which were formed in a number of the larger locals by disgruntled Progressives allied with a growing Communist minority.

Before the election of 1938 two events occurred which were to affect ITU politics for the next six years: a split in the Progressive Party, and the expulsion from the AFL of unions affiliated with the Committee for Industrial Organization. Claude M. Baker, Progressive first vice-president of the ITU, broke with the Progressive Party and accepted the nomination for ITU president from the Independents.

The developments surrounding the formation of the CIO seriously affected the ITU because its president, Charles Howard, was the first secretary of the CIO. Although Howard was one of the major leaders of the CIO, he served the group as an individual, and the ITU did not formally affiliate with the CIO. Howard's connection with the CIO was originally challenged by the Independents on the grounds that he was devoting too much time to non-ITU activities. Following the expulsion of CIO unions from the AFL, the AFL demanded that the ITU clarify its position on the issue. In the ensuing discussion within the union both political parties seemed unsure of their stand. The Progressives criticized the AFL leadership for expelling other unions, but did not propose that the ITU leave the Federation. The Independents, on the other hand, favored the AFL, but like the Progressives were afraid to make an issue out of the matter. The reactions of the two parties to the controversy within the Federation grew out of their past ideological positions. The Progressives for much of their history had given support to the idea of closer cooperation and at times even amalgamation with the other printing-trades unions. The Independents, and before them the Wahneta-Administration group, had always favored the principle of craft unionism.

The issue finally came to a head when the AFL ordered all its affiliates to pay a special tax to fight the CIO. The Progressive leadership seized the occasion to state that they were for union unity and were opposed to paying a war tax. They also argued that the AFL had no legal right to levy such a tax without the voluntary consent of its affiliated unions. Howard attempted to place the Independents and Baker in the position of defending the Federation's right to dictate to the ITU. In 1938 the membership voted 35,254 to 10,901 to refuse to pay the special assessment and the ITU was expelled by the AFL.

In spite of their endorsement of this Progressive policy, the membership in the May 1938 elections gave Baker, running as an Independent, 61% of the vote in his contest with Howard. At the same time, however, they re-elected two of the four Progressive members of the Executive Council, including Woodruff Randolph, the secretary-treasurer, who was the most aggressive of the Progressive leaders. Union observers interpreted this vote as a defeat for Howard's conservative internal policies with relation to the problem of unemployment and strikes rather than as a repudiation of his CIO policy.

From 1938 through 1944 the union witnessed a situation comparable to 1920-1928, with neither party able to win all the international offices. Baker and Randolph, the two party leaders, continued to win re-election and carried on a six-year-long debate with each other in the issues of the monthly *Typographical Journal*. The AFL-CIO controversy continued to be important, and the members were called upon almost once a year to vote in referendum on whether they were willing to accept various terms offered by the AFL to secure the reaffiliation of the ITU. In each of these votes the Progressive position was upheld.

As World War II developed the situation within the printing industry changed greatly. The principal problem facing the union was keeping up with the inflationary spiral rather than unemployment. The ITU, like other unions, signed a no-strike pledge for the duration of the war and took its collective bargaining disagreements to the War Labor Board. The War Labor Board, however, tended to be tough with the ITU. It resisted giving printers the 15% increase which most unions received under the Little Steel formula on the grounds that printers' wages were out of line with other comparably skilled workers. The Board was sympathetic also to employers' arguments that ITU laws which restricted output were hampering the war effort. The ITU membership became increasingly discontented with the fact that their real income was dropping. The Progressives, led by Randolph, began to urge that the ITU Executive Council should permit locals to strike. They argued that printing strikes would not injure the war effort and that printers were being forced to give up too much for cooperating with the government. The Independents, on the other hand, believed that the ITU could not break with the no-strike policy of the entire labor movement and that wartime strikes would injure the union.

The 1944 election was in large part fought around the issue of militancy or conciliation in wartime labor disputes. The Progressives for the first time since 1936 swept all offices, and Woodruff Randolph succeeded Claude Baker as president of the ITU. Baker was the fifth ITU president to be defeated for re-election since 1920.

Since 1944 the Progressives have remained in control of the International. In 1946 Randolph was re-elected as president of the ITU with 72% of the vote. This victory of the Progressives was the greatest obtained by any ITU party since the formalization of the Party system. In large measure it may be attributed to the sharp gains in wages and reduction in hours which were achieved following the ending of the war. Many locals which had secured little or no increase in wages during the war were able to secure increases of $10 to $20 a week, while hours of work were reduced. Although any postwar administration probably could have made equal gains, the Progressives, who had encouraged militant tactics, were able to take credit for the increases.

Given a victory of the magnitude of 1946, one might have expected a period of relative internal political peace, and perhaps a long-term eclipse of the repudiated Independent Party. Such was not to prove the case, however. In 1947 the Taft-Hartley Act was passed by Congress. The Randolph-Progressive administration decided that this new law threatened the very existence of the ITU, for it outlawed many practices which had existed in the industry since the turn of the century. The Progressive leadership decided to force the printing employers to comply with union law rather than United States law. Specifically, they insisted that employers agree informally to adhere to ITU practices which were forbidden by the Taft-Hartley law. For example, the union wanted the employers to preserve the closed shop and the rigid priority rules and was also concerned with maintaining practices which might be interpreted under the law as featherbedding. To dramatize its deep opposition to the new act the Progressive administration also refused to sign the non-Communist affidavits required by Taft-Hartley of unions which desire to be recognized by the NLRB.

The union's insistence on informal agreements led to a number of major conflicts between employers and the locals in various parts of the country. As the strikes and consequent costs to the union membership grew, the Independent Party seized on the Taft-Hartley policy of the union as its principal issue. It argued that the Progressives had exaggerated the menace of the Taft-Hartley Act, and urged that ITU officers be instructed to sign the Taft-Hartley non-Communist oath.

These issues have dominated the elections of 1948-1954. The Progressives won all four elections, but with declining majorities. At the present time the union is barely more than 50% Progressive. There is evidence that the Progressives are gradually losing control of the international union. They have already declined greatly in many of the large locals. In the past, such a shift within the larger locals has usually preceded an international change. The larger locals, as we pointed out earlier, are comparatively independent of the international and can more readily than the small locals turn against an incumbent administration.

§ Membership Control and the Party System

THUS FAR we have equated democracy in the ITU with the fact that the membership of the union has the right to choose between two parties representing opposing approaches to trade-union action. That these are real rather than formal alternatives is indicated by the fact that most shifts in ITU administration have meant sharp reversals in collective bargaining tactics pursued by the international union. For example, the defeats of the Wahneta-Administration party in 1920 and 1922 were followed by a militant strike wave and an end of the rigid arbitration agreement that had existed between the newspaper publishers and the ITU from 1902 to 1922. In its temporary return to total control of the union in 1924, the Administration group attempted to revive the arbitration agreement. This effort was finally dropped with the defeat of President Lynch in 1926.[17] The triumph of the Progressives

---

17. A similar pattern of reversal with party control may be seen in the policy of the union with regard to appeals from discharges. Under ITU law a discharged man may appeal his discharge to the chapel, the local union, then the ITU Executive Council, and as a court of last resort, the international convention. If any of these union bodies reverses the foreman's decision, the foreman or employer may then appeal to the next highest union body. In 1913 the Wahneta president of the ITU ruled that a man could not be reinstated as long as the case was being appealed. The Progressives opposed this decision, and in 1922, when in control, they

in 1944 was also followed by a greater tendency to resort to militant strike tactics.

The power of the membership to affect union policy and action is not limited, however, to its ability to choose one or another slate of candidates for international office. Since 1900 ITU members have been called upon to vote on about three hundred referenda. Referenda may be initiated by an international convention, the Executive Council, or petition from local unions. Most of these referenda have been on constitutional changes or on new assessments. There have been votes on changing the pension system, on defining the jurisdiction of the union, on the question of continued affiliation with the AFL, on adjusting the constitution to war needs, on changing the date of the convention, on the number of days a week a man may work, on unemployment relief, and on many other subjects.

The extent of membership control over the officialdom can be seen in the fact that the members have defeated twenty-nine of the ninety-nine proposals submitted by international conventions for their approval between 1920 and 1953. This figure is much more significant than it at first appears to be, for many of the proposals which were ratified involved noncontroversial technical amendments to the constitution. In most organizations, union or non-union, it is assumed that the national convention of delegates, elected by the members, represents the wishes of the members. It is clear from the record of conventions and referenda in the ITU that this assumption need not be valid. A convention in fact usually represents the local formal leadership structure, and the local leaders who go to the international conventions may and frequently do have values and interests which are different from those whom they nominally represent. This gap is generally obscured by the absence of any means for the direct expression of the desires of the membership. Referenda provide such a means of expression, *but only when they operate within the context of an institutionalized party system.* Otherwise, as in plebiscitarian one-party states or trade unions, they serve merely to legitimize the power and decisions of a ruling group. Although a large number of oligarchic unions have referenda, this has rarely resulted in the defeat of any administration proposal. In a context in which opposition and discussion of issues is not normal procedure, the average trade unionist can do little else but vote for the proposals of his permanent leaders.

---

ruled that a man must be reinstated if the local union rules in his favor. In 1925 the Administration officials returned to the 1913 regulation. Two years later the Progressive-controlled convention of 1927 restored the Progressive decision of 1922, which has remained union policy down to the present.

The power which referenda carried out within the context of a two-party system give to the membership is best seen by the votes in the ITU on salary increases for union officers. Since 1900 proposals for salary increases for international officers have been defeated eighteen times out of twenty-six (see Table 2). There does not appear to be any close relationship between the electoral strength of an administration and its ability to secure a salary increase for itself. Progressive and Wahneta-Independent officers have been equally frustrated by a membership which apparently does not believe in paying its president and secretary-treasurer more than twice what they themselves earn. In 1949 a proposal to pension union officers was defeated by more than a two-to-one majority. These referenda on officers' salaries are especially significant, for in general the leaders of the opposition party have not opposed raising salaries. Defeats of salary increases on the international level tend to have a cumulative impact within the union, since the salaries which the officials of large locals can hope to secure is limited by the level achieved by the International officers. Since the principal leaders of the opposition party usually include both local officers and men who hope to achieve international office within a year, the opposition has generally tended to share with the incumbent officers of the international the belief that they are underpaid.

Attempts by union leaders to receive a wage increase resemble in many ways a prolonged collective-bargaining session conducted by referendum between the members and the officials. The union officers, who control the convention, begin the bargaining by asking for a large increase a few years after securing their last one. As the results of the salary referenda reported in Table 2 indicate, this first demand is always refused. The officers then make a second proposal for a smaller increase which is also usually refused. Finally a third or fourth proposal is made and passes. It is significant to note, however, that every salary increase that was proposed by an international convention since 1912, except that of 1950, was defeated. The final successful referendum is initiated from below by the locals. The members apparently resent and refuse salary proposals that openly come from the administration.

In general the members refuse to give their officers a raise except during periods of great prosperity. The most recent increases took place in 1919, 1929-30, 1947, and 1950, and in each case were proportionately less than the increases in the wages of working printers. *The ability of the members to limit the gap between their own salaries and that of their officers is probably a major factor sustaining the democratic system in the ITU, for it reduces the strain on ITU officers who return to the print shop following defeat.*

Table 2—Results of Referenda on Salary Increases for Officers of the ITU, 1900-1950

		For	Against
1901—To pay president and secretary-treasurer	$1,800	9,548	6,589
1904—To pay president and secretary-treasurer	$2,000	9,436	15,275
1905—To pay president and secretary-treasurer	$2,000	9,970	12,362
1906—To pay president and secretary-treasurer	$2,000	6,401	17,837
1907—To pay president	$2,000	13,240	13,134
1907—To pay secretary-treasurer	$2,000	13,691	12,763
1910—To pay president and secretary-treasurer	$3,000	11,682	19,035
1912—To pay president	$3,500	19,850	18,010
1912—To pay secretary-treasurer	$3,500	19,427	18,052
1916—To pay president and secretary-treasurer	$5,000	10,861	24,674
1917—To pay president and secretary-treasurer	$5,000	9,779	25,499
*1918—To pay president and secretary-treasurer	$5,000	13,323	20,292
1919—To pay president and secretary-treasurer	$5,000	25,322	19,314
1920—To pay president and secretary-treasurer	$10,000	11,712	35,444
1924—To pay president and secretary-treasurer	$8,500		
and first vice-president	$6,000	15,858	30,256
1928—To pay president and secretary-treasurer	$7,500		
and first vice-president	$5,000	17,043	25,580
1929—To pay president and secretary-treasurer	$7,500		
and first vice-president	$4,200	22,882	26,794
*1930—To pay president and secretary-treasurer	$7,500	27,710	28,030
†1931—To pay first vice-president	$5,200	23,592	26,057
1935—To pay first and second vice-presidents	$5,500	11,350	31,814
1944—To pay first vice-president	$6,000		
and second vice-president	$5,400	17,223	30,443
1944—To include second vice-president among			
regular salaried officials		22,172	25,531
*1945—To pay first vice-president	$6,000		
and second vice-president	$5,400	19,360	31,363
*1946—To increase first and second vice-presidents 30%			
	(to $4,200	32,262	22,071
*1947—To pay president and secretary-treasurer	$10,000		
and first and second vice-president	$7,500	38,031	24,835
1948—To pay president and secretary-treasurer	$12,000		
and first and second vice-presidents	$9,500	26,631	33,408
July			
1949—To pay president and secretary-treasurer	$12,000		
and first, second and third vice-presidents	$9,500	32,853	34,162
Dec.			
1949—To pay president and secretary-treasurer	$12,000		
and first and second vice-presidents	$9,500	27,993	36,371
1949—ITU officials a retirement pension of $10			
weekly for each two-year term of			
service up to 50% of salary		20,898	43,423
*July			
1950—(Same as two proposals above)		33,370	36,551
Dec.			
1950—To pay president and secretary-treasurer	$250/week		
and vice-presidents	$200/week	37,341	26,864

* Proposed by locals for referendum.   † Proposed by Executive Council.
All others proposed by convention.

Table 3—Results of Referenda to Increase Union Dues, 1920-1953

	For	Against
1920—To increase the per capita tax ten cents per member	29,952	17,365
*1921—To levy a 10% temporary assessment to finance the strike for the 44-hour week	40,703	11,499
1924—To levy an additional $1 per month for pension and mortuary assessments	18,962	26,090
1925—To increase monthly per capita tax ten cents for the Union Printer's Home	32,596	17,833
1929—To raise the pensions of the aged	18,684	32,200
1932—To levy an assessment of 1% for defense purposes (permanent)	21,887	28,354
*1933—To levy an assessment of 1% for defense purposes for one year	30,025	16,336
*1933—To increase old-age assessment of 1½% and later to 2%	16,725	19,893
*1933—Above proposal resubmitted	17,595	19,508
†1934—To increase pension assessment from 1% to 2%	25,670	20,971
1935—To make 40-hour week maximum and to permit locals to levy a 3% assessment for unemployment relief	21,914	21,857
*1938—To levy one-cent-per-month assessment for AFL to fight CIO	12,101	36,760
1938—To pay 2% assessment for pensions on monthly earnings of over $30 instead of $60	22,481	24,682
1939—To reduce pension assessment to 1½%, but to raise it again to 2% if fund falls to $1,500,000	23,434	27,441
1941—To increase pension assessment to 2½% and to raise pensions from $8 per week to $10 per week	32,707	22,769
1942—To increase per capita tax by twenty-five cents	12,158	37,004
*1943—To levy special assessment for six months of 0.5%	10,047	38,474
*1943—To increase per capita tax ten cents for the Union Printer's Home	26,947	21,440
*1944—To reduce assessments for pensions	31,887	19,497
†1945—To levy a special assessment of 0.5% for six months for defense	23,778	27,899
*1945—To levy a 1% tax for three months for defense purposes	29,292	20,503
1946—To levy 0.5% defense assessment	35,106	19,960
1946—To raise per capita from eighty cents to $1	30,665	24,741
1946—To raise strike benefits to 60% of salary for married men instead of 40% and 40% for single men instead of 25%	44,539	11,203
*1948—To levy a 4½% defense assessment for one year	44,829	21,477
1952—To levy a 2½% defense-fund assessment for one year	26,463	44,344
1953—To levy a 2% defense fund assessment to last until the defense fund has $5,000,000	25,471	46,356
†1953—To limit the funds which could be transferred from one union fund to another without referendum approval to $1,000,000	34,840	33,118
*1953—To raise the defense fund assessment from 0.5% to 1%	27,690	40,061

* Proposed by Executive Council.   † Proposed by locals.

All others proposed by conventions.

Source: Reports on referenda in *Typographical Journal.*

The desire of the members to keep control over their officers can be seen in the fact that two proposals in 1918 and 1929 to increase the term of international office from two to four years were defeated by large majorities. On the first occasion, the proposal was made by the Wahnetas in a year in which they had been re-elected with 64% of the vote, while the second proposal was made by the Progressives after they also had secured 64% of the vote in the election for ITU president.[18] Clearly, a large proportion of the men who vote for a given party are not willing to guarantee the men whom they support prolonged tenure in office. This suspicion of officialdom, regardless of party affiliation, has made it difficult if not impossible for an incumbent administration to so amend the constitution as to perpetuate its hold in office.

The record of referenda on the most fundamental power of a self-governing body, the voting of funds, provides probably the clearest evidence of the ability of the working printers to keep ultimate control of their union in their own hands. On a number of occasions the members have refused to vote for permanent dues increases, though there has been, of course, an increase in union dues as the wage and price level rose. One might compare the voting record of the ITU on dues increases (see Table 3) with the historic struggles between the King and the English Parliament on the passage of appropriations. Instead of giving large sums to their officers to spend at their own discretion, the ITU members, like Parliament, are more likely to vote for a special assessment of one year or less for a specific purpose such as a strike fund. Since 1920 four proposals to secure funds for a limited period have passed, and three have been defeated. On the other hand, ten referenda proposing permanent dues increases have been defeated in this period, while only five have passed. Of the five approved, two were for negligible increases of ten cents a month for the maintenance of the Union Printers' Home, so the real score is ten defeated and three ratified. These votes do not reflect an unwillingness on the part of the membership to support the union, for two of the most heavily supported assessments were for a 10% and a 4½% tax on wages to support striking members. The 10% tax was voted by 40,703 to 11,499 in 1921 to support the forty-four-hour-week strike, while the second large tax was passed by a vote of 44,829 to 21,477 in 1948 as a means of supporting the many Taft-Hartley strikes waged by the union. The generosity of the members in supporting their fellow striking unionists, in contrast

---

18. *Typographical Journal*, 53:16-33 (1918); *ibid.*, 76:19 (1930). In 1924 the members voted 24,371 to 18,005 to fill vacancies among the officers by direct special election rather than by Executive Council cooptation. See *Ibid.*, 65:830-38 (1924).

to their treatment of their officers and union apparatus, can be seen from the above votes and also from the fact that in 1946 the members voted by 44,539 to 11,203 to increase strike benefits from 40% to 60% of the regular wage for all married men, and from 25% to 40% for all single men.[19]

Referenda have also been important in permitting union groups which disagree with the actions of conventions or of the Executive Council to appeal over their heads to the membership. And on a number of occasions the membership, by referendum, has reversed the action of a convention. The Wahneta-controlled convention of 1911, for example, repealed the law outlawing secret societies. San Francisco, which was a Progressive stronghold, then initiated a referendum to reinstate the old law, which passed. In 1915 the convention repealed the priority law of 1906, which provided that the substitute first on the priority list was entitled to the first vacancy. Two years later in 1917 the Progressive local in Spokane initiated a proposal to put the 1906 law back on the statute book. This law was also passed.

During the Great Depression, the problem of making work and/or providing relief for the unemployed was the subject of a number of referenda. The large minority of unemployed men attempted to push through legislation which would reduce the work week and permit locals to increase assessments for the relief of the unemployed. Both parties feared to take stands on these politically charged issues, preferring that they be decided by referendum. In some cases conventions presented the members with alternative proposals. At the end of the depression decade AFL affiliation became a major issue in the union, and a number of referenda were held on that.

The referendum has continued to play a major role in setting union policy. During 1953, for example, three referenda were held in connection with defense-fund policies, with the two union parties in sharp disagreement over the use of these funds. The Progressive administration had turned over a large portion of the union's defense funds to a dummy corporation, Unitypo, which is owned by the union, seemingly as a means of avoiding certain restrictions in the Taft-Hartley Act on union expenditures. This corporation has used some of its funds to establish union-owned newspapers in competition with antiunion papers. The Progressives have argued that the books of Unitypo must be kept secret to prevent the publishers from learning the facts about the economic position of the union newspapers. The Independents, however, argued that the Progressives could then use these funds for any pur-

19. *Typographical Journal,* 109:297-311 (1946).

pose, including partisan activities. Though they have not been able to win in elections or at conventions where they have argued this issue, the Independents have been successful in three referenda held during 1953. In two of these, Progressive efforts to increase the size of union defense funds by raising the defense assessment were defeated. The third referendum was initiated by Independent locals to take away the power of an ITU administration to transfer funds from one union fund to another without approval of a referendum vote. The purpose of this proposal was to prevent the large pension and mortuary benefit funds of the union from being used to supplement the defense funds, which in turn were used to support Unitypo. Though the Progressive administration and party vigorously opposed this proposal, it was passed in a membership vote by 34,840 votes to 33,118.[20]

Because of the referendum, power derived from control of the union administrative and convention machinery is always limited, for the opposition can always call for a referendum on any issue. But the sheer formal provisions would mean little if the party system did not exist. For example, a referendum proposal must first be endorsed by 150 locals before it is placed on the ballot. Without the existence of an organized national opposition, it would be extremely difficult to get 150 different groups of men scattered throughout the United States to endorse the same proposal. Even more important, the existence of institutionalized opposition destroys the monopoly over information and propaganda to the membership which the incumbent administration possesses in one-party organizations. In the ITU almost every union issue is debated from at least two sides, and the members are accustomed to discussing and weighing proposals from the leadership rather than passively accepting them. Usually at least 40% of the members have voted against the incumbent administration, while many who vote for the administration do so without being its convinced partisans. Thus there is always a large group in the union which is inclined to view with some suspicion any proposals emanating from the administration. Together, the party system and the referenda have enabled the printers to retain a large measure of control over the major policies of their union.

§ The Parties and the New York Local

WHILE THIS STUDY is concerned with the operation of the two-party system in the ITU as a whole, much of our empirical data on contemporary union politics are drawn from observations and interviews

---

20. *Typographical Journal*, 123:278 (May 1953).

with members and leaders of Big Six, the New York local of the union. This local, which has over 9,000 members, about 10% of the total membership of the ITU, is the largest unit in the international. The history of party cleavage in Big Six is therefore important both as background for the analysis of the contemporary political situation and as an example of party politics on a local level.

New York, as was indicated earlier, has a history of formal partisan conflict, which precedes that in the international. Two formal parties, the Administration and Anti-Administration Parties, contested the annual local elections from the 1880's to the first decade of this century. The two groups eventually became the local units of the international Administration and Progressive Parties. Except for a few years the conservative faction controlled New York for most of this early period. In 1915 a one-year-old Progressive administration was defeated for re-election by the man who was to remain local president until 1931, Leon Rouse. Rouse, though officially a nonpartisan, was elected with the backing of the Wahneta group and was regarded as a supporter of the Administration Party. The vacationist strike of 1919, however, drastically changed the course of New York politics. Since the International Wahneta officials helped break this strike, it became impossible for anyone seeking election in New York to be publicly identified with the Administration Party. Rouse and many of his followers joined the Progressive Party, which carried New York in every international election in the twenties by majorities of close to three to one.

Given the overwhelming supremacy of the Progressives in New York, the political struggle between the conservative and militant factions shifted from an interparty to an intraparty conflict. Rouse, who had run as a nonpartisan in local elections before joining the Progressive Party, argued successfully within the party against the party's taking part in local elections and continued to run as a nonpartisan with the covert backing of Administration Party supporters and a section of the Progressive Party. With the exception of the election of 1927 his opposition in every local contest from 1921 to 1929 came from the so-called left-wing Progressives, who felt that their party had been captured in New York by a conservative group.

The Great Depression changed the New York political scene. For most of the thirties close to half of the members of the local did not have steady employment, and the politics of Big Six naturally were in large measure oriented around the problems of the unemployed. The fairly small group of Communists, who had previously played an ineffectual role in union politics, suddenly became important. They helped to form organizations of the unemployed and also joined in organizing a new union political party, the Amalgamation Party, which had considerable success. A second new local group, the Liberal Party, was also formed about this time by a number of former Administration Party supporters as a means of breaking through the traditional antagonism to the conservative faction that existed in the local. In 1931 in a multiparty race, the Liberal candidate was successful and the long reign of Leon Rouse came to an end.

Elections in the thirties were usually contested by three or four sets of candidates. The continued discontent of the unemployed and the practical inability of any administration to do much about it provided the base for the rise and fall of new parties and candidates. In 1933 the Liberal president was defeated for re-election by Leon Rouse, who staged a successful comeback running as a nonpartisan candidate. The Progressives gradually lost strength in New York because of the discontent of the unemployed with the policies of the Progressive ITU administration, and the left-wing Amalgamation Party replaced them as the principal anticonservative group in Big Six. Gradually as the thirties went on, politics in New York narrowed down to a contest between the Amalgamation Party and a conservative group led first by Rouse and after he died in 1935 by his successor as president, William Ward. Between 1937 and 1941 the elections in New York were contests between Ward and Elmer Brown, the leader of the Amalgamationists. In 1937 Brown lost to Ward by less than 60 votes. In 1938 in a special election for vice-president Brown was victorious with a majority of 250 votes, and in 1939 Brown defeated Ward for the presidency by 60 votes. Ward, in turn, defeated Brown by a small majority in 1941.

These contests between Brown and Ward represented a basic continuation of the left-right division. The local Progressive Party was too weak in this period to even nominate candidates for president, and many of its leaders joined with the Amalgamation Party in a campaign group called the Nonpartisan Committee. Other more conservative Progressives backed the Ward group. The Brown group argued in favor of militant organizing campaigns, greater aggressiveness in collective-bargaining negotiations, and spreading the existing work among the unemployed. The conservatives, on the other hand, tended to be the party of the employed and argued that the local union could do little to alleviate the problems caused by the national depression.

The collapse of national party divisions in Big Six during the thirties was due in part to the fact that neither national party was able or willing to become the party of the unemployed. On an international level, the unemployed were politically impotent, though they were a large minority. The employed majority was not willing to reduce its own

standard of living to support the unemployed. In New York, however, those without a steady situation constituted about half the union
and could therefore constitute the base of a local party or faction.

Following Brown's defeat in 1941 and the development of wartime
prosperity, the left-wing Nonpartisan Committee dissolved and entered
the Progressive Party. From 1943 on, the New York political scene
was largely occupied by two forces: the Progressive Party and the more
conservative group led by Ward. Most of this latter group were Independents in international politics, though they did not operate formally
as Independents in New York, since they believed that they could pick
up more support if they maintained a nonpartisan guise. The conservatives remained in control of the local from 1941 until 1949, when the
Progressive candidate, Frank Barrett, was elected by a small majority.
Following this defeat the conservatives decided that the advantages of
a formal political party outweighed its disadvantages and organized a
local Independent Party, affiliated with the international Independent
Party. Since 1949 the two parties, Progressive and Independent, have
alternated in winning elections by majorities of less than 1%. The
Progressives won in 1949, were defeated in 1951, regained control of
the local presidency by seven votes in 1953 and were reelected for the
first time in 1955.

The history of New York politics points to another interesting aspect
of politics in the ITU, the fact that international and local politics may
be sharply contradictory. Since the vacationist strike in 1919, New
York has been a Progressive city in international elections, with the
exception of a brief period in the thirties when Charles Howard, the
Progressive president of the ITU, received a minority of the votes in
New York. Even in these elections, however, his running mates on the
international Progressive ticket usually received large majorities. The
conservative faction in New York, however, was able to win local elections, both under a party label, and earlier as nonpartisans or lower-case-*i*
independents. Thus local conservatism has always been stronger than
international conservatism in Big Six.[21]

The give-and-take of local politics has resulted in modifications of

---

21. This pattern in Big Six is far from unique in politics. In United States
politics, for example, the primary system serves as the mechanism through which
a basic liberal-conservative split can function within one-party states, just as in
Big Six, the special local parties permit a political struggle in what is, nationally,
a one-party local. In Holland, two Catholic provinces give the Catholic Party a
majority of from 70% to 90% in national elections. In provincial and municipal
elections, however, the Catholics break up into three parties: left, center, and
right. In Canada, Quebec is as solidly Liberal in federal elections as the American
South is Democratic. In provincial elections, however, the conservatives of the
province are organized in a provincial party, the Union Nationale, which has won
almost every provincial election since 1936.

union procedures to strengthen democracy on the local level, just as on the international level. In the first decade of the twentieth century the opponents of the Wahnetas in New York fought for and obtained a local law which limited the term of office of chapel (shop) chairmen to two one-year terms unless the chapel re-elected the chairman by a unanimous vote. This measure was designed to curtail prolonged political-clique control of a chapel, and as we shall see later, it plays an important role in sustaining the political system. The growing opposition to Leon Rouse's prolonged tenure as president of Big Six led every opposition group in the twenties to make a principle out of opposition to long tenure and to specifically commit itself to a two-term limit for presidents of the local. This law was adopted following Rouse's defeat in 1931. Before that year the local president had the power to appoint a nine-man executive committee to assist him. This procedure was also opposed by groups opposed to Rouse, and in 1931 the executive committee became an elective body. This procedure has often resulted in the election to the executive committee of men who opposed the incumbent president. On some occasions a majority of the committee has been opposed to the president. Moreover, as a further safeguard against administrative powers, the New York membership, like the membership of the international, has tended to resist giving salary increases to local officers.

The history of New York politics clearly indicates that the basic militant-conservative cleavage affects local issues as well as international ones. There are, however, some significant differences between international and local bases of division. For one thing, international political issues must necessarily revolve around over-all policies which affect the entire union, such as the issues of how to meet the Taft-Hartley Act or what to do about AFL affiliation. Local issues, however, are almost exclusively concerned with the negotiation of local scales and with such day-to-day problems of contract administration as the processing of grievances. Clearly the major arguments of a local opposition, regardless of whether it is conservative or militant, are that the incumbents negotiated a bad contract and that they are lax in enforcing union laws. Thus where the Progressives have been in office for a number of years, one will find the Independents attacking the Progressives for being too conciliatory in dealing with the employers. A local conservative party cannot be as consistent in its conservative position as can the conservative party on the international level.

Another difference between international and local politics is the greater frequency of nonpartisan or lower-case-*i* independent candidates in local as compared with international elections. This is in large measure related to the ease of communicating with members situated in one city as compared with the difficulties of reaching 100,000 men throughout North America. It is obvious that no one can hope to contest an international election without the equivalent of an international party organization. One man with a few friends, however, can reach a good part of the membership of a local. Consequently, in New York and other locals many lower-case *i*'s have won election for various posts.

Political discussion and conflict in the locals are not limited to campaign situations. The union has regular monthly membership meetings which are attended by most of the political leaders. Rank-and-file attendance at such meetings may vary from a few hundred to three or four thousand, depending on the issues up for discussion and the season of the year. The high figure is often reached at the meetings which discuss contract negotiations. The different parties and union politicians attempt to use these meetings to create issues. They may question an action of the president with regard to the handling of an overtime dispute, seniority, or some other grievance. The principal source of controversy, however, is the handling of collective bargaining or scale negotiations. While contracts usually last for two years, separate contracts are negotiated for the newspapers and commercial shops at different times, so that the local is involved in negotiations almost every year. The procedure followed during negotiations is quite prolonged. The administration begins by appointing a scale committee, which after drawing up the union's demands must submit the proposed contract to a membership meeting. Following the beginning of negotiations with the employers the scale committee must report back any agreement or change in union proposals to another meeting. The final contract must again be submitted. The opposition usually attacks the administration proposals and agreements. Often the issue is submitted to a referendum of the men in the shops.

Final settlement of union contracts usually occurs only after prolonged negotiations, often lasting half a year or more. During such periods, attendance at membership meetings runs into the thousands and special meetings to discuss the latest phases of negotiations are often called between the regular monthly meetings. Since these negotiations are also the lifeblood of union controversy and are of crucial importance to the members involved, the union is faced with a prolonged period of internal discussion and partisan controversy.

§ Conclusion

THE HISTORY of internal politics in the ITU over the past seventy years is the story of the development of an institutionalized party system. But the historical continuity of the party system in the ITU and its gradual institutionalization do not explain why the ITU is the only national union whose early factional cleavages developed into a party system. Many international unions have had competing political groups within them. The United Automobile Workers were divided among themselves until 1950, when Reuther's victory became complete. The CIO Textile Workers witnessed internal cleavage for several years preceding 1952, when the minority group left the union. The United Mine Workers had recurrent factional fights for many years until Lewis was finally able to destroy opposition groups in the early thirties. The Printing Pressmen, the second largest union in the printing trades, had periodic internal conflicts until George Berry, its president for four decades, was able to consolidate his dictatorship in the twenties. Many AFL unions witnessed conflicts between Socialists and non-Socialists before World War I, while a number of the CIO unions were divided in the late forties between supporters of the Communist Party and their opponents; but none of these internal divisions, nor the many other factional fights that have occurred in American trade unions, developed into a generally accepted party system.

Thus the central problem in explaining the ITU's unique political system is not "How did it begin, out of what series of events did it emerge?" but rather "How has it been perpetuated, what factors and forces have sustained and supported it, given it legitimacy and permanence?" Therefore in the succeeding chapters we view the ITU as a social system, focusing on its contemporary political structure and processes and looking for those elements in the occupation, the structure of the union, and the economics of the industry which in their intricate interrelations operate to sustain the network of institutions, behavior, and sentiments composing the union's internal political system.

The Social Setting of Trade-Union Democracy

CHAPTER 4

Secondary Organization and Trade-Union Democracy

THE TWO-PARTY SYSTEM is perhaps the most striking characteristic of the ITU. Scarcely less striking, and as unique among American unions, is the vast network of voluntary organizations within the ITU, created by its members to satisfy their social and recreational needs.

In most large ITU locals, such as those in New York, Chicago, and San Francisco, there are printers' social clubs, lodges, sport clubs, veterans' groups, and many other groups. On the international level there are three sports organizations of printers, for baseball, golf, and bowling. These hold annual tournaments to which teams and men come from different parts of North America. So numerous have voluntary local printers' organizations been that it has proved impossible to compile an exhaustive list of all the printers' organizations that have existed in the last half century in New York City alone. Many had short histories or disappeared without leaving any records. Without even exhausting the sources more than a hundred different organizations have been located, and we are certain that this list could be more than doubled.

The formal functions of most of the groups are primarily social. Some, at different times, have maintained regular headquarters where men could gather to talk or play cards, chess, or checkers and get something to eat and drink. Some are primarily sports organizations, though they may run occasional social affairs such as dances. Still others, such as the typographical societies, link their social affairs to benevolent activities. Some have brought together printers who are members of

(*69*)

the same ethnic or religious group, such as the Dublin Society or the Jewish Printers. Union Label Clubs have enabled printers living in the same neighborhoods to come together to further union objectives. Common past experiences have been the basis for groups such as war-veterans' posts or former employees of defunct newspapers. In this bewildering variety, trade and skill distinctions are another basis for grouping. Fraternal orders, such as the Masons, have also been the basis for printers' organizations.

Often within a single large printing plant, such as the large metropolitan newspapers, microscopic versions sprout up of the groups that exist for the occupation as a whole. Veterans' posts, lodges, and social and athletic clubs composed of workers in the same plant are common. Some of the smaller shops or shifts often constitute themselves extravocational social or recreational units.

Until fairly recently, regular weekly and biweekly newspapers were published, devoted largely to reporting the activities of the union and the various subgroups. Like the clubs these newspapers (and there have been at least three major ones) had no official relationship to the union and were published by private individuals. The most recent of these in New York, the *Typographical Forum* (1932-1943), reached a peak circulation of 3,500, or more than one-third of the working members of the union. It ceased publication during the war because overtime work did not leave enough free time available to put out a newspaper.

Social clubs, organized leisure activities such as bowling leagues, and union newspapers are of course not unique to the printers, although we know of no other occupation which has as many and diverse forms of organized extravocational activities as the ITU. What must be significant about the printers' occupational community is that *it developed without any formal connection with the union.* The various benevolent organizations, newspapers, social clubs, athletic teams, and lodges have for the most part been organized by working printers in their spare time, by men who felt the need to engage in such activities with other printers.

The formal community of printers' clubs is paralleled by an informal one. That is, large numbers of printers spend a considerable amount of their leisure time with other printers. In interviews many printers reported that their best friends are other printers, that they regularly visit the homes of other printers, that they often meet in bars, go fishing together, or see each other in various places before and after work.

Without data on other workers it is difficult to judge whether there are more of these informal social relations among printers than there are in other occupational groups. We do know, however, that few, if any, manual or nonmanual occupations have developed as extensive a network of formal social activities limited to persons working in the occupation. And when we consider that these activities draw printers together from distant parts of the metropolitan centers in which most printers work, we must assume that they find these extravocational social relations rewarding.

Is it possible that these two major differences between the ITU and other unions—that is, the incidence in the ITU of a democratic political system and of an extravocational social system—are related? that the intraorganizational social relations operate in some way to sustain the political democracy of the ITU? Or alternatively, is it possible that the same factors which shape the occupational community also operate independently to make possible the democratic political system? Or that the existence of a democratic political system is necessary for the existence of an extensive leisure occupational community? These various possibilities are dealt with in subsequent chapters.[1]

In addition to the extensive social relations between printers away from the job, there is also more socializing among printers on the job than we find in most occupations. On the large newspapers in particular, the need to put out different editions means that there are long periods between editions in which men either have no immediate work or can arrange their work so as to stop and talk for a while. In addition, many printers work nights. Night work is normally less demanding in terms of production than day work, and produces an atmosphere of greater cameraderie than the normal routine of day employment.

An important element which contributes to the feeling of freedom to walk around and talk in the print shops is the fact that both management and union administration have little control over the men in the shops or their elected leaders, the chapel chairmen. Management's power is limited by the power of the union, which is made explicit in rules which bar nonmembers of the union from the floor of the print shop during working hours. The union officialdom's control over the members or chapel chairmen is minimized by the existence of strongly-

---

1. Comparative data, however, clearly suggest that a printers' occupational community can and does exist without the presence of a highly developed democratic political system. As was indicated in Chap. 2, printers' leisure-time communities are reported in the literature of European unionism as early as the middle of the sixteenth century and throughout the nineteenth century in various European countries. German printers indicate a similar pattern in printing centers in that country. The printers of Leipzig, Germany's traditional printing center, most of whom are Social Democrats, were able to maintain group solidarity all through the Nazi period through their afterwork meetings in beer parlors.

held union norms which inhibit efforts by union leaders to punish men for their opinions or to influence the election of chapel (shop) officers. Thus both on and off the job, in clubs, in the print shops, and in informal get-togethers printers are engaged in a variety of informal social relations with each other.

In general those men who are active in the printers' occupational community, whether informally or formally, are also those who are involved and active in the union.[2] (See Figs. 1-4.)

Figure 1—Relationship between Informal Social Relations with Other Printers and Interest in Union Politics*

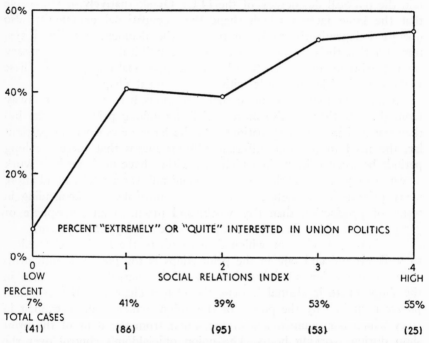

	0 LOW	1	2 SOCIAL RELATIONS INDEX	3	.4 HIGH
PERCENT	7%	41%	39%	53%	55%
TOTAL CASES	(41)	(86)	(95)	(53)	(25)

* The social relations index is a measure of the printer's informal contacts with other printers outside the shop: See Appendix I, p. 000, for details of construction of this index.

Though these data indicate that the printers who are socially active with fellow printers are also more likely to be politically involved, the question remains, Just what is the relation between the social activities of the printers' community and the active political life of the union?

---

2. The data relating participation in clubs and formal affairs to union activity show the same pattern as those reported in Figures 1-4 for informal social relations.

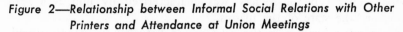

Figure 2—Relationship between Informal Social Relations with Other Printers and Attendance at Union Meetings

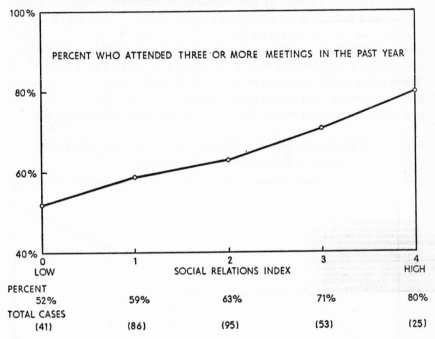

	0 LOW	1	2	3	4 HIGH
PERCENT	52%	59%	63%	71%	80%
TOTAL CASES	(41)	(86)	(95)	(53)	(25)

We will go into this relationship in some detail in Chapter 5; but before presenting the data we will describe here the theoretical approach which suggests just what this relationship is.

§ The Mass Society

IN ATTEMPTING TO LOCATE the sources of totalitarianism in contemporary society, various theorists have suggested that the political forms of nations are in large measure related to the type of organizational life which exists within them. Emil Lederer, for example, has suggested that the many organizations that we regard as normal and generally irrelevant to politics as such—religious groups, veterans' associations, fraternal orders, labor organizations, farm groups, and so on—have a definite function in the development and preservation of democracy. He argued that a society without a multitude of organizations *independent* of state power has a high dictatorial as well as revolutionary potential. That type of society was characterized by him as a *mass society*, or "the state of the masses."[3]

The current interest in the relationship between voluntary organizations and politics is an outgrowth of the concern with totalitarianism and most of the scholars who have become aware of the relationship are German anti-Nazis, but it is significant that one of the earliest efforts to specify a relationship was made over 120 years ago by Alexis de Tocqueville while attempting to solve a problem comparable to the one that we are dealing with in this book. Tocqueville wanted to find out why the United States alone among the countries of his day had

Figure 3—Relationship between Informal Social Relations with Other Printers and Talking about Union Politics

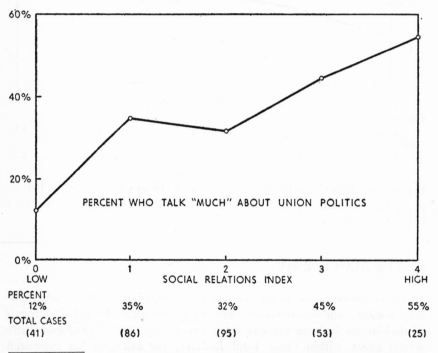

0 LOW	1	2 SOCIAL RELATIONS INDEX	3	4 HIGH
PERCENT				
12%	35%	32%	45%	55%
TOTAL CASES				
(41)	(86)	(95)	(53)	(25)

3. See Emil Lederer: *The State of the Masses*, New York, W. W. Norton and Company, Inc., 1940. This approach has been employed by an important group of contemporary scholars. Cf. Hannah Arendt: *Origins of Totalitarianism*, New York, Harcourt, Brace and Company, Inc., 1951; Max Horkheimer: *Eclipse of Reason*, New York, Oxford University Press, 1947; Karl Mannheim: *Man and Society in an Age of Reconstruction*, New York, Harcourt, Brace and Company, Inc., 1940; Philip Selznick: *The Organizational Weapon*, New York, McGraw-Hill Book Company, Inc., 1952; Jose Ortega y Gasset: *The Revolt of the Masses*, New York, W. W. Norton and Company, Inc., 1932.

a successful and stable democratic political order. He pointed to the fact that as compared with Europeans of his day, "Americans . . . constantly form associations."[4] Tocqueville then goes on to raise the question, just as we have, "Is the coincidence of a democratic political system

Figure 4—Relationship between Informal Social Relations with Other Printers and Reading Typographical Journal

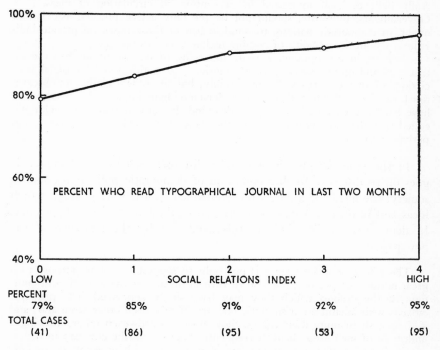

PERCENT WHO READ TYPOGRAPHICAL JOURNAL IN LAST TWO MONTHS

	0 LOW	1	2 SOCIAL RELATIONS INDEX	3	4 HIGH
PERCENT	79%	85%	91%	92%	95%
TOTAL CASES	(41)	(86)	(95)	(53)	(95)

with a highly developed organizational life the result of accident? Or is there in reality any necessary connection between the principle of association and that of equality?"

Tocqueville concludes that the coincidence of democracy and such organizational life is not accidental:

When the members of an aristocratic community adopt a new opinion, or conceive a new sentiment, they give it a station, as it were, beside themselves, upon the lofty platform where they stand; and opinions or sentiments so conspicuous to the eyes of the multitude are easily introduced into the minds or hearts of all around. In democratic countries the governing power alone is naturally in a condition to act in this matter; but it is easy to see that its action

4. Alexis de Tocqueville: *Democracy in America*, New York, Alfred A. Knopf, Inc., 1945, pp. 376-86 for this and the quotations below.

is always inadequate, and often dangerous. A government can no more be competent to keep alive and to renew the circulation of opinions and feelings than to manage all the speculations of productive industry. No sooner does a government attempt to go beyond its political sphere and to enter upon this new track, than it exercises, even unintentionally, an insupportable tyranny; for a government can only dictate strict rules, the opinions which it favors are rigidly enforced, and it is never easy to discriminate between its advice and its commands. Worse still will be the case if the government really believes itself interested in preventing all circulation of ideas. . . . Governments, therefore, should not be the only active powers; associations ought, in democratic nations, to stand in lieu of those powerful private individuals whom the equality of conditions has swept away. . . .

Nothing, in my opinion, is more deserving of our attention than the intellectual and moral associations of America. The political and industrial associations of that country strike us forcibly; but the others elude our observations, or if we discover them, we understand them imperfectly, because we have hardly even seen anything of the kind. It must, however, be acknowledged that they are as necessary to the American people as the former, and perhaps more so.

In the same chapter in which he discusses associations Tocqueville goes on to discuss a further condition of democratic politics in complex society, the need for a means not controlled by the state through which ideas and information may be presented to thousands of people at once. In democratic society he sees this need met by the existence of the newspapers.

The effect of a newspaper is not only to suggest the same purpose to a great number of persons, but also to furnish means for the execution in common of the designs which they may have singly conceived. The principal citizens who inhabit an aristocratic country discern each other from afar; and if they wish to unite their forces, they move towards each other, drawing a multitude of men after them. It frequently happens on the contrary in democratic countries, that a great number of men who wish or want to combine can not accomplish it, because they cannot see, and know not where to find, one another. A newspaper then takes up the notion or the feeling that had occurred simultaneously, but singly, to each of them. All are then immediately guided towards the beacon; and these wandering minds, which had so long sought each other in darkness, at length meet and unite.

Large national associations too find "means . . . to converse every day without seeing each other, and to take steps in common without having met. Thus hardly any democratic association can do without newspapers."

In fact, "a newspaper . . . always represents an association that is composed of its habitual readers."

The existence of large numbers of voluntary associations thus serves two needs of a democratic society. They are a source of new opinions independent of the state and a means of communicating these new suggestions to a large section of the citizenry. Two other important functions are the training of men in the skills of politics and the consequent increase in their actual participation in political organizations. Men who "never acquired the habit of forming associations" will not learn suddenly to do so because a crisis has occurred. "The greater is the multiplicity of small affairs, the more do men, even without knowing it, acquire facility in prosecuting great undertakings in common." Or as Emile Durkheim put it:

A [democratic] nation can be maintained only if, between the states and the individual, there is intercalated a whole series of secondary groups near enough to individuals to attract them strongly in their sphere of action and drag them, in this way, into the general torrent of social life.[5]

A union can be considered, of course, one of these necessary secondary organizations within society, one of the mediating organizations between the individual and the state. But here we consider it as a social system in its own right, and ask whether *within* this social system we have a state of the masses or the kind of complex, articulated structure that, according to this theory, is necessary to support democracy. Most large unions and many other associations approximate the state of the masses in their lack of mediating organizations between the administration and the individual members. The average large trade union contains only one formal organization, the union apparatus itself, and a mass of individual members. There are no autonomous suborganizations which can function as centers of opposition or as independent sources of organizational communication. It is perhaps paradoxical that the very organizations which allow workers to act collectively in their relations with employers are ordinarily so constructed that *within* them the members are usually unable to act collectively in dealing with their leaders.

---

5. Emile Durkheim: *The Division of Labor*, 2nd ed. Glencoe, Ill., Free Press, 1947, p. 28. Durkheim also pointed to the relationship between mass society and dictatorship long before the rise of modern totalitarianism. "Collective activity is always too complex to be able to be expressed through the single and unique organ of the State. Moreover, the State is too remote from individuals; its relations with them too external and intermittent to penetrate deeply within individual consciences and socialize them within. Where the State is the only environment in which men can live communal lives, they inevitably lose contact, become detached and society disintegrates. A nation can be maintained only if, between the State and the individual, there is intercalated a whole series of secondary groups near enough to individuals to attract them strongly in their sphere of action and drag them, in this way, into the general torrent of social life. . . . A hypertrophied State is forced to oppress and contain . . . a society composed of an indefinite number of unorganized individuals."—*Loc. cit.*

The qualifying adjective "large" is deliberately used in the paragraph above; it is obvious that there is a limiting size below which organizations can act democratically without any groups mediating between the members and the association. In our judgment these limits are determined by the possibilities of communication. As long as an individual can reach every member of a group personally and the group is small enough for men to know and judge the work and policies of their leaders through firsthand observation, democracy can flourish. And in fact many small union locals are highly democratic. (Small unions also cannot usually give their leaders much income or social status, so the leaders are less tempted to maintain power at the cost of restricting democracy.)

There is one further qualification to the description of trade-union members as a mass of isolated individuals. Actually there is one mediating group within large union locals, the shop organization. The extent to which this group can operate as a politically significant secondary group is limited, however, by the communications system. In most one-party unions the only means of communication among shops or with the union administration is through the bureaucracy of the organization itself. A shop group is also usually dependent on the officers of the union for support against the employer and thus ordinarily cannot constitute a basis for organized opposition. As we shall see in subsequent chapters, the autonomy of the shop organization in the Typographical Union is in part a consequence of the historic power of the individual shop and in part a consequence of the continuing power of the members to dislodge their union leaders.

Up to now we have spoken of the functions of secondary organizations for a democratic society or private government. Superficially similar organizations exist in totalitarian societies, but their function is quite different. The totalitarian leader wants the citizens to attend meetings, read political literature, listen to broadcasts, and belong to and be active in age, occupational, sex, sports, and various other groups, since by this means he can reach them with his point of view. Similarly, some trade unions, especially those under Communist control, have made strenuous efforts to increase interest in the union by establishing various forms of union-controlled leisure-time organizations and making attendance at union meetings compulsory. It is fairly obvious that Communist labor leaders are not anxious to encourage and deepen internal democracy in their unions, but rather recognize that by multiplying the controlled activities of the members they are increasing their own chances to reach and indoctrinate the membership and so reducing the possibility that it will develop hostile attitudes and withhold support in a crisis situation. As a general hypothesis, one might suggest that the greater the changes in the structure of society that a governing group is attempting to introduce, or the greater the changes in the traditional functions of unions that a union leadership is attempting to effect, the more likely the leadership is to desire or even to require a high degree of participation in various groups by citizens or members. The radical changes that accompany social revolution, or on a smaller scale the transformation of a trade union into a political weapon, put severe strains on group loyalties and create a potential for strong membership hostility toward the leadership. A high level of controlled and manipulated rank-and-file participation is perhaps the only way, given the leadership's purpose, of draining off or redirecting the discontent created by violent changes in traditional patterns and relationships.

It should be noted, however, that many nontotalitarian movements and organizations also attempt to encompass the total life of their membership. Ever since the Catholic Church has been threatened, either by anticlericalism and secularism in Catholic countries or by opposing religions in other countries, it has established networks of unions, lodges, social groups, youth groups, and other association to prevent Catholics from being exposed to values and associations which may threaten their religious beliefs. Similarly, the Social Democratic Parties of Europe, especially those of Germany and Austria, built the first total political environment, which in many ways resembled that of the Catholic Church. A number of political observers have suggested that the efforts of the Communists and Nazis to completely involve their members and supporters in activities bound to the party have been modeled on the practices of the Catholics and Social Democrats. In this country a number of trade unions led by present or former socialists have made smiliar although less successful efforts to involve union members in activities bound to the union.

It is important, therefore, to differentiate between communities or associations which have consciously organized the daily lives of their members through a variety of groups which are linked to themselves, and groups formed in relative independence of the central authority. Both situations will probably lead to a high level of participation in the affairs of the community or of organizations. The first situation, however, will be negatively related with political democracy, while the latter is one of the requirements for the institutionalization of democracy. More generally:

A. *Nonexistence of secondary organizations,* or a *mass society,* helps maintain

    a conservative oligarchy, such as is found in South American
    dictatorships, in Europe before the nineteenth century, or in
    the average stable American trade union
B. *Existence of secondary organizations*
    1. *controlled* by the government helps maintain
        revolutionary totalitarianism, intent on making changes within
        the society which it governs, as in Nazi Germany or Soviet
        Russia
    2. *independent* of the government helps maintain
        democracy, such as is found within the ITU or in the United
        States or most European democracies

To recapitulate: It is suggested that democratic politics necessarily
rests on a multitude of independent organizations, the manifest functions
of which need not be political. Such organizations serve in society as a
whole or in unions (1) as arenas within which new ideas are generated,
(2) as communications networks through which people may learn and
form attitudes about politics, (3) as means of training potential opposition leaders in the skills of politics, and as places in which they can
attain the status necessary to become political leaders, (4) as one of
the principal means of getting individuals to participate in the larger
political arena, and (5) as bases of opposition to the central authority.

The necessary characteristics of such a system of organizations, according to this theory, are clear. They must be able to mediate between
the individual and the state, or union, which means: (1) They must
have sources of power *independent* of the central body. Of course, this
power can be of several kinds. The political power of the church, for
example, resides in its popular support plus the existence of strong
cultural sentiments protecting it from interference; while that of an
organized gambling syndicate is completely different. (2) The power
of these groups relative to the central body must be considerable. A
nation or a union which is composed entirely of very small communities, isolated except for communication through government or central
union channels, would be nearly as atomized as separate individuals as
far as any possibility of democratic political opposition or collective
action is concerned.

The political functions of secondary organizations, as set forth
above, may be divided into two important classes: the *external* power
functions, by which they may oppose the power of the central body,
and the *internal* functions of increasing the political involvement of their
own members. Now the exercise of power and the encouragement of
political participation are such different functions that rather different

social organizations may perform them. It is possible for a society to have a wide variety of secondary associations which play the important role of countering the power of the state, and not have an underlying structure of primary groups to provide the second function of increasing political involvement. In some respects we may think of urban society in the United States as being a mass society in this sense. Social relations *within* the groups which exercise important pressure in politics are often attenuated. Groups such as war-veteran associations, automobile clubs, consumers' cooperatives, medical plans, and the typical trade union all operate to maintain democracy by acting as independent bases of power, while few of their members attend meetings or engage in informal social relations with other members.[6]

In this respect the ITU is different; its suborganizations are often capable of performing both functions. Compared to most trade unions and important political units, the ITU is quite small; the total membership in the United States and Canada is only about 100,000, of whom 10% are in the New York local. Therefore, organizations within the union are usually of a size that will permit them to carry out both the function of countervailing power and that of activating members through primary group contact. A club or a print shop can be small enough to maintain a high degree of contact among its members and at the same time large enough relative to the administration to give prestige

---

6. Two students of voluntary organization have summed up the available evidence on participation in such groups as follows:

"In the 'service clubs,' for example, there is a very active nucleus and a large group who are 'just members.' . . . The American Legion was founded in 1919 by a small group and is run by a self-perpetuating oligarchy. . . . Goldhamer summarized the situation for fraternal organizations as follows: 'Though fraternal organizations are subject to democratic control, it appears that the actual formulation of policy . . . is largely the function of a few interested individuals, with the great bulk of the membership acquiescing so long as these policies do not interfere with their private lives.' The Consumer Cooperative Movement, which stresses equal and active participation by all members more than most other associations do, is no exception to the active minority pattern. . . . Even in avowedly activist organizations, there is minimal participation. . . . In the most powerful and deeply rooted People's Organizations known in this country the degree of popular participation reached a point varying between five and seven per cent!"—Bernard Barber, in Alvin Gouldner (ed.), *Studies in Leadership*, pp. 484-85.

"In McKean's study of interest groups in New Jersey he repeatedly notes cases in which activity is confined to a few individuals in a group. In the National Association of Manufacturers, even among those belonging to the key policy-making bodies, participation varies widely. It is estimated that less than half the board members regularly attend meetings and that committee attendance is even lower. In the medical societies lack of participation has been a matter of some concern to the active elements from the very beginning. A similar situation has characterized labor unions, especially at the local level."—David Truman, *The Governmental Process*, p. 154.

to opposition leaders recruited from it and to defend the rights of individual members. Of course, in relation to the international union a club or a single print shop is not likely to have such power. But on this level the union's political parties and, as we shall see, the large locals appear to play the necessary role of counteracting administrative power. The locals, however, would not be in a position to do so if they were not part of a democratic international union; international democracy is in turn dependent on the persistence of organized politics within most of the large locals of the union.

CHAPTER 5

The Occupational Community
and the Political System

IN CHAPTER 4 WE ANALYZED from the point of view of the theory of the mass society the relationship between the printers' social community and the ITU's political system. Here we approach the question empirically. Formally there is no relation between the organized printers' community and the political system. The printers' clubs are explicitly nonpolitical and even antipolitical; in some cases, officials of such groups refused to discuss their own political beliefs on the grounds that union politics had nothing to do with the social organizations. Yet the connection exists.

Earlier data showed that those men who are most involved in formal or informal relationships with other printers are also more likely to be active and interested in union politics. At the same time participation in the leisure activities of the occupational community is in large part determined by factors which are independent of the political system, as the following chapters will show. This fact suggests the following process: After men enter the trade, some are motivated or even pushed into taking part in the occupational community. A high degree of interaction with fellow unionists in turn serves to motivate them to greater interest and participation in union politics.

The occupational community is of course not the only means by which individuals are stimulated to participate in union politics.[1] Gen-

---

1. For example, Kovner and Lahne point out that the "higher degree of participation among the members of the International Typographical Union as against those of the pressmen is not unrelated to the fact that the former can talk while they work, whereas press work discourages conversation." Joseph Kovner and

eralized political interest or awareness and the specific political ideologies of men (liberalism-conservatism) prompt some participation in union politics. Some men also enter union politics to satisfy personal ambitions. The occupational community should be seen then as only one of a number of routes leading to similar behavior. These varying processes are of course interrelated, and as we shall see, tend to reinforce one another.

§ The Short-Term Process

GIVEN THE COMPARATIVELY SHORT PERIOD in which we could secure data from members of the union, it was necessary to test a number of our hypotheses on the process of involvement by examining what happened to the political activity and interest of the printers during a six-month period. The members of the sample were interviewed in December 1951 and January 1952. Six months later, at the end of May, the same men were sent a questionnaire in which they were asked a number of questions concerning their activity and interest in the international election of May. About 70% of the members of the sample returned their questionnaires. Several of the interview questions concerning involvement in and knowledge of union politics were repeated in the May questionnaire. By examining the changes in responses during an election campaign we can study the effects of participation in the occupational community on behavior in union politics.[2]

The questions asked allow us to examine changes in the level of knowledge from January to May. One such question was on the positions of the parties on signing the non-Communist Taft-Hartley affidavits. The Progressives, in power, opposed signing the affidavits; the more conservative Independents favored it. This difference in party position was a major issue of the 1950 and the 1952 international elec-

---

Herbert J. Lahne: "Shop Society and the Union," *Industrial and Labor Relations Review,* 7:5 (October 1953). See Chaps. 8 to 10 below for a discussion of social relations in shop and union politics.

2. Unfortunately the variation in method by which the two sets of data were collected affected the change of response to the same question. In answering questionnaires at home, men were more likely to admit low levels of interest and activity in the union than in the face-to-face situation of the interview. Many respondents, for example, told interviewers that they were "very interested" in union politics, but then in the following May during the election campaign indicated a lower level of interest. It is extremely unlikely that these men lost interest as a result of the campaign. We are forced to conclude, therefore, that as a result of the interview situation men conformed to democratic or union norms. As might be expected, however, the replies to questions eliciting *knowledge* of specific union issues were less affected by the shift from interview to questionnaire.

tion campaigns. An examination of the response to this over the period of the campaign is consequently a good test of the communications function of the printers' social community.

Figure 5—Relationship between Active Membership in Printers' Clubs and Knowledge of Party Positions on Taft-Hartley Affidavit

CHANGE IN KNOWLEDGE OF PROGRESSIVE POSITION

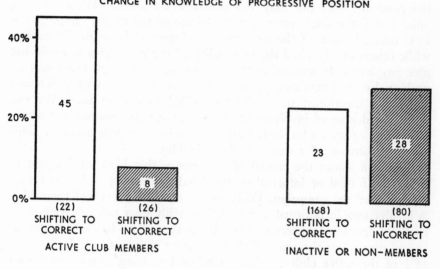

CHANGE IN KNOWLEDGE OF INDEPENDENT POSITION

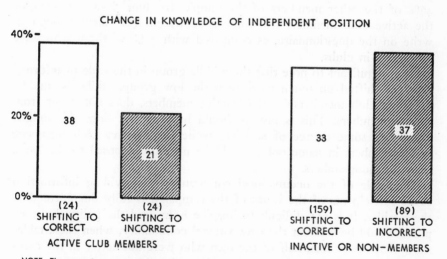

NOTE: The percentages computed are the percentage who changed their answer in a given direction of all those who could change in that direction, not of the complete groups. The totals on which they are computed are given in the parentheses.

It is clear that the clubs not only had an effect in increasing the knowledge of those who did not know the correct answer in January, but also that the active club members who were right during the interview were less likely to slip into an incorrect position in May.[3]

Another question asked at both times concerned knowledge of issues between the parties. In January the men were asked "What do you think are the major campaign issues between the Progressives and Independents?" In the May questionnaire we asked, "What in your opinion was the single most important issue of the recent campaign for ITU office?" Some of the men mentioned specific issues or differences, while others simply cited the personality of the candidates or could not give any issues. In answering the questionnaire, although there was no probing by an interviewer, more men mentioned issues or differences and fewer mentioned personalities or failed to cite an issue. We can relate the degree of involvement in the occupational community to the proportion of men who shifted up from no issue or personality in January to a mention of a campaign issue in May.

Figure 6 shows the remarkable difference that high involvement in either the formal or informal occupational community makes in seeing the issues of the campaign. While active club members and those high in involvement in informal social relations with other printers were more likely in January to perceive more issues than those less active, the involved group was also more likely to increase its knowledge. In January, 56% of the active club members mentioned an issue, as compared with 46% of the other members of the sample. By June, however, 81% of the active club members had some issue which was salient enough to write on the questionnaire, as compared with 49% of those who were not active in clubs.

It is significant to note that the middle group in the scale of informal relations shifted up much more than the low group, while the middle group in club membership, the inactive members, does not differ from the nonmembers. This is just as should be expected, since this middle group has some degree of activity, while the inactive club members, being members in name only, would be no more exposed to the issues than the nonmembers.

The role of the occupational community in providing information to its participants of the issues of the campaign is fully documented in these tables. It is not difficult to imagine how dead the political atmosphere would be without the occupational community, when these tables show that fewer than half of the men who were not active in the com-

---

3. The men were asked, "Would you have any idea what positions each of the two major parties take on the question of signing the non-Communist affidavit?" Thus some men could have guessed correctly.

Figure 6—Relationship between Increased Awareness of Election
Issues and Involvement in the Occupational Community

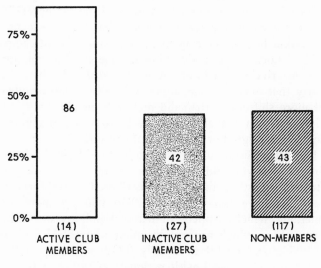

PROPORTION OF MEN WHO "SHIFTED UP" FROM
JANUARY TO MAY

CLUB MEMBERSHIP

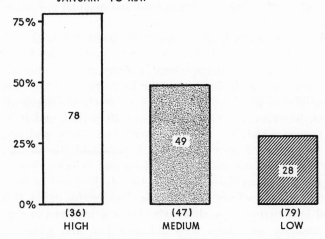

PROPORTION OF MEN WHO "SHIFTED UP" FROM
JANUARY TO MAY

POSITION ON SOCIAL RELATIONS INDEX

NOTE: As in Figure 5, the percentages are calculated on a base of those who could
change in the given direction, rather than the entire population.

munity could name a single issue of the campaign less than a month after it was over.

But not only do club members show an increase in *knowledge* in the campaign; relative to the nonmembers they also show an increase in interest and involvement in union politics. We asked these men in the January interview, "During union election campaigns, do you talk about union affairs with your printer friend much, little, or never?" Again in the June questionnaire, the same question was asked, except that this time the question began, "During this past union election campaign——." At both times more of the active club members report talking "much" than do the inactive members or the nonmembers. Further, the analysis shows clearly that over the campaign fewer active club members shifted down and more shifted up than did non-club members.[4]

The time between January and May in 1952 was not only a period of the union campaign but also one of mounting interest in national politics. The Republican and Democratic Presidential primaries were held during this period, and the national conventions took place a few weeks after the questionnaires were distributed and returned. In both January and May we asked the men, "Do you get more worked up about something which happens in national politics and public affairs or about something which happens in union affairs?" Men could answer "National," "Union," or "Both equally." Overall, the members of the union were more concerned with national politics, and between January and May more men shifted from replying union politics to national politics. But among the active club members, there was a greater shift towards concern with union politics than toward national politics, while among all others, the shift was greater toward national politics, as Figure 7 indicates.

The foregoing analysis documents one basic point, that regardless of the manifest purposes of those who take part in the formal or informal activities of the occupational community, these activities do play an important role in increasing the knowledge of and involvement in union politics of previously inactive or relatively uninterested printers. These data, however, only cover a six-month period, and it is obvious that the factors which are related to such knowledge and activity are operative over much longer periods. It is reasonable to project the implications of our analysis and suggest a long-term process. New members of the union would on the whole be relatively ignorant of union affairs and uninterested in politics. After some time in the union they would be divided into two groups, those who become involved in the occupational community and those who did not. The first group would be

_____
4. The data are similar to those in Figure 5.

Figure 7—Relationship between Club Membership and Change in
Concern for National or Union Politics

PROPORTION OF THOSE CHANGING IN INDICATED DIRECTION COMPUTED
ON BASIS OF THOSE WHO COULD CHANGE IN THAT DIRECTION

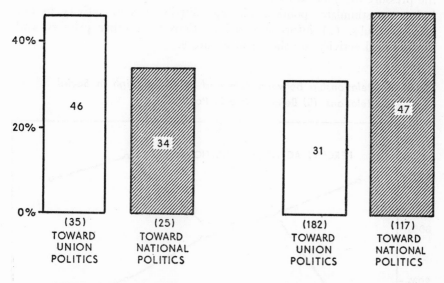

ACTIVE CLUB MEMBERS   INACTIVE OR NON-MEMBERS

NOTE: Change towards the union includes men who changed from "National" to either "Union" or "Both," and those who changed from "Both to "Union." Change towards national politics includes those who shifted from "Union" to "National" or "Both," and those who changed from "Both" to "National." As in Figure 5, the above percentages are calculated on a base of those who could change in the given direction, rather than the entire population.

more likely to get involved in discussions about union matters, meet people active in union politics, and gradually develop more knowledge and interest concerning union politics. Those who remained outside of the occupational community would be subject to less stimulation, would take longer to learn about the union and its politics, and as a group would remain less knowledgeable and interested. With the passage of time a larger proportion of the former group would become active in union politics and thus help to continue the system.

It is not necessary, however, to rely solely on this inference from the short-term panel data to support the hypothesis of the long-range activation. There is other evidence.

§ The Long-Range Process

THE CLOSEST APPROXIMATION to the logic of a long-term analysis is to compare the behavior of union members at different age levels. If the assumptions about the long-term process are valid, then more younger men than older men should be involved in the occupational community without being active politically. This follows from the hypothesis that the pressure to "join" the occupational community comes first, and that it in turn stimulates politics. The age distributions of activity in (1) printers' clubs, (2) informal social relations with other printers, and (3) political activity are shown in Figure 8.

Figure 8—Relationship between Age and (A) Being High in Social Relations, (B) Being Active in Politics

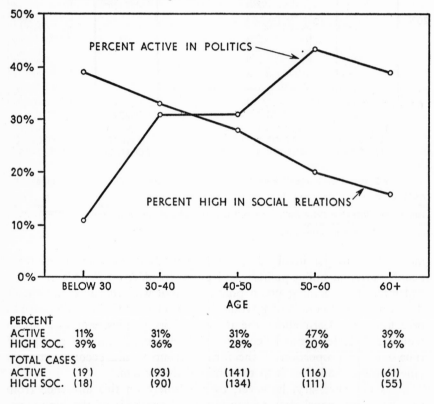

PERCENT	BELOW 30	30-40	40-50	50-60	60+
ACTIVE	11%	31%	31%	47%	39%
HIGH SOC.	39%	36%	28%	20%	16%
TOTAL CASES					
ACTIVE	(19)	(93)	(141)	(116)	(61)
HIGH SOC.	(18)	(90)	(134)	(111)	(55)

This figure shows clearly that the peak of occupational social activity, both formal and informal, is among a younger age group than is the peak of political activity. It strongly suggests, then, that men

become active and involved in the printers' community *before* they
become active and involved in politics. The peak of activity in the occupational community, both formal and informal, seems to be at age
twenty to forty, while party membership is concentrated around a peak
twenty to thirty years older. It could be, of course, that the men who
grew up twenty years earlier have lived in a more "political" period than
the twenty-to-forty-year-old group. They may have been as politically
active as they are now shortly after their entrance into the union. There is
no evidence to reject this hypothesis, but all the related evidence points
to the previous explanation as the correct one: that men generally become active in the occupation community before becoming active in
politics.

The data reported in Figure 8, however, suggest an additional stage
in the process—that men who grow older and reduce their participation
in the occupational community nevertheless continue to remain active
and interested in politics. That is, union political interest and involvement have a self-maintaining function, even after the stimulus and support of the occupational community ceases. It may, however, be suggested that the greater political activity of older printers is primarily
a function of other factors related to increased age and is not related
in any way to past membership in the occupational community. This
alternative thesis may be tested by comparing reported *past* participation in printers' clubs and *present* political activity at the same age levels.

Figure 9—Relationship between Age, Union Political Activity, and
Present and Past Club Membership

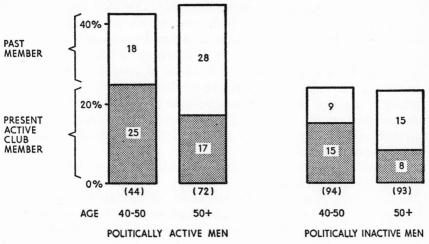

It is clear from the data that older printers who are now active in politics but are not members of printers' clubs are more likely to be past club members than are politically inactive printers; this supports the relation between club membership, age, and political activity suggested in the last paragraph.

§ The Role of Ideological Sensitivity

How ARE WE to account for those men who, while deeply involved socially with other printers, are not interested in union politics, or who, while active in union politics, have few other social relations with printers? Both these groups are atypical, yet important for understanding the whole system. These men, we suggest, are to be understood principally in terms of the two factors of generalized political awareness and specific ideology.

Printers like other men differ in their general interest in and orientation to politics. Later in the book we shall discuss in detail some of these differences. Perhaps the most crucial, and certainly the most important in our later analysis of political behavior of printers, is a general sensitivity to things political. Men differ widely in their sensitivity to and concern with matters of policy or ideology when they vote or take part in politics. Some men think largely in terms of policy differences or ideological differences, while other men's orientation to politics is based more on personal or other matters.

In order to distinguish these kinds of men we used answers to open-end questions in which the respondents told what they thought union politics was about, and why they favored one party or candidate more than another. If the questions were answered in ideological terms, that is, in terms of issues, the men were characterized as high in ideological sensitivity. If they were answered in terms of nonpolicy matters such as past specific failures of a party or attributes of its leaders or with a failure to see any real differences between the parties, the men were characterized as low in ideological sensitivity. The sample was then divided into three operationally defined classes—high, medium, and low in *ideological sensitivity*.

Appendix I describes in greater detail the way in which this index was constructed. At present we shall simply state that while it is operationally only a measure of the propensity of men to view politics in ideological terms (regardless of direction) the data indicate that most men who see union politics in such terms have a strong positive orientation towards politics, whereas many of those who reject ideology as a basis of differentiation are not interested in politics itself.[5] This does not mean that ideological sensitivity is synonomous with union political involvement or activity; the highly sensitive men are of course more likely to be active in union politics, but some of them are not, while many active and interested men, including a few of the party leaders whom we interviewed, are low in ideological sensitivity. Figure 10 indicates the relationship between ideological sensitivity and various indices of union political interest and activity.

Figure 10—Relationship between Ideological Sensitivity and Interest and Activity in Union Politics and Social Relations

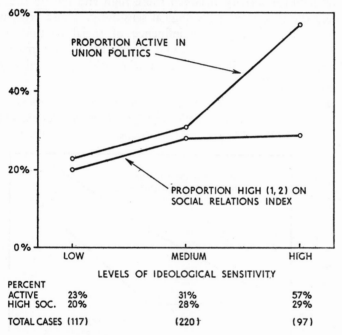

PERCENT			
ACTIVE	23%	31%	57%
HIGH SOC.	20%	28%	29%
TOTAL CASES	(117)	(220)	(97)

The findings in this figure conflict in one way with what might have been expected on the basis of earlier data. They show that ideological sensitivity is correlated with political interest and activity, yet shows little relationship to social relations with other printers. Since these latter two elements—political activity and social relations—are highly correlated, an item which correlates with one and not with the other may

5. We shall make the assumption, which will be defended in Chap. 15, that ideological sensitivity is in large part an orientation towards politics which men bring with them, and that it is not specific to or derived from union politics.

have an independent role in producing or supporting an interest in union politics.

This apparent conflict suggests that the relationship between informal social activity among printers and union political behavior is not a consistent one. That is, it is possible that involvement in the social community affects some printers more than others, and that variations in ideological sensitivity might be the clue to this differential effect. The extent to which involvement in social relations differentially affects men of different degrees of ideological sensitivity may be seen in Figure 11.

We find an interesting result. There is almost no difference (3%) in level of political activity between those high and low in social relations among the men *low* in ideological sensitivity. Those *high* in ideological sensitivity do reflect the influence of social relations (13%); but the greatest effect (20%) is found among the *middle* group in the scale of ideological sensitivity: the men who neither see union politics

Figure 11—*Effect of Ideological Sensitivity on the Relationship between Participation in Informal Social Relations with Other Printers and Participation in Union Politics*

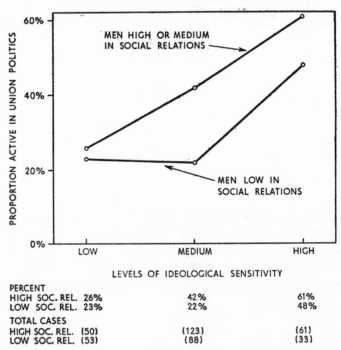

LEVELS OF IDEOLOGICAL SENSITIVITY

	LOW	MEDIUM	HIGH
PERCENT			
HIGH SOC. REL.	26%	42%	61%
LOW SOC. REL.	23%	22%	48%
TOTAL CASES			
HIGH SOC. REL.	(50)	(123)	(61)
LOW SOC. REL.	(53)	(88)	(33)

wholly from an ideological viewpoint nor are completely insensitive to ideological party positions.

When we examine the role of these three groups of men in the formal organizations of the occupational community, the printers' clubs, we find somewhat different results. There is still some differences (11% and 13%) among the ideologically *high* and *medium* groups in union political activity, but the group which is low in ideological sensitivity seems greatly affected by membership in such clubs (22%). These differences among the three groups of printers enable us to specify in much greater detail the way in which the occupation's social community operates to stimulate political interest and involvement.

The group lowest in ideological sensitivity or political concern is especially interesting since, apparently, informal social relations have no influence on their involvement in politics (see Figure 11) while club membership seems to have a great deal of influence (see figure 12).

We can understand the differential effect of informal and formal social relations on the group of low ideological sensitivity in the follow-

Figure 12—Relationship of Club Membership to Participation in Politics among the Three Ideological Groups

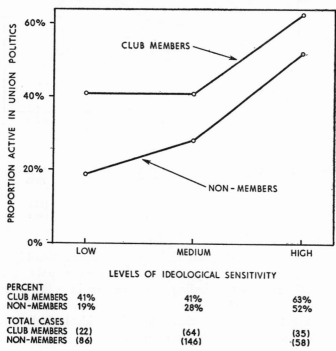

PERCENT			
CLUB MEMBERS	41%	41%	63%
NON-MEMBERS	19%	28%	52%
TOTAL CASES			
CLUB MEMBERS	(22)	(64)	(35)
NON-MEMBERS	(86)	(146)	(58)

ing way: In the ITU we would posit the hypothesis that attitudes towards union politics are one of the decisive factors which influence choice of friends. The group high in ideological sensitivity will most probably have friends who are comparable to themselves in orientation and in political interest. The low group, on the other hand, are likely to have friends who, like themselves, are repelled by or are uninterested in politics.

Figure 13—Relationship between Ideological Sensitivity and
(A) Talking Union Politics; (B) Knowing Union
Politics of Printer Friend

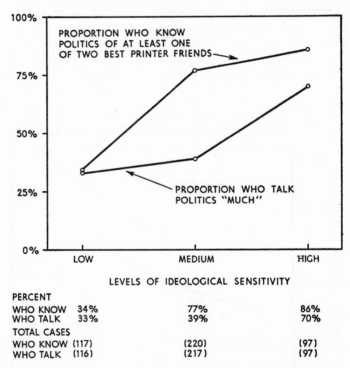

PERCENT			
WHO KNOW	34%	77%	86%
WHO TALK	33%	39%	70%
TOTAL CASES			
WHO KNOW	(117)	(220)	(97)
WHO TALK	(116)	(217)	(97)

Figure 13, which shows that there is a strong relationship between ideological sensitivity and propensity to discuss union politics, supports this hypothesis, as does the finding that men low in political sensitivity do not even know the politics of one of their best printer friends. So we should not expect the printer friendships of the ideologically insensitive to affect their political knowledge or interest.

Formal social relations—membership in clubs—however, have a great effect in stimulating political interest.

Table 4—Relationship between Participation in Informal and Formal Occupational Community and Political Interest, and Activity, for Men Low in Ideological Sensitivity

| | INFORMAL SOCIAL RELATIONS | | CLUB MEMBERS | |
	High	Low	Yes	No
Active in union politics	27%	23%	41%	19%
N	(50)	(53)	(22)	(86)

But how do the ostensibly nonpolitical clubs operate to increase the political involvement of apolitical union members? Apparently in this way: The club members are not a representative sample of the union's membership. They are disproportionately composed of members who are active in union politics. About one in every five club members is also a member of a union political party, a proportion which drops to one in ten for the union as a whole. Of the club members, 21% are high in ideological sensitivity, as compared to 13% of those not belonging to such groups. And in addition to the active leaders and other members of the union parties, there are many nonparty independents who are often active in union election campaigns (see Table 5).

Table 5—Relationship between Political Activity and Membership in Printers' Clubs, for Those Who Do Not Belong to a Union Political Party

	Club Members, %	Nonmembers, %
Contributed to campaign funds	27	15
Worked for the election of a candidate	21	10
N	(96)	(203)

Now union politics can be effectively kept out of the *informal* relations of men who share a common lack of interest or downright antipathy for union affairs, and whose friendship may be, in part, based on this feeling. But talk about union affairs and politics cannot be so easily excluded from the social relations that develop in and around printers' clubs. The clubs, the men who are active in them, and the talk and activities in which they engage are relatively independent of the sentiments or desires of any given member. So the man who joins a glee club or a bowling team or a local printers' social club, or any other printers' organization unrelated to union politics, will find that a large proportion of its members are involved in and talk about politics. Men who do not get to union meetings nor read political circulars may thus be exposed to political talk before and after the club meeting, while riding home on the subway, or while waiting to bowl.

Some findings in communications research and political behavior are relevant here. *Experimental* studies of the influence of educational broadcasts indicate that audiences can be greatly influenced by such efforts. Yet studies of *actual* listening habits of radio audiences indicate little positive effect of such programs, for the simple reason that the listening audience which the educational broadcasts are designed to reach simply does not tune in. Once it can be made a captive audience, whether in experiments or through sugaring the educational pill, then these programs have an effect. Similarly in the ITU, men come to the clubs for social reasons, but thereby also become a captive audience for the political activists.

In *The People's Choice*, Lazarsfeld, Berelson, and Gaudet report that voters are more likely to be affected by interpersonal contact, especially by political "opinion leaders," than by formal propaganda. They also indicate that middle-class persons who belong to ostensibly nonpolitical organizations such as women's clubs are more likely to be politically active than those who do not belong to such groups. Among workers, however, only membership in trade unions has the same effect. The analysis of the effect of printers' clubs suggests a possible explanation of these findings. Given the known fact that a larger proportion of middle-class persons than workers take an active interest in politics, one would expect middle-class clubs to contain more politically interested individuals than would most workers' social organizations. Consequently members of a middle-class group would more likely be politically stimulated than members of workers' clubs. If this is correct, then one should find in European countries, where the existence of a large labor political movement has stimulated the political interests of many workers, that workers would show the same tendency as middle-class individuals here.[6] In effect we are suggesting that increased contact, between individuals who are politically active and those who are not, increases the possibility that the latter will be politically stirred.

Thus far we have not spoken of men who are high in ideological sensitivity. If we turn to these men, we find a puzzling phenomenon. Participation in printers' clubs makes for some difference in their political activity, but still less than among those who are low or in the middle

6. One study which tends to confirm this hypothesis is Stephanie Münke: *Wahlkampf und Machtverschiebung—Geschichte und Analyse der Berliner Wahlen vom 3. Dezember 1950.* Introduction by A. R. L. Gurland. Berlin, Duncker and Humblat, 1952, in a series *Schriften des Instituts für politische Wissenschaft*, Vol. 1; see also Herbert Tingsten: *Political Behaviour: Studies in Election Statistics*, London, P. S. King, 1937 and Jean Stoetzel, "Voting Behavior in France," *British Journal of Sociology*, 1955, 6, p. 115. These studies indicate that in a number of European cities with strong socialist movements, workers have a higher rate of political participation than middle-class persons.

on the scale of ideological sensitivity. Our initial efforts to explain this phenomenon rested on the assumption made in an earlier draft: If one is highly responsive to issues and ideas in politics, then the additional stimulation provided by social relations is not important. The printer with a strong ideological bent is motivated to participate in union politics. He has less need of the occupational community to inform him of issues and to awaken his political interests.

This interpretation, while plausible, still left unanswered questions. Given the assumption that these men are more likely to talk about politics than any other group in the sample, it was difficult to accept the finding that high rates of involvement in the occupational community did not lead to greater involvement in politics.

When we pressed our analysis farther we did discover, for one group of men high in ideological sensitivity, that participation in the printers' social community had the expected effect. We had classified men as politically conservative or liberal on the basis of their answers to a given item scale of political attitudes on national issues,[7] and as we see from Figure 14, among the group high in ideological sensitivity, liberal-

Figure 14—Effect of Ideological Sensitivity on Relationship between Liberalism and Participation in Union Politics

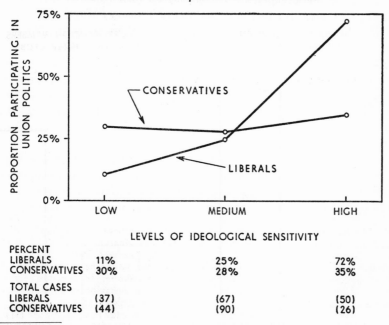

PERCENT	LOW	MEDIUM	HIGH
LIBERALS	11%	25%	72%
CONSERVATIVES	30%	28%	35%
TOTAL CASES			
LIBERALS	(37)	(67)	(50)
CONSERVATIVES	(44)	(90)	(26)

7. The construction of this scale is described in Appendix I.

ism or conservatism makes a difference in participation in union politics. The highly politicalized conservative, who accepts many of
the values of the middle-class or business community, is much less likely
to be directly motivated to participate in union politics than the highly
politicalized liberal. Since their values are more nearly allied to those of
the business community than those of militant unionism, these ideologically sensitive conservatives may even tend to dissociate themselves from
union political activity.

Now it is among those conservatives who, while high in ideological
sensitivity, are nevertheless active in union politics that we find the
printers' social community playing a role. These men must be channeled
toward political activity, and one way of doing this is through the occupational community. Although the small number of cases available for
analysis precludes any definite conclusions, the large differences in participation in the occupational community between liberals and conservatives who are high in ideological sensitivity and also politically active
warrants reporting the findings (see figure 15).

These data suggest that two distinct processes underlie participation

*Figure 15—Relationship between Liberalism-Conservatism and Participation
in the Occupational Community for Men Who Are High in
Ideological Sensitivity and Active in Union Politics*

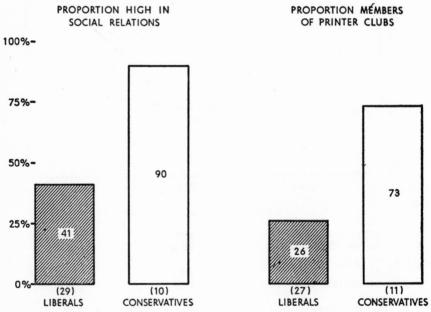

in the occupational community and political activity for the ideologically sensitive men. Conservatives come to participate in union affairs through first participating in the nonpolitical occupational community, while liberals and radicals are motivated more directly by their values towards participation in union politics and are not dependent on social relations as an activating force.

It is now easy to understand the rather low participation in printers' clubs by the politically active ideological liberals. If men bring a strong concern with liberal or radical political issues with them to the union, they will early find an outlet for their interests in the activities of the union. For such men, union politics is a highly satisfactory form of leisure-time activity. The conservatives, on the other hand, are more likely to look first to the nonpolitical social and athletic clubs for a social outlet if they seek their social satisfactions among printers.

It is thus not surprising that some of the ideological liberals are low in informal relations with other printers in spite of their being active in union politics. Some of them are active members of the American Labor, Liberal, or Socialist Parties, or belong to other general community groups which have political objectives. Their participation in union politics is only one aspect of a general concern with politics.

The political activation of the ideologically sensitive conservatives by the clubs indicates an important function of the occupational community. Since the leisure system recruits politically aware conservatives who might otherwise not be active in the union and its politics, it helps establish a balance between conservatives and liberals in union politics. It is significant that four of the Independent Party leaders interviewed had served as presidents of printers' clubs before becoming active in politics. None of the Progressive Party leaders had come into union politics from this channel. They characteristically came up through the more directly political means of chapel chairmanship and party activity.

Thus far we have dealt with the channels through which the two extreme groups of ideologically sensitive men, the highs and lows, are drawn into the political system. Among the low group the clubs play the major role, while informal social relations *per se* have little importance. In the high group, on the other hand, a differentiation must be made between liberals and conservatives in order to locate the role of the occupational community. The men who fall in the large middle group seem to feel the effect of the occupational community much more than those in the extremes. That is, they are activated both by the formal activities of printers' organizations and by informal social relations (see Figures 11 and 12). This might be expected, for these men will not tend, as do the lows, to exclude politics from their informal discussions; they will tend to have friends who, like themselves, are mildly aware of political matters. An association, whether informal or formal, between two such mildly aware and involved men should tend to increase the involvement of each. For them interest in the union is not actively dissociated from interest in its politics, as it is for the low group, so that talk of the union naturally increases their political involvement.

In contrast to the highly ideological liberals (but like their conservative counterparts) the middle group does need this stimulation and intensification. We should expect therefore that many in the medium group would have friends who are concerned with union politics, and that these social relations would serve to stimulate their own interest, activity, and knowledge of politics. Evidence for this hypothesis concerning the selective character of friendship and informal social relations may be found in the fact that the middle group is also clearly the mid-group in terms of frequency of political discussions. The hypothesis has also been verified in another context by Robert K. Merton, who found in a housing project that persons who were ambivalent in their attitudes towards race relations had friends who were often either "liberal" or "illiberal" on such issues.[8] "Liberals" and "illiberals," however, tend to have friends who had the same attitudes as themselves.

The findings in this section may be restated in terms of the propensity to exposure to a politically stimulating set of social relations. Table 6 sets forth the situation for the different groups discussed earlier.

Table 6—Kinds of Social Relations with Other Printers Necessary to Stimulate Political Activity among Various Groups of Printers

("Yes" If These Social Relations Do Bring about Political Activity, "No" If They Do Not)

	Clubs	Informal Relations	No Relations
Low ideologues	Yes	No	No
Medium ideologues	Yes	Yes	No
High-conservative ideologues	Yes	Yes	No
High-liberal ideologues	Yes	Yes	Yes

§ Conclusions

IN THIS CHAPTER we have dealt with the relationship between participation in the occupational community and involvement in union political activity. Making men politically active is not the only impor-

8. Cf. R. K. Merton, P. S. West, and M. Jahoda: *Patterns of Social Life: Explorations in the Sociology and Social Psychology of Housing*. Forthcoming.

tant contribution of the social community to the political system. The clubs, especially, also serve as the means through which men may learn the skills of politics by serving as officials of clubs; they also enable men to build reputations and win recognition throughout the union.

Though the clubs are nonpolitical, the party leaders are aware of their political functions. One present party leader said that he first became involved in union politics while serving as president of an active printers club with 300 members. The president of the union appointed him a member of the union benefit board. Though this man was nonpartisan at the time, he understood the reasons for his appointment, since "anyone who was a member of the benefit board was expected to try to get the president re-elected." A recent union president boasted to us of a political coup in getting the head of the printers' bowling league to serve as chairman of an important union committee. He pointed out that the man was well known throughout the union and in his capacity as head of the league was esteemed as a capable administrator.

Leadership in a printers' club is, however, only one of the means by which men become political leaders, and as we shall see later, is much less important than outright political activity or involvement in shop political affairs. This is understandable, since outright partisans are rarely elected presidents of the nonpolitical social clubs, and many men make careers out of club rather than union activity. The president of one of the printers' veterans posts was positively hostile towards discussing any questions about his union politics, since he felt that his role required him to be completely neutral.

The clubs take particular care not to allow politics to be introduced on an explicit level, for the introduction of partisan politics can be time-consuming and corrosive of personal friendships, and for the great majority of men they offer insufficient reward to be a major part of off-the-job social relations. The recreational and welfare activities that do bring men together in the occupational community are sufficiently rewarding in themselves to make it important to the members that they resist efforts to openly use these organizations for political purposes. But if political discussion is informal and constitutes only part of the casual talk of the printers' community, then it may be permitted. The condition placed on the use of the printers' organizations for political discussion seems to be that it must not threaten the manifest rewards of fellowship, recreation, welfare, and service.

The significance of the printers' clubs in helping to maintain the conditions supporting an institutionalized party system may be seen by comparing the situation in the ITU with other more typical, one-party unions. Occupationally limited social clubs are not unique to printers, though they seem more prevalent among them than among many other groups of workers. In fact many unions spend a great deal of union money to create and maintain such groups. In a one-party union, however, there is clearly no need to keep them nonpolitical, since there is no overt intra-union politics. These groups often become part of the communications system of the administration machine. Educational directors or other union officials attend club meetings and use the meetings as a means of reaching the membership with the administration viewpoint. In such a situation, only a new opposition will be accused of using such clubs for political purposes. The fact that these clubs exist in the ITU makes it easier for opposition to maintain itself, but this is true only because there are two legitimate parties and because the clubs have autonomous existence, not being fostered by the union administration. This is a clear example of a functional interrelationship between two factors. Independent nonpolitical clubs facilitate the existence of such opposition, and the existence of opposition in turn facilitates the political independence of the clubs.

It is possible to imagine a two-party system and institutionalized democratic political procedures in the ITU existing in the absence of these craft-linked independent organizations, or of extensive informal social relations. The several functions which the occupational community fulfills for the political system are paralleled and duplicated by other institutions. The autonomous union shop political structures (chapels) might by themselves provide a sufficient base for an opposition political party. Or an opposition party with finances or motivation provided by outside groups and loyalties, such as the Association of Catholic Trade Unionists or various radical political parties, could perhaps by itself offer sufficient competition to the administration's control of the organs of information and opinion. Informal social relations on the job might, independently of leisure-time social relations, provide contexts in which some sizable proportion of the rank and file could be stimulated to some active involvement in the union's affairs.

But what is a sufficient base for an opposition party in trade unions? How much partisan activity would constitute "sufficient" competition in the market place of ideas? What is the degree of rank-and-file interest and involvement required to support democracy in a union? In short, what are the minimum functional requirements for internal union democracy? It is easy, and at this point unfruitful, to say that these requirements vary in different unions and situations; the fact is that we cannot define these minimum requirements even in the present case, and certainly not by an inspection of any one union by itself. In the present case we can only say that the independent printers' organizations clearly work counter to the structural mechanisms which Michels identified as inherent in large organizations and on which he based his iron law. The ITU represents a case in which the secondary associations which Tocqueville saw as necessary for a democratic system *do* exist, and these groups, together with other patterns which characterize printing as craft and industry, function to support the party system which is the ITU's most striking contribution to the trade-union movement.

CHAPTER 6

Determinants of the
Occupational Community: I

IF THE ITU'S POLITICAL SYSTEM is strongly supported by the
printers' occupational community—and the evidence of Chapter 5 shows
that it is—then the question still remains, Why do printers have an occupational community? It is one thing to suggest that the existence of an
occupational community strongly increases the chances for democracy
within unions; but it is quite another to identify the conditions which
generate the community. So in taking up in this and the next chapter
the question why printing gives rise to an occupational community, we
are taking a step toward answering the question why the ITU is a
democratic union.

A comparative analysis of different occupations would be the most
direct approach toward understanding why printing gives rise to an
occupational community. Our resources, however, limited the collection of systematic data to the New York members of the ITU. Lacking
comparative data, we can utilize another approach and replace a comparative analysis with an internal analysis. Thus if we seek the determinants of a behavior pattern—in this case, activity in the occupational
community—we can compare individuals within the union who differ
widely with respect to this behavior pattern and so find out what characteristics are related to it. In large part our hypotheses for internal
analysis derive from our inferences about the ways in which printers
differ from other occupational groups; thus in some ways, *imputed*
comparison of different occupations serves as the starting point for
the actual comparison of different men within printing. For example,

suppose we want to test the proposition that printers will be motivated to associate with other printers more than most other manual workers will be motivated to associate with their fellow workers. The direct test of such an hypothesis can be made only by a comparative analysis of printers and other workers.[1] But an indirect test can be made as follows. One mechanism through which we believe this relationship to be true concerns the relative prestige of occupations. Thus the original hypothesis would be derived from:

A. Men who feel their occupation to have high prestige will be motivated to associate with fellow workers more than will men who feel their occupation to have low prestige.

B. Printing has higher prestige for its members than most other manual occupations have for their members.

THEREFORE

C. (Holding all else constant) printers will be motivated to associate with other printers more than most other manual workers will be motivated to associate with their fellow workers.

Among the members of ITU, we can test Proposition A. If those printers for whom printing has high prestige want more to associate with fellow printers than those printers for whom printing has low prestige, then Proposition A is confirmed.[2] If Proposition B is accepted on the basis of prior knowledge about prestige of occupations, then Proposition C is confirmed. Much of the analysis which will be carried out in this and later chapters involves implicitly this kind of logic, substituting two propositions for the original one, one of which can be tested by our data, and the other making use of prior knowledge about attributes of printing relative to other occupations.

In attempting to locate the determinants of the occupational com-

---

1. The only direct evidence which we have found in comparing the propensity of people in different occupations to associate with one another, is a curious one, a study of intramarriage within occupations. Using a measure based on the potential interval marriage rate (which differs according to how many women are employed in the occupation) Donald Marvin found that printers had the second highest rate of occupational intramarriage among a large number of manual and middle-class trades and professions. While we would not have thought of studying comparative intramarriage rates as a means of testing our belief that printers are more prone to associate with one another than are people in other occupations, Marvin's results help to validate the proposition. Cf. Donald M. Marvin: "Occupational Propinquity as a Factor in Marriage Selection," *Publications of the American Statistical Association, No. 122* (June 1918), pp. 131-50.

2. We will not test propositions here in any sense of a statistical test of significance. For a number of reasons the ordinary tests of significance are inapplicable here. See Appendix I for a discussion of the general problem.

munity, we shall in effect be asking why men select and are selected by one group of associates rather than another. Among the factors which may affect leisure-time behavior we may distinguish facilitating and motivating variables. For example, the many printers who work on night shifts are cut off from finding recreational outlets with people who work days and thus may be more likely to associate with other printers who also are on night shifts. Night work would thus serve to *facilitate* involvement in the occupational community, regardless of whether or not a man was otherwise motivated to associate with printers. On the other hand, a political radical who is disposed to participate in union politics might presumably be more *motivated* to associate with other union printers even though it were objectively difficult for him to do so. Of course many factors serve both to facilitate and to motivate a given behavior pattern, but this distinction will help clarify the mechanisms which lead to the choice of one alternative rather than the other.

§ The Status of Printing

THE LITERATURE OF THE HISTORY of printing around the world suggests that printers have always thought of themselves as the aristocrats of labor, as somewhat higher than other skilled workers. Given the fact that until the nineteenth century literacy was confined to members of the middle and upper classes, it is probably true that the necessarily literate printers were accorded far higher status than other presumably illiterate manual workers. If these assumptions are valid, printers have been faced historically with a conflict flowing from the conflicting demands of their class and status positions. On the one hand many of them had higher status than other manual workers and also had broader intellectual interests; on the other hand they have always been manual workers and, the historical records would suggest, either were not accepted as equals by members of the middle class or did not have many of the background factors and interests which would have facilitated their feeling at ease while participating in middle-class community life.

Does this situation still exist? There is evidence which suggests that there is still a gap in educational background and cultural interests between printers and other workers. For example, a study made in the early thirties in Austria indicated that printers who attended adult-education classes were more likely to take the type of cultural courses patronized by middle-class persons than any other group of manual workers.[3] Similarly, with regard to formal education a study of 400,000

---

3. Lotte Radermacher: "Zur Sozialpsychologie des Volkshochschulhörers," *Zeitschrift für angewandte Psychologie*, 43:461-86 (1932).

persons on home relief in the United States in 1934 reported that "compositors, linotypers, and typesetters," the constituency of the ITU, had received more years of schooling than any other manual occupational group except pattern and model makers, who were as well educated as the compositors.[4] Clearly some of the historic factors underlying printers' high social status still exist.

How does this distinction between printers and other workers affect the social life of printers? In this way: a printer is faced with the choice of mingling socially with members of middle-class-status groups, with other manual workers, or with printers. To associate with workers may mean an acceptance of lower status and also a lower cultural level. Everything that we know about the operation of status distinctions indicates that these distinctions are in large measure maintained by persons with a claim to high status refusing to associate with persons who are defined as being lower.[5] While the printers presumably will tend to reject other manual workers, middle-class persons may tend to reject printers as friends since they are manual workers. In addition, association with middle-class persons may be difficult for some printers since it may mean mingling with people whose educational and cultural level is higher than their own. Consequently printers will tend to associate more with each other than will workers who do not possess this ambiguous status.

While we have no systematic data about the status accorded to printers by various groups in society, it is possible to make some inferences about the printers' assumptions concerning their own status. The ITU members were asked to compare the prestige of printers (compositors and typesetters) with that of printing pressmen, who have for most of the past half century received almost as much pay as compositors. These men, who usually work in the same shops as the typographers, are skilled in their own right in the operation of the complex printing presses in newspapers or print shops. But 64% of the ITU sample stated that they thought the prestige of pressmen was lower than their own. Many typographers seem to think of pressmen—and of other skilled workers—as "merely" operators of machines, not real craftsmen who know the rules of spelling and grammar, can lay out pleasing advertisements, and read while they work. Many seem to think of printing, on the other hand, as a real craft or art and are willing, on purely type-of-work basis with no considerations of pay or security,

---

4. Gladys Palmer and Katherine D. Wood: *Urban Workers on Relief*, Washington, D.C., WPA Division of Social Research, 1936, pp. 137-40.

5. Cf. Carey McWilliams: "Does Social Discrimination Really Matter?" in Wilson and Kolb, *Sociological Analysis*, pp. 500-8.

to compare it with jobs of much higher status. In interviews men seldom compared it to ordinary white-collar occupations; they either compared it to other skilled jobs, almost always with a positive reference to printing, or to "the professions," usually in this case remarking that it was "not much lower than" the professions, or was semiprofessional.

A number of printers stated that the prestige of printing is lower than it was in the past. This is probably true. The increase in the importance of the linotype and other typesetting machines has removed some of the handicraft aspect of printing; some of the men who are linotype operators responded to the question about their principal printing job by stating that they were linotype operators and then swiftly added something like: "But I'm not just a machine operator; I'm an all-around printer, although I'm working on the machine right now." In the same way many of the old-timers will refer disdainfully to the young men in the trade as "just men working at a job, who have learned to operate the machine and then passed the union exam, without being real *printers*."[6]

But whatever the trend may be, many printers still consider themselves above most other skilled trades and do not aspire to ordinary white-collar work. In view of this high-status image held by printers, one might expect them to associate more with middle-class persons or with printers, and less with other workers. This seems to be the case when we examine the distribution of the "three best friends" named by each of 412 men in our sample. Of the 1,236 friends named, 35% were printers, 21% professionals, business executives, and independent business owners, 20% white-collar or sales employees, and only 25% other manual workers.[7]

Without comparative statistics for friendship choices of men in other occupations it is impossible to determine just how different this is from the friendship pattern of other workers; it seems very likely, however, that few other manual workers find as many of their friends among nonmanual workers as these printers do. It seems also likely that few

---

6. How much of this feeling among the older men may be due to nostalgia for the good old days which have been distorted by an obliging memory, and how much corresponds to actual fact it is difficult to assess. It is true that similar sentiments are often expressed by older workers in many occupations.

7. The respondents were not asked, "What are the occupations of your three best friends?" since such a question might have produced value-biased responses: that is, men might have mentioned higher occupations to impress the interviewers. To avoid this, we asked the men to give us the first names of their three best friends so that we could talk about them. Then they were asked for each one in turn, "What is his job?" We believe that this method of securing the data reduced the errors in reporting.

occupational groups of any kind are as evenly divided between manual and nonmanual workers in their friendships as printers are.

The fact that almost two-thirds of the nonprinter friends of the persons of the sample are *not* manual workers is consistent with the expectation that printers as a group where *possible* would prefer to be accepted as members of the middle class. The fact that a large minority does associate with other manual workers does not necessarily disprove the hypothesis, for these data represent not only what the printers *prefer* but also what is *available*. Friendship, as we pointed out at the beginning, requires facilitation as well as motivation.

§ The Preferences of Printers

IT IS OUR SUGGESTION that printers are more motivated to associate with members of the middle class than most other manual workers, and we would further suggest that when prevented from doing so, either by want of opportunity or by factors in their background such as low education or membership in certain ethnic groups, they will then prefer to associate with other printers rather than with other manual workers. To demonstrate this from the data is not easy; however, it is possible to test deductions which can be made from the hypothesis.

If we consider the hypothesis that printers tend to avoid association with other manual workers, it is possible to set up a testable deduction by using the responses to the question, "If you had your choice, would you *rather* spend your free time with other printers or with people not in the trade?" The key to the situation is the fact that the "people who are not in the trade" are quite different kinds of people for different groups of printers; that is, the comparison groups or reference groups which different printers use in answering this question will differ.[8] The man who lives next to the corporation president in the

8. We should make clear here just what the sense is in which we are using the term *reference group*. This term has been used in at least two quite different ways by different theorists. These two meanings may be conveniently distinguished as *comparative* reference group and *normative* reference group, terms used by H. H. Kelly, in G. Swanson, T. Newcomb, and E. Hartley, *Readings in Social Psychology*, New York, Henry Holt and Company, Inc., 1952, pp. 410-14. To use a group of people as a comparative reference group is to use them as an orientation point, as a frame of reference within which to make some judgment. This is clearly our use of the term here, for the very question suggests, with its "people who are not in the trade," that certain other people must be used as a frame of reference or a comparison group in answering the question. To use a group of people as a normative reference group, on the other hand, is to take over their norms, to emulate them. It is not in this sense that we use the term reference group at all, although we could use the term in this sense at other points in this

wealthy suburb will think of different "people who are not in the trade" than will the man living in a street in the Italian section of Greenwich Village.[9]

It is reasonable to assume that those whose nonprinter friends are primarily workers will think of these workers when they answer the question, while men whose nonprinter friends are in middle-class non-manual occupations will think of those friends in answering the question. Thus if it is true, as has been hypothesized, that printers would prefer not to associate with manual workers, those printers in the sample for whom manual workers were the reference group when they answered the question will be less likely to say that they prefer to associate with nonprinters than will those for whom nonmanual workers were the reference group. In behavior terms, those who are able to find middle-class friends will have less desire to participate in the printers' occupational community than those whose nonprinter friends are largely in low-status occupations. In Figures 16 and 17, the relationships are shown between the occupational status of the nonprinter friends of printers in the sample and the attitudes of these printers toward associat-ing with fellow printers, as well as their actual association with them in the occupational community.

The data presented there clearly indicate that the printers with low-status nonprinter friends (manual workers) are much more likely to prefer to associate with printers than are the men who associate with higher-status middle-class persons. These results are exactly those which would be expected if the assumption is valid that printers view

---

analysis. For example, when printers view white-collar workers as having higher status than skilled workers, they are accepting the dominant middle-class values of our society, and using the middle class and upper class as a normative reference group. Those printers who disdain to associate with white-collar workers, who do not choose their friends on the basis of values of middle-class society, are not using the middle class as a normative reference group. If our analysis were more refined and our data more complete, we would be able to make this latter dis-tinction between various normative reference groups. It can be easily seen that this acceptance of middle-class criteria of status (using the middle class as a norma-tive reference group) is an important variable in determining association of printers with other printers. It seems to be largely a shift to the acceptance of middle-class values which is responsible for whatever lowered image of printing there is among printers. It is this acceptance or rejection of middle-class values which seems to determine the decision to dissociate from manual workers or to use some other criteria of association. In this analysis we have implied at least partial acceptance of this middle-class value, which in a more refined analysis would be taken as problematical.

9. Our sample in fact did contain men answering to each of these descriptions. The former had the middle-class hobbies of sailing, skiing, and woodworking; the latter, none.

Figure 16—*Proportion of Printers with Varying Friendship Patterns who Prefer to Spend Their Free Time with Nonprinters*

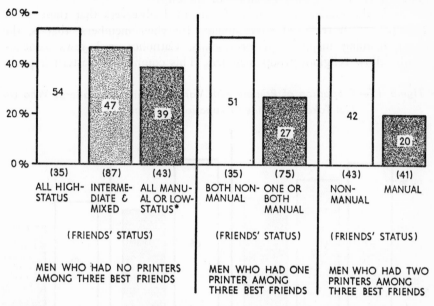

their own status as higher than that of manual workers and consequently, when unable to associate with middle-class people, prefer to associate with printers. And similarly, as the figures show, the men who do not belong to printers' clubs or attend occupation-linked social affairs tend to be individuals who associate with persons in nonmanual occupations.

§ The Opportunities of Printers

WE HAVE NOT ASKED—nor answered—the question, How does it happen that some printers associate with middle-class persons while others associate with printers or other manual workers? The data do indicate how these different opportunities arise; and with this knowledge, we may understand how different printers develop different friendship patterns.

The major single factor in the background of New York printers, affecting their opportunities to associate with middle-class persons, is religious affiliation. The population of New York City is divided into three major religious communities: Protestant, Catholic, and Jewish, each of which is represented in our sample in approximately the same proportion as in the total population of the city.[10]

It is the general consensus of informed observers that these three groups constitute social environments for their members: that is, the overwhelming majority of Protestants, Catholics, and Jews associate with fellow religious-group members. This community pattern is prob-

Figure 17—*Proportion of Printers with Varying Friendship Patterns Who Do Not Take Part in the Occupational Community*

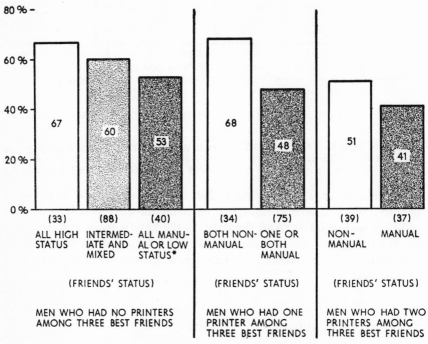

NOTE: "Low-status nonmanual" refers to white-collar workers and salesmen. "High-status" includes professions, business executives, and independent businessmen.

10.

Table—*Distribution of Three Major Religious Groups Among Printers and in the Population of New York City*

Religious Group	Printers	New York Population*
Catholics	40%	44%
Protestants	32%	22%
Jews	29%	28%
Other		1%
None		4%
N	(427)	(699)

* These percentages are from an area probability sample of the New York City population, taken for a study conducted by the National Opinion Research Center in 1951. There were 699 persons in the sample. Other studies also show roughly this breakdown.

ably related more to the persistence of ethnic communities and to social discrimination than it is to religious faith. Catholics and Jews are comparatively recent immigrants and tend to retain the pattern of in-group association of the immigrant.[11] In addition, both Catholics and Jews have been subject to social discrimination which has served to strengthen and perpetuate in-group association. Both groups also strongly oppose intermarriage and thus seek self-segregation. The Protestants, on the other hand, who are on the whole older Americans and are the majority and dominant social group in the nation as a whole, are not a self-segregated community in the same sense as the other two groups. We would guess, however, that the New York situation forces them into a segregated pattern.

The three religious groups differ considerably in their occupational

Figure 18—Occupational Distribution of White Male Members of the Three Religious Groups in New York City

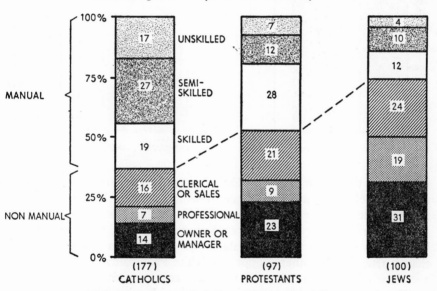

NOTE: Data from a study by the National Opinion Research Center.

11. The immigration history of the members of the sample would suggest that the printers reflect the patterns found in each group in the city as a whole:

Table—Immigration History of Three Religious Groups among Printers

Immigration Pattern	Catholics, %	Protestants, %	Jews, %
Father born in U.S.	34	49	7
Respondent born in U.S., father abroad	48	33	63
Respondent born abroad	17	18	29
N	(169)	(135)	(123)

structure. The overwhelming majority of Jews in New York are in nonmanual occupations, a large majority of Catholics are in manual jobs, while the Protestants fall between the two groups.

Given the fact that most Jews are in middle-class occupations, we would expect that Jews as compared with Catholics would be more likely to rate occupations on a scale in which all types of manual work would be considered low. In succeeding sections, therefore, we shall

Figure 19—Variations among Catholics, Protestants, and Jews in Friendship Patterns and Occupational Aspirations

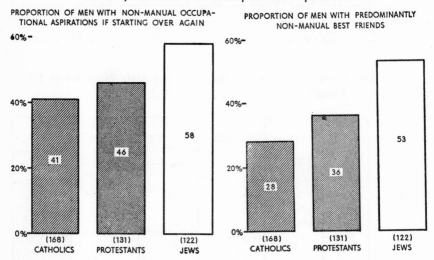

PROPORTION OF MEN WITH NON-MANUAL OCCUPA-
TIONAL ASPIRATIONS IF STARTING OVER AGAIN

PROPORTION OF MEN WITH PREDOMINANTLY
NON-MANUAL BEST FRIENDS

operate on the assumption that Catholics tend to evaluate status within a working-class frame of reference in which printing is accorded high status, while Jews evaluate status within a middle-class framework, in which printing is rated much lower. Knowing that a man is a Protestant, however, is likely to tell us less about the status of his reference group than is true for the other groups, for white Protestants are members of a variety of subcommunities of very different statuses.

The data support the assumptions that Jewish printers are much more oriented toward middle-class patterns of behavior and values than are the Catholic or Protestant groups. Two indicators of these variations in behavior and outlook may be seen in Figure 19.

Three other variables contribute to the status frame of reference and the available pool of friends: father's occupation, education, and the number of generations one's family has been in America. The printers come from diverse family backgrounds: 49% have nonprinter manual workers as fathers, while 34% are of nonmanual origins, and 17% have followed in the occupational footsteps of their fathers. They vary also in their educational backgrounds. The better educated a printer is, the more likely he is to desire a nonmanual position if he were starting his career all over again and to have middle-class persons among his three best friends.[12]

The data also show (though we do not here reproduce the tables) that the printers whose fathers were printers or in nonmanual occupations tend to have a middle-class frame of reference, while printers whose fathers were manual workers have a working-class frame of reference; and that the longer one's family has lived in America, the more likely it is that a printer has absorbed the middle-class norms of American society.

The original hypothesis is that printers in general are more motivated to associate with middle-class persons than other manual workers, and in so far as they are unable to secure middle-class friends they will tend to choose other printers as friends over other manual workers. This hypothesis can be tested by comparing workers of Jewish background, nonmanual or printing parentage, high school or better education, and native origins with the others. For those with these attributes should use the middle class as a status reference group, have better opportunities to find friends in nonmanual occupations, and will consequently be less apt to associate with other printers. Conversely, the others should use other manual workers as a reference group, have fewer opportunities to associate with middle-class people, and consequently find association with other printers desirable and status-enhancing. According to the hypothesis, Catholic printers, having less chance of finding Catholic nonmanual workers to associate with, are more likely to be active in the printers' occupational community than are Jews. Figure 20 shows this to be true.

If we now consider *which* Catholic and Jewish printers take part in the printers' social community, we come to some interesting conclusions. We should expect that Jewish printers who have high-status attributes—nonmanual parentage, good education, birth in the United

---

12.

Table—Relationship between Education and Various Characteristics of Printers

Job Aspirations	Grammar School	Some High School	High-School Graduate	Some College
Printing	54%	43%	41%	31%
Other Manual	13%	16%	13%	12%
Nonmanual	33%	42%	45%	59%
Three best friends				
predominantly nonmanual	20%	38%	38%	63%
N	(117)	(149)	(80)	(57)

Figure 20—Participation in the Occupational Community of Jews and Catholics

PROPORTION OF MEN HIGH OR MEDIUM ON SOCIAL RELATIONS INDEX

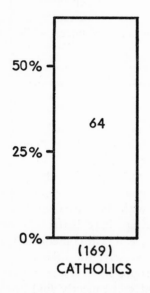

75% —

50% —

25% —

0% —

64	54
(169)	(123)
CATHOLICS	JEWS

States—will be the ones who are most interested in seeking and most successful in finding middle-class friends; whereas Jews without these high-status background attributes will be less motivated or less able to associate with persons in nonmanual occupations and will be the ones most likely to participate in the printers' community. Among the Catholics, desire and opportunity to associate with men in nonmanual occupations will in general not be as great. Those Catholic printers with high-status attributes, however, will presumably be most concerned with the status of their associates, and finding it difficult to locate middle-class Catholics with whom to associate, will be likely to associate with other printers, who are at least of equal status. Catholic printers with low-status background attributes will probably be less concerned with occupational status as a basis for friendship and should be more likely to accept or retain friends from among the large group of working-class Catholics with whom they grew up. To put our expectation in another way: Jewish printers are faced with a choice of associating with men in nonmanual occupations or with printers, while

Figure 21—*Differences in Participation in Informal Social Relations with Other Printers of Jews and Catholics with Varying Status Attributes*

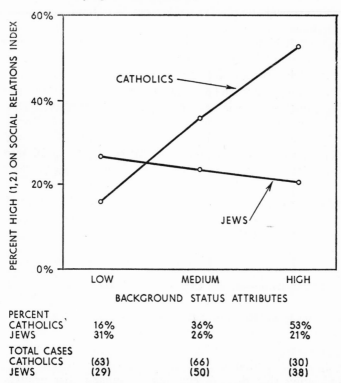

PERCENT			
CATHOLICS	16%	36%	53%
JEWS	31%	26%	21%
TOTAL CASES			
CATHOLICS	(63)	(66)	(30)
JEWS	(29)	(50)	(38)

NOTE: *Low* and *high status* refer to printers with low- or high-status attributes, such as education or family background. The above classification of low- or high-status characteristics was constructed by considering nonmanual or printing parentage and high-school graduation or better as high status, and the opposite characteristics as low. The *mediums* are high on one characteristic and low on the other.

Catholics must choose between printers and other manual workers. Those who are most oriented towards high status—the better educated, those with middle-class fathers and of native origin—will be likely to choose that pattern of association which is, for their group, of higher status; specifically, Jews will choose middle-class associates, Catholics will choose printers. Consequently, low-status Catholics should have fewer printer friends than high-status Catholics, while low-status Jews should have more printer friends than high-status Jews. These hypotheses are validated by the data in Figure 21. Thus the same status background attributes have opposite effects on the associational patterns of Jews and Catholics. But these results, rather than being contradictory, are demanded by the hypotheses when they are applied to groups with different frames of reference.[13]

While the same empirical factors—education, father's occupation, immigrant status—have diverse consequences for Jews and Catholics, it should be clear that when viewed on a conceptual level, they have similar effects. A high-status factor does not operate to produce association with persons of low status in one case and persons of high status in another. In each case, the high-status factors—education, father's occupation, and immigration background—operate to increase the propensity of an individual to associate with the group of highest status that is available to him. For Jews this means middle-class people, for Catholics it means printers, but in each case it represents a choice of the higher group. This analysis suggests anew the necessity for social research to move beyond the level of empirical generalization, that is, the correlation of empirical variables with each other. It is only when a given factor such as age, sex, or occupation is used as an indicator of a concept of higher level that we can begin to specify the complex dynamics of the social structure.[14]

§ The Marginal-Status Hypothesis Restated

LET US RECAPITULATE the basic reasoning underlying our analysis of the relationship between the status of printing and the propensity of printers to associate with one another. We begin by assuming that association is a function of two factors, motivation and opportunity. After indicating that there is evidence to suggest that printers regard

---

13. In writing this section we have presented the hypotheses and the data in the manner and order in which we developed and found them. These hypotheses are not *ex post facto* interpretations, but rather were posited as deductions from the original propositions concerning the relationship of the printers' marginal status to their tendency to find their social life within the occupational community. Protestant printers have not been discussed in any detail since we were unable to use religious affiliation as an indicator of status frame of reference for this group. As suggested earlier, evidence drawn from the attitudes of Protestant printers, and the occupational structure of the Protestant community in New York City, suggests that the Protestant printers form a middle group between the working-class-oriented Catholics and the middle-class-oriented Jews. An analysis of the relationship between status attributes of Protestants and participation in the occupational community also indicates that knowing a man is a Protestant does not enable us to make any assumptions about his probable status reference group.

14. For a number of other examples of such analysis, see S. M. Lipset, P. F. Lazarsfeld, *et al.*: "The Psychology of Voting," in Gardner Lindsey (ed.), *Handbook of Social Psychology*, Cambridge, Mass., Addison-Wesley Publishing Company, 1954, pp. 1124-76.

OCCUPATIONAL COMMUNITY: I

themselves as the elite among manual workers, and that they are better educated and more likely to have middle-class cultural tastes than other manual workers, we suggested that their status position will motivate printers as a group not to associate with other manual workers, whom they will consider of lower status.

The rejection of other manual workers as status equals is in turn related to the propensity of printers to associate with one another. Those status-oriented printers who do not have the opportunity or the ability to associate with middle-class persons will prefer to associate with other printers rather than with manual workers. Evidence for this proposition was adduced by comparing the social preferences, whether printers or nonprinters, of men whose nonprinter friends are manual workers with the preferences of those who have middle-class friends. As expected, those with manual worker friends were more likely to prefer association with printers than those with friends in nonmanual occupations.

Following the same logic of analysis, we then went on to indicate that the extent to which printers took one of the three paths of association open to them would be related to their opportunity and motivation. Factors such as religious affiliation, education, parental status, and recency of immigration would affect both the motivation of printers to seek out friends of higher status and the pool of available friends. Religious affiliation proved to be the most important single variable affecting both motivation and opportunity.

The results of the internal analysis tend to validate the utility of the conceptual approach employed in this chapter in locating the determinants of friendship patterns. It should be clear, however, that this analysis *per se* does not demonstrate any necessary relationship between the status of printing and the existence of the occupational community. To completely verify the hypothesis about printing and friendship patterns would require comparable data on the leisure-time patterns of a number of occupations, which we do not have.[15]

---

15. In a current study of the flow of scientific information within the medical profession being conducted by the Bureau of Applied Social Research, precisely the same two questions were asked of a sample of 216 practicing physicians as were asked of printers concerning their associations with fellow-workers. Both groups were asked whether they would *rather* associate with printers (doctors) in their leisure time, and whether they *actually* associate more with printers (doctors) or nonprinters (nondoctors). Doctors, who seem to have about as high an intra-occupational association as any occupational group, answered almost exactly the same as printers. This is further evidence that printers tend to associate among themselves more than most occupational groups.

§ Identification with Printing

ANOTHER FACTOR quite independent of the status of printing which might lead printers to associate with fellow workers is job satisfaction. If men like and are interested in their work, they will be more likely than those who dislike the work to associate with others in the occupation. Early in the research we were struck with the number of spontaneous expressions of liking one's job and thinking of it as a craft. In describing how they happened to enter the trade, men would talk of how lucky they were to have become printers.

One measure of job satisfaction is in the response of individuals to the question, "All things considered, how do you like printing as an occupation?" The answers to a check list are tabulated in Table 7.

Table 7—How Well Printers Like Their Occupation

Like it very much	73%
Like it fairly well	23%
Dislike or feel indifferent	4%
N	(434)

Another indication can be found in the responses to a different type of question: "Is there any occupation you would like to have other than the one you now have, either in or outside the printing trade?" A large majority of the men, 64%, said they preferred to remain in printing. Of the remaining 36%, many mentioned some higher-level position within the printing or newspaper business.[16]

---

16. Comparative data are extremely difficult to locate in this field. Three other studies, however, do suggest that printers are more likely to like their work than are other groups of workers. A study based on a random sample of employed men in the United States attempted to test degree of job satisfaction by presenting respondents with alternative answers comparable to the ones used in the present study. The results are presented in the following table:

Table—Per Cent Satisfied and Dissatisfied with Their Jobs by Occupation among American Male Workers

	Very Satisfied	Satisfied	Dissatisfied		
Trades (Skilled	32	57	11	(100%)	84
Operatives (Semi-skilled)	25	60	15	(100%)	80
Unskilled	25	54	21	(100%)	24
Service	19	50	31	(100%)	16
Total All Workers	27	57	16	(100%)	204

NOTE: Table is taken from Nancy C. Morse and Robert S. Weiss, "The Function and Meaning of Work and the Job," *American Sociological Review*, 20, 1955, p. 198.

A study of railroad workers which also used comparable alternatives found only 19% choosing the highest category of "very well satisfied," as compared to 73% of the printers. About 22% of the railroad workers were indifferent or dissatisfied, compared with only 4% of the ITU members. See Daniel Katz *et al.*, *Productivity*,

What is it about printing that printers like? There are some obvious and some complex answers. The volunteered answers of the printers themselves provide some clues.

Table 8—What It Is about Printing that Printers Like

Lack of monotony	38%
Creative aspects	37%
Pay and security	29%
Educational	21%
Working conditions	21%
Prestige	6%
Other	18%
N	(434)

NOTE: The replies total more than 100% since some men gave more than one reason.

By itself, Table 8 shows a preponderance of answers which indicate intrinsic rewards of the job. What is perhaps more meaningful is that only 11% of those answering gave wages or working conditions as their sole reason for liking printing. The overwhelming majority of the workers gave answers intrinsic to the craft nature of the job. The most common comment was that the job is "challenging," that, as one printer put it, "no two jobs are alike," or another, that "you always have to use your imagination." One is struck here by the feeling that among these men "the instinct of workmanship" is not dead. Work itself can be rewarding.

Very frequently mentioned as a reason for liking the work was its educational value. Many men reported that they read what they print and often discuss it with fellow workers. In the newspapers the talk is of the news of the day. In the book-and-job shops, content will vary

Supervision and Morale among Railroad Workers, Ann Arbor, Survey Research Center, 1951, p. 28.

In yet another study, a random sample of the Detroit population was asked, "Which of these four (choices listed on a card) best describes how you feel about your job? Very satisfied, fairly satisfied, rather dissatisfied, very dissatisfied."

Since the respondents were not allowed a neutral choice, we would guess that this form of the question resulted in higher proportions in the "fairly satisfied" group. Nevertheless, the results by occupation are as follows:

Table—Job Satisfaction of Detroit Residents in Different Occupational Categories who Vary in Ideological Sensitivity

	Manager; Owner	Professional; Semi-professional	White Collar Upper	White Collar Lower	Skilled	Unskilled and Semi-skilled
Very Satisfied	73%	55%	72	53	60	60
Fairly Satisfied	24	45	28	39	32	38
Dissatisfied	3	—	—	8	8	2
N	34	29	39	36	62	120

NOTE: Table is taken from Arthur Kornhauser, *Detroit as the People See It,* Detroit: Wayne University Press, 1952, p. 55.

greatly, but many printers have the opportunity to read and discuss magazine articles and books.

We do not wish to exaggerate the idyllic aspects of printing or to suggest that there are no disagreeable elements to the occupation. Many men, especially those who work on the linotype machine in large newspapers, do engage in routine work. For some of them printing is little more than a complex version of typing. The new typesetting machines have reduced the skill required and eliminated the creative aspects which give a man pride in his work. Indeed, a number of men complained that the increased mechanization of printing has lessened the attractiveness of the job. Yet for the great majority of printers the positive aspects of the craft outweigh the disadvantages.

This brief discussion of the attitudes of printers to their work is relevant because of our assumption that positive attitudes to one's work generate a desire to associate with workers in the same trade. Men who are proud of their work, who view it as interesting and important, will not be "bored" with taking their job into their leisure activities. A good job is a tie that binds. That this is actually the case is indicated by Figure 22, which compares printers according to their responses to the question, "If you had your choice would you *rather* spend your

Figure 22—Relationship between Liking Printing and Preferring to Spend Leisure Time with Printers

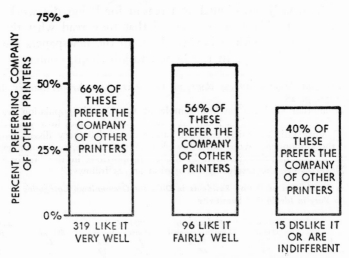

free time with other printers or with people who are not in the trade?"

Liking printing is clearly correlated with preferring to spend time with fellow workers, and as other data show, it is correlated as well with actually associating with them.[17] Conceivably these results may reflect the fact that men whose social contacts are with other printers become more satisfied with their jobs. This may certainly be true. But it seems at least as reasonable to assume that men who are really interested in their job as such, who do not simply view it as a necessary but burdensome way of earning a living, will want to continue to talk about affairs related to the job after work, just as persons in professional and intellectual occupations often do.

The assumption that men who have a positive craftsman orientation to their jobs will be more likely to want to talk about their work may be tested by comparing the attitudes and behavior of those men who gave craftsman reasons for liking printers with the minority who like their work but cite only economic reasons.

Table 9—Relationship between Orientation to Printing as an Occupation and Propensity to Talk about Printing with Nonprinters

	REASONS FOR LIKING PRINTING	
	Craftsman Reasons	Economic Reasons Only
Talk about printing with nonprinters*	65%	52%
N	(274)	(46)

* Based on replies to the question: When you talk with your friends who are not printers, do you ever talk about printing or union affairs?

The "craftsmen" are more likely to project their interest in their occupation into their social relations with others than those who view printing as simply a good-paying, secure job. If we assume that these men find pleasure in discussing craft matters, then it is fairly logical to conclude that they will seek at least some social relations with printers. Interest in and satisfaction with the occupation, therefore, are probably strong motivating as well as strong facilitating factors in the propensity of printers to associate with each other: motivating in the sense that printers will want to find friends with the same interests, and facilitating in that the occupation itself will serve as a fruitful subject of common interest for them when they get together. Further evidence for these assumptions may be found in Table 10.

Three separate indicators of liking one's job—liking one's work

---

17. A further indicator of job satisfaction may be found in the replies to the question regarding job preferences. Those who desired to remain in printing if they had a choice of jobs were much more likely to prefer printers as leisure-time associates and to actually spend more time with other printers than were those who would like to leave the trade.

Table 10—Relationship between Orientation to Printing as an Occupation and Propensity to Associate with Other Printers

	REASONS FOR LIKING PRINTING	
	Craftsman Reasons	Economic Reasons Only
High in social relations with printers*	59%	33%
Have two or more printer friends	32%	22%
Prefer some printers among friends	66%	50%
N	(271)	(46)

* High and medium groups were combined for this table.

"very much," desire to remain in printing if given a choice, and liking printing for "craftsman" reasons—all are related to a high degree of association with other printers. It is not possible, however, to demonstrate with the available data which factor is prior in time: Do men who develop a craft orientation toward their work then search out other printers as companions, or do men who develop friendships with other printers then develop positive attitudes to the craft? Actually, of course, it is probably true that both processes occur. Interaction with printers over time increases the attractiveness of the occupation, while the fact that the job is attractive stimulates interaction. The chicken-or-egg dilemma is actually, therefore, not a serious problem. There can be little doubt that the attractiveness of the job itself is one of the factors contributing to the propensity of printers to associate with each other.

CHAPTER 7

Determinants of the Occupational Community: II

WE HAVE SUGGESTED that the relatively high status of printers and their positive liking for their craft are two of the principal factors contributing to the existence of an occupational community among printers. Yet the widening of popular education, reducing the status claim of the printer, and the increased mechanization of printing, limiting his variety in work, indicate that the occupational community might be less significant today than in the past. Our impressionistic judgmen, based on reading printers' papers and magazines for the last fifty years, is that there has been a decline. Yet two unique factors, apart from status and craft pride, continue to provide the mortar to keep the occupational community together. These are the conditions under which men secure and maintain employment in a print shop, and the fact that a large proportion of printers work nights.

§ The Substitute System

ONE OF THE CHARACTERISTICS of the printing industry is the fluctuating work loads on different days of the week and at different periods of the year. Newspapers, for example, require additional printers on days, such as Thursdays, Fridays, and Saturdays, when advertising is heavier. They also expand their labor force considerably during the pre-Christmas season. Many book and job shops which specialize in advertising, magazine, or election work have comparable hiring problems. Printing tends to be seasonal, with a major slack period in the summer and the greatest amount of work between September and January.

These extra loads are filled by substitutes and by overtime. The substitutes are either beginners in the industry who, having finished a six-year apprenticeship, go to the bottom of the priority (seniority) list and must wait out an opening in the regular work force, or other printers who have lost their regular jobs.

Substitutes are hired by the day. Every printer working in a print shop, regularly or as a substitute, has a priority number within that shop, assigned according to the length of time he has been in the shop. New situations are filled or regular men discharged according to one's position on the list. When a substitute deposits his union card in a particular shop, he is assigned a number at the bottom of the list and waits his turn for a regular situation.

However, the *daily* hiring of subs is not carried out in accordance with this list. Instead, the chapel chairman holds a lottery in which each sub draws a numbered ball. Those men with the highest numbers get the positions for the day, while those with lower numbers are out of luck for that shift.

The first consequence of this procedure is that every man feels constrained to show up every day.[1] Those subs who do not get work find themselves downtown with nothing to do for the rest of the day. Subs are permitted to show up on all three shifts if they like. Many men who do not get work in the morning will often show up for the evening shift as well. If a man needs money badly, he may show up for all three shifts, trying his luck each time.

The men who have failed to get work have to kill six to eight hours between shifts. During the period when printers' clubs had full-time headquarters, many subs went there to talk, play cards, or drink.[2] Then and now, many of them go to the union headquarters, which has rooms for cardplaying or sitting around and talking. Others may meet at a

---

1. One important function of this system for the employer is that it supplies him each day with a full "reserve army of unemployed," so that unanticipated work schedules may be filled. If there were another system of hiring so that one man's chances were less than another's, either due to position on the priority list or the foreman's favor, those men with less chance would tend to stay at home.

2. Full-time headquarters disappeared during World War II, when there was full employment in the trade for the first time since World War I. Without patronage of subs, with most men working long overtime hours, and with the younger men in the military services, there was a sharp decline in occupational-community activities. The *Typographical Forum*, the occupational-community newspaper, also ceased publishing in this period. Since the end of the war the situation has gradually returned to "normal." Club and other occupational-community activity has revived, but is still far from the point reached in the thirties.

local bar and socialize. Many of the newspapers have large lounging rooms which were set up for the benefit of subs or workers who have come downtown early to see their friends. In all these ways the subs are thrown together throughout their entire substitute period.

But this is not the only consequence of the substitute hiring system for the occupational community. A second method of hiring subs also operates as a force for association. The hiring system we have described, in which the sub's job is dependent on chance, operates only for that extra work which is created by the employer. But when a job-holder is ill, he decides to take a day off, or when he has accumulated overtime and must take a day off in accordance with union rules, the job holder himself determines who will replace him. The employer has no control over the hiring in this case, nor does the union. The job-holder, in effect, owns his job, and determines who will replace him in it. Naturally the man will tend to give the opening to a friend or to the friend of a friend, or in some cases to a man who pays him a few dollars for the day's work.

Throughout a man's substitute career his work opportunities will depend on his ability to make friends among other printers in the shop. Subs are under strain to ingratiate themselves with job holders.[3] This, of course, may be done by doing favors for such men, participating in

---

3. And as would be expected, the situation-holder sometimes does manipulate the sub, in any of several ways. The pressures put upon a substitute are well illustrated by some comments made during the interview by a sub who was in our sample.

In a probe following a question about security:

No, I've felt the same about that [the security of printers, which he had characterized as "only fairly good"]. It's called to my attention every time I draw one of those balls, or whenever somebody slips one of the old sots a pint so he'll put his name up on the board as a substitute.

Q. Is there anything about the ITU which could stand improving?

Yes: the priority law. If you came into a shop and then there was a layoff, the last man still works every day, and the others who are laid off don't work at all. In the ILGWU if there's not enough work for everybody, they share it. Unionism should provide an equalization of work rather than gambling every day for a job. In hiring subs a man can pick whoever he wants, which is the *worst* form of unionism in the world. Favoritism is very prevalent. You can give a lush $2 and still make $18 a night.

Q. Do you think people like you have a lot of influence on how the union runs things, some influence, or not much influence?

Not much. [Q. Why?] Because a sub is considered a step lower than the rest, and any opinions or gripes are politely turned down. . . . He's afraid to voice his opinion because he might antagonize men giving him work and become known as a troublemaker; men who are off once in a while will not put him up as a sub for them when they are off.

Running through these statements is (along with a bitterness toward the priority system) awareness of the pressure to make oneself liked by the printer on the job and painful awareness of the substitute's dependency on the situation-holder.

printers' social affairs in which they may make friends, trying to join shop cliques, going out bowling, and other similar devices. While the stress is on making friends in one's own shop, knowing printers in a number of shops may help. Subs are permitted to work temporarily in a shop other than the one in which they have their card, if there are no subs available for work in the other shop. Many small shops have few or no subs since the opportunity to secure extra work or a steady situation is related to the size of the shop. These smaller shops must therefore call upon men from the larger plants. Here acquaintanceship pays off, since a friend may let one know in advance that his shop will need people. Attending club meetings or occupational-community affairs may pay real dividends for the substitute.

It is difficult to document on the basis of our data the precise consequences of the above two mechanisms—the need to show up every day and the dependence on friendship for employment. This is especially true since these factors were not considered in our initial formulation of the study when the interview questions were developed.[4] Nevertheless, it is possible to differentiate among the members of the sample between those men who had more substitute experience in their background than others, and to compare their social relations with that of other printers. One indirect indicator of length of substitute experience is the response to the question asking how long a man has been without steady work.[5]

It is clear that the more unemployment a man has experienced and presumably the more time he has spent as a sub, the more likely he is to be active in the occupational community. In addition, the men in the sample who were substitutes when interviewed were more involved in informal and formal social relations with other printers than the fully employed men.

If the substitute period were short or if only a few men went through the trials of a substitute, this system would not be too important for the social system of the union. But the substitute period may last from

---

4. It should be noted that even if we had considered these factors before beginning our field research, it would not have been possible for us to distinguish quantitatively between the two processes. This is because both processes are postulated to operate in the same direction for the same men. If we knew precisely *who* the substitutes associated with most, and under what conditions, we would then have the information to analyze which process contributed most to socialization into the occupational community.

5. While responses to this question are undoubtedly related to the extent of substitute experience, it is clear from the totals that many men who were substitutes did not tell us that they were without steady employment. We would guess that the difference is a result of the fact that men do not consider substitute periods, in which they may work an average of two or three days a week, as being without a job.

Figure 23—*Relationship between Reported Periods of Unemployment
and Activity in the Occupational Community*

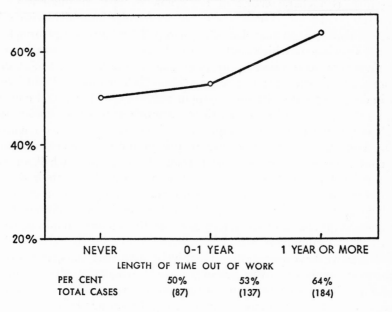

PROPORTION HIGH OR MEDIUM ON SOCIAL RELATIONS INDEX

	NEVER	0-1 YEAR	1 YEAR OR MORE
PER CENT	50%	53%	64%
TOTAL CASES	(87)	(137)	(184)

LENGTH OF TIME OUT OF WORK

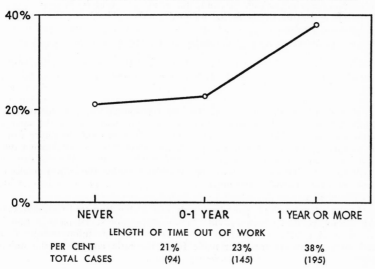

PROPORTION WHO ARE MEMBERS OF A PRINTER CLUB

	NEVER	0-1 YEAR	1 YEAR OR MORE
PER CENT	21%	23%	38%
TOTAL CASES	(94)	(145)	(195)

LENGTH OF TIME OUT OF WORK

three to five years on the large newspapers, and except for the war years it has been virtually impossible to get a job on a newspaper or in a large book and job shop without being a sub. This experience, therefore, is a characteristic of the whole occupation and not simply of a few men in it. This pressure to get involved socially with other printers ends once a man has a regular position, but the informal and formal associations which he has formed may continue for many years.

There are many other occupations, such as the building trades, longshore work, and the entertainment fields, which are seasonal and irregular in character and in which job opportunities depend on social contacts. And indeed, the workers in all these occupations tend to associate with each other. Painters, for example, must find something to do when it rains, and one finds hangouts where painters or bricklayers are known to cluster. These are often in restaurants, bars, the union hall, or even occupational social clubs such as exist among printers. In these occupations the men do not own their jobs nor do they have a system of picking substitutes like the lottery, and the power to pick workers becomes a source of power in the hands of the union administration, or foremen and employers.[6]

While we have not studied intensively any other comparable occupation, it seems clear that irregular work, while contributing to the existence of an occupational community, is most often a source of strength for the incumbent union administration.[7] Workers are so

---

6. One interesting exception occurs among the musicians. Band leaders who are members of the union hire pickup hands from men in the union hall. In this union and occupation, which resemble those of the printers in many ways, the band leaders constitute the basis for political conflict. The New York local of the union has two regular parties, much like those in the ITU, which are based on the cliques around different groups of band or orchestra leaders. A comparison of two unions in the same occupation adds further weight to these interpretations. Longshoremen, like substitute printers, must show up daily for employment, and many work only a few days a week. Longshoremen also have an occupational community. Many of them live near the docks in close proximity to each other. East Coast longshoremen are hired through the shapeup system. Each man shapes up at the dock, and the hiring boss, who is often a union official or part of the same machine that controls the union, selects the men to work. In San Francisco the longshoremen are hired in rotation, and neither the union nor employer can affect a man's chances to obtain work. The East Coast union is one of the worst dictatorships in American unionism, whereas the West Coast union, though Communist-controlled on the international level, is very democratic. The San Francisco local has two permanent political groups, which alternate in power much as do the parties in the ITU.

7. On the other hand, Shepard in a study of the Amalgamated Clothing Workers considers slack periods which provide "opportunities for social participation in the union hall and developing interest in and knowledge of union problems" to be one of the objective factors that made for democratic control in the union. Cf. Shepard, *American Journal of Sociology*, 54:315.

dependent on the union for employment that they do not dare to participate in opposition activities. It is only when workers have the security of protection from discrimination by the union that such associations may form the basis for political opposition.[8]

The difference between the printers and those occupations in which there is control over hiring by the union or the employer or a combination of both, makes possible a fairly precise statement of the consequences of variable work requirements in conjunction with different types of hiring policies. The consequences for printers, as described in the preceding pages, are summed up in Diagram A.

Diagram A

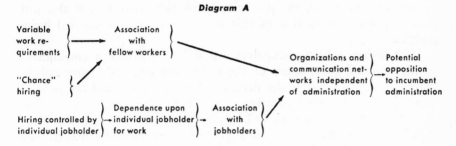

That is, the variable work requirements in conjunction with the hiring policies of the union combine to make the substitute associate with other subs and with regular printers in his shop; this in turn helps support the institutions of the occupational community, which form a basis for a continuing opposition against the incumbent administration.

In unions in which the hiring policies are controlled by the union administration, however, the same variable work requirements can have quite different consequences. Diagram B indicates the processes which

---

8. The freedom from manipulation on the part of the employer and the union gives rise among some of the printers to real feelings of exuberance and expressions of a sense of freedom. Several of the men in interview expressed these feelings. As one man happily put it: "How free is free? How free can a man be?" Although some of the practices of the printers which engender this feeling are not workable in more highly rationalized industries, some certainly are. The resulting feelings of security and well-being among printers indicate a partial solution to the problem of the worker's ever-increasing subjection to the manipulative forces of big business, big unions, and big government. One of the most appealing consequences of the ITU's democratic process, including the laws making for autonomy of the individual printer, is this feeling of freedom from manipulation, the power of self-determination.

If such grass-roots democracy with its concomitant feelings of freedom from manipulations is not possible on the national level in civil politics because of size, it is not inherently impossible in other spheres of a man's life, especially the crucial sphere of his occupation. A lessening of the manipulative power of management and of the union over a man's work would be one step in the realization of a liberal society.

Diagram B

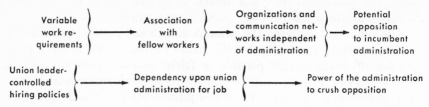

we suggest are operative. Thus while potential opposition is produced by the variable work, the power to crush this opposition is also produced by the combination of this with union leader-controlled hiring policies.

The hiring policies themselves are at least partially a consequence of the type of government of the union, the printers' hiring policies having been instituted at the demand of the members and the political opposition to the administration in order to eliminate such a union-foreman combine within the ITU. Before the priority system was introduced (and its introduction was gradual, each step eliminating some of the power of the foreman) control over hiring was completely in the hands of foremen. And as the reader will recall from Chapter 3, the old Wahneta organization is reputed to have built its power by recruiting foremen, who then gave preference to fellow Wahnetas. The predecessors of the present Progs led the fight for the priority system as a means of reducing the power of the Wahnetas and the foremen.

This historical note, together with the processes diagramed above, provides an excellent illustration of the self-maintaining mechanisms of a democratic system. The democratic control of the ITU led to the institution of a hiring system free from union leader control, which in turn helps perpetuate the institutions which give power to a political opposition. The other pattern is, conversely, a self-maintaining one for oligarchic control.[9] Oligarchic government gives the administration power to control hiring policies, which in turn gives the administration control over potential oppositionists.

Another socializing agency which affects many printers is apprentice school. While most of an apprentice's time is spent in the print shop at which he is apprenticed, there are regular classes which he attends as well. Since the whole apprentice period is six years, this means that an apprentice will get to know his classmates well. The apprentices in New York State take a trip to Albany together for a special training

---

9. Of course other factors enter in. If they did not, the printers would never have managed to free hiring from administration control.

session in each of the last two years of their apprenticeship, which further acts to increase their cohesion. The major difference between this and other school periods which produce the same kind of cohesion is that these men never separate to go their various ways as do college classmates. Many of them stay in the same city, so that their apprentice friends are fellow union members in the same local for the rest of their career. These friendships are long-lasting, as several of the members of our sample testified. One of the union political leaders clearly indicates the socializing function of the apprentice school as well as the political relevance of social groups in his answer to the question, What was the first political meeting you attended in the union?:

Some of the boys I went to apprentice school with were associated with the Liberals and I went along to observe. This was 1932 [while still an apprentice]. A fellow who serves as an apprentice in New York is different from one coming from out of town. There are groups in apprentice school, and you form opinions there and get interested. By the time you're out, you're interested and active. It's like college in a way—you make close friends and do things in and out of school together that you have fond memories of. The thing you remember most is the fun you had in school. When you see the same fellows now, you have sort of a spontaneous greeting. Going around campaigning now, I see some of them every once in a while, and we go over old times.

§ Night Work

MANY PRINTERS must work nights and week ends, thus breaking the normal pattern of family life and leisure life. About 45% of the membership of Big Six are night workers. Every newspaper and a large number of book-and-job shops have night shifts. Most newspapers actually have two night shifts, one from about four in the afternoon to midnight and the other from midnight to some time in the morning. In many industries which require night work, workers alternate between periods of night and day work. A printer, however, must remain on the night shift until he has accumulated enough priority to claim a day job. Thus, almost every printer has spent some time on the night shift. The only exceptions are the small group of men who have always worked in small shops, which do not have night work. Only 8% of the members of our sample reported that they had never worked on a night shift.

One of the primary consequences of night-work is the breakup of normal leisure patterns. Neighborhood and other organizations are built around the "normal" nine-to-five working day and meet in the evening. Mass entertainment is similarly organized to meet the needs of people who work days and want to relax in the evening. The night worker's social relationships must in large measure be limited to people who are in his same situation. For a printer the pool of other night workers most easily available to him is other printers. Printers working on the night shift will thus seek out other printers and become involved in the occupational community.

Table 11—Relationship between Work Shift and Involvement in the Occupational Community

	Night Workers	Day Workers
High in social relations	30%	23%
Two or more printer friends	38%	27%
Members of printers' clubs	36%	26%
N	(200)	(234)

Thus whatever the varied consequences of night work are, the data indicate that night work increases the likelihood of printers' associating with fellow craftsmen.

New night workers probably attempt to continue as much of their past social life as possible after going on the night shift, and these men initially show even lower levels of social interaction with other printers than do day workers. The longer, however, that they are on the night shift, the more likely they are to evidence a high level of leisure-time social relations with printers. The success that a man has in adjusting to the social requirement of night work greatly affects his attitude to working nights. When asked whether they preferred working days or nights, 62% of the night workers indicated a preference for the night shift. When we compare the leisure pattern of those preferring nights with those who would like to be on the day shift, it is clear that these responses are, in part at least, a reaction to success or failure in adjusting one's social life.

Table 12—Relationship between Preference for Night or Day Work among Night Workers, and Involvement in Social Relations with Other Printers

	NIGHT WORKERS WHO	
	Prefer Days	*Prefer Nights*
High Social Relations	22%	37%
N	(70)	(114)

Earlier we suggested that the substitute system was important in initially integrating printers into the occupational community, and that friendship patterns formed in this early period continue after men get regular jobs. Night work has a similar effect. As printers grow older they gain priority, and eventually many, though not all, claim situations on the day shift. When printers who have been on the night shift for a decade or more change to day work, they have difficulty in readjusting their leisure habits. A number of men pointed out that a printer working in a newspaper hardly gets to know his children, who are in school while he is not working. Often the children are adults before he gets a chance to work days. He has also lost contact with many of his non-printer friends during his long period on the night shift. Such men will continue to associate with other printers, given the difficulty of making new friends after forty.

To verify the long-range effects of night work, we compared the social relations of night and day workers who have spent varying amounts of time working nights.

Figure 24—Relationship between Time Spent on Night Shift and
   Social Relations with Printers

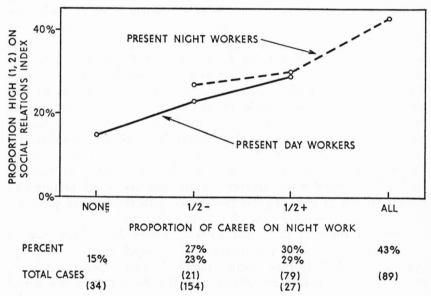

It is clear from the above data that past experience on the night shift continues to affect men's social behavior after they leave it.

There are a number of processes which underlie the propensity of night workers to associate with printers. First, we would suggest that the day worker is subject to the structured pulls of mass entertainment, of neighborhood organizations, and of nonprinter friends away from the printers' community, while night workers on all these counts are subject to a push toward the printers' community. Thus while night workers take *less* part in nonprinter organizations, they take *more* part in organizations associated with printing than do day workers.[10]

A second element in night work leading to greater social relations with fellow printers is the effect of night work on family relations. As one printer put it in an interview, "Night workers don't have to punch the family time clock." Day workers, finishing work in the late afternoon, are under pressure to rush home to dinner and to conform to a time schedule set by their children or by plans for evening activities of the family. For the day worker, the end of the day's work often means the end of relations with fellow workers unless special arrangements are made to return or to stay over for a meeting later in the evening. Thus it requires an added effort and inconvenience to see other printers after work—either missing a meal at home or leaving again after supper.

Night workers, on the other hand, finish work after their wives and families are asleep. Their schedule is so completely in conflict with that of the children that they are not expected to conform as are day workers. If a fellow worker suggests that a group go down to a local bar or go bowling or talk for a while over coffee in a cafe, no one at home will object. Many night workers, in fact, have reported such a pattern of afterwork activity. Similarly, the night worker can take his time going to work. Unlike the day worker, who is usually rushed in rising, breakfasting, and reaching work on time, the night worker customarily does not go to work for many hours after he has risen. He may and often does arrange to meet his friends downtown before work. One worker who had spent most of his time on night work reported having had a regular pattern through the summertime of meeting two printer friends in the early afternoon, going to the baseball game together, and then coming to work together afterwards.

Some of the data show that working nights does disrupt normal family schedules, making the printer freer to associate on his own. For example, we asked the men whether they visited other printers at home, and if so, how often. In accordance with the above pattern, we would expect that night workers, though they *generally* associate more with printers, do not visit them as often at home. That is, in this one area of

---

10.

Table—Recruitment of Members of Printers' and and Nonprinters' Clubs from Day and Night Shifts

Present Shift	Members of Printers' Clubs Only, %	Members of Nonprinter Groups Only, %
Days	36	61
Nights	64	39
Proportion of Career on Shift		
Most on Days	55	77
Most on Nights	45	23
N	(73)	(155)

association among printers, night workers should associate *less* than do day workers. Table 13 shows this to be true although the differences are small.

Table 13—Effect of Night Work on Home Visits

	Night Workers	Day Workers
Do you ever visit other printers at their homes? Yes	71%	76%
N	(199)	(234)

A third factor which seems to contribute to greater informal social relations among night workers is the different pace of work on the night as compared with the day shift. In many printing plants, especially the middle-sized book-and-job shops, the night shift is regarded by the men as an easier shift to work on. The pace of work is more relaxed. Supervision is less strict. This easier pace of work may have two consequences. In many shops there is no representative of management present except the night foreman, who is a fellow union member. A number of printers indicated that absence of any management personnel on the premises serves to reduce tension. A second factor present in the situation is the "abnormality" of night work itself. It is therefore more difficult for a supervisor to press a night worker hard, given the fact that he is working during what are legitimately sleeping hours.

The greater freedom of night workers from normal industrial routines tends to facilitate socializing on the job. In addition, the easier pace of night work may facilitate the development of interest in union affairs. Active partisans find it easier to walk around the job discussing elections or union issues with night men than on days.

§ Conclusions

THESE, THEN, are some of the factors within printing which seem to make for a high degree of social relations among printers:

1. Printers have been and are among the elite manual occupational groups in terms of social status. The marginal (between manual and nonmanual or working-class and middle-class) status of printing seems to be one factor which has been unique to printing all through its history and has been of major importance in motivating printers to associate with one another.

2. The craft aspect of printing gives printers a basic ground of common interest, which is probably not the case in most other manual occupations.

3. The union's substitute system operates to heighten interaction among printers, first through motivating printers to show up for work every day, and second through the fact that a substitute's chances for

employment are directly related to the number of friends that he has among regular situation holders.

4. Finally, the night work (and most printers work nights for at least part of their careers) tends to increase printers' associations with each other. It reduces printers' opportunities to associate with non-printers or to take part in neighborhood activities and mass entertainment; early in a man's career, it habituates him to occupation-linked leisure activities and releases him from the pressure of regular family life.

These four factors clearly do not exhaust the variables which could be considered possible determinants of the printers' social community. We considered at least two others, but did not have the data necessary to test them. We thought that the lack of status differentiation among the union's members and the possibility that printers might be more skilled in organizational techniques than persons in other occupations might tend to increase socialization among printers. Status differentiation within a union should operate to reduce the amount of free interaction among all members of the union. Thus we would guess that pressmen's assistants, who comprise a large minority of the membership of that union, do not mingle much socially with pressmen. In the ITU, on the other hand, almost all members are of about equal status, skill, and salary, thus permitting the choice of friends among the entire membership. We would assume also that the higher educational and cultural background of printers as compared with other manual workers means in part that they will have more know-how on setting up and managing organizations. Neither of these hypotheses, however, can be tested without comparative data from other occupations.[11]

A further determinant of printers' social relations is the nature of their work itself and the chances for informal relations at work. This factor will be discussed later, when we take up the impact of social relations within the shop on the union's political system.

We also have not attempted to take up the factors which might make some printers more social than others but which are not unique to printers. For example, it is quite possible that those printers who associate with other printers have different personalities from those who do not.

Gregarious printers, we find from our data, are, not surprisingly, more likely to associate with other printers than nongregarious ones. But there is no reason to expect that printers as a group are any different in their personality traits from followers of other occupations, nor that personality characteristics as such would help explain the high level of formal and informal social organization among printers.

---

11. An indirect test of the latter is possible and was carried out: we found that, within printing, those with most education and highest status background were disproportionately active in printers' clubs.

CHAPTER 8

The Structure of
the Printing Industry
and Democratic Politics

IN THIS AND THE FOLLOWING CHAPTER we turn from the printers' leisure-time occupational community and its significance for the union's political system to the work life of printers. The working experience of a printer, which forms half or more of his waking hours, is on the one hand largely determined by the technological and economic organization of the printing industry, and on the other hand, is of great consequence for the political life of the union. Thus the next two chapters deal with the bearing of certain characteristics of the printing industry on the structure and political processes of the ITU.

In our society the economic organization of work has for workers many of the aspects which nature bears for man in nonliterate societies. The patterns of ownership and technology, which define work relations and organization, are part of the modern worker's environment, to which he can respond and adapt within a narrow range of possibilities, but which he cannot easily change or significantly affect. If we find a relationship between aspects of the formal organization of work and the behavior and attitudes of workers, we can generally assume that it is the organizational or structural factors that determine—or help to determine—the behaviors and attitudes, rather than vice versa, for there is little a worker or even a union can do to change the way an industry is organized. Yet there has been little empirical research on variations in work environments in different occupations, and even less about how these variations affect the behavior of workers in other areas of activity, for example, in their unions.

As we point out various relationships between the economic organization of the printing industry and ITU politics, we do not suggest that there are specific elements unique to print shops which *require* the existence of a democratic political system in the ITU. Other unions in the printing trades operate under similar conditions and are highly oligarchic in their union government. There is no reason to believe that an oligarchic union could not operate in the same industrial environment as the ITU. On the other hand, the patterns of ownership and technology in printing do appear to have large and clear consequences for the internal politics of the union. Even if they do not strictly determine the character of union politics, they do affect the *chances* for internal democracy. In particular, two important aspects of the organization of the industry seem to have a bearing on union politics: the division of labor among the men who make up the union, and the degree of physical concentration and centralized ownership in the industry.

§ The Division of Labor

The politically most important aspect of the division of labor among printers is that *all of the members of the ITU share a roughly common income and status.* Printers are skilled workers. With the exception of a small group of machinists who service the printing machines, almost all the members of the ITU are men whose primary skill is composing or setting type, though they do generally work at only one of the jobs that are part of their training. A printer may be a linotype-machine operator, a proofreader, a "handman" who sets ads or other complicated work by hand, or a monotype-machine operator. In the smaller shops the same man may work at a number of these jobs, while in the larger newspapers a man will probably be limited to only one kind of work. Some kinds of jobs in the composing room, like hand composition, call for a higher level of skill than others, such as the operation of a linotype machine, and these skill differences are generally recognized by printers. But these skill differences do not make for sharp cleavages among printers because all printers are nominally able to do any kind of composing-room work and most printers have had some experience with different kinds of jobs. Most important, these different subskills do not command any appreciable difference in pay or in status. By and large, all the members of a given local receive the same pay. Some men are given small but consistent bonuses above the union scale by their employers for their high performance on the job or for extra responsibility. But the only differences in wage scales—and they are not large—written into the contract are those between the workers in the newspapers and book-and-job shops, and those between day-, night-, and lobster-shift (the second night shift) workers.[1]

The ITU is thus, insofar as this is possible, a community of equals, and there is consequently no "underprivileged" group in the unions.[2]

Figure 25—Political Participation of Various Subgroups in the Union

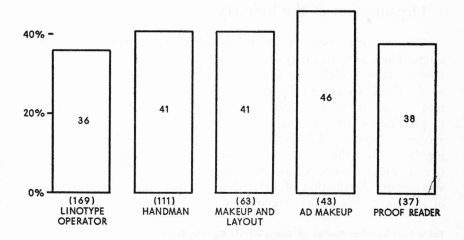

PROPORTION ACTIVE IN UNION POLITICS

RESPONDENT'S PRIMARY JOB

In this respect the ITU differs greatly from many other unions whose members vary widely in skill, income, status, and work experience. The printing pressmen, for example, contain a large group of pressmen's assistants who have less skill and earn lower pay than the pressmen who apparently dominate the union. Where we have a visibly higher status group, it is often the cadre from which the organization's officials are recruited and on which the administration machine is based. In the ITU,

---

1. In 1954 in the newspaper shops, day workers received $115 for 36¼ hours a week; night workers, $120 for 36¼ hours; lobster shift, $125 for 35 hours. In book and job shops, day workers received $107.25 for 36¼ hours; night workers, $112.83 for 36¼ hours; lobster shift, $112.83 for 32½ hours.

2. The only group of ITU members whose participation is limited by their status is the foremen, who for obvious reasons are not active participants in union politics even though they appear to be loyal union members.

however, all subskills contribute roughly equal proportions of active leaders and one finds no tendency for a high-status group to monopolize and dominate internal politics. If we look at all of the subskills represented in the union for which we have twenty cases or more—that is, which comprise at least 5% of the membership—we see very little difference in the proportions of the different subgroups which are politically active in the union.

None of the subskills plays a subordinate role in union politics, nor does any one dominate ITU affairs. We will consider the significance of this fact more fully in Chapter 10.

§ Organization of the Industry

THE PRINTING INDUSTRY is composed of small and medium-sized shops. These are of two types: newspapers, and book-and-job or commercial shops, which print books, magazines, circulars, and other such work. The latter are usually quite small, employing on the average fifteen or sixteen printers and ranging in size from one-man shops to shops which employ one to two hundred ITU members. The roughly 280 union book-and-job shops in New York employ about 4,500 ITU members, while the score of newspapers, the biggest of which use over five hundred printers, together employ about 3,500 ITU members. The approximate distribution of print shops in New York by the number of Big Six members they employ is shown in Table 14.

Table 14—Size Distribution of Shops within Big Six Jurisdiction

ITU Members Employed per Shop	3-10	11-30	31-99	100-199	200+
Approximate total of men employed by shops	1180	1825	1415	750	2155
Percentage of membership employed by shops in category	16	25	19	10	30
Shops in size category	130	100	29	5	6

Source: Official vote, Typographical Union No. 6, election of May 21, 1952, ITU officers and ITU delegates. Use of the voting records makes this table a rough approximation which underestimates the absolute numbers in each category and probably disproportionately underestimates the numbers of small shops and small-shop men. It also omits entirely consideration of the unlisted shops, the shops employing one or two ITU members, which are not organized as chapels.

In every shop employing three or more members of the ITU, union law requires the organization of a union unit, traditionally called a chapel. Each chapel elects officers, and holds regular shop meetings. Large plants such as the *New York Times* may have as many as twelve chapel officers, all elected in annual elections by the chapel members. The chapel organization is the basic unit of the union; its chairman is roughly comparable to the shop steward in many other unions, with one major difference. Whereas in other industries shop stewards rarely have much independent power or authority, the chairmen of the ITU chapels have a relatively independent position vis-à-vis the local union administration. As we shall see, the political autonomy of the chapel and the chapel chairman is one of the important structural supports of the democratic political life of the union.

The democratic political processes of the ITU operate not only on the international and local levels, but also within the chapel. Chapel officers are elected to serve for one year, and in most of the larger chapels these annual elections are hotly contested. Two or more men usually run for each of the major chapel offices, and the period immediately preceding a chapel election witnesses real campaigns, with personal canvassing and the distribution of literature. Unlike local and international elections, however, chapel elections are never conducted along formal union party lines. Though no written law exists which would prevent the union political parties from nominating candidates for chapel offices, an unwritten but powerful tradition prohibits overt party contests within the chapel. In practice, of course, the different union parties are concerned with having their members or sympathizers in chapel office, since these positions are important sources of political influence. As we shall see in Chapter 9, the parties do take part in chapel elections covertly.

§ The Autonomy of the Chapel

THE AUTONOMY OF THE CHAPEL in the ITU, as is true of so many of patterns we have identified in and around the union, is a product both of the structure of the printing industry and of the political structure and processes of the printers' union. We can see the effect of the structure of the industry most clearly if we compare the chapel chairman's position with the corresponding post in an industrial union.

Howe and Widdick, in their book on the UAW,[3] have noted how the decline of international political life in the UAW over the past decade has been accompanied by a change in the function and behavior of the shop stewards. In the early days of the union, shop stewards were generally the informal leaders of their shop, men who had gained their positions through their militant leadership in the organizing struggles and through their personal influence and prestige with the men in the

---

3. Irving Howe and B. J. Widdick: *The UAW and Walter Reuther*, New York, Random House, Inc., 1949, pp. 238-93.

shops. But as the union settled into more stable working relationships with the companies, these informal leaders, whose hotheaded militancy and distaste for routine became increasingly embarrassing to union officials, tended to be replaced by men more amenable to directives from above.[4]

It would be quite misleading to see this development solely in terms of a union leadership's tendency to maximize its power over the membership. Large-scale industries put their organizational stamp on the unions with which they deal, and rarely do their structures allow room for the administrative decentralization and shop and local autonomy that we find in the ITU. In the highly rationalized automobile industry, as in other concentrated industries, the operation of every shop affects the operation of a whole plant or firm. In such a context the union, if it is to be "responsible," i.e., to fulfill the obligations of its working relationships with the companies, must behave in as dependable and calculable a fashion as the firms it deals with. And the archetype of the calculable social organization is not a democracy but a bureaucracy. Howe and Widdick point out how these structural and institutional requirements affect the shop steward:

As a union becomes stabilized in an industry, its relations with the employers rigidify into fixed patterns. Whatever management may think of unionism in general, it realizes that only by maintaining smooth day-to-day relations with the union can steady production be guaranteed. Simultaneously, the internal structure of the union tends also to be rigidified, and the functions and authorities of its subgroups to be more precisely defined. As a consequence of these two linked developments, the shop steward's power as a union leader is bound to decrease, though he may still process many grievances.[5]

A recent study of the local union[6] included a chapter entitled "The Decline of the Steward," in which it is noted that the steward's decline in power and importance coincides with the decline in authority of his opposite number in management. On the one hand, the foreman with whom a steward deals usually has little authority to settle shop grievances, while on the other hand, the local union officers restrict the authority of the steward to settle grievances for fear that they may

---

4. Some vivid descriptions of the replacement of overmilitant first-line leaders as part of the centralization of union power that accompanies the stabilization of relations with management are found in Clinton S. Golden and Harold J. Ruttenberg: *The Dynamics of Industrial Democracy*, New York, Harper & Brothers, 1942, pp. 48-81.

5. Howe and Widdick, *op. cit.*, p. 238. Cf. also pp. 240-41 and C. Wright Mills: *The New Men of Power*, New York, Harcourt, Brace and Company, Inc., 1948, pp. 234-39.

6. Leonard R. Sayles and George Strauss: *The Local Union*, New York, Harper & Brothers, 1953.

inadvertently establish precedents unfavorable to the union. Add to this the fact that shop stewards are rarely equipped to deal with the technical problems of job evaluation and time study, or know in detail the body of precedents in grievance cases that comprise the common law in union-management relations, and it is no wonder that workers with grievances usually bypass the shop steward and take their problems to someone higher in the union who has the knowledge and the authority to get things done.[7]

As the shop steward is increasingly subject to discipline and regulations from above in the interests of over-all union "responsibility," calculability, and efficiency and is increasingly bypassed in the grievance procedure, he is less and less able to function as a source or expression of rank-and-file opposition to the incumbent administration. Rather, he tends to become the lowest rung in a centrally controlled administrative hierarchy, with the additional function of serving as an informal channel of communications upward and downward within the union structure. One of the consequences of this erosion of the shop steward's autonomy is that within the huge locals that make up the UAW (and most unions in centralized industries) one finds no structural sources of opposition power and leadership. The locals themselves become the smallest units with sufficient independent power to support an opposition group against the international administration, and they have not been able to sustain continuing democratic politics even in unions in which they have been the sources of factional opposition.

In contrast, there is little structural pressure on the ITU to develop a bureaucratic administration. The industry it deals with is neither highly rationalized technologically nor concentrated in ownership. Since a dispute in any single chapel generally has no repercussions throughout the industry, the danger to the union of relatively autonomous chapel organizations is much less than it is, say, in the UAW. Moreover, in contrast to the immensely complicated contracts of the big industrial unions, which require the services of large technical staffs and engender continuous complicated grievances, the ITU contracts are simple matters which any member of the union can understand and which some rank-and-file members help to negotiate. Since the union enforces an almost traditional body of work regulations, rubbed smooth over years of union-management relations, these contracts in operation provide little occasion for basic conflicts over interpretations or for threatening innovations by either management or the chapel chairman.

But this general agreement does not make the chapel chairman an automatic administrator of rigid rules. The many separately owned print

7. *Ibid.*, pp. 35-36.

shops of different types require the chapel chairman, in all but the smallest shops, to function like a kind of labor lawyer, applying the general provisions of a local-wide union contract to the special circumstances which obtain in his shop. Some measure of autonomy on the part of the chapel chairman is almost demanded by the difficulty of administering the contract in detail from local headquarters.

Yet many unions which operate in comparatively decentralized industries have developed oligarchic, one-party structures, in which the shop stewards are part of the administrative machine, much like precinct captains in big-city machines. Their allegiance to the union's administrative machine is secured primarily through the fact that promotion in most unions occurs *within* the union hierarchy, and comes in large part as reward for past loyalty. When top union leaders select men for higher union posts, at least one of the requirements for such promotion is evidence that the shop leader has accepted the norms and disciplines of the administration machine. A shop leader who maintains his independence in opposition to the administration group has little hope of promotion unless he becomes part of a successful insurrection. In unions in which factional uprisings rarely occur, a shop leader who chooses to be independent is in effect making the decision to remain at the bottom of the union structure. Union officials in such one-party organizations have other weapons besides control over advancement for bringing recalcitrant shop leaders into line. They can refuse to help him in shop disputes, bypass him in dealing with the employers, and generally place such obstacles in his path as to make his carrying out of his leadership role difficult or impossible.

If the chapel chairmen in the ITU are not as vulnerable to such controls from above, it is not simply because the printing industry is relatively decentralized and unconcentrated, but is at least as much a consequence of the operation of the union's two-party system. The autonomy of the chapel chairmen in the ITU is indeed one of the supports of the union's political system; but its continued existence is in part a consequence of the political system. The existence of competing union parties, and the turnover this engenders in local and international administrations, prevent any given administration from dominating the chapel chairmen. This is another example of the interdependence of elements in a functional relationship: The political independence of the chapel, which could only exist in a democratic union, contributes to the maintenance of democracy in the union. And the value system which defines administrative control of the chapel as illegitimate is a product of the union's intense internal political life.

The most striking evidence of the lack of control by the administration over chapel chairmen may be seen in the distribution of union political preference among the chairmen. As can be seen in Figure 26 there is little difference in the distribution of party support between chairmen and nonchairmen.

Figure 26—Local and International Party Preferences of Chapel Chairmen and Rank-and-File Members

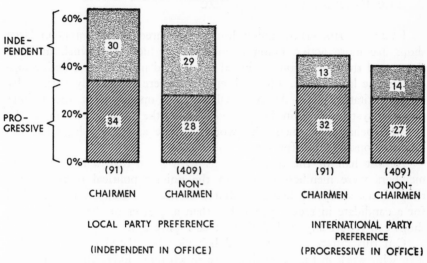

Chapel chairmen reflect the distribution of party sentiment among the members rather than that of the local administration. If anything, more chairmen at the time of the study were opposed to the local administration, which was then controlled by the Independent Party, than supported it. On other questions too—whether, for example, it is good for the local to limit the local president to two terms in office and whether the union would be better off without organized parties—our data show that chapel chairmen shared the views of rank-and-file members.

As we will see shortly, the chairmen of large shops differ in many and important ways from the chairmen of small chapels, and large-shop chairmen differ in many respects from the rank and file in their own shops. But in their union political preferences, neither large- nor small-shop chairmen show a greater degree of loyalty or submissiveness to higher union authority than rank-and-file members. This independence of the body of first-line union officers has many consequences for the operation of the union's political system, as we will see, but among other things it means that they cannot be counted on to "sell" union-administration decisions and policies to the members, or to uncritically transmit information slanted in favor of the administration. On the contrary, the independence of the chapel chairmen from the discipline of an administration machine means that administrative acts may be subject to as much criticism as support in the process of being transmitted to the members.

§ The Relevance of Shop Size

EARLY IN THE STUDY union leaders indicated that printers in large shops are more active union members than men who work in small shops, and that the union's political parties had much greater active support in the large shops. These observations were abundantly verified by the quantitative data. As we analyzed the operation of the union's political system, it soon became clear that the great variation in the political behavior of men who work in large and small shops has significant consequences for union politics.

Almost half of the men in shops with more than a hundred ITU members were members of one of the union's political parties at the time of the study, or had contributed funds to a campaign or worked for a candidate in recent years; less than a quarter of the men in small shops can report any such activity (see Figure 27).[8]

Can this difference in political behavior be related to the fact that men who work in the large shops are much more likely than small-shop men to associate with other printers in their leisure time? We tested our data for this possibility but analysis showed clearly that large-shop men are more likely to be involved and interested in union politics than small-shop men, *independently* of whether they participate in the printers' occupational community.[9] What is the explanation? What aspects of shop size help account for the higher levels of political involvement of large-shop men? Through what mechanisms and processes does shop size operate to influence political involvement, and how do these processes differ in large and small shops?

8. On inspection of this and other data bearing on the involvement in union politics of men in different-sized shops, it appeared that the sharpest falling off in the average level of involvement occurred at about a shop size of thirty ITU members. In much of the following analysis we will be comparing men who work in shops having fewer than thirty ITU members with men in shops having more than thirty ITU members. Of course, where we find it necessary in the analysis, we use narrower shop-size categories. In addition, and by way of warning, the rough approximation of "large" and "small" shops which we use in this and the following chapter, is very sharply qualified in Chap. 9, where the differences between small, medium, and large shops become, at one point, the focus of our analysis.

9. Moreover, this relationship persists when tested in a variety of ways for spuriousness (e.g., age, religion, education).

Figure 27—*Proportion of Men in Different-sized Shops Who Have Engaged in Some Union Political Activity Recently*

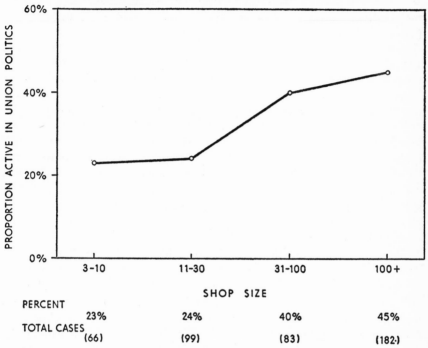

	3-10	11-30	31-100	100+
PERCENT	23%	24%	40%	45%
TOTAL CASES	(66)	(99)	(83)	(182.)

NOTE: Political activity includes being a member of a union party, contributing funds, or working for candidates.

The remainder of this chapter and the following one deal with the ways in which the size of the shop a man works in affects his relationships with three important elements in his work environment: his employer, his shopmates, and his union. For purposes of analysis it is convenient and useful to distinguish the effects of shop size on these different aspects of a man's work experience and relationships. In social reality, of course, these forces operate in conjunction.

§ Shop Size and Worker-Management Relations

AT LEAST PART of the lower interest and involvement in union politics of small-shop men as compared with large-shop men is the result of processes familiar to students of the labor movement and industrial relations. Over a hundred years ago Marx noted that workers in small craft shops, who work side by side with their employers, associate with them informally and develop personal ties with them, are markedly less class-conscious and less involved in workers' organizations than are workers in large industry.[10] The personal ties of small-shop men with their employers tend to weaken their identification with organizations predicated on a conflict of interests between workers and employers. To the small-shop man the problems of the boss are more persuasive, and the chances for individual recognition and rewards through personal relations with the shop owner are felt to be greater than in larger shops of even fifty or a hundred workers, where such direct and unmediated relations between employer and employee are not possible.

In many small print shops the owner himself is a union member, and in the smallest shops he may even work at the trade in the old craft tradition of the master surrounded by his journeymen. In contrast, the printer in the large shop is one worker among many; his employer is the firm or the newspaper rather than John Jones; his foreman is a full-time work supervisor, who, though a member of the union, is more likely to be perceived as a representative of management than as a fellow worker.[11]

In the smaller shops the union is much less in evidence, both because it has fewer functions (for example, it need not be on hand to manage a complicated priority list since few men are substitutes) and also because the workers themselves look to it less to govern their relations with management. When violations of union rules occur, the close relations between owner and worker inhibit the worker from calling the union to enforce their rules: the union might protect a man's right to his job, but it cannot enforce a set of social relations. And not infrequently, minor violations of union law are mutually advantageous to worker and owner. Men who work or have worked in small shops report that such violations are winked at by the union members in the shops.

In the larger shops management is remote and the union is near, visible, and important; in the small shops the union is remote and the owner and foreman bulk large. In the small shops not only are the foreman and owner closer to the worker as persons in their daily relationships, but also they are closer as statuses to which a small-shop man can realistically aspire. The small-shop man has a better chance of becoming a shop foreman or opening his own shop than the large-shop worker;

10. Cf. "Germany: Revolution and Counter-Revolution," in V. Adoratsky (ed.), *Selected Works of Karl Marx*, New York, International Publishers, Inc., n.d., Vol. 2, p. 470.

11. Cf. Donald E. Wray: "Marginal Men of Industry: The Foremen," *American Journal of Sociology*, 54:298-301 (1949).

indeed, he may well have already held those positions himself at one time or another in his career. About 40% of the small-shop men say that they would like to own their own shops, as compared with only about a quarter of the men in shops with more than thirty printers.

Figure 28—*Proportion of Men in Different-sized Shops Saying That They Would Like to Own Their Own Shop*

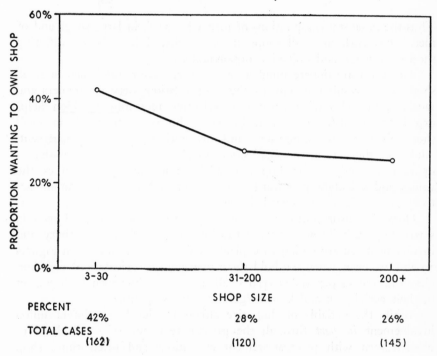

Similarly, about twice as great a proportion of men in small shops, as in large (40% compared with 20%) say that they would like to be a foreman.

It is not that small-shop men are more interested in bettering themselves than large-shop men. About the *same* proportion of small- and large-shop men—one-quarter—named some nonmanual occupation when asked what occupation they would like to have. But when asked whether they would rather be a foreman or a union officer, men with white-collar aspirations who work in large shops opt for *union officer*, while in the small shops white-collar aspirants would choose *foreman*.[12]

---

12. Whatever the size of the shop a printer works in, an orientation towards advancement through management and ownership has, as we would expect, a clear relation to interest and involvement in union politics. Those printers who have

Table 15—Shop Size, and Foreman-vs.-Union-Officer Preference among Men who Aspire to White-Collar Occupations

	SHOP SIZE	
Prefer to Become	3-30	30+
Foreman	53%	39%
Union officer	23	45
Neither	18	13
"Don't know" and no answer	6	3
N	(47)	(69)

Thus the same status aspirations of men who work in large shops and of men who work in small shops are channeled differently by differing shop experience and objective opportunities.

The disproportionate number of management-oriented men in small shops is the result not only of the close relations between owners and workers, but also of a pattern of selective recruitment which helps explain these differences: that is, men who come to work in small shops already have aspirations and orientations toward management. And once they are in the small shop, the absence of a highly politicized or even strongly union-shop atmosphere undoubtedly reinforces the values and orientations toward management and away from union activity which these men may bring with them.

Does the disproportionate number of management-oriented men in small shops *wholly* account for the lower rates of union activity and involvement we are trying to explain? It does not. As we see in Figures 29 and 30, even when we hold these management orientations constant, clear differences persist between small- and large-shop men with respect to their activity in and knowledge about union politics.

While the variable of shop size affects the level of printers' union involvement *in part* through the greater tendency of small shops to contain men with pro-management aspirations and orientations, shop size also affects the level of union activity and involvement through affecting the relations of ITU members *with each other* in the shop.

§ On-the-Job Social Relations

IN ANALYZING THE CONNECTIONS between group membership and in-

---

aspirations to be foremen or to own their own shop undoubtedly have undergone what Merton calls a process of "anticipatory socialization"—that is, they have assimilated the values and perspectives of the group to which they aspire, and have little interest in union activities.

Table—Attitudes towards Becoming a Foreman and Index of Activity in Union Politics

Political Participation	Prefer Foreman	Prefer Union Officer	Prefer Neither
Active	26%	51%	37%
Inactive	74	59	63
N	(159)	(132)	(117)

Figure 29—*Proportion of Men in Large and Small Shops Who Are Active in Union Politics (Union-Management Job Aspirations Held Constant)*

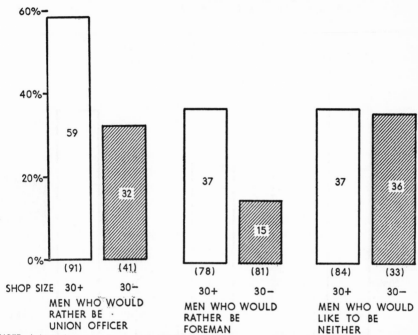

SHOP SIZE   30+   30—   30+   30—   30+   30—
            MEN WHO WOULD   MEN WHO WOULD   MEN WHO WOULD
            RATHER BE ·   RATHER BE   LIKE TO BE
            UNION OFFICER   FOREMAN   NEITHER

NOTE: A large-shop man who responds "Neither" to the presented alternatives is, in his union involvement, more like the large-shop man who opts for "Foreman," while the small-shop man's "Neither" response looks more like the small-shop man who responds "Union officer." In both cases the "Neither" response appears to be a rejection of the objectively more possible channel of mobility, and thus a denial of aspirations for mobility, at least within the occupation.

dividual behavior, sociologists have traditionally distinguished between primary and secondary groups. As an ideal type, the former is characterized by a strong sense of "weness"; by the personal, voluntary, and inclusive character of the relationships among its members; and by the identity of ends held by its members, among which are the primary relationships themselves. In contrast, secondary groups are characterized by more impersonal relations between members who interact fleetingly, often indirectly, and in terms of specific roles rather than as total persons. These secondary relationships are not seen by the members as ends in themselves, but as means to some defined ends which vary among the members.

In any print shop, whether large or small, the relationships among the printers in the shop are neither of the ideal primary form nor purely formal and impersonal, kept to the bare minimum required by the flow of work in the printing process. Men who have frequent and enduring

Figure 30—Proportion of Men in Large and Small Shops Who Are High in
Knowledge of Union Politics (Union-Management
Job Aspirations Held Constant)

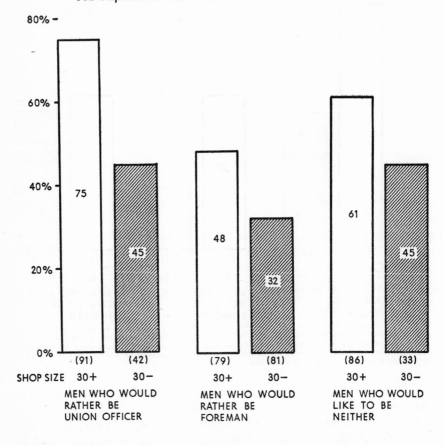

relationships with each other invest those relationships with some measure of affect and sentiment. A high frequency of interaction among men
on a job or in a residential neighborhood, as Homans and others have
emphasized, serves to increase the likelihood that friendly relations will
develop among them. Such interaction tends to generate common sentiments and group norms and frequently some sense of group solidarity,
especially if the participants are on the same status level. The informal
group relations that inevitably grow up within formal structures of
relations may become of great importance to those who participate in
them as well as being necessary to the very operation of the formal
structure. Such informal networks of relations not only act as defense

or security organizations which support their members against external groups or authority, but also provide for their members' self-esteem and open an arena for self-expression.

If, on the one hand, simple experience and numerous studies tell us that men who work together soon break through and elaborate the formal and impersonal relations which brought them together, on the other hand, the social relations which develop among men in a common work place do not inevitably assume the classic character of ideal primary group relations. For one thing, work relations are necessarily, to some degree, involuntary: the men with whom one can develop close personal relations on the job are limited to those who work in the same shop, and often to those who work in close physical proximity so that frequent interaction during working hours is possible. And the more those relations are involuntary—that is, the smaller the pool of available *choices* for close personal relationships—the narrower the *scope* of the relationship is likely to be in terms of the shared values that are part of its content. Or to put it another way, the fewer the people from whom a worker can choose on-the-job friends, the less likely he is to find people who share his salient values and attitudes, and the less likely are those relations to develop into close and intimate friendships.

Thus, on-the-job social relations may vary considerably in the degree to which they approximate the close friendship relations of the primary group. The significance of this fact for union structure and politics may be indicated in two propositions:

1. The degree to which on-the-job social relations among printers are involuntary will vary with the size of the shop. They are on the average less involuntary in large shops than in small.

2. The more that social relations have a voluntary and self-selected character—that is, the more they are based on shared values and sentiments rather than physical propinquity—the closer those relations are likely to be, and the more likely they are to be able to function as arenas of political discussion and mutual stimulation for their participants.[13]

In the larger shops, on-the-job social relations are likely to be more

---

13. A third proposition, which will be explored later in this chapter, would suggest that the likelihood that social relations on the job will in fact function as arenas of political discussion does not continue to increase with increasing opportunity for selectivity to enter into the relationship. If we raise the question, under what conditions are social relations on the job likely to be penetrated by union politics so that politics becomes part of the content of the relations, one provisional hypothesis would suggest that some measure of self-selection in the relationship, coupled with some measure of involuntary exposure to political activists, makes for more highly politicized social relations in the shop than where the chances are greatest for self-selected networks of social relations. See below, Chap. 9.

voluntary than in the smaller shops, first because there are simply more men to choose from, and secondly, because the work schedules in larger shops are not as tight, and their economic margin of operation not as narrow, as in the small shops. As a result, men in the larger shops generally have more free time during working hours to leave their benches and machines and move around the shop.[14] This freedom from close supervision reaches its maximum in the big newspapers, where a man may often have an hour or two during his shift without a work assignment, because the concentrated work involved in getting out an edition does not last for the entire working period. Night workers, who are concentrated in the large shops, are under especially light supervision (except in morning newspapers). The relative freedom from close supervision and the recurrence of slack periods during the shift allow men in the large shops to engage in a great deal of socializing during work hours. As one old-timer, who has worked in both large and small shops, noted: "In the newspapers you get a chance to discuss the union more than in the book-and-job shops, where it is all production. There you can't buttonhole a man and convince him of something because there just isn't time."

The looser, more variable work schedules in the larger shops make the larger number of printers in them physically available as potential shop friends to any given printer who works in a large shop.[15] Size and work schedule together bring each printer in the large shops into direct contact with more printers than the small-shop man is exposed to during his working hours.

The statistical data show that the larger a shop a man works in, the more likely he is to have close friends in the shop. In response to the question, "Do the printers whom you see off the job work in the same shop as you do?" men in the large shops reported that they see their shopmates off the job, men in the small shops do not.

Similarly, large-shop men, when asked whether their best printer friend is a *close* friend or not, are more likely than men working in small shops to identify friends working in the same shop as themselves as close. This finding confirms the assumption that men have more inti-

---

14. During the course of the study, we had an opportunity to verify this observation. Our interviewers were usually given permission by foremen in large shops to conduct hour-long interviews with the men during their working time. In the small shops, however, foremen were much less willing to give such permission, stating that their work schedules simply would not permit the men to do this.

15. Cf. J. Kovner and H. J. Lahne: "Shop Society and the Union," *Industrial and Labor Relations Review*, 7:3-14 (October 1953), for discussion of work schedules and union politics.

mate social relations with other printers in large plants than they do in small ones.[16]

Figure 31—Relationship between Shop Size and Place of Employment of Printers Seen Off the Job

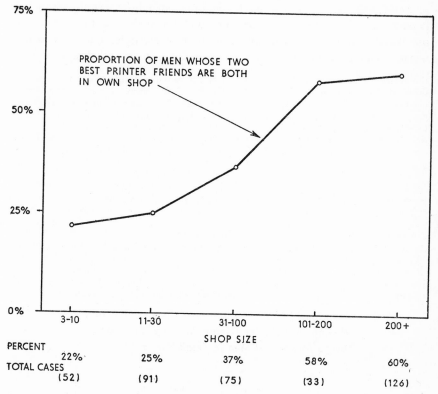

PROPORTION OF MEN WHOSE TWO BEST PRINTER FRIENDS ARE BOTH IN OWN SHOP

SHOP SIZE	3-10	11-30	31-100	101-200	200+
PERCENT	22%	25%	37%	58%	60%
TOTAL CASES	(52)	(91)	(75)	(33)	(126)

16. There is at least one other important factor which affects the difference in the character of social relations in large and small shops. Men working in small plants are more likely to have worked in a number of print shops in the past, while large shop men are much less mobile. This occurs because seniority does not give much job security in small shops, and men who are laid off will often surrender their priority to take positions elsewhere. Consequently, small-shop men are more likely to be friendly with printers now working in other shops than are large-shop men. Nevertheless, when the number of jobs which men have had is held constant, the data clearly indicate that men in large shops are more likely than small-shop men to have their best printer friends in their present place of employment.

On the average, the tendency for men to have shopmates for their best printer friends increases during their first seven, eight, or nine years in a shop, leveling off at a stable maximum *which varies with the size of shop* (see the accompanying figure). After seven or eight years in a shop, a man has probably made as good and close relations on the job as he is going to. And as we see in the curves of

Aside from the variations in freedom of interaction on the job between large and small shops, there are, of course, many other factors which determine whether men will form close friendships or not. Basically, the previous discussion of the relation of shop size to the likelihood of having friends in the shop has been an analysis of the effect of propinquity. But there are some kinds of men whose requirements for friendship are so stringent that they will be unable to find friends in the limited universe of one print shop. For example, one man whom we interviewed is intensely interested in the history and design of type

---

the relationship, it is only after a man has entered into stable and enduring relations with other men in his shop that his shop's size shows its greatest effect on his tendency to have shopmates for best friends. We have suggested earlier that the larger numbers of printers present in the larger shops allows a greater voluntary component to friendship choices, which in turn permits closer friendship ties to develop among men in the large shops. But the larger pool of men in the shop offers, for a new man in the shop, only *potential* friends; for the average man it is years before the slow and subtle processes of friendship selection and the growth of affective ties have finally established him in some roughly stable equilibrium of relations with other men in his shop. During the first few years in a large shop, little of the greater "friendship potential" inherent in them has been realized by most printers, and there is little difference between large- and small-shop men in their tendency to have their best printer friends in their shop. The difference between large- and small-shop men increases to a maximum somewhere around seven years on the job, when presumably most men have explored and fully realized, so far as they are going to, the friendship potential of their shop. Thus we see that propinquity begins as a friendship *potential* which has increasing importance as a determinant of on-the-job friendships, until after some years the full potential of propinquity for friendship choice has been realized.

Relationship between Length of Time on Job and Having Best Printer Friends in Shop, for Men in Large Shops and Men in Small Shops

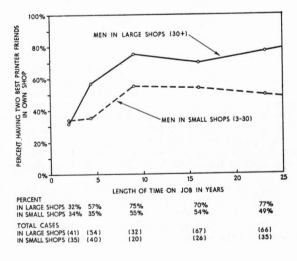

PERCENT				
IN LARGE SHOPS 32%	57%	75%	70%	77%
IN SMALL SHOPS 34%	35%	55%	54%	49%

TOTAL CASES				
IN LARGE SHOPS (41)	(54)	(32)	(67)	(66)
IN SMALL SHOPS (35)	(40)	(20)	(26)	(35)

faces. Apparently he shares this interest with a handful of men scattered in different print shops around the city. Since this common interest is salient and important to these men, they sought each other out, and on the basis of this shared interest developed close relations with each other in their leisure hours.

While such unusual interests may be rare as a basis for friendship, there are other more common values and interests which affect printers' choice of friends. For example, the members of the union differ in their political values. In terms of the scale of political attitudes in national issues, the men were divided among liberals, conservatives and moderates.[17] The liberals among printers are more interested in politics, both national and union, than are conservatives. Liberals, therefore, should be more likely to use similarity in political belief as a criterion for friendship, while conservatives should be less selective. Hence liberals, as Figure 32 shows, are less able than conservatives to find close friends inside their shop.

Figure 32—For Large-Shop and Small-Shop Men: Relationship between Political Attitudes and Having Best Friends in Same Shop

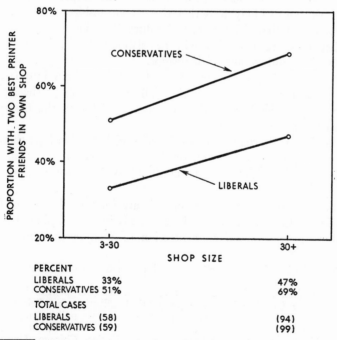

PERCENT		
LIBERALS	33%	47%
CONSERVATIVES	51%	69%
TOTAL CASES		
LIBERALS	(58)	(94)
CONSERVATIVES	(59)	(99)

17. This distinction is purely an operational one, based on responses to a six-item liberalism-conservatism scale. For discussion of this scale see Appendix I.

Social-political attitude is, of course, only one of the many value and interest orientations which may affect friendship selection. In a society in which a large proportion if not the majority of people are relatively uninterested in politics, these values may actually be used far less than others as criteria and bases for friendship.[18] For purposes of this analysis, however, it is not necessary to consider, even if it were possible, all the other possible criteria for friendship selection. It is clear that the smaller a group into which a man is placed, the less likely he will be to find like-minded individuals within the group, and thus he will be forced to seek out friends elsewhere.

The foregoing analysis of the variations in friendship patterns in shops of different sizes may be summarized in the following propositions:

1. The larger the pool of men available for social relations during working hours, the greater the chances for men to have more "voluntary" self-selected relations with other men in the pool. In print shops the number of men available is determined by the number of printers in the shop, their physical location, the degree to which the work process makes for interaction among the men, and the amount of freedom on the job for socializing during working hours.

2. The greater the chances for voluntary self-selection of friends in the shop, the more likely it is that these relationships will be based on a wider range of shared interests and values. This in turn makes it more likely that these relationships will be elaborated and intensified over time into close and genuine friendships.

3. The deepening and elaboration of social relations into friendship relations takes time, so that in both small and large shops the likelihood of having close friends in one's shop increases during the first years a man is in the shop.

4. The fewer alternative networks of social relationships that a man has recently been part of, or currently belongs to, the more likely it is that his closest friendships will be confined to the group or pool in near proximity.

5. The more stringent a man's criteria are for the selection of friends, the less likely he is to have his best friends in his propinquitous pool, unless there is an unusual concentration of men in the shop who fill his requirements.

In the printing industry the several processes noted above work to-

---

18. Nevertheless, data from a recent study of national politics indicates that most adults have friends with the same political affiliations as their own. Over two-thirds of the voters interviewed supported the same political party as their three best friends, while approximately one-tenth had a majority of friends with differing affiliations. See Bernard Berelson *et al.: Voting*, Chicago, University of Chicago Press, 1954, pp. 94-95.

gether to make it far less likely that a small-shop man will have close friends in his shop than that a large-shop man will. There is a smaller pool for voluntary friendship choices, there is less freedom on the job, and there is less likelihood of having been in the same shop for a long time with others who have also. Moreover, those men with stringent criteria for friendship are far less likely to find people who meet those conditions in the small shops than in the large. The net effect of these processes is to make the on-the-job relations among printers in small shops less close within the shop and less likely to be continued outside the shop.

§ The Political Relevance of On-the-Job Relationships

RELATIONS AMONG PRINTERS on the job in the large- and medium-sized shops have more of the voluntary character of friendship relations, are more the product of choice than chance, while the small-shop men much more frequently work side by side with printers with whom they are neither very close friends nor whom they care to see after hours. These findings help provide an additional answer to the question, Why are men in large shops more active in union politics than men in small shops? Social relations within large shops resemble printers' leisure-time relations, by serving as forums or arenas within which union politics are discussed. In the small shops, however, the social constraints inherent in the greater involuntariness of interpersonal relations tend to prevent the development of informal arenas for the discussion of union affairs. As is demonstrated in Figure 33 and 34, where these informal political arenas exist (in the occupational community or on the job in the larger shops) they act both independently and cumulatively to stimulate and sustain the political involvements of their participants.

§ Consensus and Dissensus in Large and Small Shops

THE APPARENT INEFFECTIVENESS of on-the-job relations in the small print shops in stimulating political interest may also be related to the fact that the physically close but relatively involuntary relations among printers in the small shops are highly vulnerable to such potentially divisive issues as union politics. It is important to men who must work together every day that they maintain good informal relations with one another,

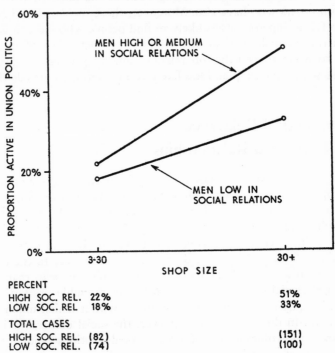

Figure 33—Access to One or Both Major Informal Arenas of
Political Discussion (Off the Job and within the Larger
Shops), and Participation in Union Politics

PERCENT			
HIGH SOC. REL.	22%		51%
LOW SOC. REL	18%		33%
TOTAL CASES			
HIGH SOC. REL.	(82)		(151)
LOW SOC. REL.	(74)		(100)

and such work groups usually develop a certain amount of group solidarity, as students of industrial sociology have shown.[19] Such a group can place great pressure on its members to accept the salient attitudes and loyalties of the group—for example, the group's norm for production—and such acceptance is usually a condition for admission into the group. But a small group, in order to preserve good interpersonal relations and solidarity on matters of importance to it, need not and cannot enforce consensus with regard to all values and attitudes held by its members. A group may much more easily exert pressure on its members to *reduce* their interest or involvement in activities and attitudes which are peripheral

19. Cf. Everett C. Hughes: "The Knitting of Racial Groups in Industry," *American Sociological Review*, 11:512-19 (October 1946); F. J. Roethlisberger: *Management and Morale*, Cambridge, Mass., Harvard University Press, 1941, Chaps. 2 and 4; Thomas N. Whitehead: *Leadership in A Free Society*, Cambridge, Harvard University Press, 1937, Chaps. 3 and 4; William F. Whyte: *Human Relations in the Restaurant Industry*, New York, McGraw-Hill Book Company, 1948.

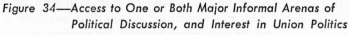

Figure 34—Access to One or Both Major Informal Arenas of
Political Discussion, and Interest in Union Politics

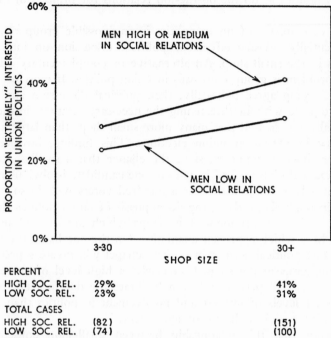

PERCENT		
HIGH SOC. REL.	29%	41%
LOW SOC. REL.	23%	31%
TOTAL CASES		
HIGH SOC. REL.	(82)	(151)
LOW SOC. REL.	(74)	(100)

to the group's own functioning and which may place a strain on solidarity if introduced into it. The value to the group of reducing the
saliency of issues upon which group consensus does not exist is clear:
what is a matter of relative indifference is not a source of internal
cleavage.[20]

We should expect, therefore, that workers in small shops will for
this reason be less likely to engage in hot discussions about union affairs
with shopmates than will printers in larger shops, whose more voluntary shop cliques tend to be of one mind regarding union politics, or
who can argue about union politics with other workers in their shops
outside their work groups without danger to their work-enforced relations. In the small shops as in the large, division in voting in union
elections can and often does occur, but such dissensus involves least
strain for the small-shop work group when the issues of union politics
are defined by the group as being of little significance. It is in part

---

20. It is usually much easier and less dangerous to de-emphasize an issue than to
attempt to enforce consensus on some strongly felt norm or attitude which is not
central to the group's functioning.

because of this kind of group de-emphasis of politics that the small-shop work groups do not tend to stimulate or sustain their members' interest in union politics as do the on-the-job relations for printers in the larger shops.

The de-emphasis of union politics is one possible group response to the potentially divisive effects of political discussion on interpersonal relations in the small shop. An alternative or complementary adaptation to this problem is group consensus in union politics. If most of the men in a small shop agree politically, then political discussion and activity may take place without threatening the necessary relations in the group. Empirically we do find that many more small shops than large approach unanimity in voting in union elections. This finding, however, is in part an artifact of numbers, since the chance that a small shop with a few voters will give 75% of its vote to one candidate is obviously greater than that a large shop with over a hundred voters will do so.

But in *small shops alone*, the de-emphasis of union politics should be stronger and more pronounced in shops which are divided politically than in those which approach unanimity. On the one hand, the presence of even one political activist in a given chapel will create a pressure towards consensus in the shop. Conversely, a high level of consensus on union politics will permit and even facilitate the development of somewhat higher levels of interest and involvement in politics than in small shops without such a degree of agreement.[21]

Evidence that this relationship between small-shop consensus and membership involvement does exist can be found by comparing men working in small shops in which there was a high measure of consensus (more than 63% of the shop vote for one party in the local election of 1951) with men working in shops which were more evenly split in the 1951 election. The proportion of men working in the high-consensus small shops who have recently engaged in some form of union political

---

21. Festinger *et al.*, in their study *Social Pressures in Informal Groups* and elsewhere, place great emphasis on the importance of what they call "a pressure toward uniformity" which operates in small groups. They see this pressure arising out of the group's need for mutual identification and solidarity, and also out of the need for conformity as a basis for group action. That such pressures exist in small groups cannot be denied. But these studies do not explore the correlative problems. What kinds of groups exert pressure on their members toward conformity with regard to what kinds of norms, values and attitudes, and in what circumstances? Neglecting these questions allows these writers to overlook such alternative group responses to the problem of normative variation and conflict among its members as a pressure toward the de-emphasis of given areas of concern or sentiment which are not central to the group's activities but yet are potentially divisive of its relationships. This de-emphasis response may be especially characteristic of such involuntary groups as are found in small shops and workplaces, in which a high rate of interaction is enforced by the context and the type of work.

activity is four times as great as the proportion of politically active men working in the divided shops.

Table 16—Relationship between Shop Political Consensus and Men in Small Shops (under 30 ITU Members) Recently Active in Union Politics

	In Shops with High Consensus	In Shops with Low Consensus
Men active in union politics	29%	7%
N	(125)	(28)

It is, of course, impossible to tell from the data whether political activity is increased by political consensus in the small shops, or whether consensus is in part a result of the fact that the political activists bring most of the relatively uninterested men in their shops into line on election day. Undoubtedly both processes operate. The data do indicate, however, that in those small shops which are almost evenly divided in party voting, very few men are active in union politics. In such shops, dissensus in union politics can be tolerated by the small work group because it is accompanied by a very strong de-emphasis of union politics.

The same relationship should not exist in large shops, where the more voluntary networks of on-the-job social relations segregate into politically homogeneous cliques, and thus not be endangered by political involvements of their members, while the shop as a whole divides politically. And this is indeed the case, as can be seen in Table 17.

Table 17—Relationship between Political Consensus and Men in Large Shops (More than 30 ITU Members) Recently Active in Union Politics

	In Shops with High Consensus	In Shops with Low Consensus
Men active in union politics	43%	43%
N	(105)	(160)

While in the small shops the absence of consensus in voting probably means an extremely apathetic shop politically, one which both tolerates dissensus and discourages political involvement, the large shops, with their many cohesive and probably near-unanimous subgroups or cliques, do not need shop-wide apathy as a correlate to lack of shop consensus on union politics.

It is true, however, that a minority of men in the small shops characterized by high political consensus are able to deviate from the general voting pattern of their shop. These men are, as might be expected, the least integrated in the social life of the plant, for the deviants are much less likely than the conformists to have shopmates among their two best printer friends.

Figure 35—*Relationship between Conformity to Shop Political Atmosphere and Having Friends in Shop (Small-Shop Men Only)*

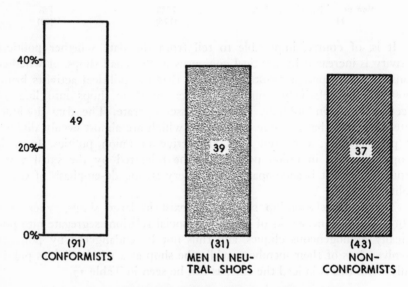

PROPORTION HAVING BOTH OF TWO BEST
PRINTER FRIENDS IN SHOP

NOTE: Conformists are men in high-consensus shops (those giving one party more than two-thirds of the vote) who voted with the majority in their shops. Deviants are men in the same type of shop who opposed the majority.

The data in Figure 35 suggest that where consensus rather than de-emphasis is the group response to the problem of the divisiveness of union politics, the man who deviates from the group's political preference often meets with the most common group sanction, some measure of exclusion from the group. At the same time, such deviants may themselves look outside their shops for friends who share their political sentiments.

If these suppositions are correct, then the tendency of small-shop deviants to have their best printer friends outside their shops should be much greater among those printers who take their union politics seriously, are most sensitive to union political issues, and probably choose their printer friends on the basis of shared political sentiments than among those to whom union politics are relatively unimportant. That this is in fact the case is shown in Figure 36, which indicates that the tendency of nonconformists to find their best printer friends outside their shop is wholly supplied by men who are on the upper half of the ideological-sensitivity scale.

The men low in ideological sensitivity, for whom union politics is not as salient or important and who would not be expected to choose their printer friends on the basis of shared political sentiments, have their best printer friends in the shop about as often when they deviate from their shop majority preference as when they accord with it.

These results may be summarized in a few generalizations.

1. When and where a given issue or sentiment (for example, preference in union politics) is important and salient, nonconformity to the prevailing or majority sentiments can usually be maintained only if the

Figure 36—*Relationship between Conformity to Shop Vote and Having Best Friend in Same Shop, for Men High or Low in Ideological Sensitivity (Small-Shop Men Only)*

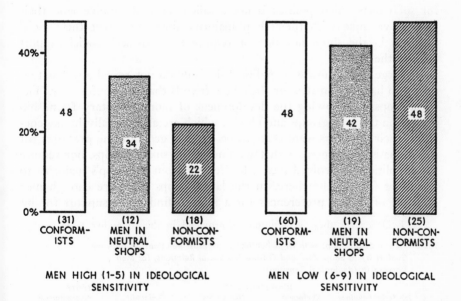

nonconformists have some kind of social support—i.e., are in some kinds of relations with others who share their sentiments on the issues in question.

2. In the small shops, a nonconformist voter to whom union politics is important cannot find that support in the shop itself; the small shops are usually too small to allow the creation within them of subgroups which stand against the political sentiments of the majority in the shop. In the small high-consensus shops there may be only two or three men who vote against the shop majority, and these men may have nothing in common with one another except their political preference. Thus the small-shop nonconformist who takes his union politics seriously is unlikely to be able to find close printer friends in his shop. More likely his social relations off the job sustain his nonconformity with the majority in his small-shop work group. (It is also probable that he came to have the political preferences that appear deviant in his shop through being involved in social relations off the job.)[22]

The deviants who are low in ideological sensitivity in the small shops —men to whom union politics is not important or salient—are nonconformists in a very different sense. The high deviant in the small shop holds a *salient* sentiment at variance with that of his shop majority, so that his nonconformity affects his relations with other men in his shop, decreasing his chances of forming friendships with them. In contrast, the low deviant is a nonconformist in the statistical sense only. Since for such men union politics is not a salient area of involvement, their vote at variance with their shop majority does not affect their social relations in the shop, nor does it require them to seek social support outside the shop.

In large shops, however, political deviants do not reveal any less tendency to have shopmates for their best friends than do conformists. The large shops, by allowing the development of more voluntary friendship groups on the job—groups and cliques which are as politically homogeneous as their members want them to be—neither generate the pressures for de-emphasis and consensus that we find in the smaller shops, nor require those politically involved men who deviate from the shop's majority to find their friends elsewhere. In the larger shops there are enough men available of similar preferences for a man to find social support for his

---

22. Evidence for these assumptions is provided in the following table.

Table—Men in Small Shops with High Political Consensus: Relationship between Conformity to Shop Vote and Off-the-Job Social Relations, for Men Varying in Ideological Sensitivity

Off-job Social Relations	HIGH SENSITIVITY		LOW SENSITIVITY	
	Conformist	Nonconformist	Conformist	Nonconformist
High	16%	56%	17%	17%
Medium	35	17	33	26
Low	48	28	50	57
N	(31)	(18)	(60)	(23)

nonconformism, which, like that of the man low in ideological sensitivity in the small shops, is more a statistical fact than a felt social reality affecting his social relations.

§ Appendix: Friendship and Small-Group Theory

OUR PRIMARY CONCERN, in this section as elsewhere in this book, has been to contribute to the overall analysis of the ITU and its unique political system. But since some of our findings appear at first glance to be at variance with propositions that have been put forward by sociologists working in the developing area of small-group theory, it may be valuable to re-examine briefly the findings in the light of that body of theory, and part of that theory in the light of our findings.

In his valuable book, *The Human Group*, George Homans reanalyzes a section of the classic study of the Hawthorne plant of Western Electric[23] which deals with the men who worked in the bank wiring room. After exploring the development of group norms and friendly sentiments among the fourteen men who regularly worked in the bank wiring room, Homans points to the development of two cliques within the larger group:

> Just as all the members of the group, thrown together in the room, were to some extent friendly (with one exception), so individuals within the group, thrown together by the geography of the room, the nature of their work, and common membership in soldering and inspection units, were friendly to an even greater extent. . . . We can, then, sum up the relationship between interaction and sentiment both in the group as a whole and in the subgroups by saying once more that *the more frequently persons interact with one another, the stronger their sentiments of friendship for one another are apt to be.*[24]

Why should the same thing not happen in the small print shops? We have argued that the men in the small print shops do not tend to develop as close friendship ties with their shopmates as do men who work in larger shops. Yet in the bank wiring room, very much like a small print shop in size, we find friendship ties among almost all the men, with even closer relations among the members of the two distinct subgroups. In the work relations of the bank wiremen there was a large measure of that element of "involuntariness" that we have suggested

---

23. F. J. Roethlisberger and W. J. Dickson: *Management and the Worker*, Cambridge, Mass., Harvard University Press, 1937.

24. George Homans: *The Human Group*, New York, Harcourt, Brace and Company, Inc., 1950, p. 133.

reduces the chances of such relations developing into close friendship ties. Homans, in contrast, suggests that such involuntary relations are the very breeder of friendship, by requiring a high rate of interaction between men. In fact, the more narrowly constrained relations between men are, in Homans' view, the more likely they are to become friends: we see that the cliques in the bank wiring room develop among those who are thrown, by the chance accident of the work process, into most frequent relations with each other on the job. Now, how does all this fit what we have said in this chapter?

The apparent contradiction hinges on the term "friendship." The original observers in the bank wiring room, and Homans after them, took as evidence for friendship, interactions among the men on the job: they noted that the men talked to each other in friendly fashion, and not only about matters related to the work at hand; they helped each other in their work, traded jobs with each other, shared candy with each other, played games with each other during lunch hour. By noting with whom an individual had such relations over and above those required by the work process, how frequently they occurred, and what kinds of sentiment were associated with the interactions, the patterns of friendships among the men in the bank wiring room were identified.

Let us compare these indicators of friendship with the operational criteria of friendship we have been using in our analysis of on-the-job relations among printers. We have used two criteria, both of which give us the same kind of results and which appear to us to be different indices of the same kind of friendship; whether a man's two best printer friends worked in his shop, and whether a printer associated with his shopmates off the job.

It is immediately apparent that the Hawthorne study (and Homans in his re-analysis of it) on the one hand and the ITU study on the other were looking for different things, were in fact investigating two very different problems which translated themselves into differing criteria and indices of what is loosely referred to in both studies as "friendship." The former were interested in on-the-job relations both for their own sake and for their bearing on the relations between the workers and the "formal organization" of the plant. These interests are not central to our analysis of the political system of the ITU and the relations between the men and their union. We have not the slightest reason to doubt, and some reason to believe, that in every print shop, even the smallest, we may find the same kinds of social relations that are pictured in the Hawthorne studies. But we are interested in on-the-job relations among printers only insofar as they are relevant to the union's political system, and especially insofar as they can function as arenas of discussion and debate about union politics.

The conditions making for the kind of "friendship" that Homans talks about are not the same which make for the kind of "friendship" we talk about, the kind that is relevant to union politics. Indeed, we have argued that the constraint and involuntary relations which led to "friendships" among the men in the bank wiring room are precisely the conditions least likely to make for the kind of "friendship" that can function as arenas of political discussion and debate in the shops where printers work.

If the ITU study has little direct knowledge of what actually goes on among men in the print shops, so the Hawthorne study and Homans know practically nothing about what the bank wiring room workers do off the job. Specifically, they do not know whether the relationships that they recorded and identified so carefully in the shop have any consequences for the behavior of the men outside their shop. Could it not be that these "friendships" that we see in the bank wiring room are restricted to the shop? In contrast, our problem forces us to look beyond these kinds of friendships and ask whether interpersonal relations in involuntary groups are likely to be elaborated beyond and outside the circumstances that initially enforced the interactions. And our findings suggest that the more that relations among men are involuntary —i.e., the less chance there is for voluntary selection to operate in the choice of associates—the less likely it is that those relationships will be elaborated beyond the contexts which give rise to them, in this case, the workshops.

For Homans, propinquity, with one important qualification,[25] is

---

25. Homans' major qualification of this hypothesis states that "when two persons interact with one another, the more frequently one of the two originates interaction for the other, the stronger will be the latter's sentiments of respect (or hostility) toward him, and the more nearly will the frequency of interaction be kept to the amount characteristic of the external system." Homans here is talking of relations between those of different rank or status.—*Ibid.*, p. 247.

We might suggest that the relationship between the superior and subordinate is a special case of what we have called involuntary relationships, which, as we have seen, can take other forms between status equals. Homans himself notes that it is not just the status inequality that prevents the emergence of friendly sentiments, despite frequent interaction. Rather, he cites specific aspects of the relationship and its environment: the need for unquestioned obedience arising out of a dangerous and uncertain environment, an inability on the part of the subordinates to escape from the relationship, and a superior who has not been chosen by those he leads—all these will decrease the likelihood that the status unequals will develop ties of friendship between them. But at the other end of the continuum, Homans everything. People who are thrown together, if status equals, will become friendly. But not all interpersonal contacts become interpersonal ties. People have statuses and values which are not wholly the creations of their immediate interpersonal situations, but are products of prior experiences and circumstances. These prior factors serve to select persons from one's environment. The important problems then become: Under what conditions are friendships determined more by propinquity and when more by shared values and statuses? When are values shaped more by association patterns, and when are association patterns more shaped by prior values? And when are shared values of greater significance in shaping patterns of friendship than shared statuses?

The present study allows us to examine different situations in which the objective chances to exercise selectivity in the choice of friends vary. In the smaller shops there is clearly less opportunity for the selection of friends on the basis of any prior statuses or values than in the larger shops with their larger pools. Our guiding question has been, What are the consequences of more or less selectivity for the character and consequences of the ensuing interpersonal relations? Our answer is that the greater the opportunity for men to select their friends from a large pool of other printers in physical propinquity in their shops,

---

points out that Doc (W. F. Whyte, *op. cit.*), who was leader of a voluntary neighborhood group, the Norton gang, which had informally chosen him its leader, did have close friendship ties with his "subordinates." The key variable in Homans' analysis of why status unequals frequently do not develop friendship ties even when they have a high rate of interaction seems to lie in the degree of constraint, of forced and involuntary interaction, which can, as we have seen, also exist among status equals.

In the case of involuntary relations between status unequals, there is a double measure of constraint—a constraint to interact, and a constraint to obey; while among status equals there is only the constraint to interact. And status unequals are less likely to develop even the casual informality that develops among status equals who are constrained in interact. We might summarize this in a table:

Table—Types of Interaction as Affecting Relationships

Type of Interaction	Type of Sentiment to Develop	Degree of Elaboration of Relationship Likely to Occur
1. Involuntary interactions between status unequals	Respect or hostility, but little affection or friendship	Restricted to that required by the situation
2. Involuntary interactions between status equals	Casual friendships	Elaborated in norms and activities directly associated with the context which requires the interaction
3. Voluntary interactions between status equals	Closer friendships	Elaborated more widely to include a wide range of participants' values and interests and activities outside the context which first gave rise to the interaction

the more likely it is that these friendships will be deeper and closer, and their activities elaborated more widely, both on and off the job.[26]

---

26. Speaking of American society, Talcott Parsons notes: "Particularly between men, we institutionalize a diffuse 'friendliness' among occupational associates, to a markedly higher degree than is the case, for example, in most European countries. This is symbolized in such ways as the use of first names, various informal social relationships such as 'having a drink' together, and often a 'kidding' relationship. But such expressive orientations are not permitted to go too far in particularistic exclusiveness; there is an obligation to manifest them relatively impartially toward all associates or colleagues, and the corresponding expressive symbols and rewards are organized this way. The conspicuous thing about this pattern is the limit placed on its particularism and hence its integration with the universalism of the occupational system. It readily becomes evident how breaking through these limits could be threatening by providing occasions for 'favoritism' in the instrumental aspects of the same concrete relationships."—*The Social System,* Glencoe, Ill., Free Press, 1951, p. 418.

We would agree with Parsons' observations regarding the prevalence of "diffuse" and casual relationships among men in American shops and offices. It may be that the pervasive universalism of the occupational system is partly responsible for this, but we hold that the objective chances of finding men in one's shop or office with whom one shares values or interests are of greater influence on the kinds of friendships one develops around one's workplace. We live in a heterogeneous society whose members use highly differentiated criteria in their choice of friends. Men do not deepen the diffuse friendly relations they have with others in their workplace, not only because of the functional requirements of their occupational roles, but more simply because there is often nobody in the office or on the job they care to associate with more closely. And as we have suggested, the greater the chances for selectivity, the greater the likelihood of closer friendships developing between shopmates.

CHAPTER *9*

The Chapel
as a Political Unit

THE PREVIOUS CHAPTER has dealt with the way the size of a printer's shop affects his relations with shop management and with other printers. How does shop size affect relations with the union? For the men in the small shops, management is near and important and the union remote. For men in the larger shops the union is closer and shop management more remote, and dealt with through the union. Beyond these patterns, however, differences in the content of union shop organization, the chapel, constitute another important part of the printer's work environment and experience which varies with different-sized shops.

§ Chapel Chairmen in Different-sized Shops

UNDER THE REQUIREMENTS of the union constitution, about one thousand men currently hold chapel office in New York. This means that about one out of every eight or nine men holds this union post. A much larger proportion of the membership have held chapel office in the past. Over half of the random sample of Big Six members report having held some chapel office during their union careers. Turnover in these posts is high, since a local law prescribes that no chapel chairman may hold office for more than two consecutive one-year terms, except with the unanimous consent of the members of his chapel. Such consent is rarely given in the larger shops, while in the smaller shops, where unanimous consent might be obtained more readily, the position tends to be regarded as an obligation to be passed around and shared among the chapel members.

Although the formal organization of the union makes no distinction between the chairman of the *Daily News* chapel, with some six hundred ITU members, and the chairman of a three-man shop, the actual characteristics of the office and of the men who fill it are so different in large and small shops, that to continue to talk about chapel chairmen as if they could be distinguished from nonchairmen without regard for the size of the chapel they head, would be both misleading and unfruitful.

The chapel chairmen in large shops are much more deeply involved in union affairs than either their own rank and file or small-shop chairmen, as is clear in Figures 37A and 37B.[1]

As can be seen from these data, chairmen of shops with more than thirty ITU members have markedly higher rates of union political interest, activity, and knowledge than the rank and file in their own shops, while by way of contrast, the chairmen of the smallest shops, with fewer than ten ITU members, are almost indistinguishable from their rank and file in these respects.

Chapel chairmen should be expected to differ from their rank and file where the job *recruits* members who possess special characteristics, and where the post of chapel chairman gives a man different kinds of *experiences* from those of the ordinary member. Both of these factors operate to make chairmen in large- and medium-sized shops markedly different from their rank and file in their relation to the union, while neither of these factors works to differentiate the small-shop chairmen from their rank and file. The chairman of a small shop has little to do with the union besides collecting dues once a week

---

1. Further evidence may be found in the figure below.

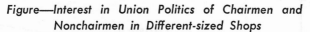

Figure—Interest in Union Politics of Chairmen and Nonchairmen in Different-sized Shops

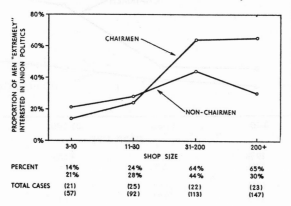

and keeping the financial records for the chapel. The post offers no special status or rewards, nor does it take the chairman away from his bench or machine during working hours. The post in a small shop is rarely a step upward in the union hierarchy, since it provides neither the leadership training nor the popular following that would recommend a man for higher union posts to union leaders or men in other shops. So it is not surprising that the small-shop chairman typically holds the job because nobody else wants it; frequently not even he wants it, and he has become chairman only because he protested slightly less vigorously than anyone else in the shop. When selection for the job occurs in this random way, chairmen will not differ appreciably from nonchairmen in their involvement in union affairs.

In contrast to the chairman in the small shop, the large-shop chairman usually *wants* his job. Over two-thirds of the chairmen in shops with more than a hundred ITU members say they would rather be a union officer than a foreman, while only a third of the chairmen in shops with fewer than thirty members show the same preference. Moreover, many of the large-shop chairmen have served an apprenticeship in lesser chapel posts, while none of the small-shop chairmen have done so—there are no other chapel posts in small shops. The clearest evi-

Figure 37A—*Knowledge of Union Politics of Chairmen and Nonchairmen in Different-sized Shops*

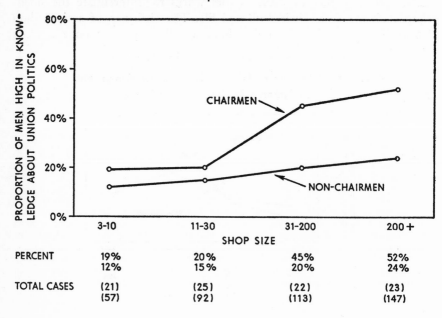

	3-10	11-30	31-200	200+
PERCENT	19%	20%	45%	52%
	12%	15%	20%	24%
TOTAL CASES	(21)	(25)	(22)	(23)
	(57)	(92)	(113)	(147)

Figure 37B—Rates of Union Political Activity of Chairmen and Nonchairmen in Different Shops

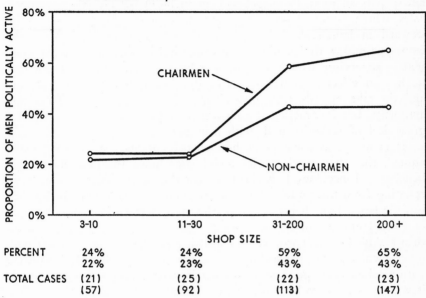

PERCENT	24%	24%	59%	65%
	22%	23%	43%	43%
TOTAL CASES	(21)	(25)	(22)	(23)
	(57)	(92)	(113)	(147)

dence that large-shop chairmen want their jobs may be seen in the fact that most large-shop chairmen have to run for their office against opposition. The percentage of those who have held chapel office and were elected against opposition increases with the size of the shop in which they held office, with about two-thirds of the men who have held chapel office in shops with more than a hundred members reporting that they were opposed for office.[2]

2.

Table—Proportion of Chapel Officers in Different-sized Shops
Who Were Elected Against Opposition

(Asked of all those who have held chapel office: How many men were there in that chapel where you held office?)

Did Someone Run Against You for That Office?	SHOP SIZE			
	100+	50-99	10-49	Under 10
Yes, %	64	58	31	10
No, %	36	42	69	90
N	(88)	(33)	(108)	(63)

The above table both confirms the fact that chairmen in large shops usually want their jobs, and throws light on the relationship between the size of a shop and internal political cleavage. As noted earlier, the small shops are much less likely to develop cliques or subgroups which oppose each other on union politics. In the small shops few men want to be chapel chairmen, few men care much who is chairman, few men want to create the severe strains which contested chapel elections would introduce into the cohesion and work atmosphere of the small shop.

In the larger shops the chairman of the chapel is actually a union officer who spends at least part of his working time, and in the large newspapers all of it, in chapel and union business.[3] He enforces union rules which cover almost every aspect of work. In contrast to the steward in large-scale industry, the chapel chairman deals with the employer and with his direct representative in the shop, rather than with a supervisor who is so low in a long management structure that he has no effective power or authority. Workers and employers can and do take appeals from the chairmen's decisions to higher union authority, but in practice the chairmen in these larger shops wield a great deal of authority both with management and the men.

It is likely, as some large-shop chapel chairmen have persuasively argued, that they work harder and longer hours than do the men at benches and machines. It is also true that they are subject to the strains resulting from their role as the first arbitrator of any intrashop dispute.[4] But the large-shop chapel chairman clearly is engaged in a different type of work from that of the ordinary printer. He is a man-manager rather than a skilled manual worker: his working hours are spent dealing with other men—arguing, persuading, exercising power—rather than working with machines or type. And his job carries with it special rewards which, it is clear, are felt to be considerable. A chapel chairman in a large shop has a greater measure of personal control over the content and scheduling of his work than other workers have. His work is more varied, and to him, more interesting. Although printers on the whole seem to find their work interesting and "creative," nevertheless many chapel chairmen indicated that one of the major rewards of the job for them was the chance to deal with people rather than with machines and type. In addition, considerable status accrues to the job in large shops—status deriving from its stature as an elective post, as a recognition of talent and ability, as a position which commands a certain amount of power and influence, and as a form of work which is much more "middle-class" and managerial than manual labor. Such a job recruits a body of able, informed, and ambitious men, who in the course of gaining and holding chapel office acquire many of the skills of politics and leadership. These men learn how to organize a political campaign, to preside over

---

3. A chapel chairman, whether working full- or part-time for the union, continues to be paid by his employer. In addition, he receives for his services twenty-five cents per week per member. This sum is paid from chapel dues. In the largest shops, it is distributed among several chapel officers.

4. For a discussion of the role such strains play in the democratic control of labor unions, cf. Shepard, *op. cit.*, p. 313. On the other hand, another solution to such strains is oligarchic control. Cf. Philip Taft: "Understanding Union Administration," *Harvard Business Review*, 24:246 (Winter 1946).

meetings and speak in public, to gain and use a personal following for political ends. They learn union law, the administration of union affairs, and how to negotiate with management. In short, the chairman of a large shop learns a great deal about the job of a union officer.

The existence of this body of skilled, politically active, and ambitious men in relatively autonomous elective union posts has a variety of consequences for union politics. For example, in the formal organization of the union, the chapel chairman is one of the major links between the union administration and the rank and file. Supplementing the direct links between the member and his union—the union meeting, and the ITU *Journal* and Big Six *Bulletin*--the chairman is nominally a key in the two-way channel of communication between leaders and led, explaining and amplifying administrative policy and action to the members, and communicating rank-and-file problems and sentiments to the union leaders. On the whole, large-shop chairmen perform these functions, while small-shop chairmen do not. A chairman must himself have accurate information to be able to communicate it, and the fact that small-shop chairmen are almost indistinguishable from their rank and file in their level of knowledge about union law and politics would indicate, even if no other evidence were available, that small-shop chairmen could hardly act as a channel of communications to and from the membership.

But the influence of the chairman in his chapel goes beyond passing information up and down the line. For those chairmen who do transmit information, *how* they transmit information to the men in their shops —whether critically or uncritically, as a shop leader or as first-line administrative office—is as important a part of their influence in their shops as is the fact of transmission itself. As has already been noted, the autonomy of the chapel chairman and his independence from administration control make it at least as likely that he will transmit news of union administrative actions or policies with a critical commentary as with a reinforcing one.

Apart from his communications functions, a chairman who himself is active and involved in union politics and affairs can stimulate members of his chapel to also become active. The predominance of this type of chairman in the large shops is certainly one of the reasons for the comparatively high levels of political involvement among the large-shop rank and file.

This pattern of active and capable large-shop chairmen has other important consequences for union politics. *It breeds men hungry for union office.* After his constitutionally limited two-year term (if he is re-elected for the second year) the chapel chairman must return to the ranks. If he is working in a large newspaper, this means that he moves from a white-collar, better paid position back to a bench or machine. But these are men who are ambitious and who have had the experience of holding a position of higher status and power. The principal remaining avenue of further mobility and continued high status and leadership is union politics. Thus the turnover in chapel office in the larger shops creates a pool of trained and ambitious men who are motivated to seek higher union office, most of them through the union's political parties.[5] One result is that almost every union officer and candidate for office is a former chapel chairman. But most important, this pool of men who have had the taste and experience of chapel office provides recruits for the *opposition* party, men who possess political and administrative skills and experience, and who have a popular following in their own chapels or in the union at large. Thus in the ITU, in contrast to many unions, the administration in power never has a monopoly on the members of the union who have had training in political skills or experience in union office.[6]

The larger chapels, by generating and supporting a body of union activists who have gained political and administrative skills and a personal following independent of the union administration, thus perform perhaps their major function for the union's political system—providing sources of power and leadership outside and independent of the union administration. In Chapter 4 we discussed the relevance of the concept of the mass society for our analysis of the ITU. There we noted the importance for a democratic political system of the existence of sources of power independent of the state, or in our case the union administration, which mediate between the individual and the central governing body. In the ITU the independent chapels, along with the printers' organizations, play this mediating role and provide structural bases for the two-party system which is the heart of the union's democracy.

§ Politics in the Chapel

IN THE COURSE of this discussion it may have been forgotten that in the chapel as in the clubs, the open introduction of union politics is in-

---

5. This is the push tending to involve large-shop chairmen even more deeply in union party politics. There is also a pull provided by the party leaders, who are continually on the lookout for a chance to recruit active men who have a personal following and have shown vote-getting talents. We discuss this pull in Chap. 11.

6. In a later chapter on union leadership (Chap. 11) we show in more detail how the large-shop chapel officers provide the primary source of union and party leaders.

formally prohibited. Many union leaders explain this prohibition by noting that the issues of chapel politics—personalities and the administration of chapel affairs—are not related to the differences and issues between the two union parties. But as can be seen at the local and international levels of the ITU, almost any issue can be converted into a partisan issue. Few issues that arise in the union are intrinsically party issues; they are *made* political issues by the parties and their spokesmen. The maintenance of the rule has other and better explanations. For one thing, chapel chairmen must deal with the union administration regardless of which party is in power; if they were openly partisan, a strain would be introduced in dealing with a local or international administration of the other party, and the help and services which the local administration can render the chapel might be jeopardized. Secondly, a chapel chairman is frequently called upon to decide issues between members within his chapel, and again open partisanship might strain harmony within the shop. Finally, the nonpartisanship of chapel chairmen helps sustain their independence in their relations with the union officialdom. A chairman is expected to be primarily the representative of the men in his chapel in dealing with the employer *and* with the union, and he is supported by union norms in resisting efforts to make him a representative of the union administration. Chairmen who ignore this normative prescription and attempt to further the interests of their party at the expense of chapel interests or harmony lose support in their chapels.

Despite the fact that union politics are nominally excluded from chapel elections, it is clear that the union parties have a strong interest in trying to elect men who are sympathetic to them to chapel office. Chapel chairmen hold strategic and influential positions which assure them of getting more of a hearing than anyone else in the chapel on union affairs. They communicate and interpret the actions and policies of the local administration to their members, preside at the monthly chapel meetings, and informally influence political sentiment, especially among the least active members.

The party leaders recognize the power of the chairmen to influence votes; in interviews, leaders of both union parties acknowledged that their members in the larger shops work consciously to influence chapel elections. Most often, party influence takes the form of organized but covert support of candidates who are sympathizers and supporters but not members of the party. While sanctions against party politics in the chapel appear to hinder the candidacy of overt party members in chapel elections (only one-quarter of chapel chairmen in shops with more than thirty members are party members) being a party sympathizer and consistent supporter will gain a man a party's organized support and the support of partisan factions in the chapel, without alienating the independent voters who would be wary of electing a too openly partisan chapel chairman.

PARTY STRENGTH IN THE CHAPELS

Just how numerous are party members and partisan factions? Table 18 shows the support for each party in the large shops.

Table 18—Party Members and Supporters in Large Shops with Thirty or More ITU Members, Per Cent

Consistent Progressive supporters*		28
Prog Party members	8	
Nonparty actives†	10	
Inactive supporters	10	
Consistent Independent supporters		17
Ind. Party members	6	
Nonparty actives	4	
Inactive supporters	7	
All independents‡		50
Party members	2	
Nonparty actives	12	
Inactives	36	
"Don't know" and no answer		5
		100%
N		(265)

* A consistent party supporter is one who supports the same union party both locally and internationally.
† Nonparty actives contribute campaign funds and work for candidates.
‡ Lowercase "independents" are all those who do not support the same union party both locally and internationally. They include a few party members.

First, with regard to the distribution of party strength, Table 19 shows that in the large shops, the Progressives have more partisans of all degrees of activity than do the Independents, though at the time of the study the Independent Party was in power locally. The Progressives are stronger than the Independents in the small shops as well.[7] Taking small- and large-shop men together, the local membership as a whole seems to be divided among three groups: a large minority of between 25% and 30% of the membership who back the Progressives consistently in both local and international elections; a small minority of about 15% who do the same for the Independents; and a large group,

---

7. In this section we focus on the relative party strength in the large shops, since, as we have noted, in the small shops chapel office is rarely important enough to be contested or to engage the union parties. Morover, union politics in the chapel is carried on by the active partisans and party members. Not only are there fewer of them in the small shops, but those few are distributed so thinly among the hundreds of small shops that most small shops have none at all.

Table 19—Party Members and Supporters in Small Shops with Fewer than Thirty ITU Members, Per Cent

Consistent Progressive supporters		25
Prog Party members	7	
Nonparty actives	4	
Inactives	14	
Consistent Independent supporters		9
Ind. Party members	2	
Nonparty actives	1	
Inactives	6	
All independents		58
Party members	2	
Nonparty actives	7	
Inactives	49	
"Don't know" and no answer		8
		100%
N		(165)

comprising about half the membership, who do not consistently support either party, but tend to vote Progressive in international elections and to fluctuate between the parties in local elections.

A number of factors help explain the difference in the relative strength of the two parties in New York. Big Six has traditionally been a Progressive local in international elections: since 1920 the New York local has given a majority to the Progressive presidential candidate in fourteen out of eighteen international elections. Though the Independents won the 1951 local election, the Progressives carried New York in both the 1950 and 1952 international elections.

The lack of strength of international Independent candidates in New York caused the leading local conservatives to delay setting up a formal local party organization for many years. Since the local politicians are primarily concerned with winning local office, they refrained from using an international party label which might weaken them locally. Between 1941 and 1949 the local anti-Progressive group, which controlled the local administration during these years, had no formal party structure of any kind, but worked through campaign committees. After their defeat in 1949 the Independent leaders in New York decided that the advantages of systematic organization outweighed the liabilities of the party label in New York.[8]

The organizational weakness of the Independents has greater conse-

8. They have not yet been able to build as strong a party organization as the Progressives, who have had a party organization in New York since 1911. The comparative weakness of the Independent Party organization in New York has meant that in most of the larger chapels there has been a larger and better organized nucleus of Progressives working to influence the chapel's vote.

quences for chapel elections than for local elections. In spite of their organizational weakness, the Independents are often able to win a majority of the votes in the large shops in local elections, by reaching the nonpartisan majority with an intensive election campaign. But those election issues—such as a local contract or welfare benefits—which can make enough Progressive supporters and nonpartisans vote for the Independent ticket to win the local elections for them are not present in chapel elections. This allows candidates for chapel office in the large shops who are Prog sympathizers to profit from the stronger Progressive party organization and the larger reservoir of Progessive sentiment in the shops, without having to carry any responsibility for the Progressive Party's record in local administration. The result is that the chairmen of the large shops are more often Progressive Party supporters (though not members) than are the rank and file or the small-shop chairmen. The disproportionate number of Progressive supporters among the large-shop chairmen is in large part a result of the fact

Figure 38—*Progressive Party Supporters among Chairmen as Compared with Rank-and-File Members in Large and Small Shops*

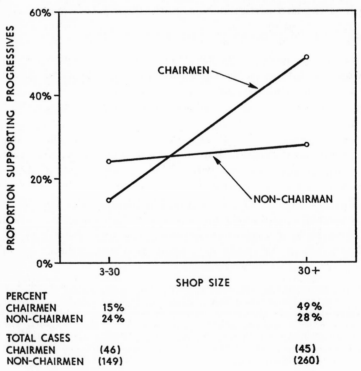

PERCENT		
CHAIRMEN	15%	49%
NON-CHAIRMEN	24%	28%
TOTAL CASES		
CHAIRMEN	(46)	(45)
NON-CHAIRMEN	(149)	(260)

that in the large shops the sizable number of members and active partisans of the Progressive Party form a group well-organized enough to get men who are sympathizers elected to chapel office.

It is a curious fact that in the larger shops, where chairmen are usually elected against opposition, the men who are elected to the post differ markedly, in their political sentiments and union party attachments, from their constituents, while in the small shops, where the chairman's post is filled more casually and often by self-appointment, chairmen are more representative of their rank and file. (For example, there was almost no difference in voting between chairmen and nonchairmen in small shops in the 1951 local election; in the large shops, the chairmen voted much more strongly than the nonchairmen for the Progressive candidate.) This apparent anomaly, however, is evidence of the fact that the seemingly nonpolitical chapel elections in the large shops actually do involve a covert struggle for power between the union parties for control of the chapel, with the political sentiments of the chairmen a product of the relative party strengths in the chapels. Though the chapel chairman is defined as nonpartisan, the chapel election tends to favor that party which has the strongest organization and the most political resources.[9]

THE ACTIVE PARTISANS IN THE LARGE SHOPS

A further examination of Table 18 shows that about 16% of the men in the shops with more than thirty members belong to one of the union parties. But the parties can count on another 14% of the membership, men we can call active partisans, who consistently support one of the union parties by contributing funds to it and working for its candidates. Another 17% are inactive partisans, supporting one party both locally and internationally without actively engaging in union politics. Taken together, these partisans comprise some 45% of the membership in the larger shops.

The earlier analysis of the relationship between the size of a shop and the level of interest and involvement in union politics among the men who work in it largely ignored the active role of the union parties and their partisans. Working in a large shop increases the likelihood

---

9. Studies of nonpartisan elections in civil politics point to the same conclusion. In one such study it was found that a conservative group which had the support of the press was usually able to win nominally nonpartisan elections in situations and places where the majority of the voters were voting liberal when faced with party labels and issues. Cf. Arthur Naftalin: "The Failure of the Farmer-Labor Party to Capture Control of the Minnesota Legislature," *American Political Science Review*, 38:71-78 (February 1944).

that a man will be concerned with the affairs of the union and that he will have the kind of social relations with other printers on the job which encourages such interest. But these social relations would not by themselves involve men in union politics if there were not other processes at work making the issues of union politics part of the content of those relations. By bringing union politics into the chapel in ways that force them upon the attention of less active and partisan men, the active partisans are important to the union's political processes far out of proportion to their numbers. These active partisans convert *potential* political arenas into *actual* ones by channeling union concerns into union politics and by injecting political issues into the networks of social relationships that flourish in the larger shops.

In describing their entry into union politics, many of the men now active in both union parties indicated that the political atmosphere in their chapels first brought the union parties and union political issues to their attention:

> I worked in a chapel out of which came a number of officials of the local. . . . When you see big men like that coming out of your own shop, as a young man you learn a lot. . . . You had to be a dumbbell not to know what's going on. They were always discussing things, they were political-minded and made us interested.

> The first shop I worked in in New York had an active Prog and Independent—each wanted me to join. The Independent took me around to headquarters and introduced me to the big shots there.

> I was working in the M—— [a newspaper]. C [now a local officer] and D [later an international representative] worked there. They would round up the young fellows to get votes for themselves or on an issue. These men being union politicians got me interested. Both were undoubtedly aspiring for union jobs. The results were obvious, they attained them in later years. I had no interest in politics at all before; I think it was created there. It started me attending union meetings.

> I was at the N—— [a newspaper] then. Naturally you talk to fellows, there were different viewpoints, and they ask you, "Going to the union meeting?" and we went. I worked nights and was unmarried then.

> I got interested in a chapel fight over a man's priority, which the politicians in the shop were fighting over. You get interested first in the shop, and then branch out afterwards.

These reports indicate how the party men bring union politics into the shop. Active partisans attend union meetings regularly and bring back to the majority of less active members news of what went on. The issues brought up in the meeting are debated all over again in the shop,

with the opposition party attacking administration measures and administration supporters defending them. Thus men who never attend
union meetings nor bother reading the *Typographical Journal* or the
Big Six *Bulletin* are often forced to listen to discussions of local or
international issues.

Political discussion in the shops is to some extent consciously organized. Party leaders in many of the larger shops make certain that
their point of view reaches the membership. Men without party allegiances are consciously approached for their support. One party leader,
who is also an elected member of a high union body, described the
operation of politics in his chapel as follows:

In the T—— [a newspaper], we have two completely separate groups.
Workers either consult me or consult A, who is L's man. [L is a leader
of the other party.] Anyone can find out who is an Indie or a Prog
in the shop by watching who they associate with. . . . A large part of
the differences between the Indie and Prog followers is a result of personal
contact. Many members follow me because I did them a personal service in
the shop or in relation to their rights in the union. Most of our members lean
in one or another direction, but can shift because of some immediate issue.
The differences in voting in different plants are also a result often of personalities. Our party workers in [newspaper A] and [newspaper B] are very
good. They can demolish the other side's arguments better than the equivalent [opposing party's] leaders in their shops. In [newspaper C] on the other
hand, we do not have an able person on our side.[10]

This same man reports one of the ways a partisan can attempt to shape
political sentiment in his shop. "I often stand at the chapel bulletin
board, and when somebody reads an [opposition party circular] I
point out the lies in it." Undoubtedly there is somebody on hand to
rebut him, and the casual reader at the bulletin board is thus exposed to
or drawn into a political debate on the spot. This kind of interaction
between active partisans and the less active men goes on constantly and
works to stimulate political interest and raise the general level of knowledge about union politics among the men in the larger shops.

SIZE OF SHOP AND INVOLVEMENT IN
UNION POLITICS: A CURVILINEAR RELATIONSHIP

The fact that active party members and partisans are key men in
making other men's social relationships on the job relevant to union

---

10. This respondent, like most union activists, probably overestimates the influence of chance relationships and personal favors in shaping party allegiance. In
chapters 15 through 17 we explore a range of factors which affect party allegiance
and voting behavior.

politics requires a re-examination of the analysis of the connection between the size of shops and the union political involvements of the men who work in them.

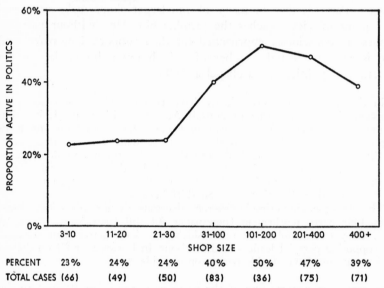

Figure 39—Relationship between Size of Shop and Activity in Union Politics

	3-10	11-20	21-30	31-100	101-200	201-400	400+
PERCENT	23%	24%	24%	40%	50%	47%	39%
TOTAL CASES	(66)	(49)	(50)	(83)	(36)	(75)	(71)

Up to this point we have been talking about "large" and "small" shops. In so doing we have implied that the relationship between shop size and political behavior is linear in character, such that the larger the shop, the greater the political involvement of the men.[11] But is the assumption of linearity valid for all of these relationships, for the whole size range covered by our sample, and hypothetically, for shop sizes greater than those studied? For example, can we assume that the relationships found between shop size and various factors making for greater political participation show themselves operating most strongly in the very largest print shops? And would they continue to hold if there were print shops employing thousands of men as do single plants in other industries? There is evidence in the study that this is not the case, and some additional data suggesting why it is not.

---

11. Often we made a dichotomous break between large and small shops because of the need for a sufficient number of cases in the several categories to allow us to test more refined relationships. A shop size of thirty members was chosen as the breaking point after an examination of variations in certain crucial attitudes and behaviors, such as participation in and knowledge about union affairs, which revealed a sharp break at about that shop size.

If a more refined breakdown than the simple one of "large" (more than thirty) and "small" (less than thirty) shops is made, the actual relationship between the size of the work unit and participation in union affairs turns out to be curvilinear rather than linear. The highest level of involvement in union politics occurs not among men who work in the very largest shops in New York but rather among those in shops employing between one hundred to two hundred ITU members.

The number of cases in each group is fairly small, and in the largest-size categories we are dealing with very few shops. There are only two shops with more than 400 members, the *New York Times* and the *New York Daily News,* and the men in these two shops are very different in their level of involvement in ITU politics. But in spite of this, we believe that the pattern revealed in Figures 39 to 41 is not the product of sampling error or idiosyncratic shop factors. Rather, the increase in the proportion of politically inactive and uninterested men in shops of more than one or two hundred men is a necessary result of the factors we have already described.

In Chapter 5, where we explored the processes of political activation and stimulation that take place in the printers' clubs and in their informal relations off the job, we noted that having informal social rela-

Figure 40—Relationship between Size of Shop and Interest in Union Politics

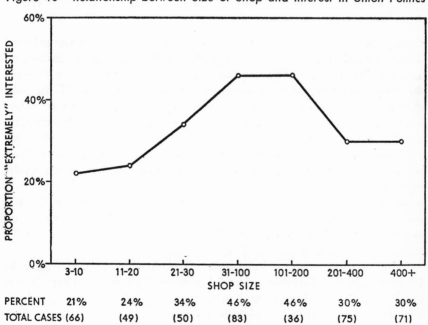

	3-10	11-20	21-30	31-100	101-200	201-400	400+
PERCENT	21%	24%	34%	46%	46%	30%	30%
TOTAL CASES	(66)	(49)	(50)	(83)	(36)	(75)	(71)

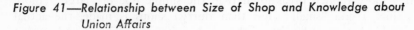

Figure 41—Relationship between Size of Shop and Knowledge about Union Affairs

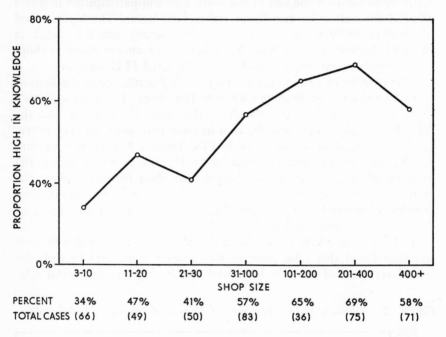

	3-10	11-20	21-30	31-100	101-200	201-400	400+
PERCENT	34%	47%	41%	57%	65%	69%	58%
TOTAL CASES	(66)	(49)	(50)	(83)	(36)	(75)	(71)

tions with other printers off the job did not tend to affect the political interest or involvement of the group of men who were *least* sensitive to union political issues. We explained this by suggesting that if such politically uninterested men associate with other printers off the job, they are likely to associate with men as politically insensitive as themselves and thus successfully screen union politics out of their leisure-time social relations with other printers. By way of contrast, those ideologically insensitive men who belonged to union clubs were markedly more politically active and knowledgeable than nonmembers. In the clubs men of little political sensitivity are, (according to our hypothesis), involuntarily exposed to political stimulation from the more active and partisan men who are fellow club members, and are less able to screen politics out of their club relationships than out of their almost wholly self-selected relations off the job.

The question of the voluntariness of relationships came up again in Chapter 8, in the discussion of social relations on the job. There it was noted that the relations among printers on the job in the small shops seem to be involuntary to a high degree and do not tend to develop into the close friendships that can function as arenas of political stimulation and discussion. In contrast, the "large shops" (and in Chapter 8 we did not distinguish, as we do now, between medium and large shops) permit a greater measure of self-selection in the informal relations among shopmates on the job, and more frequently tend to develop into the kinds of close relations that have consequences for the participants' union political interest and involvement.

Juxtaposing these two analyses, it may be suggested that *social relations among printers are most likely to stimulate political involvement among men who are initially uninterested in politics where there is enough selection possible in the choice of associates so that the relationships are likely to ripen into close friendships, and yet little enough selectivity in the relationships to ensure that men who are little interested in union politics are exposed in personal ways to men who are highly involved in union politics.* These conditions appear to be best fulfilled in the medium-sized shops.

The shops which employ the most ITU members are the big newspaper plants. Not only are these shops very large as print shops go, but also the men in them do not work steadily the whole time of their shift, having free time during working hours to circulate around the shop. This allows a member of such a shop to actually have social relations with men in any part of the shop, not just those in physical proximity

Figure 42—Relationship between Size of Shop and Personal Acquaintanceship with Active Party Supporters

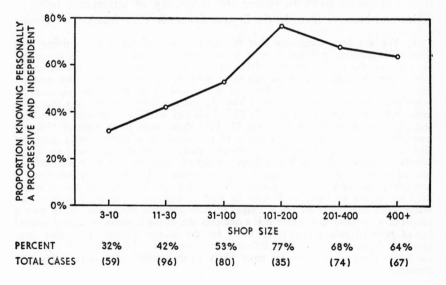

	3-10	11-30	31-100	101-200	201-400	400+
PERCENT	32%	42%	53%	77%	68%	64%
TOTAL CASES	(59)	(96)	(80)	(35)	(74)	(67)

to his bench or machine. The very large measure of voluntariness and self-selection in these social relations on the job allows many of them to ripen into friendships. On the other hand, the number and variety of men available in these shops is so great that men who are not at all interested in union affairs or politics are able to restrict their on-the-job relations to others like themselves, screening union politics out of the social relations they do have while avoiding politically stimulating contact and relations with union activists and partisans. Thus the inactive men in the largest shops are less likely to have personal relationships *with politically active men* than are men in the medium-sized shops.

Twice the proportion of the men in the two biggest newspapers, as compared with the men in these medium-sized shops, do not know personally *either* an active Progressive or an active Independent. It is not that the union parties are stronger in the medium-sized shops—on the contrary, it is likely that the parties are better organized and more active in the very larest shops—but that the party members and active partisans have greater difficulty in reaching all the workers in the largest shops on a personal level. The ten most active partisans in a shop of a hundred men may know all their shopmates. In a shop of four hundred, the forty most active partisans probably do not know personally as large a proportion of the men in the shop as do the ten in the medium-sized shop.[12] The larger number of activists in the larger shops tend to interact more with each other; if the inactive men in the largest shops are able to associate more with each other, this is true of the activists as well, and both these tendencies work to reduce the frequency of interaction between active and inactive men. In the largest shops the very freedom of choice

---

12. We are here suggesting that the effectiveness of the party activists in a shop in stimulating political interest among the less involved men is dependent not only on the *proportion* of activists in a shop but also on their absolute numbers. Georg Simmel touches on this same point when he cites examples showing that "the *absolute* numbers of the total group and of its prominent elements so remarkably determine the relations within the group—in spite of the fact that their numerical ratio remains the same."—*The Sociology of Georg Simmel*. Translated and edited by Kurt Wolff, Glencoe, Ill., Free Press, 1950, p. 98. One of Simmel's examples suggests that the importance of ten rebels in a parliamentary party of fifty is greater than that of four rebels in a party of twenty. It would seem that whether a numerically smaller or larger group of "prominent men" has greater or less influence or power in a larger mass organization in which they constitute a constant proportion depends, among other things, on the nature of the influence they are trying to exercise. It may be that an organized group of twelve men could more effectively govern a chapel of four hundred than could three men a chapel of a hundred. But where it is a question not of the exercise of formal control but of *personal* influence, it seems likely for the reasons we cite above that three men will have greater personal influence in a shop of a hundred than twelve in the larger shop, where they are more likely to monopolize each other's time and attention.

allows the subgroups and cliques to be more homogeneous with regard to their involvement in union politics and at the same time more insulated from one another, thus reducing the effect of the active partisans in the shop on the inactive men. Further, the greater visibility of the parties and of party competition in these largest shops somewhat reduces the effectiveness of their partisans' efforts. Studies of personal influence, especially in politics, find that the more formal efforts of party campaigners to sell a party are less effective than the kinds of relations more commonly found in the medium-sized print shops where party workers talk to other workers as shopmates rather than in a quasi-official role of party representative.[13]

§ The Political Relevance of Personal Relations in Differing Contexts

WE HAVE IN VARIOUS PLACES discussed the political relevance of printers' social relations as they occur in five different contexts: in the small, medium, and largest shops, in the printers' clubs, and in the various settings where printers get together informally in their leisure hours. We can summarize and relate our findings about social relations in these various contexts if we characterize each type of context in terms of the degree to which a printer is able to choose the men with whom he has a continuing relationship—what we have spoken of as *voluntariness* of social relations. In Figure 43 we make no attempt to suggest just where along this continuum of voluntariness our several contexts are located, but we do indicate what we believe to be the relative positions, or rank order, of these contexts.

Figure 43—Location of Contexts along Continuum of Voluntariness of the Relationships within Them

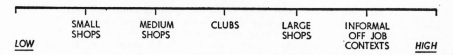

	SMALL SHOPS	MEDIUM SHOPS	CLUBS	LARGE SHOPS	INFORMAL OFF JOB CONTEXTS	
LOW						HIGH

The most completely self-selected and voluntary relations are those among printers who get together casually and informally off the job

13. P. F. Lazarsfeld *et al.*: *The People's Choice*, pp. 150-58. This study stresses the importance of casual personal relations in affecting the direction of political sentiment. Such relations, we suggest, have their effects not only on the *direction* of political attitudes but also on the level or degree of interest and involvement of those exposed to them.

in their leisure hours. A printer does not have to associate with any other printers outside of working hours, and if he does, it is because he and his friends want to get together and enjoy each other's company. People enjoying such a relationship are likely to share a wide range of values and interests. These relationships serve best to stimulate and sustain the interest of the participants in union political affairs, *if*, to begin with, one or more of the participants have some interest in union affairs. But the same factors which will cause some interest in union politics to spread and affect the entire group of friends, will also insulate from union political affairs if there is no such interest in the group to begin with. So among printers in close, informal social relations with each other off the job a sharp dichotomy exists, with the members of some groups very interested in union politics, and members of other groups not interested at all.

On-the-job social relations in the largest shops resemble these informal social relations among printers off the job. The large number of fellow workers available for casual socializing in the shop allows men to select others as friends who are much like themselves in their interest and involvement in union affairs. Of course even in the largest shops the work situation limits freedom in forming social relations, and there is a somewhat greater chance that inactive and uninterested men will be exposed to or drawn into political discussions with activists who work in the shop. But the least interested men are generally able to escape such exposure.

At the other extreme the relations among men on the job in the small print shops are highly limited by the small number of men working. Men in the small shops should constitute potentially the very best kind of captive audience for stimulation and proselytizing by union activists.[14] But the earlier findings and analysis suggest why small shops so rarely are successfully converted into captive audiences by and for political activists. For one thing, there are relatively few activists in the small

---

14. A very few of the small shops do in fact seem to constitute such a captive audience for a political activist, who usually is the shop chapel chairman. As we see in the table below, where the chapel chairman of a small shop is politically active, he may be able to drastically influence the men in his shop, since he can reach them so easily and frequently in his role as chairman and activist.

Table—Influence of Active Chapel Chairmen (Small-Shop Men Only)

Political Participation of Men in the Shop	Active Chairman	Inactive Chairman
Active	46	18
Inactive	54	82
N	(26)	(85)

No such relationship would be expected, nor is it found, in the large shops, where the level of activity of the chairman is no indicator of the political environment to which the large-shop men are exposed.

shops, and none at all in most of them. Secondly, as we have also noted, the highly involuntary nature of the small-shop men's on-the-job relations tends to prevent them from ripening into the closer kind of relations that can include union politics as part of its content. Men in the small shops who have the casual occupational friendships with one another that are found in workshops and offices everywhere tend to resist the introduction of the potentially divisive issues of union politics.

Social relations among printers in the medium-sized shops in some ways resemble those in the printers' clubs. In the medium-sized shops there are enough men available so that printers can often find men on the job with whom they can develop close friendships. Moreover, there are enough activists in the shop to constitute an important source of political knowledge and stimulation. These shops, and the printers clubs they resemble, constitute captive audiences for political activists. In the small shops a potential captive audience exists, but there is seldom any active partisan in the shop to try to capture it, while the very heterogeneity of the audience makes it tend to resist the introduction of union politics. In the larger shops there are partisans aplenty, but they may have difficulty in capturing the audience—that is, in penetrating the networks of social relations formed by the apolitical. In the medium-sized shops and the printers' clubs, where everyone knows everyone else, it is difficult for even the most politically apathetic man to completely insulate himself from contact with the more active men in his shop; or looking at it from the other side, the active men can more easily reach all the men in the shop or club. In these two kinds of contexts there is sufficient range for social relationships to permit them to develop into closer friendships, while at the same time there is a limit to the degree to which individuals can restrict their relationships with others like themselves. It is in these contexts, where social relations are in party free and voluntary and in part limited, that union activists can reach down farthest into the hard core of politically uninterested men.[15]

---

15. Further evidence for this is provided in the following table, which shows the proportions of politically insensitive men in different-sized shops who know an active party man personally.

Table—Size of Shop, and Personal Acquaintance with Active Party Men,
of Men Low in Ideological Sensitivity

Low IS Men Who Know Personally An Active Prog or Ind.,%	SHOP SIZE					
	400+	200-400	100-200	30-100	10-30	3-10
Both Prog and Ind.	38	55	64	36	36	5
Prog or Ind.	16	28	..	14	16	24
Neither	46	17	36	50	48	71
N	(13)	(18)	(11)	(22)	(33)	(21)

Since these men are little motivated to seek out active party men, the fact that a much larger proportion of those of them that work in medium (as compared with large and small) shops know an active partisan supports our analysis of the nature of interpersonal relations in different union contexts.

Union Politics in Operation: Leadership and the Legitimacy of Opposition

CHAPTER 10

Leadership in a Two-Party Union

I: Requirements of the System

IN ATTEMPTING TO EXPLAIN the persistence of an institutionalized two-party system in the ITU, we have up to now concentrated on the printers' occupational community and on their social relations inside the shops. We have shown how the social relations between printers, formal and informal, on and off the job, tend to involve members in the political life of their union. The nominally apolitical printers' clubs, chapel organizations, and informal social groups create an informed and interested rank and file. But this is only one of the requirements of a democratic political system. A democratic political system also requires leaders—leaders who have independent sources of power, independent bases of status, independent channels of communication through which ideas bearing on union affairs and politics can flow. Democratic politics requires that the opposition be strong enough to successfully resist being crushed by any arbitrary action of those in power; in addition, it requires a social atmosphere in which opposition is considered legitimate and not properly the target for repressive administrative action.

Many of the same elements in the union and industry that create an informed and interested rank and file also contribute to the security and effectiveness of the organized opposition. In a sense they thus make possible the democratic political processes into which printers are drawn in all the ways we have described. Just how the structural and normative conditions necessary for democratic politics have been created and maintained in the ITU is the subject of the next four chapters.

Under what conditions are there likely to be men in a union who are willing, prepared, and able to take an active part in internal organized opposition groups? In the following discussion this question is separated into two parts:

1. What factors tend to increase the *size of the pool* of potential union activists? Under what conditions is there likely to be a relative abundance of men who are at all inclined to be active in union affairs? Under what conditions a shortage?

2. Under what conditions will some of these *potential* activists be enabled to take part in organized opposition groups or parties within a union?

§ Factors Affecting the Number of Potential Union Activists

THE TWO GUIDING QUESTIONS are distinct but not wholly independent: The size of the pool of potential leaders is in some measure affected by the internal political structure of the union and the opportunities it affords potential leaders. Nevertheless, despite the influence of the political structure, it does appear that workers in different industries and occupations vary in their tendency to take active roles in their union. In such unions as the ILGWU there are apparently more opportunities and openings for active union work than there are members who are inclined to fill them. Leaders of the ILGWU report that almost any reasonably capable member who is strongly motivated to secure some union office and is prepared to work for it can gain it, but so few are, that the union administration has to make strenuous efforts to recruit new leadership by conducting leadership schools and by continual exhortation of the membership to play more active roles in the union.

In other unions, which are oligarchic, centrally administered, and without a traditional commitment to industrial and union democracy, the leaders are just as happy that there is relatively little interest among rank-and-file members in gaining union office. There is no leadership "problem" in such unions (which include many of the old-line AFL craft unions) because the scarcity of available positions coincides with apathy on the part of the membership, apathy which is left undisturbed by the incumbent administration since it ensures continued monopoly of leadership.

The ITU differs from both these kinds of unions. In unions like the ILGWU the union organization requires relatively large numbers of first- and second-rank leaders in the shops and scattered locals, but there are relatively few aspirants for these posts. In unions of the second type few aspirants are needed or wanted, and few try to obtain union office. In the ITU many leaders are needed, and they exist in abundance. Why should the pool of potential activists be large in the ITU as compared with other unions? Part of the answer lies in the relatively high rewards of printing as a craft and as a source of status in the larger society. It is not surprising to find a greater abundance of union activists and leaders in those occupations—like music, journalism, acting—whose members consider their occupation an appropriate and rewarding sphere of activity. Similarly, a large proportion of printers, as compared with other manual workers, see their occupation and its institutions as a rewarding area of activity outside working hours. The relatively high level of satisfaction of printers not only helps maintain an active occupational community (which we have seen is one of the structural pillars of union democracy in the ITU) but also helps more directly to retain *within the union* the very men who are most likely to contribute actively to its political life. Job satisfaction works to increase the size of the pool of potential political activists inside the union by slowing the mobility of ambitious and talented men out of the occupation.

High job satisfaction is only one aspect of the printers' status implied in the term "labor aristocracy." For the overwhelming majority of printers the relatively high status of the occupation, the stake they have in it if they hold priority in a steady situation, and its relatively great rewards in income and security all tend to turn attention and aspirations away from the uncertain rewards of other occupations and back toward printing and its union. And it is precisely the most ambitious men, the men who are the most likely to aspire to leadership status in the union, who are thus saved for the union. In other manual occupations the potential leadership is often lost before it ever enters union affairs because of the greater rewards offered by other occupations. As Howe and Widdick write, the UAW "often faces the problem that precisely the men who are the most alert and serious and hence most likely to be active unionists, are also usually most eager to get out of the plants."[1]

In the ITU the "most alert and serious" men are likely to be chapel chairmen, who have, as a group, higher occupational aspirations than do nonchairmen. The chairmen of large shops, from whom the bulk of union leaders and activists is recruited, have the highest occupational

---

1. Howe and Widdick, *The UAW and Walter Reuther*, p. 17.

aspirations of any group.[2] The ambition of the able men finds its outlets in chapel and union office. One former international officer explicitly stated that mobility in the union structure was a conscious adaptation to being stuck as a printer. He had at first spent most of his spare time training for a profession. When he realized he was not going to get there, he shifted to the union as a path of upward mobility:

Once you are a printer, there's no other job you can get except that of union official. . . . I had once intended to go into business for myself, but once I realized that I would always be a printer, I became interested in the possibilities of working for the union.

One local activist further illustrates the point in his reply to the question, Have you ever thought of leaving printing for some other type of work?

Yes, often; but the recompense is not as secure. Maybe family responsibility or lack of initiative is the cause. It's not the dislike of the work motivating me; it's because you're limited economically by the scale and contract —limited that is, if you'd like to do better. The pay isn't bad in our line. I wanted to do a number of things—not too practical—but I wanted to study law. I would like to do organizational work, and I like to write. After thinking it over, I see they are a dime a dozen and not as good pay. I also thought of going into business. I was in my own grocery store for three years during the depression. Things got better in printing and I went back completely to it in '40. Before this I worked in the store days and printing at night. I didn't like dealing with women and the financial returns and the hours weren't as good. I would like to own my own business in the future, but the thing holding me and other boys down is the uncertainty of business, knowing you *do* have a skill. People successful in business usually *have had* to go into it, by accident or other reasons. But when you work 36¼ hours per week and make close to $5600 in the trade, you think ten times before leaving, and ninety-nine out of a hundred don't make the break.

To the question, What kind of business would you like to go into? L replied:

I wouldn't care for a printing plant, but I'd like to be a publisher. . . . Also I like public relations and entertainment. I do it for the union and the party: in fact, I'm putting on the Anniversary Dance and Variety Show for the Prog Club.

2.

Table—Occupation Preferences of Chapel Chairmen and Nonchairmen

	CHAIRMEN		NONCHAIRMEN	
Size of Shop	30+	30—	30+	30—
Percentage preferring white-collar job or profession	49	35	26	28
N	(45)	(46)	(259)	(150)

The indicator of occupational aspirations is the response to the question: Is there any occupation you would like to have other than the one you now have—either in or outside the printing trades?

Given L's abilities and his strong inclination to improve his position, it is very likely that he would have left any less attractive manual occupation at the first opportunity, either to open a small business, or failing that, to enter the lower white-collar world. To a printer these alternatives look much less attractive, and he is thus "saved" for printing and its union. Held to the occupation by its manifest rewards as compared with realistic alternatives, he is by temperament, inclinations, and ability a potential union leader. Given the structure of the ITU, L makes his practical adjustment and exploits the available ways, in chapel and union office and party activity, of using his skills, gaining status, and registering achievement within the institutions of the union's political system.

The ambitious printer can usually look to only two available channels of mobility: shop management or ownership, or leadership in the union. In practice, the option between working for foremanship or seeking union office is largely determined for the ambitious printer by the size of the shop he works in. We have already seen that ambitious men in small shops look to foremanship, while their counterparts in the larger shops, where there is much less chance of becoming foreman, focus their aspirations on chapel posts and union office. Even more striking evidence of this may be found by examining the answers of chapel chairmen to the question, Would you rather be a foreman or a union officer? Two-thirds of the chairmen in shops with more than thirty men, as compared with only a little more than a third of chairmen in smaller shops, indicate a desire for union office.

Table 20—Answers of Chapel Chairmen to "Would You Rather Be a Foreman or a Union Officer?"

	30+	30—
Prefer foreman, %	19	44
Prefer union officer, %	65	37
Neither, %	16	19
N	(43)	(43)

While the size of a shop heavily affects whether an ambitious printer will be oriented towards becoming a union officer or a foreman, it is clear that the most consciously mobile members of the union tend to become active in union politics. In contrast, the scatter of evidence bearing on the union behavior of upward mobile men in other occupations indicates that ambition to secure a higher-status position is related to nonparticipation in union affairs.[3] Thus the attractiveness of

3. See S. M. Lipset and Joan Gordon: "Mobility and Trade Union Membership," in R. Bendix and S. M. Lipset, *Class, Status and Power*, pp. 491-500; see also A. Tannenbaum and R. Kahn, "Participation in Local Unions," forthcoming.

printing as an occupation, the relatively limited chances for mobility within the occupation, and the real opportunity for advancement through union work are among the crucial factors helping to make the body of especially ambitious printers into a group of potential union activists and leaders.

While many men become interested in union politics as a solution for their high-status aspirations, others develop the same union goals as a result of having been "born into" the union. A significant minority of the union's members, 17%, are the sons of printers, while 30% have relatives other than a father in the occupation. Many of the leaders of the ITU are recruited from the ranks of printer families. These men have in common early and prolonged association with printers and their union in their own families, and apparently as a result of these associations come to see the ITU and its institutions as an appropriate and rewarding area in which to invest their leisure time and energies. Some of these men grew up in what amounted to a printer subculture; for example one leader reports:[4] "My stepmother and all her sisters had been printers, and I heard the conversation at home so much that it was just the natural thing to do. Hearing it at home so much made it so that I really didn't know anything else. I don't know how they started in printing. . . . I think it was in their family before them." Still another leader notes: "My stepfather was a very old member of the printers' union. . . . After my mother married him I learned unionism at home."

Union leaders are aware of the influence of printer origins on union involvement, and one young leader, himself the son of a printer, refers to the informal union policy of encouraging and facilitating the entrance into the ITU of boys from printer families.

My father is a pensioner in the union, and it was through him that I got into printing. A lot of fathers in printing are anxious to get their sons into it because it's given them a good living and they would like to see their sons in it. . . . I have three brothers and all four of us started out in printing. . . . My uncle is in printing too. . . . We feel it's highly desirable to have sons of printers, sons of Big Six men, come in. The father can teach his son unionism from the beginning.

For men whose fathers and other close relatives were printers, printing is not simply something they work at for a living, but is the repository of strongly held norms, sentiments, and affective ties. For such

---

4. The senior author can testify to the reality of this subculture from his own experience. As a young boy he was taken by his father to meetings of Big Six. This practice of printers' bringing their children to union meetings continues today. It is another example both of the pride which printers have in their union and of the significance of the union to them as a leisure time activity.

men, union activity is in effect *prescribed* as a legitimate form of leisure-time activity; and to gain leadership status in the course of such activity is, for such men, to gain prestige in the eyes of an important reference group. We would expect a good proportion of men from such origins to become part of the pool of potential union activists almost from the moment they get their union cards, if not earlier in apprentice schools.

The occupational community plays a role analogous to that of printer relatives in the creation of a large pool of potential union activists. Elsewhere (Chapter 5) we have dealt in detail with the nature of the process of activation to union politics through the occupational community. At this point we need only re-emphasize that those printers who become active in printers' organizations acquire norms which define union activity as appropriate and prestigeful. Just as participation in the occupational community increases the union political involvements of the rank and file, so it tends to enlarge the pool of potential union activists from whom the party and union leaders are recruited.

A very different kind of factor making for union activists and leaders is a left political ideology which prescribes active participation in trade unions as part of a general social-political orientation. Mr. —— is a clear example of this kind of ideologically motivated leader. He is active in local political affairs and a former officeholder in a local administration; he has also apparently long held Communist sympathies and uses the jargon of Community Party organizational tactics in describing the formation and liquidation of the Amalgamation Party, which functioned locally as a Communist Party front exploiting the unemployment issue during the thirties.

My first office was chapel chairman [in a small shop] in 1926. I had no interest in [union] parties then. . . . The first [union] party that I joined was the Amalgamation Party in 1932. The Amalgamation Party had begun functioning in 1931 when I attended my first meeting. . . . The Progs were then a reactionary group and didn't become progressive until we moved in and took them over—about 1937-38. This was connected with our period of struggle in the depression and the thirties. We had the goal and the political bug. We became a minority group in the Prog Club, expanded and took it over. We bored from within. The [international] vice-presidency was vacant then. Ralph Wright wanted it and was entitled to it as a Prog man. But we split it up and I was instrumental in this: Elmer Brown was the man we backed. We made a diversion so that our man got in by a slight number. We infiltrated more until more progressives joined, and the reactionary group [in the Prog Club] had to find its political allies elsewhere.

Though today this sounds like a parody of Communist Party primers, the men who spoke it and used its prescriptions had some real success in ITU politics during the thirties. Men with this kind of orientation constitute a tiny fraction of the local membership—at a guess, perhaps 1%—and an even smaller fraction of the international membership. But they are disproportionately active in union politics. Of the thirty-four local union leaders and activists we interviewed intensively, four or five appear to be basically motivated towards union politics through commitments to a social and political ideology which resembles ——'s.

The contribution of a left ideology to the pool of potential activists is one which might be expected to operate in almost any union, and in the ITU it acts as a basic motivation towards union activity quite independently of the characteristics of printing as occupation and industry. Ideology differs in this respect from the influences of the high status of the occupation, of printer origins, and of the occupational community, all of which are factors intimately related to specific characteristics of the printing crafts and industry.

But all of these factors, including a left ideology, operate independently of the ITU's political structure. That is, all of these factors would work to dispose men to be active in the affairs of the union even if the union were not run through the democratic machinery of a two-party system. There is, however, at least one important mechanism operating to increase the pool of potential activists and leaders which is very largely a product of the union's democratic structure: the large number of first- and second-line union posts in chapels and local union committees, which breed union activists by drawing men into the political life of the union. It is not simply the large number of such posts (for this can be matched by the large number of shop stewards needed in other unions) but rather the autonomy of these posts and the high rate of turnover in office which make them an ideal seed bed for union leadership. Both their autonomy and high rate of turnover are consequences of the union's over-all democratic political processes; and insofar as they operate to draw large numbers of men into the active life of the union, and thus increase the size of the potential pool of leaders, they are helping maintain the system of which they are part.

§ Requirements for the Recruitment of Activists to Opposition Groups

THE SEVERAL FACTORS CITED ABOVE—the high status and other rewards of printing as compared with most manual trades, printer family connections, the lively occupational community, a left ideology, and the need to fill many autonomous first-line union posts—all lead printers to consider their union as a legitimate and rewarding sphere of activity and involvement, and thereby tend to increase the number of men who can, under any given circumstances, be drawn into participation in union affairs.[5] But how do potential leaders become actual leaders? What leads some of them to ally themselves with a group which is openly in opposition to the incumbent union administration? The example of the ITU suggests that if a continuing opposition group is to recruit support at all comparable in numbers and strength to that of the incumbents, it is necessary that such support by a union member should not endanger (1) the man's material security nor (2) his security of status.

§ Material Security

INDEPENDENCE IN UNION POLITICS is a luxury that only men with some economic security can afford. The exceptions, the men who willingly suffer marked personal disadvantage by opposing authority for a principle, are rare enough to excite our admiration, but too rare to maintain a going opposition party. Principled opposition may enrich democracy with ideas, ideals, and issues, but economic security for most of the oppositionists is essential to its continuance.

Theoreticians of democratic society have observed that opposition in civil politics bases itself on different parts of a highly differentiated and diffuse economy. Since in classical liberal theory the ownership of property is the base that provides the security to resist political oppression, it is generally argued—as writers from Locke to Hayek have argued—that the preservation of or return to a wide dispersion of ownership of small holdings is necessary for the maintenance of democratic political institutions. The connection between ownership of property and political security (as a factor in political power) is a point of agreement between classical economic theory and Marxist theory, since both see in the economic sphere the central source of social power. For the former it was private property that gave political independence; for the latter it was the relationship of a whole class to the means of production that defined its political role and power. But neither of these traditions gave much thought to the political situation of the property-

---

5. While the factors cited above all affect the motivation of printers to engage in union activity, the relatively high level of formal education among printers makes itself felt in somewhat different fashion, as a broader distribution of the minimum verbal skills necessary for organizational leadership than is found in most trade unions. However, as the level of education rises throughout the population, this distinguishing characteristic of printers as a group is likely to become less important than it has been in the past.

less employee *within his own class organizations*. What may ensure his material security if he expresses and works for his political preferences inside his trade union, for example? The union may protect his job if he engages in civil politics against his employer; but who will protect him from his union administration in his opposition to *it?*

Economic security for an employee is job security. He has it only if he has guarantees that his job tenure is not endangered by his political activities. These guarantees could take the form of civil law or they could be part of the union's own normative system. Let us consider each of these possibilities.

Most civil law bearing on trade unions regulates their relations with other institutions, primarily with business management. Civil law, e.g., the Taft-Hartley Act, has only very tentatively and without much apparent success attempted to intervene in internal disputes in trade unions —between a member and the union administration or between opposing union factions. The civil courts may insist on a union conforming to the appearance of due process; but the courts do not seem interested in passing on either the substance of any given case or on union judicial processes in general. Unions make very little distinction between executive and judicial power and will often assign the judicial function to agents of the administration which is bringing a member up on charges. The member-union relationship remains one largely governed by the law and practice of each union.

What protection can the worker have within his union? The evidence in the ITU suggests that the requisite security for a worker can flow from the general acceptance of a set of "universalistic" norms and rules governing the procedures for gaining and holding job positions, norms and rules which are relatively invulnerable to manipulation by the incumbent administration.

In the ITU the rules which govern getting and holding a situation are based primarily on the universalistic criterion of seniority. The priority system, whose major purpose and manifest function is to protect the worker against management, also functions to provide the ordinary member with job security against a resort to arbitrary and repressive sanctions by the union administration.

We might underline the fact that it is not the *absolute* security of a man's job that affects the likelihood of his supporting opposition groups in union politics. If anything, the unemployed were among the most active political groups in the union during the Great Depression. The crucial question is whether this security can be taken away by the union administration.

In some unions a man gets his job through the union office, and to be out of favor with the administration is to be passed over when jobs are distributed. In other unions, expulsion from the union serves the same purpose. The Taft-Hartley Act has tried to intervene in this latter kind of situation, but where there are no safeguards internal to the union, a man has little practical redress by turning to the courts. He may save his own job, but at so much cost and trouble that the effort involved is almost as much a deterrent to dissenting or oppositionist behavior as the loss of the job itself would be.

In the ITU a man's job is usually obtained directly from the shop. In principle, a man can put his card in at any shop, and he will get a situation in that shop by strict seniority. Actually, as was noted earlier, if a man has good personal relations with the men in a shop it will help him, but these deviations from the universalistic rules are not exploitable by the administration for political purposes. As a matter of fact, the danger that the hiring process will be systematically manipulated for the benefit of one group was at the heart of the political uprising against the Wahnetas, out of which the present party system developed; since then there have been no important changes that would allow the power of job distribution to be used for internal political purposes. Thus in the ITU the combination of strongly held norms and union rules which govern the getting and holding of jobs insulates the job market from administrative manipulation.

§ Security of Status

THE MATERIAL SECURITY that flows from the separation and insulation of the whole system of employment from internal political pressures is the first but not the only prerequisite for the regular recruitment of men to an opposition party in a union. Perhaps as important is what may be called *status security*—psychological security based on the expectation that active opposition to the incumbent administration will not be penalized by a marked loss of prestige and standing in the union. For union activists to have enough status security to support an opposition party, it is desirable: (1) that there not be too great a gap in status between union officers and the rank and file (the breadth of this gap, in turn, depends on the relative social status of the occupation as compared with the status of union officer in the larger social structure); (2) that there be independent sources of status for union leaders outside the union administration.

In almost all unions there is a sharp distinction between the status of the members who work at the trade and those who are officers of the union. In general, the status of officers of local and international unions does not come from their association with their particular trade or industry, but derives from the quite different roles they play in their occupation of "trade-union official." And this status is very much higher, both in the eyes of the general public and of their own rank and file than is the status of almost all working-class occupations. The NORC study of the relative job prestige of different occupations as ranked by a national cross section of the population indicated that "official of an international union" ranks about the same as "proprietors, managers, and officials," and considerably higher than any manual occupation.[6] Howe and Widdick note that in the UAW:

> The status of the union official can be very high; . . . he is usually highly respected by the workers for his presumed superior knowledge and greater articulateness; he earns a larger and more steady income than they do; he does not have to submit to factory discipline and can keep comparatively flexible hours; and he enjoys what is for most Americans a very great privilege and mark of social authority: he can wear "white collar" clothes rather than work clothes.[7]

Each of the grounds on which this deference is accorded the leader —knowledge, skills, income, job control, head instead of hand work— tends to separate the official from the ranks in his style of life, social perspectives, and so forth. But in addition, the status differential they create serves to *justify* the leader's monopolization of power in the union which his position in the union hierarchy only makes *possible*. The familiar self-reinforcing pattern of power and status begins to operate: union office carries with it power, develops skills, supports a middle-class style of life, and is in fact a middle-class occupation. All this makes it easier for the leader to maintain his power, first because he thereby becomes abler, but more important because the high status he is accorded by the rank and file serves to legitimate his authority.

The higher, more secure income, together with the different range of experience that is involved in being a union official—desk work, travel, association with business, government, and other union leaders— provides the basis and substance for styles of life markedly different from that of the men in the shop.[8] At the local level there usually is not a large difference between the official's income and the worker's pay, but still the local officer has a securer income, a better chance to rise within the union structure, and a much pleasanter, more varied, and more rewarding kind of work.

---

6. Cecil C. North and Paul K. Hatt, in Wilson and Kolb, *Sociological Analysis*.
7. Howe and Widdick, *The UAW and Walter Reuther*, p. 257.
8. Michels in his *Political Parties* made this cleavage a central element in his analysis of oligarchy.

The high status of leaders compared to the rank and file in most unions gives the union official a very great stake in the retention of his job, driving him to attempt to reduce in every way the insecurity of his tenure. These efforts, of course, are often directly contrary to the democratic values of the trade-union movement. And it is precisely in unions that the strain between the incumbent's desire for security of status (i.e., of office) and the democratic processes is uniquely great, as a result of the size of the official's status stake in his job and of the nominally democratic character of his organization.

With few exceptions, almost every trade-union official has moved up in the status hierarchy through his own achievements. The occupation of trade-union leader is one of the few of high status which is filled almost wholly by achievement and in which family help plays almost no role. Most high-status positions carry with them some security of tenure once a given position is reached. Democracy, however, implies permanent insecurity for those in governing positions; and the more truly democratic the governing system, the greater the insecurity of the incumbent. Thus every incumbent of a position of high status within a truly democratic system must of necessity anticipate the loss of his position by the operation of normal political processes.

People cannot be expected to accept this insecurity with equanimity. Once high status is achieved, there is usually an interest in protecting and retaining it. This is especially true if the discrepancy is very great between the status of the office held and that of the position one is likely to fall back to upon defeat. This is very much the case for most trade-union officials.

It is quite true that insecurity of tenure is faced by holders of elective public office in any democratic society, but there are important differences between the political situations in the state and in a union. Politicians in democratic societies are generally drawn from what Max Weber termed "dispensable" occupations, such as the legal profession or (more often in Europe than in the United States) journalism.[9] A practitioner is able to leave these occupations for long periods to enter politics, and can return to his occupation without much loss of status or earning power when he loses his elective post. Indeed, far from being penalized by a return to civil life, many former public officials are able to capitalize on the skills and informal relations established while in office.

In contrast, those relatively few trade-union leaders who are defeated after serving in high union office cannot return to a position

---

9. Max Weber, "Politics as a Vocation," in H. H. Gerth and C. Wright Mills, *From Max Weber*, especially pp. 94-99.

which will enable them both to retain their high-status position *and* to continue to be active in union politics. To return to the style of life of the rank and file is too great a change for the defeated union leader; this is why so many union leaders who lose office leave the occupation entirely and either go into management or secure an appointive office in some other union hierarchy.[10]

The absence of an experienced trained cadre of potential leaders in the ranks (which defeated office holders could provide), makes very difficult the maintenance of an active opposition in the ranks which could present alternative sets of leaders and policies at union elections. When all the men of experience in union affairs are either in the administration or out of the union, there is no nucleus of skills, ideas, and reputations around which an opposition can crystallize. The history of the UAW illustrates this pattern: their three former international presidents, a former international secretary-treasurer, and a number of past vice-presidents and other high officials have left the union upon defeat to take jobs in private industry or in other unions. Thus, unions in low-status manual occupations not only lose potential leaders who fail to enter union affairs, as we have noted earlier, but they also often lose experienced leaders who refuse to return to the shops if they can do better outside the occupation.

The internal political consequences of the relatively "flat" stratification system in the ITU are now clear. Its members have an income and status which minimizes the disparity between the perspectives and styles of life of workers and union leaders. The current union scale of journeymen printers in New York (conditions are very similar elsewhere) is approximately $110 a week, with slight variations between the different shifts and the newspaper and commercial shops. During a period of full employment this amounts to nearly $6,000 a year before taxes and union charges. Very many union printers, however, make considerably more than this minimum; many shops pay premiums and bonuses to their more experienced men.[11]

Side by side with the high average wages earned by journeymen printers is the tendency of the union's political system to operate to keep the income differential between workers and union officers small.

Official salaries can be raised only by referendum of the whole membership of the local or international, and the membership persistently refuse to give their officers large or frequent raises. Union officers

---

10. Cf. Lipset, in Berger *et al.*, *Freedom and Social Control*, pp. 92-98.

11. Shop foremen and superintendents, all union men, naturally get much higher wages than the union standard, in some cases up to $10,000 and $12,000 a year.

do make more than working printers, but even that differential is less than it appears, since holding union office in the ITU involves a great many extra expenses which officials in other unions either do not have or else are able to charge off to generous (and frequently unexamined) expense accounts. ITU officers are almost always party men and have to contribute a sizable proportion of their salaries to their party's campaign chest; and when they "have a drink with the boys" they are expected to pick up the tab. Since all expense-account items must appear in the *Typographical Journal*, for international officers, or in the local monthly bulletin, for local officers, it is difficult to pad the expense account to accommodate these necessary political expenses. One respondent reported that a former international vice-president refused to run for re-election because he could not afford the additional expenses that went with the job. Although few union leaders refuse office or leave it for this reason, the fact is that they have very little financial stake in union office, and are that much less inclined to entrench themselves in office to the detriment of the democratic process.

The fact that the incomes of international and local officers cannot support a style of life much different from that of the average member is an important factor, though not the only factor, tending to minimize the cleavage between leaders and led. Printing is a skilled trade with rich traditions and a relatively high status for a manual occupation. Within the trade itself the status of journeyman printer is probably even higher than in the society at large, and working printers themselves have very much the sense of meeting their union officers as status equals, with nothing like the deference paid by most semiskilled workers to their white-collared middle-class union officers.

Moreover, the union officer's work is not always very attractive to the skilled typographer with pride in his craft. Most industrial wage work is physically wearing, monotonous, without much intrinsic meaning or reward for the worker. Printers are not the body of free and unalienated craftsmen that traditionally some of them once were, but they still seem to derive important rewards and gratifications from their work itself. The dull smoldering hatred for the machine, plant, or shop which is characteristic of many wage workers in industrial society is simply not present among printers in any noticeable degree.

The relatively high income, status, and job satisfaction of the printer as compared with ITU leaders (and of trade-union officials generally) introduces an amazing freedom and flexibility into the union's internal political life. Where return to the ranks, either voluntary or upon defeat in an election, involves no great loss in style of life, job rewards, or status, the union officer has very much less of a material and psychological stake in his job. The return of a union official to the ranks is further eased by the absence of any feeling that he has been repudiated, for changes of fortune are frequent in the ITU's two-party system, and defeat is generally by a small margin.[12] Almost invariably, men in the ITU who serve a term in local or international office do return to the ranks upon defeat, fulfillment of a statutory term of office, or voluntary retirement. Over the past twenty years, or as far back as we checked, almost every officer of the ITU and its two largest locals, New York and Chicago, who has left office has returned to the trade, except for a few who have gone on the retirement list of the union.[13] Within the ranks these men form a body of skilled and experienced union activists who engage in union politics outside the formal administrative structure.

The narrowness of the status gap between officers and rank and file in the ITU not only facilitates the flow of men from office back to the ranks, but also affects the relationship between superiors and subordinates in union office. In most unions the wide status differential between leaders and led provides the unity of purpose, the common perspectives, and the disciplinary sanctions and rewards for conformity which help convert a union administration into a political machine. The special interests, activity, and experience of union officials, both on and off the job, create bonds of sentiment, common orientation, and perspective which sharpen the cleavage between officials and rank and file and serve as important cohesive elements within the leadership group. The members of a union officialdom, who share far more in common with each other than with the rank and file, appear to develop a self-consciousness regarding their common interests which finds expression in their use of the organizational machinery for the defense of their individual tenures and group power.

The organizational machinery is most effective in the defense of an incumbent administration when the administration has achieved the partisan discipline of the political machine. And the special privileges and status of the union official as compared with the rank and file can be a potent instrument for the achievement of this partisan discipline. The hold of a union machine on officials does not lie solely in the fact that lower- and middle-level leaders retain their jobs at the pleasure of the top administrative leaders; it is rather the fact that these jobs are so attractive, as compared with work in the shops, that gives the union officeholders their huge stake in their positions, and correlatively makes them dependent upon and subservient to their union superiors.

---

12. For further discussion of this point, see Chap. 11, pp. 233-36.

13. There is no loss in seniority status for men who serve as full-time union officials.

As a corrollary of this fact, a union which draws its members from an occupation whose status is equal to or higher than that of union leader shows less tendency to develop a strong and cohesive administrative political machine. The dictatorial power of leaders of unions of professional workers and artists rarely approaches that of the leaders of unions of manual workers. Similarly, in the ITU, where the personal stake of the union officer or aspirant is so much less than in most unions of manual workers, the administrative machine has a much weaker hold on him. It cannot expect his blind devotion or enforce his single-minded service in defense of the administration's power and tenure. Thus politics in the ITU become far less a matter of machine discipline and far more the free interplay of ideas, issues, and personalities.

But as was noted earlier in this chapter, the security of status that allows union activists to be in opposition is affected not only by the narrowness of the status gap between leaders and men in the shop, but also by the chances of achieving the status associated with union leadership in other ways than through holding a union office. If this is possible, an individual who wants to be active in union affairs is made that much more independent of the incumbent administration.

The relevance to union politics of independent sources of status for potential union activists is pointed up by Michels' analysis of oligarchy. For Michels, the widely observed cleavage between leaders and led in large, nominally democratic organizations, plus the monopoly of status held by the administration and its bureaucratic offices, is a central element underlying the iron law of oligarchy. Michels' analysis of organization is in part a theory of social stratification within large democratic organizations, especially those which draw their members from the working class. If we look at the bases of this stratification system we see that Michels assigns greatest importance to the factor of "position within the formal organizational hierarchy" and treats other variables of stratification, such as power, accorded status, and income, as largely dependent upon and derived from this position within the administrative hierarchy.

Looking at large bureaucratized working-class organizations in general, this is probably an accurate observation. As Michels notes, it is the fact that leaders of conservative and bourgeois parties derive their status in large part from sources *outside* the parties—from their economic position or professional status—that reduces the tendency of these parties to become bureaucratized and develop the administrative discipline and oligarchic control which characterize the working-class organizations. The ITU, which does not conform to the iron law, is a case where power, status, and income are not always nor inevitably dependent upon formal position in an administrative hierarchy, even in a working-class organization. For as we have seen, the chapel and the printers' social organizations break the monopoly of prestige which ordinarily is held by the union administration. Or put in terms of social stratification, these independent structures create alternative sources of status for printers outside the administrative bureaucracy, thus nullifying one of the assumptions underlying Michels' iron law. The chapels and printers' clubs are arenas of activity in which men can gain the status rewards of leadership without accepting the discipline of the administration machine and without being dependent on its approval. In this respect the existence of alternative sources of status in a union operates in similar and parallel fashion to the rough equality of status between working printer and union leader: *Both work to reduce the status stake that union activists have in holding union office, and by reducing that stake reduce the dependency of officials on the incumbent administration and increase the chances of their supporting opposition groups.*

These alternative sources of status have two important characteristics: first, they are autonomous or independent status systems; and second, they are not themselves bureaucratized. The first of these characteristics allows men to acquire the status and prestige of leaders outside the administrative machine; the nonbureaucratic character of these small structures means that status and prestige acquired in them attaches more to the men as persons than to any office they hold in them. Thus a man who is openly opposed to the incumbent union administration can both acquire prestige and leadership status in union-related affairs and *retain* that prestige through the vicissitudes of a career in union politics—in union office and out of it—as a chapel chairman or working at a machine.

CHAPTER 11

Leadership in a
Two-Party Union
II: The System at Work

IN THE LAST CHAPTER we observed that a party system in a trade union requires that there be first a body of men who are inclined to invest their time and energies in union activities, and second, that these men have enough security to engage in these activities outside of and in opposition to the administrative organization. We have shown how these requirements are met in the ITU. But to demonstrate that the fulfillment of these and other requirements make party politics possible does not show us concretely the ways in which potential leaders are brought into the active political life of the union.

The specific channels of leadership recruitment are not themselves determinants of the party system; they are among its consequences, but are in that important class of consequences which also help to maintain the system. Thus in what follows we will take the party system in the ITU as given, and see how it operates to maintain a continual flow of new leadership at all levels of the union where the necessary activities of an internal democratic system are carried on.

Let us examine the careers of two typical union leaders.

Mr. M entered the trade in 1924 and the union in 1929. A man of considerable intelligence, talent, and ambition, he very early looked towards the union as an arena for activity and channel of advancement. He began attending union meetings, became active in his chapel, was elected vice-chairman of a big newspaper chapel in 1933 and chairman in 1937. He became active in local union politics in 1935, when a group of more militant and radical men who appealed especially to the unemployed printers were pushing Elmer Brown for president of Big Six. Brown had worked in the newspaper plant where M was vice-chairman. M by this time had a personal following not only in his own shop but in others where he had worked, and Brown asked for his support. Whether on his own initiative or Brown's, M was one of the organizers of the Nonpartisan Committee, which developed into a local party, supporting Brown and other candidates for local office. M continued active in the NPC, becoming its chairman, until its amalgamation with the local Progressive organization in 1940, after which he continued his activity for the Progs.

After his election as chairman of his newspaper chapel in 1937, M was appointed to the local discipline committee by Brown, then local president, in 1939. M was elected to the local executive committee in 1941 and again in 1943. He was local delegate to several international conventions, ran for the office of local vice-president in 1947 but was defeated, and was appointed to the full-time paid post of local organizer by a Prog president in 1949. He returned to his shop when the Progs were defeated for local office in 1951, but continues active in local union and party affairs.

M has strong leanings toward legal work, and this has constituted an important part of his activities in the union. He has studied union law closely and is an effective advocate on the floor of the union meetings. He has served as counsel for the local union in appeals to the ITU Executive Council, played a judiciary role as member of the local disciplinary committee, which hears and tries members on charges of infraction of union rules, and has also been on the other side of the bar as defense counsel for members, appealing decisions of the union to the local meeting.

The important elements in M's career were his activity in his big newspaper chapel, his knowledge and skill in the use of union law, and his close association with a vigorous group of political activists who had connections and a following throughout the local. Behind the specific activities composing his career lay a strong motivation toward achievement and advancement, and a political ideology which on the one hand defined the union as an appropriate channel for achievement and mobility and on the other hand allowed him to use one of the major local political groups as the vehicle for his aspirations.

M's opposite number in the Independent Party, N, is a very different kind of man, although his union career does not look very different from that of M.

N entered the union in 1925. He very quickly started going to meetings and became union label representative in his chapel almost immediately. He lost interest for several years, and then with the depression again became active in the various chapels he worked in. During the thirties N acted as defense counsel for different men who were up on charges for one reason or another. Very early in his career, in 1926, he joined the Monotype Club, a nominally apolitical subcraft organization of three to four hundred members which looks after the special interests, and especially the job situations, of monotype operators. He became very active in the Monotype Club, was on their board of governors, and was secretary and chairman of several committees. Largely through his friends and connections in the Monotype Club, he became active in the early thirties in the Big Six Liberals, a group which supported candidates for local union office, most of whose members later joined the local Independent Club when it was organized in 1949. N was active in support of one of the candidates in the 1939 election and was chairman or vice-chairman of the several book-and-job chapels he worked in during the forties.

N came to wide prominence in the local during the forties when, as chapel chairman, he attacked what he deemed a recurring violation of union law in another chapel. He had a man go into that shop and then make a complaint. Two successive local presidents, the man he had supported in 1939 and the man who later appointed him local organizer, ruled against him. He fought the case to the ITU Executive Committee on appeal from the local ruling twice, finally gaining a clear-cut victory. An effort to discredit him boomeranged in his favor, and he was elected to the local executive committee in 1947. Since he was not wholly committed to any party, he was appointed to a scale committee by the Progressive local president in 1949. He ran as a lower-case independent for local vice-president in 1949 and lost to the Progressive candidate. N was elected chapel chairman in his shop again in 1950, and local delegate to the ITU convention in 1951. He was invited to join the Independent Club in 1950 and accepted. He lost the club's nomination for local vice-president but was appointed full-time organizer when the Independents won the election.

N is a conservative, soft-spoken man who comes from a printer family and likes to spend his leisure time with his printer friends. His entrance into union political activity was much more the result of social relations and personal pulls than of any strong ideological commitment to union work. The original source of his involvement in important local union affairs was apparently his activity in the Monotype Club, a nominally apolitical craft and social-fraternal organization. The close friends he made in the Monotype Club drew him into a local Independent Club. His important chapel offices apparently came largely as a result of this involvement in local union politics. But chapel office, and the opportunities it gave him to get deeply involved in cases of what he believed to be infractions of union rules in neighboring shops, gave his personal stock in the union a boost at the same time that it stimulated his own political ambitions. Finding it impossible to gain local office as a lower-case independent, N affiliated with the Independents and was rewarded with the union post he held when interviewed.

The union careers of these two men cover the range of personal and organizational activities which, in different combinations and sequences, constitute the career lines of almost all of the active leaders in the union. If we examine the biographies of these and other leaders we find in each some or all of the following kinds of activities, often, though not always, in roughly the sequence in which we list them:

1. Early and regular attendance at local union meetings.
2. Interest and activity in the affairs of the chapel.
3. Speeches from the floor at local meetings.
4. Election to chapel office.
5. Service as "counsel" in behalf of a member, a chapel, or the local in trial proceedings or appeals held under local or International union law.
6. Appointment to minor local union committees or posts.
7. Membership and activity in a union political group or party.
8. Membership and activity in a "nonpolitical" printers' club or organization.
9. Appointment to paid full-time local office—organizer, benefit clerk, etc.—and election as delegate to International conventions.
10. Election to the local executive committee or higher local office.

The career of Mr. M which is sketched above shows all those activities except for membership in a nonpolitical printers' club, while the career of Mr. N included all of these activities at some point or other in his career.

Not all of these various posts and activities are equally important in understanding how the party system recruits leadership. It does not greatly contribute to our understanding of the operation of the union's recruitment machinery to note that after twenty years of varied kinds of union activity, an active party member who desires it can usually count on an appointment to one or another of the local union committees when his party comes to power. The crucial events in the recruitment of union leaders occur at the beginning of an active union career; it is at that point that we can see that the factors which make for a pool of potential activists and the factors which provide the necessary personal security for opposition activity are but the necessary conditions for the recruitment of a union leadership. Let us look more closely at some of the concrete mechanisms through which these underlying conditions are translated into a continual flow of party and union leaders.

§ Attendance at Union Meetings

A PRINTER WITH AN INTEREST in union affairs, with or without ambitions for union office, will ordinarily and most naturally pursue this interest first by attending local union meetings. Meetings of Big Six, held monthly in a large high-school auditorium in downtown Manhattan, are very far from the routine, manipulated, and predetermined local meetings so common in other unions. On the contrary, every event and policy of any importance to printers sooner or later comes to the floor of the Big Six meeting for discussion; these discussions are full and often heated; the presence of an opposition caucus ensures the debate of policy proposals; and often on matters of real consequence there are close floor votes. The meetings, as we note elsewhere, are both consequential and dramatic, and attendance can be quite rewarding to a man with an interest in union affairs and a taste for public debate and organizational politics.

The union meeting provides, among its many functions for the union's political system, a link between the personal ambitions and inclinations of individual men and the union institutions. Regular attendance at these meetings is almost invariably the first step on a career in union affairs. The meeting is the place where a potential leader's private motivations start to become relevant to union politics, not only for the role he plays there, voting and speaking, but also for the larger role of "union active" that he begins to acquire for himself, a role which begins to equip him for further involvement in the union's political system.

Regular union-meeting attendance can by itself bring a man to the attention of established union leaders. And speaking on the floor is one way to begin gaining a reputation outside one's own chapel. Mr O apparently first came to the attention of leaders of both parties in this way.

O got his journeyman's card in 1934 and from the very beginning attended meetings regularly and followed union affairs closely. Very soon he attracted notice by speaking on the floor at a union meeting on the unemployment situation, in a way that earned him, by his own report, "prolonged applause." He became active in his chapel at the same time and learned union law. He was elected secretary of his chapel in 1937 and chairman a year later. In 1939 he was appointed to the book-and-job investigating committee by the then local president, a leader of the faction which later organized the local Independent club. O reports that this appointment came as a great surprise to him and he has no idea why he was chosen, but it seems likely that this was an effort by the conservative group to size up and perhaps gain the support of a promising young activist who was not yet committed. But O didn't bite, although appointed to several trial committees in addition.

In 1950 O was appointed by the then local president, a Progressive, to be chairman of the committee in charge of arrangements to celebrate the Big Six centennial. Up till this time O had not joined either political party though he had received appointive posts from both. But in 1950 O reports that the Progressive leaders told me I was being talked about and insisted they wanted me in there; that they "knew my sympathies were there; and why wasn't I in there? I thought about it and decided that I couldn't sit on the fence if active. Therefore I joined the party to give room for the expression of my opinion." O continues to work in the shop, but is active in Progressive Party and union affairs generally and is very much available for future union posts.

But even Mr. O, who made a speech on the floor of the local meeting earlier in his career than most printers, had to prove himself by gaining chapel office before he became the object of competitive recruitment efforts by the two parties. Some leaders who have a special flair for parliamentary debate keep themselves before the eyes of the membership throughout their careers by frequent speeches on the floor of the meeting. But in most cases, regular attendance at local meetings is more important to a man's political career *indirectly*: by attending meetings regularly a man can demonstrate his union interest to his shop-mates and also gain the special knowledge about current union affairs which enables him to play an active role in his chapel.

A man who exhibits interest in union affairs and a willingness to work in these affairs in his leisure time is valued by union leaders both for the concrete services he can perform and for the political value of his support of the party in his shop. But before the processes of institutionalized recruitment begin to operate, a man must show some evidence of interest in union affairs on his own. He must define *himself* as a union activist before he can be defined by others as a potential leader or political partisan. Regular attendance at local meetings is the first, almost obligatory step in this self-definition.

§ Chapel Office and a Union Career

AN AMBITIOUS MAN who has begun to take an active interest in union affairs can, if he wants, immediately identify with one of the union political parties, begin to do party work, and hope for eventual recognition of some kind as reward for good and faithful party service. This is the ordinary way party workers are recruited into parties which compete for control of the state. But in the ITU the parties have relatively little patronage at their disposal. There are only seven full-time appointive posts available to the President in the local union—four business representatives, a benefit clerk and assistant, and a label representative —and those posts generally go to active party men who themselves have a personal following. The much more common pattern for political activists in the ITU is to seek chapel office on their own *before* affiliating with a political party. The chapel office is the pivot of a union career; rewarding in itself to the union activist in status and experience, it can be gained without organized political support, while equipping him with skills and a following which enhance his value to the parties.

Of the thirty-four union leaders interviewed intensively, only three had never held elective chapel office at any time in their union careers. Two others, who had held elective chapel office, had been lower-case independent (nonparty actives) throughout their union careers. Of the twenty-nine leaders interviewed who had held elected chapel office *and* had been active party men, eighteen had held their first chapel office *before* becoming active in a union party, five apparently became active in party politics before gaining their first chapel office, and for six men the sequence is uncertain or else the man became active in party and chapel almost simultaneously. This pattern, whereby most active union men serve in some chapel office before identifying with a party, seems to be the result of two factors. First, the nominal prohibition against the overt introduction of union politics into chapel affairs, which we have discussed earlier, inhibits the union activist from identifying with a party too early in his career, before he has gained a following in his own chapel. Party membership is associated with partisanship and self-seeking, while chapel office is seen rather as a kind of public service; there is a general sentiment, among rank and file and actives alike, that a man ought to earn the right to be partisan by serving in chapel offices or other nonpolitical posts before making a partisan commitment. Party membership does not appear to hurt a man's candidacy for chapel office if he has a long union career behind him, but it is felt to be inappropriate and narrowly partisan for a young man to make his party commitment before demonstrating his willingness to take on nominally nonpolitical posts.

The second factor behind the chronological priority of chapel office to party membership is that becoming a party member seems to be rather a process of recruitment to the party by other party activists than a man applying for membership on his own initiative. And this recruitment usually takes place after a man has gained chapel office on his own, because it is there that he takes on value for a party as a man with a following, and also there that as chapel officer he begins to come in contact, at chairmen's meetings and other union functions, with the party men who are always on the lookout for new men with a following in the ranks.

We can see this pattern of recruitment of chapel chairmen to the union parties in the careers of the leaders themselves.

P entered the union in 1940 and a few years later became chairman of his shop, a book-and-job shop employing about twenty-five ITU members. Some trouble developed with the shop management, and P turned to the local union administration for help. P reports, "I got the help of the union leadership then, and became quite friendly with it—Bill R [then one of the local organizers] especially." R, in addition to being a local organizer, was one of the leaders of the local Progressive Party organization. P then joined the Progressive Party and became active in its work. P explains his commitment to the party thus: "During that condition in the shop, R was helpful. I promised to be active, attended party meetings, and promised to deliver the [shop] vote if he was helpful. I took assignments after that in the party." The connection was mutually advantageous: P later became member of the executive committee of the local Progressive Club and was also appointed to local union committees.

P's case shows very clearly how the ordinary working relations between local officers and chapel chairmen can be turned into opportunities for getting new blood into the union political parties. In a union with live democratic political institutions, partisan politics tends to permeate all union relations and functions.

Local officers get to see chapel chairmen at monthly chapel chairmen's meetings and in the course of union business. But they also make it their business to get around to the shops as often as they can, and especially at election time. Even while campaigning for votes in the shops, they keep a sharp eye out for chapel chairmen who look like good prospects for recruitment to their party organizations. One local activist, who had long been active in the Independent Party, broke with them when, as he charges, "the leader of the international Independents came to New York and dictated putting on a man to run from New York for an international office without consulting the local party organization." Mr. S continues:

For ten years I didn't go exclusively to either party. I would give donations to both—it didn't obligate me to either. Then during the 1949 campaign, Barrett [the Progressive candidate for local president] came to see me at the shop and asked me as chapel chairman to show him around. He hadn't known me before. . . . I asked him some questions; he looked at me because he thought them good questions. Next thing I knew, when he was elected I was appointed to the political education committee. This functions during the [civil] elections. It recommends candidates for political office outside the union. Right after that I was appointed to the local benefit board. I joined the Progs . . . after I met Barrett and he appointed me to the political education committee. . . . Now I'm on their policy committee, chairman of their membership committee, and God knows what else they'll have me do if I don't say No.

S was an especially attractive recruit: as both a former Independent activist and a chapel chairman, he probably commanded a substantial following in the local. His rapid rise in the party organization also suggests that he is a man of energy and ability. The important thing to note is that his talents were not permanently lost to the political life of the union after his break with the Independents, as they almost certainly would have been in a one-party union. He could continue to be active in his chapel, quite apart from his involvement in party politics, and his post in the chapel eventually provided the circumstances for his re-entry into union politics.

§ The Printers' Clubs and Union Leadership

MANY OF THE LEADERS we interviewed have been members of one or more printers' clubs or organizations at some time during their careers. Club memberships usually help a union career; at the very least, membership in a printers' club whose members are recruited from the whole local widens a man's acquaintance in the union and helps him gain a circle of friends outside his own chapel whom he can count on to actively support him when he runs for union office.

Among the leaders we interviewed, three had been presidents of large city-wide clubs having a hundred or more members. In each of these cases, this club presidency was an essential factor in their political activation, pushing them in different ways into the political life of the union.

For example, D joined the union before the First World War. From the beginning he was interested in union affairs and regularly attended the monthly union meetings, although in these early days he took no active part in discussions on the floor or in union politics. However, he very early became interested in the problems of his subcraft, and a few years after joining the union he helped organize the Monotype Club.[1]

D soon became president of the Monotype Club, and continued in that office for fourteen years. During these years both he and his relations with the union changed in a number of ways: (1) He was gradually drawn more closely into union politics. The administration of the union affected the members of his club, who increasingly looked to him as their spokesman in their relations with union leadership. (2) His

---

1. This club was formed primarily to meet the problem of job placement for the men who operated the monotype machines. Before its formation, shop owners would call the manufacturers of the monotype machine when they wanted to hire a skilled monotypist. Many of the monotype operators had gotten their training in a school run by the manufacturer, who thus could act as intermediary between employers and the operators. Such an arrangement, of course, was vulnerable to all kinds of favoritism and corruption, and the Monotype Club, when formed, took over the function of placing monotype operators in jobs. This is not an official function, since the Monotype Club has no more official status in the union than any other printers' club. Nevertheless, the Club's role at the point of job distribution is an important one for its roughly two hundred members.

role as club president, and as a key man in job procurement for monotype operators, gave him a great deal of prestige and power among the
monotypists, and this prestige carried over among members of other
subcrafts. (3) This prestige among the members was recognized by the
union leaders. (4) While D was gaining a name and a wider prestige
among the membership, he was also acquiring skills of a sort that are
not learned at the monotype machine: administrative and political skills
which earn added prestige among manual workers while being indis-
pensable qualifications for a career in union politics.

In the middle twenties D was appointed a member of the local benefit board by the local president at that time, Leon Rouse. This is a
part-time, unpaid job, but, like all committee jobs in the union, is esteemed by active unionists. The reason Rouse appointed D seems clear:
it was primarily to obtain the support of the monotypists and any others
with whom he had influence. As D notes, "Anyone who was a member
of the benefit board was expected to try to get the local president
elected."

This appointment illustrates one of the "self-maintaining mechanisms"
of a democratic as compared with an oligarchic system. If Rouse had
been more strongly entrenched in office, had not faced an internal organized opposition, and had not needed extra votes wherever he could
find them, he would have had no need to gain the support of men like
D. But the committee jobs the president distributes to club leaders and
chairmen of larger chapels in return for their support enable them to
gain additional union-wide prestige. In the long run, this acts as much
to defeat the incumbent as to help him, for the independent status of
these men means that they can desert him whenever they become dissatisfied with him or his policies.

In the election of 1931 D did become dissatisfied with Rouse, and
because of his independent status did not feel obliged to continue to
support Rouse. As he says, "Conditions had changed. I felt we should
have a change in elective officers to meet the new conditions, just to
see if we couldn't change conditions in the trade—although to be fair,
the administration wasn't responsible for the conditions." (The conditions he speaks of were the unemployment which was growing in 1931.)
By this time, D's club leadership and initial involvement in union politics had made a real political activist out of him. Since then he has
helped organize various local parties, in the thirties and forties, and has
been active in them. At the time we interviewed him, his party was in
office, and he held a full-time appointive office in the local administration.

D did not have to be intensely ambitious for union office (as indeed he was not); his many friends in the union took the initiative in drawing him into union politics. His presidency of the Monotype Club led him directly to a place on the opposition ticket in one local election. D explains how he came to run for vice-president in 1936 very simply: "Well, I was president of the Monotype Club; I had a lot of friends; they would come after me. I was picked because I was president of the Monotype Club and was well known." D's position in the union's social structure and the requirements of leadership of a significant subgroup in the membership provided the social pressure directing him into union politics, an arena into which his personal motivations and aspirations might not have led him by themselves.

If internal politics in the ITU can take the form of an alternation in office or competing union parties, rather than of occasional explosive factional fights leading to the replacement of one entrenched oligarchy by another, it is in part because an opposition in the ITU does not have to gain union office quickly or die. The existence of independent printers' organizations which remain active between elections and are not affected by the outcome of any given union election gives an opposition a source of strength to which it can return time and again for both leadership and rank-and-file support. Thus in the ITU a candidate or an active political group can *lose* a number of union elections and still remain alive, active, recognized, and unintimidated. For example, the various political groups and parties which D supported lost more elections than they won between 1932 and 1945, but neither the defeats of his friends nor his own defeat by a narrow margin when he ran for local vice-president in 1936 drove him out of union politics. And what is true of the printers' club is true also of the autonomous chapels and locals: these independent structures which operate to sustain ITU politics are more stable and longer-lived than any single issue. Without such enduring bases, it is doubtful if an internal opposition which did not win its first election could long survive the concentration of power in the hands of the incumbent administration.

§ The Distribution of Leadership Skills

THE CLASSIC MECHANISMS which Michels identified as guaranteeing and reinforcing the power of an organizational oligarchy over the mass membership are all *monopolies* of one sort or another: monopolies of power, status, channels of communication, money. At various points in our analysis we have noted how in the ITU these monopolies are broken in some fashion—by characteristics of the occupation, through the operation of the occupational community, and through the autonomous chapel and local system.[2]

In most unions one of the principal factors which operate to perpetuate incumbent power is the administration's almost complete monopoly of the chances for learning political and administrative skills. One of the few roles open to a manual worker in which he can learn such skills is that of union leader. In the political life of the nation as a whole, political leaders are recruited mainly from those occupations whose members must learn political skills in order to carry out their occupational role. The legal profession is, of course, the one which best trains its members in such skills, but many business executives also learn political skills: the successful executive must be able to make speeches, secure assent, mediate conflict, and so forth.

If one considers the trade-union movement, it is apparent that the principal school of leadership skills is usually the union administrative and political structure itself. The average worker is rarely if ever called upon to make a speech before a large group, to put his thoughts down in writing, or to organize a group's activities. The monopoly of political skills within the union possessed by union officers is one of the major factors which prevent the effective organization of opposition sentiment within labor organizations.

The one-party union organization may offer mobile office-seeking union members the opportunity to learn organizational skills through formal educational programs or through participation in unpaid voluntary positions. Such aspiring members, however, are usually subjected in the process to a barrage of administration views on economics, politics, and union organization. And since mobility within the union structure requires that the aspirant take over the norms and orientations dominant in the organizations, i.e., those held by the leaders, one would expect that active members—potential leaders—would be receptive to the viewpoint of the administration and tend to develop a loyalty to it as the source of a more interesting and rewarding pattern of life activity.

Aside from his political education or indoctrination, the aspiring leader in most unions has only one place to go if he is to go anywhere, and that is into the administration. Unless some opposition group exists, his political activity has to be within the bounds set by the administration. Union officers, who are often faced with a paucity of skilled and capable prospective subordinate officials owing to the lack of ade-

---

2. We might suggest most broadly that a two-party system within a trade union can exist only if these administrative monopolies are broken; and as we have seen, the system itself, once in operation, helps maintain itself by keeping them broken.

quate means for training them, are usually willing and even anxious to accept capable union activists into the administrative structure.

But the union administration's monopoly over the teaching of political skills is not always complete. Members of a trade union may learn political skills as a consequence of their occupational roles, or through participation in some other organization in which they are given the opportunity or are required to learn political skills. For example, actors must learn to deliver speeches effectively, and observers of the membership meetings of Actor's Equity report that there is a high degree of membership participation in discussion, as well as a long history of internal political diversity.

The average manual worker who belongs to a union, however, does not gain such abilities through his job, and research studies clearly indicate that he does not tend to belong to formal organizations outside of the union. There are, however, at least two organizations which have contributed to the training of workers in political skills: churches and radical political parties. In the United States and Great Britain many workers belong to churches whose membership is predominantly working class and whose lay leaders or ministers are themselves workers. Observers of the British labor movement have pointed to the fact that many of the early leaders of British trade unions and labor political groups were men who first served as officers or Sunday-school teachers in the Methodist or other nonconformist churches.[3] In the United States many of the early leaders of the United Automobile Workers, which had a large membership from the South, were men who had been active in Southern sects. Today the Catholic Church, through the Association of Catholic Trade Unionists, and Catholic labor schools, seeks to train Catholic workers in the skills of oratory, parliamentary procedures, organization, and administration. In situations in which Catholics as a group wish to fight the incumbent leadership, Catholics trained in these church groups often form the active core of opposition groups.

On the other side, left-wing political parties such as the Communists and Socialists have contributed a large number of the labor leaders of America. Workers who join such parties are trained, formally or infor-

---

3. "The training in self-expression and in the filling of offices and the control of public affairs which these [Methodist] Societies provided for a great host of working men and women was invaluable as a preparation for industrial combination and for the future work of Trade Unionism. The Dissenting Chapel and the Methodist Society were the pioneer forms of the later self-governing labour organizations, and they became the nurseries of popular aspirations after place and power in civic and national government."—A. D. Belden, *George Whitefield the Awakener*, pp. 247 ff.

mally, in the skills of organization and communication and become potential union leaders. During the late thirties, John L. Lewis, though a political conservative, was forced to hire many Socialists and Communists as CIO organizers because these parties were the only reservoirs of organizing talent and skill that were friendly to the labor movement. One of the assets which has enabled Communists to gain support from non-Communists within the labor movement is the fact that in many unions Communists, though a small minority, are the only persons not in the union administration who know how to organize an effective opposition.

One key, then, to the potential for an active internal political life of any organization is the availability of trained political participants within the organization. This in turn will vary with the status of the occupation, with the extent that union membership overlaps membership in other groups which may provide independent sources of leadership training, and with the opportunities for gaining leadership skills within the union and occupational institutions.

The ITU has a number of leaders who have had leadership training in various extra-union movements and organizations; for example, a striking number of Independent leaders in New York have had training in Catholic labor schools. But in contrast with most unions, whose members can get this leadership training only within the union administration or outside the union, printers are afforded a variety of opportunities to gain the political and administrative skills of leadership in union-connected activities which are not controlled by the union administration. The leaders whose careers we have sketched above give ample evidence of these opportunities: chapel office, local meetings, printers' clubs, the party organizations, all are training grounds where the skills of leadership are acquired. In these arenas, men learn to speak in public, they learn the political arts of persuasion and compromise, and the administrative skills of chairing meetings, disbursing funds, and running organizations. Not one of the printers whom we interviewed gained his training in union leadership solely through holding union office.

It would be difficult to overestimate the importance for a continuing democratic system of a wide distribution of political skills among the membership. In many unions the only men who know parliamentary procedure, union law, or how to write a political campaign leaflet are the few who occupy the union offices. In the ITU there is hardly a chapel, local, or union committee meeting at which the chairman does not face men in the audience whose knowledge of union law and skill in parliamentary debate match his own. Many of the men he addresses have chaired meetings of their own; some have occupied the very posts the speakers currently hold. In a system which provides for regular turnover in office, union office itself becomes a training ground for opposition activists and leaders.

This last point directs our attention to the phenomenon of "leadership in the ranks"; and this is a question not only of leadership skills but also of leadership status. An effective opposition requires not only that there be men outside of the administration who are equipped with the skills needed to play the role of opposition leaders, but also that these men be defined by their fellow members as legitimate leaders and spokesmen. We have seen how in the ITU a varity of arenas and channels exist in and through which men can gain the status of union leaders outside the administrative machine. It is worthwhile looking briefly at the way in which men who have held union office are able to retain their status as union leaders on their return to the ranks, and the consequences this has for the union's political system.

§ Retaining Leadership Status

ONE OF THE PRIME CONSIDERATIONS of bureaucracy as a type of social organization is that the authority, power, and prestige which it disposes inhere in the offices which make it up, and not in the persons of the incumbents of those offices. To the extent that union administrations are bureaucratized (and many of them are increasingly so) men who are active in them, except for the top leaders, have little personal reputation or prestige apart from that derived from the union office that they may hold at any given moment. This fact makes union officeholders unlikely recruits for an opposition group or for any kind of independent action.[4]

In the ITU, by way of contrast, the union administration is not highly bureaucratized. We have already spoken of the rarity of full-time appointive posts. The thirty-four local leaders we interviewed have all, without exception, run for and been elected to some chapel or union office during their careers. Uniformly they think of themselves as men with personal influence and a following among the membership rather than as loyal followers of some popular union leader. Many of them have held appointive union office, but in almost all of these cases it is apparent that they were appointed as a *political* act—as a recognition of their

---

4. The converse of this is recognized by union leaders, who have observed that the most popular first-line shop stewards and committeemen are, by virtue of their *personal* following, more likely to break bureaucratic discipline and behave independently, or as it is put, "irresponsibly." See Golden and Ruttenberg, *The Dynamics of Industrial Democracy*, p. 19.

following in the rank and file and as an effort to gain that additional support for the party holding union office.

The fact that ITU activists and leaders at every level are political men rather than bureaucrats, men who look to the ranks and to rank-and-file organizations like the chapels, printers' clubs and party organizations rather than to their hierarchical superiors, makes *leaving* union office a completely different experience for men in the ITU from what it is in most other unions, aside from the fact, already discussed in the previous chapter, that there is not a great status gap between the role of union leader and working printer. Reports by union leaders of how it feels to return to the shops after leaving union office indicate that most of them continue to function as union leaders—as opinion leaders, as prestigeful and influential and knowledgeable men to whom other men in their shops bring questions about union affairs and politics. One man who returned to the shop after holding full-time union office for seven straight years reports:

When I went back to the trade the fellows would come to me asking questions. Even when I was out of office they kept asking me questions. They came to me instead of the [chapel] chairman. I asked them, "Why come to me?" but they did, and I always helped them. All in all, it wasn't such a big letdown. I liked the work on the monotype machine. It's a great pleasure to know you're doing a good job. While I was out of office we organized the Independent Party and we had a meeting every week, and I only missed one meeting since we started.

The transition from union office to work in the shops was immeasurably eased and cushioned for this man, as it is for most ITU leaders, by his continued enjoyment of the essentials of leadership status—the respect and deference accorded him by other printers, both in his own shop and outside it, together with continued opportunity to exercise power, through informal influence leadership and more formally through chapel office and leadership in the opposition party organization.

While holding union office in the ITU almost always increases a leader's stature in the eyes of the rank and file, it is a stature that a man can substantially carry back with him into the ranks. The fact that the activists' status in the shops is so closely bound up with their informal advisory and opinion leadership functions suggests that other members continue to defer to them primarily on the basis of their personal reputations as men active in and familiar with union affairs. And their continuing activities in union affairs in opposition provide continual reinforcement for their leadership status in the shops. Another leader notes: "Even after a man leaves office, he is looked up to, he has something, he's respected as an enlightened person. Although I have no office now, if the question of [union] law comes up they say, 'We'll hear what M has to say,' and my contention carries. I give 'em the case, why it happened, why the law was enacted." M can "give 'em the case, why it happened, why the law was enacted" because he continues to remain "up on things" through his continued activity in his party organization; it is through continued participation in the more formal arenas of union activity outside the local administration that the leader in the shop continues to earn the deference he is accorded by the men in his shop.

But it is not just in their own shops that ex-union officers continue to enjoy the status of leaders. The monthly union meeting is a recurring opportunity for active members of the party out of power to fill the leadership roles associated with their status. Members of the opposition party usually sit together on one side of the large school auditorium where local meetings are held. Its members usually caucus before the meetings to work out party strategy on the agenda items. Ex-officers play a prominent part in the spirited debates on matters of policy; the power they derive from leadership of their own party, their following among the membership, and their special competence derived from past offices they have held give them a special status in the debates. This status is recognized by the incumbents, who in many ways acknowledge the legitimacy of their status and behavior. This special recognition is part of the continuing rewards of leadership status to men who do not hold any union office.

Thus leaders out of office continue to be leaders of their own parties, where they continue to deal with much the same problems that they handled while in office: formulating party policy on issues, preparing for or engaging in the yearly election campaigns for local or international office, choosing party slates and mending political fences—all the variety of tasks and problems associated with the political game. One man, currently on the executive board of the local Prog organization, said that leaving office didn't bother him:

Being a club [i.e., local party] officer, you still have work and things to do—always something to do, letters and circulars. I have written many circulars to apprise the membership [of given issues] and letters to and from other locals for general information. Also political circulars for candidates, a résumé of the individual, etc. [Did other men regard you differently after leaving office?] No, not that I could readily see. Many times someone may seek me out for information and counsel, and if I can help him I do so—on procedures, etc. During the course of everyday life there isn't a night when someone doesn't come over to me for something. I have to explain to them their requirements or rights or what to do or supply general information. Something is always going on to keep your interest.

We may contrast with all this A. J. Muste's description of those infrequent cases where a defeated union official in a factional fight returns to the shop.

The defeated ex-official will find the great mass of his fellow workers, including most of those who vilified him for sticking to his job in the union, regarding his return to the shop or mine as a humiliation and taking good care to make him feel this. He is a man who did not "make good," who "quit under fire"; there must be a nigger in the woodpile, or why should he lower himself by a return to the shop? If the circumstances preclude such judgment, then he will probably be suspected of working at the trade and staying in the union in order to make things unpleasant for the man elected to replace him and in order to build up a following for himself again among the rank and file.[5]

In the ITU, where turnover in office is frequent and part of the natural order of things, defeat in election and return to the shop is *not* viewed as a humiliation. And whereas in other unions a return to the shop and an effort "to build up a following again among the rank and file" is viewed as suspect, as self-seeking and divisive, *the same behavior* is reported by ITU rank-and-filers and leaders with pride and approval.

Printers are not so different from other workers that they spontaneously arrive at wholly different appraisals of the same leadership behavior. The difference lies in the nature of the differing political institutions within which leaders play their different roles, in office and out. Whereas ex-officials in the ranks of most unions are potential sources of division and a threat to the normal workings of one-party government, in the ITU the ambitions of leaders in the ranks and their quarrels with successors in office are harnessed to an institutionalized two-party system and are hedged around with norms and rules which make competitiveness and striving elements in a democratic political process.

The return of union officers to the shop has, as we have noted, many functions for internal democracy, not least of which is the creation and maintenance of an informed body of men in the shops who are able and qualified to comment critically on the behavior of the union administration. The existence of such a body of men in the shops is of great importance to the maintenance of the union's political system; in addition, the fact that they can continue to play this leadership role, both in and outside their shops, reduces their stake in union office and greatly increases their freedom to oppose the incumbent administration.

5. A. J. Muste: "Factional Fights in Trade Unions," in J. B. S. Hardman (ed.), *American Labor Dynamics*, New York, Harcourt, Brace and Company, Inc., 1928, p. 341.

§ Conclusion

AN OPPOSITION PARTY in a trade union, as anywhere else, is composed of men—men who publicly declare their opposition to the incumbent administration and their intention to dislodge the incumbents from office. Thus one requirement for the existence of an organized opposition is that there be such men who are willing, prepared, and able to behave like union oppositionists. The question to which the first of these two chapters on leadership addressed itself was: Under what conditions are such men likely to be found in a trade union? We answered this by indicating, first, that there must be a pool of men in the union who could under any circumstances be drawn into activity in union affairs; second, that before any substantial portion of such a pool of potential union activists can be drawn into an organized internal opposition party, it must be clear that such activity does not threaten a member's material security or his personal status.

In the present chapter we have been looking more closely at the actual patterns of leadership recruitment and behavior in the ITU. We have seen how the institutional structure of the union and occupation heavily affects the ways men gain leadership status within it; and conversely, how the patterns of leadership behavior contribute to the maintenance of the union's political structure.

At the heart of the difference between the political systems of most unions and the one we have been looking at throughout this book is the *legitimacy* of the organized opposition in the ITU. A continuing party system requires that there be continuing organized opposition; such opposition, as we have seen in the last two chapters, requires supporters and leaders. But for the opposition to function as a party it also needs to be granted the moral right to exist and to function. In the next two chapters we will look more closely at the sources, nature, and consequences of this moral right, that is, the legitimacy of opposition in the ITU.

CHAPTER 12

The Normative Climate
of ITU Politics:
Legitimacy of Opposition

AN ORGANIZED internal opposition, if it is to function in union politics as a going political *party*, must be accorded legitimacy: that is, its existence as a critical opposition striving to dislodge and replace the incumbent officeholders must be accepted as right and proper both by the men it is striving to dislodge and by some large proportion of the membership. In the absence of this ascription of legitimacy, an opposition group constitutes not a *party* but a *faction*, with characteristics and functions very different from those of a party. In this chapter we will look first at how the absence of a legitimate internal opposition is explained and justified in other unions and private organizations. We will then explore the consequences of the illegitimacy of opposition for the behavior both of dissident groups and incumbent leaderships. With this comparative reference we can then turn to the ITU to see what legitimacy of opposition looks like there, what some of its roots and sources are, and how it affects the union's political system.

§ The Cult of Unity

MANY UNIONS here and abroad have been arenas for factional fights of one sort or another; under especially favorable circumstances, as in the New York local of the Musicians' Union, some of these factional fights have developed some of the characteristics of party competition. But ordinarily, neither rank-and-file union members nor union activists see as necessary or desirable the indefinite prolongation of a state of affairs in which one or more groups of members make it their business to be continually critical of the administration's conduct of union business. This widespread feeling that organized opposition in unions is illegitimate can be traced in part to the combative posture historically forced upon working-class parties and labor organizations by external enemies.

It was in this way that the repression of opposition was justified in a crucial resolution adopted by the Communist Party of the Soviet Union in 1921:

All class-conscious workers must clearly realize the perniciousness and impermissibility of factionalism of any kind, for in practice factionalism inevitably results in weakening team work. At the same time it inevitably leads to intensified and repeated efforts by the enemies of the Party, who have fastened themselves onto it because it is the governing party to widen the cleavage [in the Party] and to use it for counterrevolutionary purposes.[1]

Harry Bridges, in the quotation cited earlier, uses a similar argument to justify one-party rule in the USSR and in his own union. This view of politics in working-class organizations is shared in practice by many non-Communists in and outside the labor movement. In a study of 154 international unions in the United States (substantially all of them), Clyde Summers reports that "two-thirds of the unions have clauses which expressly restrict internal political action, and these clauses reach a wide range of activity—from slandering union officers to issuing circulars to the members."[2] In addition to these specific prohibitions, Summers reports that "'vague and general clauses are readily adaptable, and other specific provisions may be distorted to this end."[3] Philip Taft notes: "Most unions explicitly prohibit the existence of factions, cliques, or political parties organized to discuss union business outside of official meetings as proof of the establishment of a dual or opposition union which can be penalized by expulsion."[4]

---

1. Resolution on party unity, passed by the Tenth Congress of the Communist Party of the Soviet Union, March 1921. See *History of the Communist Party of the Soviet Union*, New York, International Publishers, Inc., 1939, p. 255.

2. Clyde Summers: "Disciplinary Powers of Unions," *Industrial and Labor Relations Review*, 4:513 (July 1950).

3. Summers, *op. cit.*, p. 513.

4. Philip Taft: "Understanding Union Administration," p. 252. Efforts are sometimes made to reconcile actual one-party rule with the democratic norms of the labor movement and the larger society. For example, in the ILGWU, party activity and organization are permitted during the three months directly preceding

Now the dangers to the strength or survival of workers' organizations which lie in internal cleavage are not just bogies created out of whole cloth by Machiavellian union leaders to justify and prolong their own tenure. A view which holds internal political conflict to be illegitimate and impermissible is convenient for such leaders and is fostered by most of them, but their interests and efforts could hardly explain the widespread hold this view has on workers who have no direct stake in the tenure of their leaders. The objective insecurity of workers' organizations and their vulnerability to their enemies have made worker solidarity almost the first law of survival for their various defense organizations. The lesson has been learned often and well: when workers are united they can often improve their collective lot; when they fall to fighting among themselves, their disunity can be exploited to the disadvantage of all of them.

This position finds further support in the Marxian analysis of politics and the class struggle, an analysis implicitly accepted by many trade unionists who repudiate the Marxist label and ideology. This analysis holds that formal political groupings can exist legitimately only on the basis of "real" differences in their material interests. Such "real" differences always exist between different economic classes and may exist between different industrial and occupational groups and between different geographical areas. This view assumes however that union members have the "same basic interests," and thus sees no basis for an institutionalized party system *within* labor organizations.

It is on the basis of this general rationale of "trade-union unity" and "common class interests," insofar as any rationale is sought, that leaders of most American trade unions brand as illegitimate, as "divisive factions," any organized groups within their unions which oppose their policies and challenge their tenure. The view that factions are illegitimate is held not only by those they directly threaten, the incumbent leaders, by by most union members as well. Most members are passive spectators of factional fights in their unions, and they are generally less interested in who wins them than that they be over, in the belief that any stable administration, even a bad one, is preferable to the weakness and disunity that results from a prolonged factional fight. In the absence of rules of the game, the factional fight is generally violent and fought without quarter; it is assumed by both sides that the defeated faction is defeated permanently. One decisive defeat for a faction, whether in organizational

a union election; but since the union administration is in effect a continually organized and functioning party, this restriction actually inhibits only opposition parties and factions.

maneuvering or in an election, is generally fatal: it will rarely be given another chance.

The notion that internal political conflict may be more than an unpleasant interlude in the course of an otherwise stable and settled organizational history, the idea that political conflict may itself have value for the organization within which it is waged and that the conditions under which it may flourish ought to be created and preserved —these sentiments and values, which lie at the heart of Western parliamentary democratic theory, are not widely held in such organizations as trade unions.

§ From Faction to Party

SOME OF THE LARGEST and most progressive unions in the country are led by men whose deepest personal commitments are to the ideals both of political and of industrial democracy. But the unions these men lead do not contain legitimate internal opposition groups.[5] Democracy in a trade union does not arise simply out of the wishes or sentiments of its members or even of its leaders. As in a civil state, democracy, it seems, must have its roots and sources in social structure.

The evidence from the ITU and other trade unions suggests that *an internal opposition gains legitimacy only when it rests on independent and enduring bases of support and power which cannot be destroyed or repressed without seriously weakening the union itself.* The existence of independent and enduring sources of power and support within the union membership, we suggest, is a necessary if not a sufficient condition for the development of legitimate and effective opposition in a trade union.

We might best explore this hypothesis by raising the more general questions: First, under what conditions can an *effective* opposition (that is one capable of taking over the union administration) develop in a union? And second, under what conditions does an effective opposition come to be seen as a *legitimate* one? In summary, the evidence suggests:

(*a*) That effective oppositions in trade unions are rare.

(*b*) That an effective opposition is most likely to arise in a situation where the ordinary concentration of power and status in the hands of the administration has been disrupted.

---

5. Michels in his *Political Parties* analyzed this same contradiction between ideology and behavior in the European labor movement.

(*c*) That such a disruption usually occurs in connection with some organizational crisis.

(*d*) That such organizational crises ordinarily generate factional, i.e., illegitimate, opposition groups, but do not create the kinds of enduring independent sources of power among the members on the basis of which an organized opposition can acquire the legitimacy of a party.

By "crisis" we mean any large disruption of routine in the life of a union: its birth, militant organizing drives, hard-fought strikes, widespread unemployment of its members, and so forth. During such periods the policies of the administration are called into question, and forceful leaders may gain an audience among the relatively large proportion of the membership whose attention has been focused by events on the policies and effectiveness of the union administration. These events engender widespread interest and involvement among the members and often require something approaching mass participation on the part of a membership which in "ordinary" times need do nothing but pay its dues. In such situations the events themselves break through the customary apathy of members and alert them to possible alternative courses of action and leadership. In such a situation men who oppose the administration may gain a large (if transient) support in the ranks that would enable them to dislodge the incumbents.

The history of the UAW furnishes an example of factionalism in a union. During its birth and early struggles a number of leaders arose, each of whom had created a following, and gained a reputation on the basis of his skills and personality: his ability at rough-and-tumble organizing, his oratory, his ability to come up with dramatic and effective ideas and carry them into action. The absence of anything like a stable administration in the early days, and the problems of organization and hard strikes, created a situation in which would-be leaders looked to the rank and file for firmer bases of power and status than the feeble administration was able to dispose through its machinery. Without having yet achieved legitimacy in their relations with management, the men who were in union office were unable to achieve the monopoly of political legitimacy internally that is the prerequisite of oligarchic control. During these years every strike, every organizing campaign provided opportunities for able and ambitious men to gain power and prestige; plants, locals, and even radical political groups provided the base for another set of more or less autonomous leaders and claimants to leadership who looked to the ranks for their mass support.

The stabilization of the internal situation took the form of a series of factional fights, in the course of which the Reuther group gained supremacy. Today Reuther is solidly in the saddle, apparently invulnerable, scarcely challenged by any organized group. Stability in the government of the UAW gives the administration a near monopoly over the sources of power and status in the union. At the same time, since its relations with management are also largely stabilized and routinized, there are few if any opportunities for an aspirant to power to find a base outside the administration hierarchy or to gain significant prestige and reputation except by gaining union office. These can still be attained by able young workers, but they go up *through* the hierarchy and not outside and against it.

The unchallenged supremacy of Reuther and his group is more striking than other entrenched union administrations because of the history of internal struggle and insurgency out of which he arose, and also because of the assumed greater "independence" and militant assertiveness of his followers which some observers saw as ensuring the continuance of a lively internal political life in the UAW.[6] The triumph of administration over politics in the UAW cannot, we believe, be explained as a "sellout" or a decline in the personal toughness of UAW activists; it is rather the absence of *enduring* sources of power among the membership which best explains the disappearance of a continuing opposition.

The kind of support one can attract from the rank and file in a crisis situation is almost always a *transient* support, linked to the specific crisis which has alerted and activated the membership. If a leader is not able to institutionalize his power and status by gaining office, he is likely to find that his strength in the ranks does not survive the crisis in which it was born.

Effective factional challenge is possible so long as a union has not stabilized its relations with its environment—so long, that is, as organizational crises are frequent and recurrent. Even capture of the top administrative posts, as Homer Martin and R. J. Thomas learned, does not ensure permanency of tenure while conditions in the union and industry are so unsettled that they continually generate sources of power and status outside the administration. Conversely, the chances of effective challenge to the incumbents grow slim indeed after a union has entered the stage of "responsible" labor-management relations. The manifest impermanence of factional opposition in American trade unions has led the same observer who hopefully predicted continued internal democracy in the UAW after Reuther's victory to note, less wishfully and more accurately, that "Democracy in the unions is like the democracy

---

6. Cf. C. W. Mills: "Grass Roots Union with Ideas," *Commentary*, 5:240-47 (1946).

of some Latin-American countries, it often proceeds by upsurge and revolution rather than by smoothly operating democratic machinery."[7] But the ITU suggests that while this is true enough as a generalization, "smoothly operating democratic machinery" does sometimes develop even in a trade union.

The crucial distinctions between the kind of internal conflict that made the early years of the UAW so lively and the kind of conflict we see in the ITU is the difference between *faction* and *party*. In a party system, opposition is organized and challenges the incumbent administration continuously, in good times and bad, in times of labor peace and stable relations with management, and in times of struggle and organizational crisis. An opposition party is not in revolt, like a faction. It does not stake all on one or two big issues that stir up the rank and file on the rare occasions of crisis. It does not seek power, as a faction does, solely on the spontaneous but transient support of an undifferentiated mass membership on these occasions of crisis. We have already discussed the structural sources of strength of opposition in the ITU: the autonomous locals, the autonomous chapels, and the independent printers' organizations which make up the printers' occupational community. We have seen how, in its power bases, the party system in the ITU is rooted in the structure of the industry and union and in the social characteristics of the men who work at the trade. But in addition, the parties of the ITU, in contrast to factions, are defined as legitimate. What is the nature and basis of this legitimacy?

§ What Party Leaders Think of the Party System

MOST SIMPLY, the legitimacy of the party system in the ITU shows itself in the approval by most ITU members and leaders of the continuing existence of organized groups of members which work openly to defeat and replace the incumbent international and local administration. No important group or section of the membership is hostile to the party system, nor desires to do away with it.

It is true that about 20% of the members answer in the affirmative to the question, Do you think the union would be better off if both parties were dissolved and elections were held on a non-party basis?[8]

---

7. C. W. Mills, *The New Men of Power*, p. 106.
8. Implicit in the question is the assumption that democratic elections would continue to be held in such an eventuality.

But these sentiments, besides being held by a small minority, are (*a*) not strongly held by many, (*b*) not concentrated in a group or stratum in the union, and (*c*) not organized. As we see in Table 21, from two-thirds to three-quarters of the men in each group or category examined say that the union would *not* be better off if the parties were dissolved.[9]

Table 21—Answers to "Do You Think the Union Would Be Better Off if Both Parties Were Dissolved and Elections Were Held on a Nonparty Basis?"

Class of Respondent	Yes, %	Number
All chairmen	24	91
All nonchairmen	23	408
By degree of political participation:		
High	19	88
Low	25	95
Inactive	24	313
Consistent supporters of:		
Progressive Party	17	138
Independent Party	27	67
Nonpartisan	26	262
Members of a party	16	73
Non-party-members	25	423
By size of shop:		
Over 200	28	168
100-200	19	47
30-100	26	88
10-30	18	117
3-10	23	78

Of course the opinions of the groups differentiated in Table 21 are not all of equal importance to the political life of the union. The sentiments of the union leaders as a group are most important, since they are the men whose activity keeps the party system going, yet whose tenures in union office are permanently jeopardized by the existence of an organized opposition party. Moreover, given the structure of the union, any serious attack on the party system would have to enlist the support of at least a portion of the active leaders of the union. Therefore in our intensive interviews with the leaders of both union parties, we made special efforts to learn what norms and attitudes they held regarding the party system in the ITU.

In a series of probing questions we tried to elicit expression of any deeply held feelings regarding the opposition, feelings that might be contrary to the accepted norm of opposition legitimacy. For example,

9. About 10% of the members cannot even conceive of the possibility of dissolving the parties. They argue that "they would just spring up again under different names," and the history of the parties in the ITU agrees with them.

we asked not only how the leader felt about the party system, but specifically how he felt about the opposing party. We also asked the leaders whether they believed the union would be better off if the other party lost most of its strength. And we asked whether the opposing party ever did anything underhanded or unfair, on the assumption that if a man saw his opponent's behavior as consistently violating the rules of the game, it would be more likely that he already did or would come to see the party system as a whole as illegitimate. Moreover, if a leader cited cases of opposition wrongdoing and illegitimate behavior, we asked if he could think of anything he would like to see banned by union law, as a way of finding out whether he wished to limit the free competition of the democratic arena.

We found among the leaders of the ITU parties a uniform and deep conviction that the party to which they were opposed was "wrong" in its policies or its administration of policy and that their own party "could do a better job." But we also found, when we asked the question, Do you think the union would be better off if the other party lost most of its strength? that twenty-four of the thirty-four party leaders we interviewed gave unqualified answers in the negative.[10] These leaders gave three kinds of reasons for preferring the two-party system: First, democracy in a union, like democracy in the state, is desirable for itself: "It means democracy," says one leader in referring to the union's party system. "It's the natural, normal, healthy, or American thing," says another. Second, an opposition party is a check on "power" or "too much power": "It [the two-party system] keeps you on your toes." "It prevents you from getting a big head and slipping." "You need a watchdog; . . . otherwise you'll forget you're a printer." Third, an opposition party is a source of fresh ideas and leadership: "It's better for the union, as each side brings something new to strengthen the union." "It stimulates leadership." The ease with which arguments were produced indicates that where objective conditions allow the development and survival of a two-party system in a private organization, its leaders can find justifications for internal democracy at least as emotionally and pragmatically compelling as the counterjustifications for oligarchy produced by leaders in one-party organizations.

We do not have here a lip-service norm insulated from daily be-

---

10. This proportion, about 70%, is roughly the same as the proportion of men in our representative sample of Big Six members who did not think the union would be better off "if the parties were dissolved and elections were held on a nonparty basis (see Table 21). If these different ways of eliciting sentiments regarding the legitimacy of the party system are at all comparable, they would support our belief that the distribution of the legitimacy norm is roughly constant throughout the membership of the union.

havior. Nor do we find in most of these leaders a pious affirmation of party democracy existing side by side with attitudes toward the other party which if carried into practice would effectively destroy the party system.[11] There is, however, a minority of leaders who say they would like to see the opposing party effectively weakened, though even these generally qualify their responses by expressing their preference for the two-party system, thus explicitly distinguishing between their attitude to opposition in the abstract—which they find legitimate—and their attitude toward the existing opposing party. Leaders who respond in this way can be deeply committed to the party system while desiring some kind of party realignment. For example, one Independent who wants the Progressives to lose most of their strength makes it clear that in his view "Another party would have to come up to succeed them." But other leaders who verbally approve the party system while withholding tolerance from the opposition they face give one the impression that their approval of an organized opposition is so highly qualified as not to preclude their acceptance of a one-party situation.[12]

The minority of party leaders who nod to the dominant norm regarding two parties while withholding legitimacy from the existing opposing party are men who indicate strong antagonism to the opposition. It is doubtful if the legitimacy norm which they acknowledge acts as much of a restraint on their actual political behavior. These men do not make overt attempts to destroy or repress the opposition less because of their norms or values than because in the political climate of the ITU such efforts would boomerang against their own party and lose it votes at the next election.

The inhibitions which the political process in a democratic organization places on the behavior even of men who reject the legitimacy of

---

11. The phenomenon of lip service given to norms coupled with directly contradictory attitudes and behaviors is discussed by Myrdal in connection with race relations. See G. Myrdal, *An American Dilemma*, pp. 21-23. A list of contradictory norms in a variety of areas which are held simultaneously by Americans is found in R. S. Lynd: *Knowledge for What?* Princeton, N. J., Princeton University Press, 1948, pp. 60-62. For a psychological analysis of the contrast between ideology and real opinion, See T. W. Adorno *et al., The Authoritarian Personality,* New York, Harper & Brothers, 1950, pp. 671-75.

12. Another Independent who would like the Progs gone would want any other opposition group "to be more choosy in their membership selection," leaving vague the conditions an opposition would have to fulfill to gain his tolerance. Of the six Prog leaders interviewed who would like to see the Independents decline in strength, three qualified their views with statements about the desirability of an opposition party for expressing "minority views"; whether tolerance would be withdrawn if the opposition threatened to become a majority party is not clear. One of these Prog leaders, who would "like to see two progressive parties, and not one conservative one as now," indicated the more ideological character of these Prog leaders' reservations concerning the character of an acceptable opposition party.

the system can be seen in the responses of the three leaders interviewed who come out flatly against both the present Independent Party and the two-party system itself. These men, who in practice play the democratic political game as if they believed in it, clearly do not. One man reported that he thought the Independents were "an accident of history." Another leader thought that "two parties are not a [necessary] phenomenon," that "parties for their own sake" were not necessarily good, but that "ideas" were necessary: "If an opposition exists, it exists. If not—no need for it. I wouldn't just form it for itself. When you have an opposition it's a sign something is wrong!" The third man thought the same of opposition parties in other unions: "If a man like Bridges is unopposed, it's a sign he serves the members well."

The rejection of the democratic game by even a few leaders is a threat to democracy out of proportion to the number of leaders holding such views, even when such men are not able to implement their sentiments through repressive action against the opposition. It is not the direct attacks which such men may make on the political system that are most dangerous to it, but rather the fact that by openly repudiating the legitimacy of the opposition they invite the rejection of their own political legitimacy (and that of their party) on the part of their opponents. This observation provides a clue to the corrosive effect that Communists have on trade-union democracy. (It is significant that the three leaders interviewed who were most forthright in their rejection of the desirability of a two-party system were among the most strongly pro-Communist leaders in the union.) Communist ideology does not tolerate the existence of an organized opposition, so that any rise to power by Communists also means an attempt to destroy the opposition. These antidemocratic goals seem to pervade any intraunion dispute to which the Communists are a party. In a number of unions (the ILGWU is a notable and clear example) a merciless fight against an internal Communist faction also spelled the end of democracy in the union. The presence of a strong pro-Communist faction and the bitter internal fight to a finish that its presence often engenders are certainly factors which can destroy the chances of opposing factions developing the legitimacy of competing parties.

In the ITU, however, the Communist issue seems to be largely confined to the New York local, and even there the strength of the Communists and their sympathizers is not so great, either in the Progressive Party or in the membership at large, as to override the union's norms of democracy and the legitimacy of opposition.

§ Relations Between Opposing Party Leaders

THE ASCRIPTION OF LEGITIMACY to the opposing party by party leaders would have little practical significance if at the same time these leaders withheld their tolerance from the men who make up the opposing party's leadership and guide its activities. In a combat organization like a union, the charge of disloyalty, of serving other and prior interests to the detriment of the welfare of the organization, clearly places any member so charged outside the pale of tolerance and justifies the suspension of all rules of the game. Accusations of disloyalty against members put a severe strain on democratic political processes in any political unit, and most especially in trade unions, where party democracy is almost always fragile and where the defensive climate characteristic of fighting organizations is continually re-created by the union's relations with management.[13] Thus it is important supporting evidence for the strength and reality of the legitimacy norm in ITU politics that its parties' leaders, almost without exception, grant that "the other party's leaders are as loyal to the union" as they themselves and their own party's leaders are.

Accepting as right, proper, and desirable the continued existence of the opposing party carries the clear implication that one is prepared to live with that party and its leaders. In fact an orientation toward the opposition as a group or party to be lived with rather than destroyed is the prime distinguishing mark of leaders in a union with a legitimate party system. This orientation affects both their public and private behavior. It affects their public behavior by inhibiting political acts of extreme hostility and repression which would make continued political and administrative relations between the parties impossible. It affects the leaders' private behavior by requiring that at least a minimum of social intercourse and friendly personal relations be maintained among men who have to look forward to dealing with one another personally on a score of union committees in the future conduct of union business.

Some party leaders indicate that they have only minimal relations with opposing leaders beyond those required by union affairs; such relations go little further than the bare conventional gestures of cordiality required by the union norms. One such leader, a Prog, expresses his

---

13. This is one of the reasons why the presence of a strong Communist faction so greatly weakens the chances for the development of a legitimate party system in a trade union. Communists, both by their actions and ideology, are highly vulnerable to charges of disloyalty to non-Communist organizations of which they are part.

feelings regarding social relations with Independent leaders: "I do not visit socially with Indies, and if invited I would not go, but I would not mind having a drink [with them]." This same leader indicates how even extreme antagonism toward individual leaders in the other party is controlled by the norms operating in a party system: "I hate X [an Independent] and he feels the same about me, but we have to act friendly." Another Progressive, who is somewhat less hostile toward the Independents, nevertheless indicates the nature of the minimal social relations with opposing leaders to which he restricts himself. Asked if he has any friends among the Independent leaders, he replies: "Not close friends. There's no one there I'd really call a friend. Some I get along with, I have a drink with, and that I could be friendly with, but not that I could call friends. I don't think they'd consider me [one] either."

Independents as well as Progressives are included among those men who tend to minimize their social relations with the opposition. For these men their union and extraunion political loyalties (examples of the latter are anti-Communism and "progressivism") largely define their interpersonal relations with the opposition within the bounds set by requirements of the democratic political processes.

The democratic game itself requires continuing personal relations among political opponents. And quite apart from the genuine positive sentiments that may be generated by interaction, the norms governing those relationships in the union require at least the outward signs of friendliness. Without these minimal and conventional gestures of amiability, relationships between men of conflicting social and political values and personalities could easily lead to expressions of positive antagonisms which would threaten the continuation of the relationship. Personal relations among opposing party leaders are not wholly a matter between themselves; they are also a matter of importance to their respective party organizations and to the union as a whole. The union norms require rather more evidence of friendliness between opposing party leaders than is required, say, of labor and management representatives who meet periodically across a bargaining table, for much of the relations between opposing party leaders takes place in connection with union business in which they are expected to be able to work together and "cooperate," at least to the extent that any differences between them must not injure their conduct of union business.

While on the one hand at least a minimum of friendliness is required of opposing party leaders in their relations with one another, on the other hand too great an intimacy with leaders of the opposing party would put severe strains on their roles as party leaders. Close friendships between opposing party leaders would involve direct conflicts of loyalty and identification which could hardly be sustained in the small-town atmosphere of a local union where the close friendships of prominent members are public knowledge. Nevertheless, there are men who allow their official relations to engender warmer feelings toward their political opponents. These men are more tolerant of opposition, less rabid in their partisanship, and generally quick to use the term "friend" for leaders in the other party whom they "know" or are "acquainted with" or meet regularly in official relationships.

One old-time Independent describes this kind of orientation toward opposition leaders: "[I have] a lot of friends in the other party—people I work with here or have met in the international. I wouldn't say 'close friends,' though. More like a long-time acquaintanceship. Even Randolph [Progressive international president], if we'd meet on Forty-second Street, we would go in and have a cocktail together."

Several other old-timers in both parties report having such friendships with opposition leaders. These men limit the degree to which they allow their political loyalties and commitments to define and determine their informal interpersonal relationships; conversely, it is among these men that personal ties and loyalties play a role in shaping political affiliations and identifications: this group includes the leaders who have switched parties over personal issues in the past.

Whereas the first group's minimal relations with opposition leaders are governed by a set of social conventions which prevent basic antagonisms from disrupting relations necessary for the conduct of union business, this second group has to develop mechanisms for stabilizing their much friendlier relations with opposition leaders somewhere short of intimacy in order to preserve their political roles as party leaders. One of these mechanisms seems to be the avoidance of discussion of union politics during informal get-togethers with leaders of the other party. "Not mixing business with pleasure" is the formula for this device.[14]

The pattern of drinking together in bars and taverns is a well-established convention within which opposition leaders carry on informal relationships. The highly conventional and traditional character of this pattern allows the more antagonistic leaders who conform to it to maintain the minimal amenities with the opposition in a stylized and emotionally muted form. On the other hand, the same pattern

---

14. While the insulation of political from friendship roles protects each and allows the development of warmer ties among opposition leaders than would otherwise be possible, the exclusion of union politics—an important and central interest to union party leaders—from these relationships usually precludes their developing into such close and intimate friendships as would severely strain the party leaders' roles in the union's political system.

affords the friendlier leaders opportunities for the expression of real camaraderie with their friends on the other side of the political fence under circumstances which do not raise questions about their party loyalties. In both cases, the institutionalized pattern of "having a drink" with the opposition *disciplines personal sentiments to the needs and requirements of the union's political system.*

§ Union Above Party

THE UNION IS FIRST and foremost a defense organization for its members, and nothing, not even a two-party system, would long be tolerated if it threatened to destroy the unity and effectiveness of the organization. The party system in the ITU could hardly exist if it were not for the variety of mechanisms that have developed to permit freedom of opposition without allowing such opposition to destroy the cohesion and effectiveness of the organization.

The legitimacy norms themselves in large part perform this very function. By mitigating the intensity of conflict, by disciplining the behavior of opposition and incumbent alike, they prevent party competition from engendering the deep bitterness among opponents that would make it impossible for them to work together in shop or union committee, to the detriment of the union as a defense organization.

The norms themselves are supported by various patterns of behavior which similarly work to mitigate party competition. We have already noted how party leaders drink together, and maintain at least a minimum level of friendly relations. Moreover, when the party organizations hold social functions, such as an annual dance, it is generally expected that the leaders of the opposition party will attend. (If they do not, they become known as "poor sports," which does not help their vote-getting abilities.) Such attendance, besides having a symbolic value, brings opposing leaders together under convivial circumstances and thus blunts the edge of latent animosities; it also reaffirms their ties as union brothers and subordinates their roles as opposing party leaders.

The same function is served by recurring nonpolitical events, such as blood donor drives and charity campaigns. It is clearly understood that members and leaders of both parties will be represented on the guiding committees for these activities. A good example was the recent celebration of the centennial of the New York local. A very active nonparty man was chairman of the centennial committee with leaders of both parties serving with him.

One significant pattern working in the same direction is the annual memorial meeting for deceased members. All elections, both local and international, take place in May. This is the period in which internal conflict is at its height, partisan feelings run strongest, and tolerance is at its lowest. Just at this point, immediately after the election, instead of holding its regular monthly membership meeting during which antagonisms would likely be further sharpened, the union calls its members together to join in memorial services, in a ceremony eulogizing all departed union brothers, and especially the honored of the union's past—without reference to their party affiliations. While it is often difficult to be precise about the latent functions of a given institution, it requires no great insight to recognize that the May Memorial Service is an ingenious and effective method of reaffirming and reinforcing the solidarity of the union and its members after the strains of the election campaign.

§ Are Legitimacy Norms Independent of the Structural Base?

WE HAVE DESCRIBED the operation of the norm of legitimacy of party opposition in the ITU. But we believe it would be misleading to assign to the norms of legitimacy of opposition an independent and determinative role in the maintenance of the party system in the ITU.[15] Without the diversity of power sources on which it rests, the norm of legitimacy of political opposition could not by itself maintain the party system as a living political process. Challenges and threats from the outside, ideological and personal conflicts fed and sharpened by lively party competition internally, these continually strain the leaders' commitments to the rules of the democratic game. Our interviews with the party leaders suggest that it would not be difficult for many of them to accept repressive behavior directed against their opponents. Some of them, as we have noted, accuse their opponents of breaking the rules of the democratic game, thus implicitly disqualifying them for the protection of the norm. Others affirm their belief in the ideal of opposition, but do not feel any moral obligation to behave with restraint toward the reprehensible "radicals" or "reds" or "reactionaries"

---

15. This same error is made by those who hold friendliness and good communications to be the key to industrial peace and labor-management cooperation. This idealistic bias is basically a failure to recognize that systems of sentiments are elements in mutually interdependent functional systems, and at least as much consequences of other elements in those systems as they are determinants of them.

who actually oppose them. We can easily imagine these same arguments, which are used by leaders in other unions, justifying repression of opposition in the ITU.

The fact that there are relatively few breaches of the rules of the democratic game can be understood only *in part* as resulting from the moral binding power of the norm itself. In large part it can be seen as a practical recognition and accommodation to the political consequences—specifically, the loss of support of large numbers of members and relatively independent activists—that would follow from gross and repeated violations of the rules of the game. And the crucial fact here is *not* that many members would be made indignant by some repressive behavior by their union administration. Leaders of many unions have often braved the resentment of the rank and file to secure organizational power. The crucial difference in the ITU is that there the sentiments, indignation, resentment of the members become *politically effective* by being channeled into collective action through clubs, chapels, and autonomous locals which are not controlled by the union administration. These organizations are capable of autonomous action that an administration cannot ignore or dismiss. The resentment of isolated members facing a union administration which is violating the democratic rights of opposition, if the members allow themselves to feel any resentment, is usually politically irrelevant. In the ITU these sentiments, since they are organized, have consequences which the leaders cannot ignore.

Thus, we see, any administration in the ITU which seriously planned to repress the opposition (and it is doubtful if men with this conscious dedication could dissemble well enough to be elected) would first have to destroy the independent sources of power on which opposition bases itself and through which the membership can make its sentiments politically effective. In civil societies, totalitarian parties have had to do just this—destroy the independent secondary organizations—in order to secure their own power. In the trade unions, union administrations rarely have to be so violently repressive of all autonomous organizations, simply because such independent sources of power rarely exist in and around a union occupation.

We might also note that the repression of independent nominally apolitical organizations made up of the members of a single union is not or would not be easy. For one thing, the repressive legislation of many union constitutions could not easily be used against nominally apolitical organizations. Leaders may argue that factionalism is divisive and should be stamped out, but only in thoroughgoing totalitarian societies can there by any justification for the repression of sports teams, social clubs, and occupational groups. Yet, as we have seen in the preceding chapters, such nominally apolitical organizations do in fact perform a variety of latent political functions for the opposition party and thus help maintain the party system. In the ITU the same is true of the chapel organizations; the autonomy of their leadership, their election by the chapel members, is embedded in the traditions and norms of the union, and is almost required, as we have noted, by the economic and technological organization of the industry into many small and independent units. Thus while the chapels and the occupational community are the two basic pillars supporting organized opposition, they themselves are far less vulnerable to administrative repression than is an opposition party by itself.

§ The Legitimacy of Opposition and Union Law

THE PRECEDING DISCUSSION, which locates the roots of the legitimacy of opposition in the ITU in a specific network of power relationships, is an appropriate introduction to what at first glance appears to be a paradox. We have spoken thus far about the *informal* normative system of the union. What recognition of the legitimacy of internal organized opposition do we find in formal union law? The answer is startling: Not only does ITU law, whether constitution or bylaw, fail to guarantee the right of members to join together to try to elect a candidate or pass a referendum or oppose the incumbents; union law in the ITU flatly and explicitly prohibits such organization. Article XII, Section 1 of the ITU constitution includes an "obligation" to which every member of the union must subscribe on joining. Part of that article reads, "I will belong to no society or combination composed wholly or partly of members of the International Typographical Union, with the intent or purpose to interfere with the trade regulations or influence or control the legislation of this union."[16] But the major political parties in the union, not to mention the many smaller, more transient "combinations," continuously and avowedly aim to "influence or control the legislation of this union."

Today we know only too well that a legal system has effective meaning only in a specific context of power and sentiment. It is abundantly clear that similar laws may perform quite different functions in different social structures. But we are usually reminded of this relationship among law, practice, and social power by the contrast between some democratic constitutions and the dictatorial practice of the rulers of the polity nominally bound by the constitution. The anomaly in the

---

16. *ITU Constitution* (1950 edition), p. 17.

ITU is of just the reverse order. Instead of, as in the USSR, a democratic constitution nominally protecting the rights of organized political opposition together with an actual one-party system, the ITU shows a constitution which formally prohibits organized political opposition, together with an operating two-party system.[17]

It would be easy but erroneous to conclude from the evidence in most trade unions that any potentially repressive clause in a union constitution will effectively secure power in the hands of the administration. In the ITU, where organized opposition exists, the formal prohibition on internal political activity is not only not used as a repressive weapon by the incumbent administration; it is directly contradicted in the praises of the union's party system uttered by union spokesmen on public occasions and in official union publications.

The fact is that the contradiction between the legal prohibition and the formal affirmations of the legitimacy of internal organized opposition is just not felt by the members or leaders to be a contradiction of any significance. Many of the members do not know about this constitutional clause; those who do know about it, when questioned, often smile at the absurdity and just call the constitutional item a dead letter; a very few may go on to give an account of the historical circumstances —the battle against the secret societies—which gave birth to such a sweeping condemnation of internal "combination." The secret societies apparently were a threat to the integrity and cohesiveness of the union, and this justified, in the eyes of the membership of the day, the harshest measures against them. But the current parties are recognized to be not a threat but an element of strength in the union, and the law, which certainly could provide legal justification for proceeding against them, is wholly ignored.

Not quite wholly ignored. In rare cases a single member may attack the party system and in doing so refer to this section of the constitution in support of his position. One such case may be found in the letter column of the official ITU *Journal* in 1940. The circumstances of the occurrence are themselves instructive. At that time the two international parties were almost evenly represented on the international Executive Council and at the convention, and this near balance of power put a

---

17. In this respect most American trade unions are more consistent: they neither formally protect the rights of political opposition in their constitutions, nor do they have them in practice. We have noted earlier that most union constitutions include sections and clauses which proscribe organized internal political activity, in much the same way as does the ITU constitution. In those unions which do not have within their social structures independent sources of power, these clauses help impede or prevent organized opposition activity by *justifying* the repression that the structure of the organization makes possible.

strain on the legislative and administrative procedure of the union. Nothing came of this isolated protest, but we can guess that if this situation in the union government had persisted and had begun to impair the efficiency and effectiveness of the union in its primary task of representing its members in their relations with the employers, more sentiment hostile to the party system might have developed, perhaps crystallizing around the constitutional prohibition on organized politics. But in fact that particular deadlock did not last long.

This last observation suggests an even more general condition for the maintenance of a party system: the security of the political unit in its external environment. It appears that a party system is a luxury that only a relatively secure union can afford. Under external attack the importance of internal unity is so great and so overriding as compared with the issues of internal politics that the call for unity, coupled with the definition of internal opposition as traitorous, makes a loyal and legitimate internal opposition almost impossible.[18]

---

18. The degree to which external dangers affect the chances for internal democracy is probably related to the strength of the union itself. Although there are too few cases to test the hypothesis, we might suggest that a strong union with a loyal membership can maintain its internal democratic processes in situations where a weaker union would come under the control of a strong leader.

CHAPTER 13

Functional Consequences of Legitimacy of Opposition

TO RE-EMPHASIZE AS WE HAVE, at the end of the last chapter, that the legitimacy of opposition in a political unit is ultimately based on the existence of independent sources of power in that unit is *not* to say that the norms which define opposition as legitimate are unimportant. The norms that define opposition as legitimate can only arise when the monopoly of power is broken; but once they exist, they have real consequences for behavior, independent of their origins. Both of the questions we have been asking thus far—What are the determinants of the legitimacy of opposition? and To what degree and by whom are they held?—are distinct from a third question: Given the existence of the norms, what are their consequences for other aspects of the political system? These consequences contribute in many ways to the maintenance of the union's political system.[1]

---

1. In examining the ramified consequences of the legitimacy of organized opposition in the ITU, we may better trace the functional connections if we make some effort to specify the groups or organizations which are affected, perhaps differently, by the existence of legitimate opposition. Provisionally we can identify some of the consequences of the legitimacy of opposition (1) for the opposition group, (2) for the incumbent administration, (3) for the union as a whole, and (4) for the membership at large, the individual members of the rank and file. In the following pages we will focus on the consequences of legitimacy for the survival of the opposition, since, as we have noted, that is the central problem for union democracy. In our discussion, however, the consequences of the legitimacy of the organized opposition for other elements in the system and for the union as a whole will be apparent.

§ Legitimacy and the Survival of Opposition

IF THE LEGITIMACY of opposition guarantees to opposition elementary rights and freedom of action, it does *not* guarantee the opposition's survival. Legitimacy guarantees that the incumbents will not use any and all means at their disposal to crush or repress opposition; it does not guarantee that opposition may not wither away from its own weakness. In chapters to come we will explore in some detail the basis of diversity and division in the ITU. At this point, however, we might note that while the problem of organizational survival still exists for the opposition in the ITU, its legitimacy greatly eases the problem of survival in a number of ways: first and foremost, by sharply limiting the kinds of weapons that can be directed against it; second, by providing it with additional channels of access to the membership; and third, by making it easier for an opposition to recruit members and active partisans.

Thus the administration does not expel members of the opposition party nor does it bring them up on charges before union trial boards for their organized political activities. The principle of opposition legitimacy establishes clear if broad limits on the kinds of verbal and published attack the incumbents can make on the opposition, and on its use of the official union organs for political propaganda. The rules of the democratic game, in the ITU as in American civil politics, permit a candidate to say a great many things about his opponent, but the fact that elections do not settle matters permanently makes the use of outrageous slanders and pure fabrications extremely rare in union campaigns. To a participant the content of campaign literature may appear to be unbridled; to the observer there is noticeable a quality of restraint —a restraint which permits men and political groups to live and work with one another after the election is over.

The ascription of legitimacy to a political opposition guarantees it the elementary right to organize and function. How important this is becomes evident again and again. Only recently a factional fight in the Textile Workers Union, CIO, ended in the defeat of the challengers at a convention, followed by the order from the administration for the defeated faction to disband its organization and cease operating as an organized opposition.[2] In that case the leaders of the losing faction and some of the locals which supported them chose to secede from the union and affiliate with an AFL union rather than comply with the order

---

2. See the *New York Times*, May 16 and June 20, 1952.

to disband. In any case they no longer function as an internal opposition in the union.

In the ITU the opposition is secure in its legitimacy and knows that the attacks directed against it by the incumbents are not aimed at its destruction. Not dominated by the first problem of survival, it is able to direct its energies toward the longer-range and more constructive problem of gaining enough support in the ranks to oust the incumbents at some future election.

§ Legitimacy of Opposition and Access to the Membership

ONE OF THE most significant consequences of the norm of legitimacy of opposition in the ITU is that it gives the opposition right of access to the membership. It is generally recognized that a major source of administrative power in most organizations is the administration's exclusive control over the formal channels of communication with the members. Ordinarily a union administration's control of the union newspaper, local meetings, and international conventions, and its own full-time staff whose members are paid to travel around and talk to local members and leaders, amount to a near monopoly of the channels of communication to the membership. Lazarsfeld and Merton[3] have noted that such monopolization of the channels of communication, with the consequent absence of counterpropaganda, is one of the basic conditions for the effectiveness of propaganda. This condition, as they note, is indigenous to totalitarian states; it is also characteristic of the one-party structure of most labor unions.

Such a monopoly over the internal channels of communications works to reduce the expression of disaffection among the membership, and thus to minimize the political effect of what disaffection there is. On the one hand, the only facts and viewpoints bearing on union matters that are widely available to the membership under such conditions are those disseminated by the administration. Official policy is justified, while alternative proposals or programs, if mentioned at all, are discredited. On the other hand, even if the membership is not convinced of the correctness and efficiency of administration policies and there is widespread discontent, the discontent remains atomized, privatized, or restricted to small politically irrelevant groups, and is not focused and

---

3. P. F. Lazarsfeld and R. K. Merton: "Mass Communication, Popular Taste and Organized Social Action," in Lyman Bryson, *The Communication of Ideas*.

organized behind a single set of alternative proposals. As Philip Taft notes: "In a controversy between an officer and a member or group of members, the advantage is on the whole with officials. . . . The officers control the official organs which can be used to belabor an opponent, to impugn his motives, to question his integrity and competence."[4] Even more frequently, the opposition is ignored altogether, and is unable to provoke any recognition of its existence from the administration.

In some situations the administration's monopoly over the flow of communications is broken by groups outside the union. Although the public press is not ordinarily concerned with the internal structure or political processes of specific trade unions, there are situations in which radical political parties, churches, or ethnic groups, many of whose members are also members of a trade union, use their own channels of communication with the union members to oppose an incumbent administration. Such external support has on occasion played important roles in factional fights in unions. But the very fact that such support is *external* to the union prevents it from establishing its legitimacy as an interested party in union affairs. As a result, such external support cannot be the sole basis of a continuing legitimate internal opposition.

At various points in earlier chapters we have noted the fact that in the ITU, opposition groups have the use of independent channels of communication that are built into the structure of the union and occupation—notably the printers' clubs and informal groups that make up the occupational community, and the autonomous chapel organizations. These basic channels of communication are supplemented by a number of others, of considerable importance in union politics, which are themselves products of the legitimacy of opposition in the ITU. Among these are the party organizations themselves, the use they make of union meetings and regional and international conventions, the printed matter they mail to the membership and get posted on chapel bulletin boards, their members and supporters in the shops, and the visits of their candidates to many of the shops during local and international campaigns. Let us consider a few of these channels.

§ Union Meetings

STUDENTS OF INTERNAL union politics almost invariably observe that "the members don't attend union meetings." Usually the low attendance at union meetings is seen as both symptom and cause of oligarchic con-

---

4. Philip Taft: "Democracy in Trade Unions," *American Economic Review* 36, 2:364 (May 1946).

trol; if only the members would bestir themselves, show some interest, and avail themselves of their union rights, so this argument goes, they could increase the measure of democracy in trade unions.

If we ignore the hortatory tone in these observations and examine efforts to explain the phenomenon of low attendance at meetings, we note first that union attendance is appraised against an implied standard of 100% attendance as the characteristic of some ideal union democracy; second, that the causes of nonattendance are usually located in the members themselves; and third, that it is usually done in clearly tautological fashion. It is the members who are uninterested, more interested in other things, apathetic, and so forth.

It may be more fruitful, before examining the local meeting in the ITU and some of its consequences, to look at this question of membership attendance or nonattendance from another direction. Instead of asking why men do not attend union meetings (a question which follows on the assumption that they should) we might ask, Why do they go when they do, and what kinds of rewards are there for attendance? This will shift our attention to the character of the meeting and to the nature of union government, away from the relatively fruitless business of calling members who do not attend meetings "apathetic."

In the majority of unions which are more or less firmly controlled by their incumbent officers, union meetings offer the ordinary member very little reward for attendance. Apart from special mass meetings called in connection with some crisis, union meetings are dull sessions which deal with matters of routine administration rather than union policy. The ordinary member who attends can hardly feel himself a significant participant in any decision-making process, nor does the meeting itself, as a spectacle, usually possess any interest or human drama.

The presence in a union of a legitimate organized opposition changes the character of the union meeting. First, it increases the relevance of the matters discussed on the floor and the importance of the policy decisions made. Second, and of equal importance, the presence of an organized opposition ensures that a spectator will see and hear a clash of interest and sentiment. Conflict within a democracy not only affects the policy of the political unit, not only has all the positive consequences for the interests of the member or citizen that political theorists have identified; in addition it is interesting in ways that administrative procedures are not. The fact that his presence makes a difference in real issues that come to the floor and the fact that these issues are presented to him in forceful and dramatic ways—largely through spontaneous speech and debate—are both rewards for attendance which bring members to union meetings quite apart from some abstract feeling of a moral obligation to fulfill a democratic duty in painful and tedious fashion.

To get a better idea of who attends union meetings, we can examine the information gathered through our mail questionnaire, which asks about attendance at specific meetings. The questionnaire, as we note elsewhere, was especially concerned with learning about how the men voted in the international union election of May 1952. Preceding that election there had been a local union meeting in February to nominate a slate of international officers (actually to support the nomination of one of the two major party slates) and two meetings in April during the campaign to deal with assorted union matters. Each respondent was asked whether he had attended the February meeting and one or both of the April meetings.

On the basis of this data we can see in Figures 45 and 46 that while the majority of those who by our broad criteria are active participants in union politics do go to the union meetings, and a much smaller proportion of "inactive" members go to meetings, nevertheless there are

Fig. 44—Politically Active and Inactive Men Who Attended Three Specific Local Meetings, Per Cent

Fig. 45—Average of Active and of Inactive Men in Attendance at Any One Meeting, Per Cent*

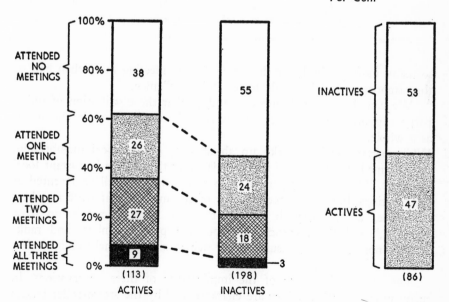

* All those in our random sample who returned the questionnaire.

Fig. 46—Members of Both Union Parties and
Non-Party-Members Who Attended
Three Specific Local Meetings,
Per Cent

Fig. 47—Average Attendants
at Any One Meet-
ing, Party Members
and Non-Party-
Members, Per cent*

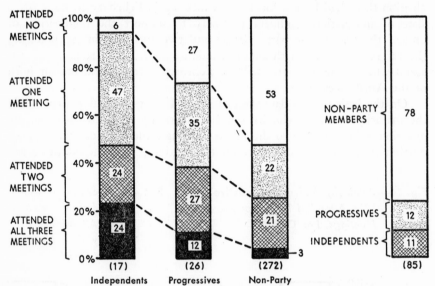

* All those in our random sample who returned the questionaires.

so many more of the latter that at any given meeting more than half of
the attendance will be made up of "inactive" men.

We can also see, in Figures 46 and 47 that the distribution of union
party supporters at the meetings is roughly the same as in the union
as a whole.

While party members make up about 14% of the local membership,
they formed about 23% of the attendance at these three important local
meetings. The opposing parties were about equally well represented at
the meetings, but over three-quarters of the men present were members
of neither union party. It is clear that the meetings are in no sense
"stacked," and the presence of opposition party members and rank-
and-file nonparty men ensures lively debate and genuinely enlightening
sessions.

Let us consider some of the implications of these observations. In
many unions, local meetings are characterized by the steam-roller tactics
of an entrenched and arrogant administration, punctuated from time to

time by the hysteria and violence of bitter factional struggle. Such meetings can function neither as instruments of union democracy nor as channels of communications between political activists and the membership. In the ITU we see most clearly how the legitimacy of opposition enables a union meeting to serve both these functions. Parliamentary rules largely prevail in local meetings: the chair recognizes opponents as well as political supporters; debate is usually thorough; votes, both hand and secret, are promptly and accurately counted, with representatives of the opposing sides doing the counting. The chair often leans over backward to avoid the impression of railroading resolutions or suppressing opposition motions, and any leading opposition spokesman who wants the floor gets it almost automatically. Though the local president, who ordinarily chairs the local meetings, often uses the power of the chair to gain political advantage through all kinds of parliamentary tactics, his maneuvers are almost always within the bounds of parliamentary law, and though they sometimes engender opposition resentment, they almost never earn the bitterness that would be associated with actions felt to be violations of the basic norms governing legitimate political conflict.

It is in such an atmosphere of heated partisan debate and maneuver within the bounds of mutually accepted rules of procedure that issues are raised and discussed. The large numbers of interested but independent members present at any union meeting are thus present at a forum given over largely to the critical discussion of opposing policies and alternative suggestions. These men are exposed to opposition ideas and criticism in ways that are not possible where debate is either suppressed or else carried on in an atmosphere of crisis. Not only do the men themselves come to know the opposition position better by virtue of their attendance at union meetings, but they also serve to carry these arguments and criticisms back into the shops with them, where they provide first hand accounts of the events which occurred at meetings. These accounts, of course, are quite independent of control by the administration.

The character of the local union meetings is part and parcel of the party system in the ITU. But the character of the meeting also works powerfully to strengthen and support the party system out of which it arises. The objective importance, drama, and unpredictability of the proceedings attract a larger steady average attendance than in many other unions. The men who come to debate or to listen are exposed to the opposition arguments, which they then carry back into the shops with them, giving the opposition point of view an additional channel of access to the membership.

We might also remark again in passing how the union meetings support the party system in still another way—by providing an arena where men with aspirations for leadership can gain the prestige and reputation that they need to play leadership roles outside the administrative machine.

In the ITU the union meeting has varied functions—as arena and instrument for making union policy, as forum of debate and criticism of administrative and opposition policies, as a source of status and prestige for union actives and opposition leaders, as a place for the recruitment of opposition actives, and as an independent channel of communications between the opposition and membership. The union meeting under the two-party system is a classic example of a social pattern embodying a set of functional mechanisms which in turn operate to sustain the pattern and the conditions which give rise to it. The international conventions work in many ways almost identically to sustain the party system on the international level.

§ The Written Word

THE UNION MEETING is only one way in which a legitimate opposition can get a hearing from the rank and file. The chapel bulletin board is another. It is not surprising that we find in each print shop a space where official union bulletins and announcements are posted and kept up to date. What is not so common elsewhere is the practice in ITU shops of posting *all* printed material bearing on union affairs, coming from any source whatever in the union, without discrimination as to space or treatment. The opposition party can print campaign leaflets, policy statements, newspapers, or any other kind of propaganda material, mail copies to all the chapel chairmen, and be pretty sure that this material will be posted on the great majority of chapel bulletin boards even by chairmen who support the incumbent administration.

The opposition also reaches the membership through the mails. Here again the legitimacy of the opposition cancels what in other unions (and private organizations more generally) is a big advantage of the incumbent administration: its exclusive possession of the organizational mailing lists and addressograph plates. In the ITU these lists and plates are, as a matter of fair play, available to the opposition party. Apart from supplementing other channels of communication to the working members, direct mailing is almost the only way of reaching the men on the retired list who, while retaining their vote and other union privileges, no longer go to work in the shops. In other unions—e.g., the Musicians—the large body of inactive or retired members, who usually hear about union affairs only from the union administration, form a solid core of automatic administration supporters, probably at least in part because of their isolation from the live current of controversy and criticism that the working member is likely to be exposed to in the shop.

In sharp contrast, the rules of the game that govern party competition in the ITU require that the party out of office be afforded *all* of the opportunities to gain access to the membership with partisan arguments that the incumbent administration possesses. In an interview, a leader of the party then in opposition locally mentioned getting the pensioner mailing list for his party's use in a campaign mailing. When asked why the administration gave it to him, he looked surprised and said, "Well, if they weren't turned over how could we reach the pensioners?" He could not even conceive of a refusal.[5]

The ITU also has its equivalent of the whistle-stop campaign tour. During the three or four weeks preceding an election the candidate takes time off from his job and personally visits as many locals (if a candidate for international office) or shops (if a candidate for local office) as he can. He usually visits the larger locals or shops, for economy of effort, and personally speaks to as many of the men in the shops as is physically possible. This is one of the rights of the opposition candidates as well, under the rules of the game; and the chapel chairman, regardless of his own political preference, conducts all candidates who visit around the shop and introduces them to the men. By and large the owners and managers of print shops have accepted these visits during working hours as part of the business of dealing with the ITU.

The strictness with which the members enforce the norm of equality of access to the membership for both parties is illustrated by an incident which occurred during the local presidential campaign of 1951. Several of our respondents mentioned that one of the reasons why the Progressives received only a minority of the votes in the *Times* chapel in that election was that they held a campaign meeting there immediately after a chapel meeting without having invited the Independent candidates. This was regarded by the members as a violation of the informal election code, which prescribes that the candidates of both parties be invited to campaign meetings held in the shops. The Progressives, who were sensitive to this charge, tried to defend themselves by saying that it was an accident, that the Progressive candidate for local president just happened to come to the *Times* chapel meeting that evening, and that someone thought it would be a good idea if he

---

5. The fact that retired members are exposed to opposition as well as to administration propaganda may help account for the fact that they are not thought, by informed leaders of both parties, to be a voting bloc in any sense.

talked to the men. But apparently that particular violation of the norm earned a swift punishment—loss of votes for the Progressives in that chapel.

The opposition candidates' personal visiting in the shops (along with party rallies, which probably persuade only the persuaded) is one of the few ways through which he can attempt to counter the advantage the incumbent has of having been seen and heard, at union meetings and functions, by a relatively large part of the membership. This is even more important in international elections than locally in Big Six. The absence of any statutory limit on the tenure of an international president allows him to run to succeed himself, and to become, in time, increasingly familiar as he is elected again and again. Locally, the two-term limit on consecutive tenure in the office of local president, the tendency of former local officers to run again, and the activity of opposition leaders at union meetings, all tend to equalize the relative familiarity of the candidates of both parties to the membership.

There is no question that the incumbent party still retains advantages. But the legitimacy of opposition works in many and subtle ways to reduce these advantages, which are elsewhere so often overwhelming and unchallengeable.

§ Is the Union Weakened?

WHAT NOW of the widely held belief that internal party democracy is incompatible with union strength; and that, since the union is primarily an economic defense organization, it must dispense with this luxury?

The members of the ITU provide the best answer to this charge through the clear distinction they make between the union as an institution and the particular sets of leaders who are currently in office. In most one-party unions, it is difficult for members to distinguish in their own minds between the organization and the leader or leaders who have controlled it for decades. If an oligarchic leadership is characterized by corruption, dictatorial practices, lack of concern for the members, or plain inefficiency, one finds that the members are not able to conceive of the organization functioning differently. As Michels pointed out, both the oligarchs and the members tend to identify the organization with the leadership. And the incumbents habitually use the loyalty that exists for the organization as a means of rallying support for themselves. In such organizations an attack on the leadership is widely interpreted as, and often of necessity becomes, an attack on the organization as it exists, and thus does weaken it as a fighting organization.

In a union with a legitimate two-party system, in which turnover in office is the rule, it becomes possible and even necessary to distinguish between the current officeholders and the organization as a whole. Moreover, all contenders for power, since they have objective chances of gaining power, have an interest in maintaining the attachment of all members to the organization. In the ITU all political groups make a fetish of the statement, "The Typographical Union is the best union in the world." The incumbents are accused by the opposition of betraying the traditions of the union, or of weakening it, but the union itself is always praised. In interviews, opposition leaders are almost as anxious to tell an outsider how wonderful the union is as they are to castigate the incumbent officials. The two-party system serves to deflect discontent among members and opposition leaders away from the union itself and toward the party in power. Thus in the ITU discontent works to maintain the party system by ensuring turnover in office, while at the same time serving to strengthen rather than undermine the unity and effectiveness of the union in its relations with management and the state.[6]

---

6. Similar patterns were found in a study of four union locals in the United Rubber Workers and the United Automobile Workers. The local with the greatest amount of internal factionalism had the highest degree of union loyalty. See the forthcoming study, "Participation in Local Unions," by Arnold S. Tannenbaum and Robert Kahn.

The Electoral Process in the ITU: Political Issues and the Vote Decision

CHAPTER 14

Bases of Political
Cleavage in the ITU

UNTIL NOW WE HAVE NOT FACED a rather difficult question: Just what are the bases for political diversity and conflict in the ITU? The union members' work is alike, their pay is essentially the same, there are no real status or prestige differences among them. Yet this group of men supports a thriving, two-party democratic system; differences are strong and continuous, with frequent changes in office.

The membership of the ITU is internally homogeneous and undifferentiated. In this respect it is in sharp contrast with industrial unions, which are composed of workers of many crafts, many status levels, many different interests. And the contrast with civil political systems is just as great. In the politics of the United States the bases of diversity are innumerable. Economic status, religious affiliation, sectional interests, racial or ethnic minority membership are among the most important bases of political groupings in national politics.

Characteristically, party differences in United States politics have their roots in such groups, and much analysis of United States politics focuses on the concordance and conflict between them. Similarly, the factional fights which continually crop up in many unions are often linked to status or craft differences absent in the ITU. These sporadic factional fights are the closest parallel in most unions to the party system in the ITU, yet the diversity which produces them is largely lacking in the ITU.

Thus, on the basis of comparison both with other unions and with the civil politics of the United States, bases for democratic political

(273)

cleavage hardly seem to exist in the ITU. Parties need issues on which to feed, issues which reflect real differences of opinion among the members. Otherwise, as is often the case with much civil politics on the city level, the parties find themselves with no real issues and with apathetic voters who either vote to continue the old administration or fail to vote at all.

All the factors in the ITU we have examined in previous chapters, such as the communication and involvement functions of the clubs and chapels, the nuclear political organization at the chapel level, the independent paths to prestige and leadership afforded club leaders and large chapel leaders—all these are irrelevant if there is nothing to fight over. These factors *support* participation of the members and the party organizations, but in order for real involvement and activity to come about, there must be a basis of disagreement on which these supporting institutions can work. We are so accustomed to the multiple disputes which exist among subgroups in the United States that it seems that cleavages such as these must exist in all organizations; but this is far from so. When an organization (like a union, or the Farm Bureau, or the American Medical Association) is formed explicitly to carry out one set of ends, unity seems the key to success and the normal state of affairs. Just as it is "obvious" that there are many differences and conflicts in a nation like the United States, it is almost as "obvious" that there should be unity in a voluntary organization formed to gain specific ends for its members.[1] And we might expect this to be especially true in a union like the ITU, which is even more homogeneous than most voluntary organizations.

Yet the political division in the ITU persists. Just what is the content of this continuing political division? From what sources either in the structure of the union, in the occupation, or in the backgrounds of the men themselves, does it derive?

In order to answer these questions, there are available various kinds of data: interview data, with information about the individual printer, permitting exploration of the factors which make a printer vote one way rather than another; voting records for locals and for shops; and the printed and remembered records of issues which have been fought out in the union as a whole.

Data on the individual tell the motives or reasons that the individual gives for his voting, as well as of some of the influences on his vote or

---

1. David Truman points out that the interest group's "cohesion will in the long run profoundly affect the extent to which the group is successful in exerting its claims upon other groups in the society."—Truman, *The Governmental Process,* p. 20.

opinion which he himself does not recognize. On the other hand, data concerning campaign issues and the history of ITU politics tell much more about the system as a whole: they show, for example, what policies or questions unite men *within* each opposing group while at the same time producing cleavage *between* opposing groups.

In the present chapter the data which characterize the union as a whole will be examined: the political history, issues of various types, party formations and dissolutions, policies of the parties when in power, and other similar data. We shall concentrate mainly on issues, however, as constituting the most important kind of data on the level of the system as a whole. In Chapter 15 we shall turn to the individual level and explore first the sources of certain stable differences in values or ideology among party leaders, activists, and ordinary union members. Then, taking these differences as given, we shall in Chapter 16 look at the actual voting behavior of men as a function of these individual differences and of various differences in social location. In Chapter 17, we take up the varying roles of local unions in international politics. Throughout the four chapters, we shall continue to focus on the same question: What is the content of political cleavage in the ITU, and what are its sources in the occupation's structure and the men's backgrounds?

Before examining the empirical data, we shall make a few general theoretical statements about political systems. These are to be used merely as *sensitizers* in our examination of the data. They suggest where to look for sources of cleavage, and how to organize our observations in a useful way.

§ The Nature of a Political Unit

PERHAPS THE CRUCIAL defining characteristic of a political unit is this: It *acts* as a unit, making single decisions on questions which affect all its members. In certain areas of behavior a collective decision takes the place of individual ones. The most obvious example of this in a union as a political unit is the single collective bargaining policy which replaces individual bargaining with management by each worker. This is the very basis for formation of a union. The advantages gained from collective decisions in the place of individual ones is one important motive for the formation of political entities generally. In civil society all sorts of voluntary organizations spring up whose members forfeit some part of their individual autonomy to gain collective ends. And civil societies themselves have the same general principle as part of their foundation: the slogan, "United we stand, divided we fall," or its equiva-

lent, has always been a rallying cry for organizing into ever-larger political bodies.

The distinguishing characteristic of a *democratic* political system
is that the collective decision which is to affect all the members is in
turn made, at least nominally, by the members themselves. In a pure
democracy, like the old New England town meetings, the members
themselves make these decisions through debate and vote. In a representative democracy the members can only review periodically, through
referenda and elections, the decisions of their representatives.

In a very simplified form we might picture the political process in
a pure democracy in a simple model (Figure 48).

Fig. 48—A Simple Model of the Political Process

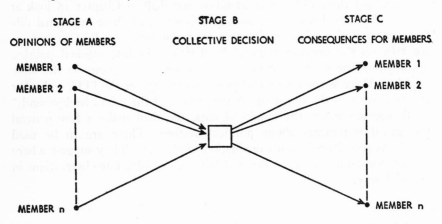

| STAGE A | STAGE B | STAGE C |
| OPINIONS OF MEMBERS | COLLECTIVE DECISION | CONSEQUENCES FOR MEMBERS |

MEMBER 1   MEMBER 1
MEMBER 2   MEMBER 2
MEMBER n   MEMBER n

All this is of course familiar, but its relevance for us is none the less
great. We are looking for sources of cleavage or conflict in the opinions
of the members, that is, in Stage A of Figure 48. These considerations
of the nature of a political unit suggest that the democratic political
process may *generate* its own diversity or cleavage in the following
way: if the decision has different objective consequences for different
members, this may feed back upon their opinions, and influence them.
Either the differential effects of a past decision or the anticipated differential effects of a future decision can feed back from Stage C to Stage A
and affect the opinions of the members.

The first general principle to sensitize us to possible bases of cleavage
in the ITU, then, is this: *If men are in positions such that they will
be differentially affected by policies of the union government, then*

this differential effect is a possible basis of cleavage. The important characteristic of this kind of cleavage is that it derives from the political system itself; it is internally generated by the fact that a political unit must often make a single decision, and is not a result of outside factors making for differences of opinion and sentiment.

We are all familiar with particular cases of this kind of political cleavage. "Interest-group conflict" is the name usually given to differences of this kind. This is perhaps the most common and is certainly the most widely recognized type of political cleavage. Questions involving labor and management, farm subsidies, tariffs, taxes, etc., generate interest-group cleavages in civil politics—cleavages between those who will profit more by one policy and those who will profit more by another. In union politics a good example of this differential effect occurs in wage policies. When there are two wage scales (i.e., two crafts, or two job grades) in the union, a *percentage* wage increase benefits the men with the higher scale, while a *dollars and cents* increase "across the board" favors the lower-paid group. At least two students of trade-union policies have noted this as a basis of cleavage in union politics.[2]

The principle above directs us to one possible basis of cleavage. But men, in addition to looking out rationally for their own individual interests, identify with social objects of all sorts—groups, organizations, values, other persons—and are concerned with *their* interests. In the union a printer may identify with his subcraft, his shop, his local, one of the union political parties, and with the union itself as a whole. When union policies affect these objects, even without directly affecting the man himself, his identification with them will again produce a possible basis of cleavage. For example, a man who is highly identified with his local may oppose a policy which would take away some of the autonomy of the local. Or for men who strongly identify with opposing parties, the differing consequences of an election for their opposing parties will put them into opposition to one another. The point here is that "identification with the party" is simply a special case, like identification with a local, of the general principle. Stated more precisely, this principle for sensitizing us to another possible basis of cleavage is: *If groups, organizations, or individuals with whom members strongly identify are in positions such that they will be differentially affected by policies of the union government, then this differential effect is a possible basis of cleavage among the members who so identify.* This

---

2. Sayles and Strauss in *The Local Union,* p. 43 and elsewhere, make this point. And A. Ross in *Trade Union Wage Policy* (Berkeley, University of California Press, 1948), makes the same point, with a number of elaborations.

is nothing more than the earlier principle coupled with the psychological principle of identification. It is still generated from within the political system, by the political processes themselves.

But these two principles, if taken alone, would lead us to view a printer's vote decision in too simple a fashion. We would be saying in effect that if a man or a group with which he identifies is objectively affected in a certain way, he will respond in a certain way. This neglects the well-known fact that a policy which *objectively* affects two men alike may *subjectively* be seen quite differently. For example, there are no policies in the ITU which objectively affect Jews, Catholics, and Protestants differently. But the effect on themselves and on the union of a decision by the union administration to call a strike is perceived differently by the average Jewish printer, the average Protestant printer, and the average Catholic printer. The differences in these men's cultural backgrounds have left them with quite different internal dispositions: different value systems, different desires, different fears and hopes. Similarly, the consequences of such a move are perceived and evaluated quite differently by those in a politically radical social context and those in a conservative one.

Besides leading him to perceive in his own way the effects of a policy decision on himself, on others, and on the union as a whole, a printer's dispositions and his social context give him different aims and goals for himself and for the union. That is, a printer with radical values will evaluate a decision to call a strike quite otherwise than will a printer with conservative values, not because the strike will objectively affect him differently nor primarily because he perceives the effects differently; his different evaluation will be based on the goals he wants to see the union attain, and the role he thinks it should play in society. Or as another example, two printers might differ strongly on the question whether to demand a pension rather than a wage increase in a contract negotiation, not because one will be objectively helped more by the pension than the other, but because having a pension is more in accordance with one man's goals and aspirations, while a wage increase is more in accordance with the other's goals.

These differentiating elements—that is, a man's internal dispositions and his social context—are of a quite different order from those first discussed. While in the first two principles, cleavage is seen as arising from the political process itself, here we see cleavage arising from sources completely outside the union (such as religious, ethnic, or cultural background, or family needs) or from sources within the union (such as a man's friends, or his experiences in strikes or other union activities which have given him a particular viewpoint). But in either case, these sources of cleavage are external to the political system of the union. These further principles to which we should be sensitized in our examination of the data are, first: *If men have different dispositions, such as different goals, aspirations, and particularly if they have different values, they will (a) perceive the effects of policies differently, and (b) evaluate these effects differently.*

Similar is the "social context" principle: *If men are in social contexts which differ on matters related to union politics, they will (a) perceive the effects of policies differently and (b) evaluate the effects differently.*

These, together with the two earlier principles, constitute our four "sensitizing principles" to guide our treatment of the data. They will aid particularly in examining union issues, but will also be of value in directing the analysis of data on the individual level.

In terms of these sensitizing principles, we may elaborate the political process diagram in Figure 48 to serve as a conceptual model in the analysis (Figure 49).

Figure 49—A Second Model of the Political Process

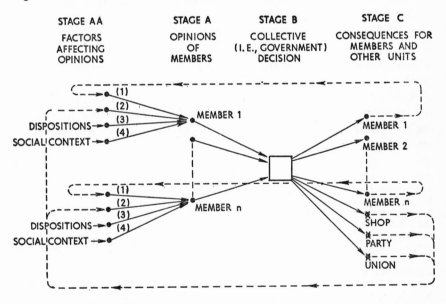

The central problem is to be of the content and sources of cleavage in Stage A, while it is those factors in Stage AA that we have delineated in the four sensitizing principles. As indicated in the diagram, Factors 1

and 2 (corresponding to the first two principles of cleavage set forth earlier) feed back from Stage C of the political process itself, while Factors 3 and 4 arise in other ways.

§ Issues in the ITU

ALIMONERS VS. INDUSTRIALISTS

IN CHAPTER 3 we pointed out that the first important political cleavage in American printers' organizations was between the "alimoners" and the "industrialists." The first group thought that the union should be primarily a benevolent society, formed for the security of its members against sickness or death. The "industrialists," the radical faction of their day, wanted a collective-bargaining instrument to regulate wages for the security of its members against the employer. These two factions existed in many printers' locals until the formation of the ITU in 1850.

In terms of our theoretical orientation, what type of cleavage does this represent, and what are its sources? One group saw as the primary foe sickness, accident, and death. The other saw as its primary foe the employer. These are certainly fundamentally different orientations. Did this early cleavage result simply from a difference in individual values, or did it derive from the self-interest of the alimoners and industrialists? That is, did it derive from the differing dispositions among the men (the third principle stated above) or from differing interests (the first principle)?[3] In the absence of other data, we simply cannot tell. Both possibilities seem plausible. Men who had no desire to organize to combat their employer might have wanted to form a benevolent society, while

---

3. We shall henceforth identify the first principle, which concerns differential objective effects of union policies on those in different positions, as the *self-interest principle*, or the *interest principle* for short. This term has been used in this way in the past, but it has been used in other ways as well, which we must be careful to distinguish. Sociologists like Small, Ratzenhofer, Bentley, MacIver, and others for whom interest was a major concept used the term in a much broader sense than ours, to denote what are now usually called "values." And we do not mean *subjectively* different interests here, but rather *objective* differences, for this is the basis on which this principle was developed. It would cause some difficulty if we were suggesting that an observer could state what a man's "objective interests" are. But we are only saying that an observer can say whether men are in positions such that a union policy (past or potential) can objectively affect them differently. We certainly do not presume, as did Marx and others, that we can as observers "tell the workers what their interests are." Probably Weber's concept of "material interests" corresponds most closely to our usage here.

We shall identify the third principle, which concerns cleavage arising from differences in men's stable dispositions, such as ideology and aspirations which stem from outside the political process, as the *disposition principle*.

others, more militant by nature, saw a need and the opportunity to bargain collectively. On the other hand, there have always been self-employed printers and some printers who are also employers. There are some today, but there were proportionally more in the past. These men may have formed the nucleus of the alimoners because they personally would have been hurt by collective bargaining rather than helped. Thus the alimoners vs. the industrialists might have been in part the self-employed and employers vs. the wage-earning printers. However, the persistence of this division throughout the union's history, continuing in modified form even today, is evidence that such positional differences among the members cannot wholly account for the cleavage.

Regardless of the actual sources of this difference, there can be little doubt that these positions, taken before 1850, differentiated between militant and conservative groups. And significantly, these differences have continued as live issues between the political parties in the ITU during the twentieth century. The conservative faction of the union has always been more inclined than the militant faction to press for the extension of the benevolent activities of the union. The Wahnetas (the conservatives after the turn of the century) placed particular emphasis on establishing and increasing union old-age pensions and mortuary benefits, as well as on building up the Union Printer's Home. There was considerable opposition in the early twentieth century to these measures. In 1909, for example, the membership voted down an administration proposal for a mortuary benefit by 17,275 to 16,368 votes.[4] The same proposal was defeated by 203 votes in 1910 and was finally ratified in a referendum in 1911.[5]

In the twenties and thirties the Wahnetas, and later the Independent Party, often attempted to use the administration of the union's benefit funds as a campaign issue. They charged that Progressive administrations were not careful in maintaining an actuarially balanced pension fund. In 1924, following its temporary return to office, the Lynch administration undertook as its major measure the revamping of the pension fund. The Progressives, on the other hand, while never opposed to benevolent activities, have not displayed much interest in them. In recent years the Independents have once again raised the issue of the handling of the benevolent funds, which make up the bulk of the union treasury, and have criticized the Progressive administration for borrowing from the pension funds in order to support defense activities, such as strikes. In 1953 the Independents initiated a referendum to amend the constitution so as to limit the power of the ITU administration to transfer funds

---

4. George A. Tracy, *History of the ITU*, pp. 949-51.
5. *Ibid.*, p. 1000.

from benevolent funds to the defense funds. This proposal was passed by the members.

Evidence that the difference in orientation of the two political tendencies in the union is related to basic variations in outlook among the members of the union may be found by looking at the membership of New York printers' benevolent societies. The two large benevolent societies in New York make a scrupulous effort to be completely nonpolitical. Yet their members are disproportionately conservative and supporters of the Independent Party. The issue of trade-union activities or benevolent activities is, of course, long forgotten—the union today is committed to both. Nevertheless, many of the current issues show this same division between those who believe that the organization should be a militant trade union and those who see the welfare of the printers best served by benevolent activities and friendly cooperative relations with employers.

THE SECRET SOCIETIES

The struggle against the secret societies, which ultimately culminated in the institutionalization of a two-party system in the ITU, is a clear example of an interest difference resulting in political conflict. The original members of the secret societies were in many ways the elite of the union: they included many officers of local unions, and a large number of foremen. Men could join only by invitation, and in the nineteenth century there were many qualifications for membership, most of which concerned activity and interest in the union. A man who had ratted on the union (by working in a non-union shop) could never join the Brotherhood.

Though the Brotherhood was probably composed of the most militant members of the union, like other successful revolutionary vanguards who succeeded to power, the secret society became a conservative force. Its members and leaders obtained the most privileged positions in the trade, as union officers, foremen, or holders of the best jobs in union print shops. Through secret signs the foremen members of the Brotherhood were able to recognize fellow members who came into their shops for a job and would give them preference in employment.[6] This was

---

6. One method used by the Wahnetas, successors to the Brotherhood, was to make out Wahneta members' union cards in green ink. When a new man came into a shop and deposited his union card, the foreman could tell immediately whether he was a fellow Wahneta or not. Two men whom we interviewed told us about this method from their personal experience. Another method employed was to select a letter of the alphabet as an identifying code. A Wahneta entering a new shop would pick out the code letter from a box of type, so that a Wahneta foreman would know that he was on the "inside." Less colorful methods were also used, such as applying to the secretary of the Grand Lodge for a letter of

important in the nineteenth and early twentieth century, when many printers were wanderers, traveling around the country, staying in one town only until they became tired of it. Tramp printers[7] were numerous until the Great Depression, though the introduction of a strong priority system reduced their numbers early in this century. The special preference given to members of secret societies was also important because of the seasonal cycle in demand for printing. Secret-society members were protected against these fluctuations in demand.

The existence of the secret societies became a major issue dividing union printers from the seventies on. From 1880 down to the beginning of World War I, efforts were made by opponents of these groups to outlaw them. At international conventions, resolutions outlawing the societies sometimes passed, sometimes failed, in either case usually by small margins. It is evident that this issue was grounded in self-interest, for nonmembers opposed the existence of an elite which could control the union and distribution of jobs, while secret-society members were fighting for the continuation of the source of their power or secure employment. We would guess that the secret-society members were over-representd in union conventions because they had the only organized international group, and if the opposition had had the right to initiate referenda earlier (a right they did not succeed in forcing through until 1896) the societies would probably have been outlawed earlier. Actually, as was indicated earlier (see p. 59 in Chapter 3), the final adoption of a permanent law outlawing such societies occurred through a referendum which was initiated by Progressive locals after the Wahneta-controlled convention of 1911 had repealed a previous law. While secret societies were officially illegal after 1912, the Grand Lodge did not disappear from the scene until sometime between 1928 and 1930.

The secret societies provided the first clear basis for interest cleavage in the union. Unlike many interest bases (such as craft or locality) this one was not intrinsically part of the structure of the union or occupation. Once the control over jobs effectively disappeared with the passage of priority laws, this source of interest cleavage vanished. The loyalties and resentments which were engendered by these bitter fights, however, have persisted down to the present. One can still find many older printers who explain their present party allegiance by referring either to past membership in the Wahnetas or to economic deprivations which they claim to have suffered as a result of Wahneta control of jobs.

introduction to the secretary of the circle in a town to which a Wahneta intended to move.

7. Cf. *A Memorial to the Tramp Printer*, compiled by John Gordon, South Brewer, Maine, Gordon Press, 1927; "History of the Famous Itinerant Printers Known as Missouri Press Printers," *Publishers Auxiliary*, July 1932.

AN ISSUE OF POLICY: THE PRIORITY LAWS

Another early issue which was still alive as recently as 1942 is the issue of priority, mentioned above. Originally, the foreman had complete control over hiring and firing.[8] He could and did hire competent men before men less competent, but also sometimes hired his friends (or fellow members in the Brotherhood) even when others were more competent. As we saw earlier, various efforts were made from the mid-eighties on to restrict the power of the foremen and to establish the principle of priority in hiring. This issue bedeviled union politics until the 1920's. The factors related to this cleavage are manifold. In the first place it was clearly an interest issue for the foremen members of the ITU. The members and leaders of the Brotherhood, and later the Wahnetas, also stood to lose if the foreman lost his power to hire: for the leaders it was a weapon for maintaining control of the union, while for the members of the societies it was a guarantee of employment. But the issue also reflected two conflicting sets of values, as is indicated in the following statements made during a debate in 1908:

The most serious effect of [the priority law] . . . lies in the fact that it absolutely destroys the independence of the man who holds a situation. In days gone by he had confidence in his ability to obtain employment wherever the services of competent printers were in demand. . . .

Furthermore, [priority] . . . absolutely destroys competition among employers for the services of men who are classed above the average in competency and speed.[9]

And just the opposite set of values is manifested in the following quotation:

Opponents of the priority law have approached me with the argument: "If it were not for this law, you, being a fast man, could go anywhere and get a situation right off the reel, should you lose the one you now have, while under the law you would have to go to the foot of the list." That is just the argument that demonstrates the selfishness of the proposition to abolish the law. My conception of trade unionism is that it means "the greatest good to the greatest number"; that it is not an institution to promote the interests of a few "swifts," but is intended to promote the welfare of the rank and file.[10]

If the first quotation were from an employers' magazine, and the second by a union spokesman, no one would find them surprising. Yet the first statement was written by the president and secretary-treasurer

---

8. See Porter, *Job Property Rights*, pp. 16-35, for detailed discussion of the development of priority in the ITU.

9. James J. Murphy, president of New York Typographical Union No. 6, and Charles M. Maxwell, secretary, in *New York Union Printer*, April 1908, p. 6.

10. Herbert Cooke, *ibid.*, August 3, 1908, p. 6.

of the largest local in the ITU, and the other by an active opponent of the Administration Party. These statements indicate a fundamental difference in values which rarely develops *within* the trade-union movement. The difference between the belief that men should share and share alike, and the belief that privilege is a reward for competence is in large measure the basic underlying value conflict between the left and the right in political life. The very fact that these union leaders faced with strong internal opposition could present the issues in such terms probably meant that they were certain that many printers agreed with them. Political statements are made on the basis of the response they will engender, and neither of these statements would have been made publicly unless it corresponded to values held by the members. This division, like the cleavage over benevolent activities, indicates the extent to which printers as a group are split between conservative and radical values.

These values were probably related to basic interests as well. Undoubtedly many men who were not involved with the Wahnetas stood to benefit from a rigid priority law, while others would suffer. Older men who had been working for many years in one plant, but whose work abilities were declining as they grew older, would have had an obvious self-interest in a priority law. Younger men who were confident about their abilities, or substitutes who were sweating out their time without steady employment, would probably have been inclined to support efforts to repeal priority laws. It is impossible to discover, however, whether the issue actually resulted in an interest-group cleavage between younger and older men. Regardless of age and length of time employed in a given shop, many men, in evaluating their feelings on this issue, probably questioned themselves as to whether they were among the especially competent men who might benefit from repealing priority, or among the less skillful who would be let out first. Since this was a matter of individual evaluation and psychological security and there was no way by which the sheep could be openly differentiated from the goats, these different self-evaluations could not have led to an open interest-group alignment. Nevertheless, such sentiments may have played an important part, operating through self-interest, in determining many men's positions on the conflict.

Many issues present the same picture of complexity. An issue engages many different kinds of interests and dispositions. It is verbalized in certain terms in an attempt to bring into play deep-rooted dispositions stemming from cultural sources outside the union, but the issue is also directly related to many sets of self-interests: those of foremen, secret-society members, older men, highly skilled printers, and less competent men, as well as the interests of candidates for office who find themselves depending on the outcome of the issue for their own election. It is clear that not all these bases of difference are in the same sense the *source* of the cleavage. It is hard to say in this case which bases were important in *initiating* the cleavage and which were instrumental in *enlarging* it, in making it a union-wide issue for many years. Some of the other issues will show more clearly that *certain bases of cleavage are characteristically those which initiate the cleavage, while other types are necessary to enlarge the issue to encompass the whole membership.* Since both these functions are necessary to a democratic political system, it becomes important to distinguish just what is the usual function of each source of cleavage in the political process. This we shall attempt later.

The priority issue is no longer a source of cleavage within the union, though (as with the issue of benevolent activities) its shadow still lingers on in the behavior in office of the two union parties. The Progressives have been continually in favor of strengthening the law, while the Administration Party and its successor, the Independents, have been against its strengthening, taking the more conservative position. There has been a general trend, however, in the basic values of the membership, so that the law itself is now accepted by almost everyone. Few printers would now respond to the argument given by the Administration Party president of the New York local in 1908 against the law—the argument quoted above. This probably is part of a general trend in this country over the past half century or so, and not specific to printers nor even to workers. Issues in national politics like social security which were once completely rejected are now almost wholly accepted.[11]

CONSERVATISM VS. MILITANCY

Though the issues discussed above began in the nineteenth century, democratic politics in the ITU did not begin in highly organized form until the turn of the century. From that time, however, the union has been divided between a militant and a conservative group.

The basic militant-conservative difference which characterized the parties at the turn of the century and has continued since that time can be seen from excerpts of the 1901 convention speech of the first international president elected as an Administration Party man, James Lynch. The official Wahneta historian of the union reports his speech as follows:

---

11. A discussion of the "natural history of issues," in terms of the secular trend in values which makes an issue to be first rejected, then accepted by some, and finally accepted by all, is presented in Bernard Berelson *et al., Voting,* pp. 207-12.

Conservative and intelligent action would win the prize; "radical, ill-advised and ill-considered propaganda will waste the opportunity and make of what should be progress, a weapon of retrogression. . . . [The membership] are cautioned as to alluring schemes and recommended to the path 'well worn, perhaps, and slow of advancement, but one that brings, nevertheless, safe returns, adds to our stability, and conserves our strength and influence.' "[12]

An indication that "conservatism" was once a more honored term among union members than it is today (another indicator of the secular trend mentioned above) is evident in the way the term was used here and elsewhere by Administration Party leaders at that time. At the same convention, for example, Lynch called the referendum vote in favor of an arbitration agreement with employers "a credit to the conservatism of the membership."[13] The turning point of this term, in terms of the values of the members, seems to have occurred in the twenties. In 1928 after defeat by the Progressives the Administration Party disbanded and a new group, the Conservative Party, with many of the same men at the center, took its place. It met with another defeat in 1930 and quickly changed its name. One of its founders, whom we interviewed, had this to say about the name:

The Administration Party was succeeded by the Independents. For the first two years we called it the Conservative Party. We changed the name in 1932 because the connotations of the word were bad for a party in the union. Personally, I think it's a good word; but it wasn't the right word for the party name.

This continuity of ideology in the Administration-Independent Party and a similar continuity among the Progressives is one of the important characteristics of the union's political system. Conceivably the marginal status of printing may help produce this division. Printers have the income and in many ways the prestige to allow them to dissociate themselves from workers and from radical movements. At the same time, because of their literacy and associated skills, they have been everywhere one of the earliest groups of workers to organize in all countries and have aided in the organization of other workers. Here is a statement by a Wahneta which will illustrate this "split personality":

For twenty years the relations between the International Typographical Union and the American Newspaper Publishers' Association were of the most friendly character. The President of the Union appeared before the publishers' convention and the labor representatives of the publishers appeared before

---

12. George Tracy, *op. cit.*, p. 662.

13. *Ibid.*, p. 664. An official history of an ITU local, written in 1907, proudly describes the then ITU secretary-treasurer, John W. Bramwood, as "one of the most conservative men in the labor movement." *Printing and Printers in Providence*, Providence Typographical Union, 1908, p. xi.

our convention. . . . The personal relations of the members were always of the best and the publishers met all points at issue in a broad and generous spirit. Now all this has changed. In the place of a friendly and cooperating group of publishers, we have a hostile combination. . . .

The present [Progressive] President of the International Typographical Union appeared before one convention of the publishers, and after listening to his speech the publishers resolved that thereafter representatives of the International unions . . . would not again be invited to address them.[14]

Just what have been the effects of this deep ideological difference on ITU politics? One of its functions seems to have been to generate institutions which have themselves become sources of cleavage. The Wahneta organization, which produced so many conflicts of interest, seems partly to have been continued because men who "thought alike" on union matters, who agreed that the union should take the conservative path, wanted to have an organization both for fellowship and to help them carry out their beliefs. And the union parties seem to have been formed and held together, not by patronage and interest coalitions, as in United States politics, but by a consistent ideology or at least by a common antagonism to the other party's ideology. The cleavage in values or ideology allows for enlargement of issues which start out as conflicts of interest among only small groups of the members. It does this through transforming interest cleavages which, as they gain legitimacy, come to be shared and articulated, eliciting responses from the members in terms of their own values and ideology. The priority issue, which could engage two opposing sets of values, illustrates this well.

Perhaps the most important consistent difference in the ideologies of the two parties has been their position on arbitration and strikes. The Administration Party favored arbitration of collective bargaining differences wherever possible. It entered into a pact with the newspaper publishers in 1901 which required all locals to arbitrate such differences. The Progressives, on the other hand, while never attacking arbitration as such, opposed long-term national commitments and demanded that local unions should be given the freedom to decide when and whether arbitration procedures should be employed.[15]

The national arbitration agreement between the ITU and the newspaper publishers was ended in 1922, the first year that the Progressives controlled a majority of the Executive Council. Between 1924 and 1926, when the Administration Party again controlled the union, efforts were made to renew the arbitration agreement. A new arbitration contract was actually agreed to by both the publishers and the ITU in

14. *Typo Blade*, Chicago, June 1923, p. 4.
15. See "Our Arbitration Policy," in the *Progressive* (Denver), April 1912, p. 2.

1926, but it was never ratified, for the Progressives returned to power in that year.[16]

From their formation in 1912 until they came to power in the twenties, the Progressives attacked the incumbent Wahnetas for being too conciliatory towards the employers. The attempt of the Administration Party to suppress the 1919 "vacationist" strike in New York was used by the Progressives as an example of the differing attitudes of the two parties. During the Progressive Party's first period of control of the ITU, 1922-1924, a large number of strikes occurred in connection with the union's effort to gain the forty-four-hour week. The then opposition Wahneta Party accused the Progressives of unnecessarily calling or prolonging these strikes, and of alienating friendly employers. They claimed, for example, that the militant tactics of the Progressives had caused the union to lose shops in many cities. As one of their spokesmen saw it:

Our [Progressive-led] union in New Orleans was during the period of union papers especially active in seeing to it that the composing room foreman walked the chalk line, and at times did not investigate very closely charges that he had deviated an inch or two before finding him guilty and applying what was called discipline. . . . It was always the principle of the thing with the union. Finally the crash came, the newspapers were lost and they are still out. It was a case of telling the employers "where they got off" until finally they made up their minds they would continue to ride without the union. . . . Result of New Orleans and other things, there is now the open shop supported by a formerly friendly association [of employers].[17]

In the late twenties the Conservative Party, the successors of the Administration Party, continued to criticize the Progressive Administration for their strike tactics, and argued that many strikes were unnecessary. For example, the party organ in 1929 commented as follows on the settlement of a strike in Albany:

There is an increase in wages and the granting of the forty-five-hour week. . . . Both of these advantages were offered and could have been obtained before the strike. If the strike had not occurred, the old contract, unquestioned priority and continued employment would have gone on, and there would not have been a valueless war with a cost of more than three hundred thousand dollars.[18]

During the Great Depression, the issue of more or less militancy fell by the wayside as an argument between the two parties. Printers, like

---

16. See Jacob Loft, *The Printing Trades*, New York, Farrar & Rinehart, Inc., 1944, pp. 239-57, for a discussion of changes in arbitration procedure in the printing trades.

17. *Typo Blade*, June 1923, p. 4.

18. *Typo Topics*, 1929, p. 6.

other workers, were forced to accept wage cuts and refrain from striking. The opposition Independents criticized the Progressives for accepting reductions in the standards of living, but no one urged the need for an aggressive strike policy.

During World War II, however, the difference in the attitudes of both parties towards strikes reasserted itself. The ITU, like most other American unions, agreed to give up the strike weapon in the interests of the war effort. There were initially no differences between the two parties on this issue. As the war went on, however, great discontent developed within the ITU over the way the War Labor Board handled their cases. The Progressives, led by Woodruff Randolph, who as ITU secretary-treasurer was the only Progressive union officer in an administration dominated by the Independent Party between 1942 and 1944, objected that yielding these rights would prove permanently damaging to the union. They therefore began to question the absolute no-strike pledge and proposed that strikes be authorized in cases where war necessity was not present. The Independents, while objecting to the WLB decisions, defended the no-strike pledge on patriotic grounds. In 1944 the Progressives swept back into office under a ticket headed by Randolph. And shortly thereafter, the ITU became the only union besides the United Mine Workers to drop the no-strike pledge.

As we shall see later, this same difference between the two parties reasserted itself with the passage of the Taft-Hartley Act. One other major issue, however, developed in the late thirties and early forties, which can only be understood in terms of the ideological commitments of the two parties: the CIO-AFL controversy.

In the middle thirties the ITU was the only craft union in the AFL whose officers expressed any sympathy for the CIO. The Progressives, though in office when the CIO began and in danger of defeat, supported the CIO, while the opposition Independents supported the AFL. The Progressives had always been strong advocates of militant and aggressive organizing policies, and industrial unionism in the printing trades. They had never pressed this latter issue, since the other printing craft unions were all conservative and opposed to unification. As a result of the Progressive-inspired resistance to paying a "war tax" against the CIO to the AFL, the ITU, alone among the printing craft unions, and craft unions in general, remained unaffiliated to either union from 1938 to 1944. CIO organizers report that when they entered cities and towns in antiunion areas such as the South, the one place where they could obtain any help was the ITU local in town. Many ITU leaders in the South became temporary, and in some cases permanent, organizers for CIO unions. This behavior by well-paid skilled craft-unionists astonished the CIO men. It can only be understood in the context of ITU politics. Through their identification with the Progressive Party, many printers and their local leaders absorbed a general value frame of reference which made them view the CIO drive with sympathy, while skilled photo-engravers, pressmen, electricians, and carpenters either did nothing or opposed the industrial-union drives.

The generally more militant policies pursued by the ITU in the last twenty-five years, as compared to every other printing craft union and almost all other AFL craft unions, cannot be understood except as a result of the emergence of ideological issues in the two-party fight. The continual need to reaffirm either a conservative or militant trade-union ideology in election campaigns has led ITU leaders to react to new situations in terms of values as well as of organizational needs. During the period of Wahneta supremacy, from 1900 to 1920, the ITU was probably more conservative than most trade-unions.[19] Progressive rule, which has lasted from 1928 to the present, with a six-year interval of Independent control (1938-1944), has seen the ITU taking positions vis-à-vis the employers, the government, and other unions, which almost invariably are more militant than those of other craft unions. These more militant positions, like the conservative positions which preceded them, have had the support of slightly over half the membership, as evidenced not only in elections, but in referenda on specific issues. This whole complex of ideological issues, we believe, represents no division in interests between union members but rather a division in ideological values.

Conflict within the ITU is not limited to ideologically linked issues. Some of the other issues reflect the kinds of interest that we have mentioned earlier, but others show quite different kinds. Among the latter is a group of issues which shows evidence of the conflict between the interests of the party that is in office with those of the party in opposition.

THE INS VS. THE OUTS

The Progressives, who were out of office until the twenties, nevertheless managed to initiate some union action before that time. One piece of legislation they successfully introduced was a law which provided for a board of auditors, three in number, elected by the membership, to audit the secretary-treasurer's books each year. Today (1955), with the Progressives in office, the tables have been turned. One of the Independents' strongest issues in recent years has been that the one

---

19. Nevertheless, though the policies and methods of the union were manifestly conservative, the ITU in this period made many collective-bargaining gains not equaled by most unions until very recently.

auditor who is an Independent has not been allowed to see how part of the union's funds (the Unitypo funds for establishing newspapers in strike-bound cities) is being spent. The Progressives, who initiated the audit system when they were out of office to keep a check on the administration, are accused, now that they themselves are the administration, of undermining it. The Progressives reply that such secrecy (which is legal for Unitypo funds) is necessary to protect the union from the employer.

There have been many policy cleavages which show a similar shift in the parties' positions as they gain or lose control of the administration. The Progressives before the twenties were strongly in favor of local autonomy, while the Administration Party stressed the need for central authority to allow more effective bargaining. The Progressives were also the party of economy during this period, keeping close watch on the administration's use of union funds and making frequent accusations of free spending. On each of these issues there has been a change. For a short time after they gained office in 1928,[20] the Progressives maintained both their former positions. The Conservative Party accused the Progressives of saving money at the expense of strikers and at the expense of successful wage negotiations. But in time the Progressives shifted on both these issues, and they became the party in favor of centralization and spending. They felt the need for both power and money to fight unemployment and wage cuts during the depression. At present, with the Progressives again in power, they are still the party of spending and centralization, while the Independents make issues out of both of these policies, claiming to be for local autonomy and reduced spending.

Such issues as these, perhaps best characterized as the "ins vs. the outs," exist in any democratic political system.[21] What are their sources? It is easy—too easy—to say that they are partisan issues, deriving simply from party activity. This is certainly part of the truth, but it does not explain other things—for example, how it is that such issues sometimes produce a cleavage among nonparty men.

These issues seem to arise in the following way. The administration acts or attempts to act in some way which benefits itself more than it does the members and the other party. Its motives for doing so may be obscure and mixed; but more important than the motives involved are the differential consequences of these administrative actions. When the administration's action tends to benefit the administration at the expense

20. Before this, from 1920 on, they had some share in the administration, but it was not until 1928 that they gained control of the Executive Council.
21. The historical reversal of position of the Democratic and the Federalist-Whig-Republican parties on the issue of States' rights should be noted in this connection.

of the members, the other party, or local unions, then the interest principle comes into play, and in a rather complicated fashion. First, the administration's interest is involved. Those members who identify with it, either through party ties or simply because it is the administration, are affected too, through the identification-interest principle. In addition, the opposition party activists, whose status as party leaders and chances for office are threatened by the action, stand to be directly harmed by the action and thus have their interest at stake. Their followers, who identify with the party, will not be directly affected if the party is affected, but through the identification-interest principle are also affected. Moreover, issues are expanded to encompass and involve nonparty members. For example, all the recent campaign propaganda of the Independents on the financial activities of the Progressive administration is expressed in such terms as "We will lower your assessments," and "The administration is spending too freely." The administration ordinarily counters in terms of the members' interests as *union members* rather than as individuals; that is, in terms of the interests of the union as a whole. Thus it brings in the identification-interest principle, the members identifying with the union as a whole. The reply made on this issue both by the Administration Party when it was in power and by the Progressive Party during its administration has been that more money and administrative centralization is needed in order to allow the *union* to carry out its purposes. On the issues of economy and centralization the opposition attempts to engage the members' *self*-interest as individuals who dislike taxes and want to guard their autonomy, while the incumbents attempt to bring into play the members' identification with the union's goals. This seems to be generally the case in democratic party conflict: it is the administration which calls for "national unity," while it is the opposition which usually appeals for protection of individual rights.

These issues affecting ins and outs are complex in view of the number of processes through which cleavage occurs. They are usually more than the simple party fights they seem to be; if they were not, they could not gain the attention of the union members as a whole. While each may *begin* as a conflict between the interests of the parties, it is *enlarged* to become union-wide through engaging each of the four principles discussed earlier: interest (of the members), identification-interest, disposition, and social context. The other issues we have discussed, such as the priority issue, or alimoners vs. industrialists, may seem to be more nearly "real issues" in the sense that they reflect and crystallize genuine difference in sentiment among the members regarding what the union's goals and purposes should be; but the ins-vs.-outs issues are just as important in their consequences for the internal power structure of the union. And it is largely because arbitrary power-grabbing acts by an administration were *not* converted by a watchful and potent opposition into issues which engage the interest of the constituents that many former democracies are now oligarchies. The histories of many trade unions (such as that of the pressmen, who work alongside the printers) as well as of many Latin American countries will serve as illustration.

CONSENSUS ISSUES

There is another important group of issues which in some ways resemble the issues affecting ins and outs but which involve no policy cleavages at all. Charges of corruption, of bad administration, and similar issues fall into this group. An apt term for these is "consensus issues," for there is complete policy consensus; the only question is some problem of fact: Is there or is there not corruption? or Who will give a more efficient administration? Questions involving personalities fall into this group of issues, too.

The parties' purpose in making such charges is to engage the identification of the electorate. In most campaigns of this type neither the values nor the personal interests of the electorate are usually involved, and personal campaigning must fill the void left by the lack of such differences.[22]

The ITU has had its share of consensus issues, as have most political systems. Campaign charges and countercharges of laxity, inefficiency, and the like are probably not as violent in the ITU as in United States civil politics, but they are produced in abundance. Their function seems largely to provide a content for the political division in those campaigns which involve no real policy issues, and also to capture the involvement of certain men who would remain uninterested in politics if it were articulated only as a value cleavage.

Some characteristic consensus issues in the union are the administration of the Union Printer's Home, which the out party almost always questions; charges that union money has been spent on other than union

---

22. Much Southern State politics in the United States seems to be of the consensus kind, and in particular, a politics of personalities. From the descriptions given by V. O. Key: *Southern Politics*, New York, Alfred A. Knopf, Inc., 1950, Arkansas seems to be nearest a pure type of personal politics. No continuing divisions exist, and campaigns are carried on almost completely in personality terms. Policy differences between candidates hardly exist.

City politics exemplify another type of consensus politics. There has been much agitation for "taking politics out of city government," on the principle that there are no (or few) policy problems (except those on which there is universal consensus) facing city governments. This, of course, is not quite true, but it is true that few city elections turn on policy differences; consensus issues of some type usually dominate the campaign.

affairs;[23] and charges that the administration uses the regional union representatives as party organizers. Another is the charge that the secretary-treasurer of the union uses the *Typographical Journal* (of which he is editor) for political propaganda.[24] This is important to the opposition party, for the *Journal* is the only international literature which most printers get, except at campaign time.

It is true that these issues involve policy in the sense that administration acts are being brought into question. But they involve no cleavage or division in policy between two groups of voters. The question is not whether the Union Printer's Home *should* be well administered, or whether the secretary-treasurer *should* abstain from putting partisan politics into the *Journal*. The electorate *agrees* on these questions. The only issue is whether the Home *is* well administered, whether the Journal *is* free from political propaganda. This is the fundamental difference between these issues and the other ins-vs.-outs issues, both of which involve at their core the interests of the out party vs. the interests of the administration. The ins-vs.-outs issues could engage the values of the electorate on opposing sides of the policy questions, Should there be more centralization or more local autonomy? Should Unitypo finance be more fully accounted for, or would this expose the union's activity to employers? There are no such problems of "should" among consensus issues, except for the election problem itself: Should candidate A or candidate B be elected? The crucial means of distinguishing consensus issues is that the party on the defensive never argues the point; it denies the charge and attempts to change the subject to another issue.

As in United States civil politics, consensus issues are much more characteristic of local elections than of national contests. The principal issue of controversy in most local contests is the collective-bargaining agreement. All printers agree that they should have higher wages for fewer hours, with longer vacations and a good retirement system. The principal question is, Was the last contract negotiated by the incumbent

---

23. These charges are probably the least true of all those mentioned. One of the attributes of their union of which printers are most proud is its honesty and full financial accounting, printed in detail in the *Typographical Journal* (and on the local level, in the local official bulletin). Even with this, there is sometimes questioning of specific items in the account. These are probably sometimes justified, but there is undoubtedly less misuse of union funds in the ITU than in almost any political system in which the possibility exists.

24. Both the latter charges are usually true, though the blatant use of the *Journal* for politics would not likely be tolerated by most printers. One important contribution to printers' democracy has come from the fact that they have not been so dependent on official journals as have most union members. With their knowledge of newspapers and access to printing equipment, printers have published many newspapers for printers, most of which have kept watch on union activities. But these have most often been on the local level, not nationwide.

local administration the best possible one? During all contract negotiations the opposition party carefully prepares the way for the next election. It puts forward greater demands than the administration believes it can gain from the employer. The opposition also criticizes the administration's handling of various grievance cases.

How do these consensus issues relate to the four principles of cleavage? There is a definite interest here—that of the candidates and party to get elected. This interest is not generated by the political process in the sense we have used the term, but by the *election* process. That is, it is not the outcome of policy questions which will affect the parties and candidates differently, but rather the outcome of the election itself. This involves a generalization of the interest principles to include not only policy questions but also election disputes as the generators of differential effects. The identification-interest principle seems to be the one which creates widespread cleavage in these issues. The members' identification with candidates and parties whose interest it is to win elections throws them on opposite sides of these consensus issues.

We shall examine the nature of these issues more systematically later in the chapter. First we need to examine other kinds of issues, in particular the ones relating to the structure of the occupation.

ISSUES GENERATED BY THE STRUCTURE
OF THE OCCUPATION

The elaboration of crafts and skills within printing which occurred around the turn of the century has had important effects on union politics. Among the pressmen, where there are the two major subdivisions, pressmen and assistant pressmen, and additional distinctions among the men according to the kind of presses they operate, the differential pay and prestige of the several skill groups seems to have reduced the chances for continuing democratic politics in the union. Among the typographers, the subcraft divisions seem not to have made much difference. Nevertheless, the very existence of these subcrafts has been enough to sensitize some printers to their possible function as sources of cleavage. One printer, the editor of the *Typo Blade* (an Administration Party journal), had this to say in 1922:

Without prejudice or carping criticism of anyone or of any group of men who believe it is to their interest to form organizations within our ranks, based on economic reasons, we question the advisability of this being done. . . .
Organizations composed of members of a local having for their purpose the support of candidates for office, or the discussion of questions of policy that are up for consideration, affecting the local or international are very

proper organizations. But these are mixed in their character and not exclusive to a particular branch of workers.

But when organizations take on an exclusive, or class, character, they are bound in the end to lead to confusion and will undermine the solidarity of the union, the one thing we should all be striving for. . . .

We now have monotype societies and linotype societies, each composed of members of the union working at that particular branch of the trade. This is sowing the seed of dissolution, conflict, controversy. Some of those participating in these organizations are not aware of this and do not mean to be associated with an organization that is bound to develop these results.[25]

This party man saw clearly the possibilities of cleavage dangerous to the union resulting from having the subcraft division in the occupation intensified by formal organization.[26] His fears were not borne out, however; today there are monotype and linotype social clubs in many locals, but there is no evidence to show that they have intensified the political conflict in the union. Certainly the political division in the union is not between these groups. Probably the reason that these fears were ungrounded was simply that these subcraft divisions are not functional divisions with respect to the political processes in the ITU. Few actions of the union administration differentiate in any way between one subcraft and another. The union has always kept the pay and prestige structure of the occupation homogeneous, and has never allowed it to develop gradations. The extreme example of occupations which have developed numerous gradations is, of course, the white-collar world. One of the most successful measures used by employers to keep white-collar employees from recognizing that they are in a common circumstance and from organizing is to proliferate the gradations of prestige and pay which separate them.[27] And of course white-collar people themselves help institute such gradations, for it is from these that many of their satisfactions (and many of their frustrations as well) derive. The various subcrafts represented among the ITU men in a print shop, all with equal pay and status, and the various jobs filled by the white-collar workers in a bank, all with different pay and status,

---

25. *Typo Blade*, Vol. 1, 11, January 1922, p. 5.

26. The fact that it was a party activist who saw so clearly the possibilities of danger in this situation exemplifies an important function of party activity in a political system. The interests of a party, whether in opposition or in power, but especially in opposition, sensitize active party men to the consequences of the political processes which are occurring. Later we will discuss in more detail this and other important functions of a party system in maintaining a democratic political system.

27. The conscious use of such measures by employers is discussed by Carl Dreyfuss: "Prestige Grading: A Mechanism of Control," in R. K. Merton *et al.* (eds.), *Reader in Bureaucracy*, Glencoe, Ill., Free Press, 1952, pp. 258-64. Dreyfuss discusses in some detail the sources and consequences of this proliferation of statuses.

are at opposite extremes in the extent of their pay and prestige gradations. That these two occupational structures also are at opposite extremes in association and common feeling suggests just how important a
determinant of occupational consciousness of kind is the extent to which
jobs are stratified in a firm or industry.

One further historical set of events illustrates what could have happened to the ITU. When new crafts began to appear in printing as a
result of technological changes in the industry, the typographers organized these crafts (just as they helped organize workers in trades
other than printing) and kept them within the union. Around the turn
of the century the union found itself with an industrial structure having
in it a number of different crafts with different contracts and different
wage scales. It is useful to note how the union attempted to integrate
these crafts and what the final outcome was. As the crafts came into
existence and became a part of the union, they were one after another
given vice-presidencies in the union, with a seat on the executive council.[28] This is a common practice in unions which comprise several crafts.
The arrangement probably works with varying degrees of success in
different unions. In the ITU it did not work at all. One by one the
crafts (which then had fewer members than the typographers) seceded
from the union, forming their own autonomous unions. In most of
these cases of secession we have no data on just why a group left. But
we do have data on one case of attempted secession which occurred
much later than the others. This is the case of the mailers.

The mailers, who are not printers at all, handle the distribution of
newspapers. They constitute a small and weak segment of the labor force
of newspapers, and were able to organize only through the assistance
of the ITU in the first two decades of the present century. Organized
and supported by the Wahneta administration of 1900-1920, they gave
overwhelming support to the incumbent international administration during this period. The president of the autonomous Mailers' Trade District
Union, who was also a vice-president of the ITU, was a Wahneta supporter who was ordinarily elected without opposition. The Progressives
were never able to get more than a tiny majority of the mailers to support them, and in fact made few efforts to win support from them.

In the twenties, however, when the union was almost evenly divided
between the Progressives and the Administration Party, the mailers suddenly acquired greater political significance. Since neither party had
complete control of all printer positions on the Executive Council, the
vote of the mailer vice-president, who was chosen by the 2,500 mailer
members, could prove decisive. In addition, the mailers, by voting al-

---

28. Jacob Loft, *op. cit.*, discusses the early structure of the printing union.

most unanimously for the Administration, could decide the election for
the presidency and for other positions on the Executive Council in a
close contest. These facts naturally perturbed the Progressives and they
began a struggle to break up the autonomy of the Mailers' Trade District Union. The autonomy of this organization meant that the mailers
had their own full-time paid officials who were all Administration Party
men, and that these mailer officials could keep the mailers united, politically and otherwise, throughout the country. The Progressives, after
coming to power in the late twenties, dissolved the MTDU, but the
mailers' leaders contested the dissolution in the courts and received a
favorable verdict, which meant that the ITU had to keep the separate
organization whether it liked it or not. The Progressives did not
press the issue strongly between 1928 and 1938, when they had complete control of the union, and the fact that the mailers were voting
Conservative and later Independent was unimportant politically.

Between 1938 and 1944, however, the issue of mailer autonomy took
on new significance. In 1938 and again in 1940 the Independents and
the Progressives divided the four printer positions on the Executive
Council. The mailer vice-president, therefore, cast the deciding vote—
in favor of the Independents. In 1940 the Progressive candidate for ITU
president actually received a small majority of the vote of the printer
members, but was defeated by the fact that the mailers voted overwhelmingly for the Independent incumbent. Mailer delegates to ITU
conventions tended to vote as a block, and in the few conventions in
which party division was close, gave the edge to the conservative faction.

The Progressives naturally had a party interest in destroying the
mailers' political strength. To have the issue put in such terms, however,
would probably have been distasteful to all but die-hard Progressives.
The Progressives therefore presented the issue to the membership as a
conflict between the printers and the mailers, arguing that the printers,
who constituted 95% of the membership of the ITU, had the right to
decide their own affairs. With the question posed in those terms, the
printers voted in a number of referenda to restrict the power and
autonomy of the MTDU. The mailers' leaders recognized that they
faced a hopeless battle, and finally seceded from the ITU in the early
forties, though a number of mailer locals in the larger cities remained
with the ITU.

The dilemma faced by a small craft within a larger body was well
presented by the president of the Mailers' Trade District Union in debating with the Progressive advocates of the dissolution of that body:

I am opposed to dissolving the MTDU because I am convinced that
mailers who are very much in the minority in the printing crafts cannot

protect and further their interests unless they have the right to govern and control the affairs of their craft. . . . It is a mathematical impossibility for three thousand of one craft to get justice from seventy thousand of another craft. . . . There are but few printers that know mailers and fewer that associate with mailers. Fewer still know anything about mailers' work. Therefore printers, regardless of their intentions, are not sufficiently familiar with mailer work to pass upon their problems or legislate for them.[29]

This statement clearly indicates the interests of the mailers, and suggest what the motives of the other crafts (all of them small minorities in the ITU) must have been when they seceded from the ITU around the turn of the century. The whole issue shows what might have happened if the subcrafts within the composing room had been differentiated by pay or separate contracts. As the editor of the *Typo Blade* feared, separate craft organizations would have produced the structural bases for political conflict between subcrafts and probably made impossible a democratic two-party system. Over fifty years ago Georg Simmel pointed out that democracy is possible within trade unions only as long as the interests of the members are homogeneous:

The best student of the federation of English trade unions says that their majority decisions are justifiable and practicable only insofar as the interests of the various confederates are homogeneous. As soon as differences of opinion between majority and minority result from real differences in interests, any compulsion produced by outvoting inevitably leads to a separation of the members. In other words, a vote makes sense only if the existing interests can fuse into a unity. If divergent tendencies preclude this centralization, it becomes a contradictory procedure to entrust a majority with the decision, since the homogeneous will, which ordinarily (to be sure) can be better ascertained by a majority than by a minority, is objectively non-existent.[30]

Translated into the political life of most trade unions, Simmel is in effect saying that democracy is difficult if not impossible in unions which represent diverse groups. In the typical industrial union, for example, internal conflict along ITU lines would undoubtedly result in cleavages between different crafts. A settlement which benefited one group could be attacked as hurting another group. Thus a one-party system is perhaps necessary for the internal unity and survival of unions whose jurisdiction encompasses many crafts.

Where interest cleavages are inflexible and built into the occupational structure of the union, it would appear that democratic processes not only lead to oppression of the minority subgroup, but that they probably lead to *more* oppression than would rule by one man. The

29. *Typographical Journal*, Vol. 91, No. 2, August 1937, p. 52. The quotation is from Munro Roberts. He goes on to propose secession from the ITU.
30. Kurt Wolff (ed.), *The Sociology of Georg Simmel*, p. 245.

seventy thousand printers, knowing they would never be in a minority with respect to the mailers, could act toward them without the restraint which comes from knowing that one may one day be a minority. The mailers, on the other hand, could see no chance of ever becoming the majority. There was little reason for them to continue to play the game. Unable to revolt, they first appealed to outside authority, and then gave up and attempted to secede. The rigid craft division thus worked in two ways to break down the democratic process: it made the majority more a tyrant, and the minority less willing to accede to majority rule.

This example suggests some of the consequences for democratic processes of permanent divisions in the economic structure of the trade. These divisions, when they become involved with policy questions, seem both too intense and too rigid for the continuance of democratic processes in a voluntary organization.

THE UNEMPLOYMENT ISSUES

The unemployment issue of the thirties resulted from a *temporary* economic structure within the union (in contrast to a permanent craft division like the mailer-printer division). In 1933 more than half the union printers in New York were either unemployed or working less than five days a week. The situation was similar in other large cities, though it was not so in small towns. Unemployment created two classes of printers, the employed and the unemployed, a potential basis for interest cleavage. This time the basis for cleavage was on two levels, the individual level and the level of locals as units. That is, some individuals were employed while others were not, and some locals had a high number of unemployed, while others did not.

Both these bases were brought into play when a four-day week was proposed in the 1933 convention and later voted on in a referendum. This proposal would have affected the unemployed and the employed in directly opposite ways. It also would have affected different locals differently. Where the union was weak, it could mean that employers might try to break with the union rather than accept the complications of a share-the-work plan. Weaker locals and the international administration, both of which would bear the brunt of instituting a four-day week, would be adversely affected by the policy, while the locals with high unemployment would be benefited.[31]

---

31. The strength of the cleavage between locals over this kind of issue is shown by the fact that the New York union went on strike in 1919 to gain the forty-four-hour week, though this was against ITU policy, while a number of Canadian locals seceded from the international body rather than agree to institute the five-day week when this became ITU law.

Neither national party took up the demands of the unemployed, probably for two reasons: both parties, but especially the Progressive incumbents, saw the difficulties arising from attempts to institute a four-day week; they were national parties, with some need to maintain consistency, while the problem was not the same everywhere. In a political perspective, the unemployed were a minority in the ITU as a whole, and the party which backed them against the employed would probably lose. A group with a strongly ideological orientation, the Amalgamation Party, whose platform and other activities indicates that it was Communist-dominated, arose in New York and a few other large cities to support the unemployed. This resulted in an odd mixture: a tiny ideological party, whose ideology had no connection with internal union issues, served as the advocate for an interest group, the unemployed. The party survived only as long as the problem lasted, but it used the issue to gain strength: it elected a president of the New York union, and some of its leaders became important figures in the New York Progressive Party after the Amalgamation Party's demise around 1940.[32]

CURRENT ISSUES

The most important recent issue in the ITU has been how to fight the Taft-Hartley Act. The act is in direct conflict with several principles which most union printers hold dear and which have been incorporated in their contracts for many years. Probably the most direct violation of their norms is the act's ban on the closed shop. Whatever the closed shop means in other occupations (and in some it undoubtedly means less freedom for the average worker) for union printers (at least, those we interviewed) any other arrangement would be intolerable. Since their union is not something imposed from above, but is completely identified with their trade, they can hardly conceive of a nonunion printer in the composing room. In newspapers and large shops even the employers are sometimes kept off the composing-room floor, so it is not hard to imagine what would happen to a nonunion printer.

The common antagonism of printers to the Taft-Hartley Act and the need to present a solid front to the employers made the Independents agree when the Progressive administration decided to fight the act. But the differing ideological perspectives of the two union parties soon

32. The history of this ideological party seems like that of many such parties in civil politics. They languish, with only a few ideologically committed men as supporters, until they find an issue which coincides with their ideology and affects the material interests of many men. The mass base of the party derives largely from interest. When this issue becomes less important, the mass base falls away, and the party is again the small band of ideologues.

led them into a bitter controversy as to how to fight the Taft-Hartley law. Both agreed that it was an obnoxious law. The incumbent Progressives argued that clauses in the law would enable employers to seriously weaken the union. They therefore insisted that all employers agree to maintain all provisions of ITU law including the closed shop, even if these provisions violated national legislation. Since contracts to this effect would have been illegal, the Progressives ruled that ITU locals should not sign any contract which contained any provisions beyond wages and hours. Employers, however, were to be required to notify the union, either by letter or through a posted list of shop rules, that they would continue to accept ITU law. As a gesture of the union's complete rejection of the Taft-Hartley law, the Progressives also refused to sign the non-Communist affidavits required by the law for recognition by the National Labor Relations Board.[33]

Many employers refused to agree to the demand of the ITU that they violate national legislation in their own shops. This refusal led to a number of costly strikes (the most serious being a twenty-three-month strike against the Chicago newspapers). In order to support these strikes, the Progressive administration asked the members to approve a $4\frac{1}{2}\%$ tax for defense purposes, and this proposal was passed by a large majority in a referendum.

The opposition Independents, on the other hand, adopted a completely different position. They argued that the employers could be trusted not to attempt to destroy the ITU. In effect, they suggested that many of the Taft-Hartley strikes were caused by the union's policies rather than by employer intransigence. They also pointed to the fact that most American unions have agreed to sign the non-Communist affidavits and to fight against Taft-Hartley at the ballot box rather than on the picket line. Various Independent-Party-controlled locals refused to strike and reached informal agreements with their employers. They were denounced by the Progressives as being allies of the employers. In this issue, as in others, the Independents have followed their less militant ideology, compromising more quickly and showing less willingness to strike.

Issues stemming from the Taft-Hartley controversy still dominate ITU politics, though the Progressive incumbents have gradually modified their policies under the pressure of lost strikes, congressional investigations, and adverse judicial decisions. The ITU no longer demands

---

33. There seems to have been no suggestion, even from rabid Independents who would be expected to fight the Progressives, that this decision not to sign was because of Communism in the ranks of the officers. The officers did in fact sign the affidavit, but refused to file it with the NLRB.

that employers violate Taft-Hartley, but seems to have won an informal agreement from most printing employers to covertly accept the maintenance of ITU laws in their shops. On the other hand, ITU officers have still not filed non-Communist affidavits, and the Independents still charge that such refusals are empty gestures which weaken the strength of the union.

§ Summary and Restatement

WHAT CAN WE SAY more systematically about the political system from this account of the issues which have dominated ITU politics? A number of generalizations seem possible.

We cannot identify particular issues completely with one or another principle of cleavage, as we pointed out earlier, because issues always seem to involve more than one principle. However, certain issues seem to be initiated on the basis of one principle, or at least seem to embody one principle more than the others. The issues which seem particularly to exemplify the two "interest" principles are these:

(1) The secret-society issues, in which the interest and interest-identification principles operated to make the secret-society members fight for the existence of their organization.

(2) The priority issue (which also activated deep-seated value systems) involved the interest principle, particularly the interests of foremen and the older or more highly skilled men vs. those of younger or less skilled men.

(3) The ins-vs.-outs type of policy issue involves several kinds of interests: those of the administration, in conserving or increasing its power and authority in the union vs. those of all members below them in the authority system, particularly (*a*) activists in the opposition party, who stand a chance for office, (*b*) local officers, from whom authority may be drained, and (*c*) ordinary members, who stand to lose some part of their independence and their power in the political process.

(4) The consensus issues (honesty, efficiency, etc.) which, like the ins-vs.-outs issues, involve the interests of the administration vs. those of the party or candidate out of power. Through the identification-interest principle, this purely partisan fight becomes a union-wide issue. The intensity of cleavage among the electorate due to such issues, however, is not usually great.

(5) The mailer issue, in which the interest division was along the lines of the occupational (i.e., economic) structure. The potential issues that existed along other craft lines may be included here too.

(6) The unemployment issue, when the occupation was temporarily characterized by these divisions. (*a*) men with jobs and men without; (*b*) local unions with high unemployment and unions with little unemployment; and (*c*) local unions which were strong and could enforce a four-day work week, and those which were weak. Issues involving these aspects of the structure brought into play interests associated with them.

These cases of interest and interest-identification conflict differ from one another in various ways. One distinction which may be relevant to a theory of democratic politics is this:

(1) Some of the conflicts cited appear to have been between groups in different positions in the *economic* (i.e., occupational) structure; the mailer and the unemployment controversies were of this kind, as was the priority issue, in part.

(2) Others of the issues arose out of conflicts between groups in different positions in the union's *political* structure. The ins-vs.-outs issues, insofar as they show differences between the interests of the administrative officers and the members, or between international and local administrations, involve this kind of cleavage, as did the secret-society issue, in which the interests of a political subgroup in the union were directly at stake.

(2a) A special case of (2) are those conflicts of interest between groups holding different positions in the union's *political electoral* structure. This, of course, is primarily the party structure: the number, nature, composition, and internal structure of electoral parties. Usually the differences generated here are those created by the election process itself, rather than by policy decisions, but at times policies may be instituted by an administration which weakens the out party's position. The electoral structure, though an informal one (the party system is outside the organizational structure of the union), is still part of the political authority structure. Since the ordinary voter has some authority in the political decisioning process, it follows that organizations like parties, which can channel their opinions into the decision-making process, have a place in the authority structure. Because this ability to channel opinions is variable, the authority position of the party is not a stable and formal one.

Besides these various interest issues, there are the issues which rest on continuing ideological (dispositional) difference among the members. Several of the issues we mentioned above to illustrate the interest principle had some ideological flavoring, but these in which ideological conflict seemed to play a particularly important part are:

(1) The alimoner-vs.-industrialist issue, which centered on the goals of printers' unions: Should they be benevolent societies, on guard against

accidents and death, or bargaining instruments, on guard against the employer?

(2) The priority issue, in which values similar but not quite the same as those above came into opposition. These were the values of individualism (foremen should have free reign in hiring) and of universalism or equality (men should be hired in the order of their arrival as substitutes, regardless of the foreman's preference).

(3) The arbitration issue. The Administration and Progressive Parties' positions on compulsory arbitration reflected the same ideological split as is seen in the above issues, with the Progressives' role the more militant one. The attitude to strikes, best exemplified by the Progressives' refusal to abide by the no-strike pledge in 1944 while the Independents agreed to it, reflects the same ideological difference.

(4) The unemployment issue and the rise of the Amalgamation Party. In this issue, we have little evidence that ideology played an important part for many men. But this issue marked the beginning of a new ideological strain in union politics. It was not so much that Communist ideology was different in content from the earlier radicalism. It took much the same attitude toward the employer, except that it was probably more militant. But it differed in that it did not so much operate within union politics as attempt to *use* the union as an instrument in gaining civil political ends. The platform of the Amalgamation Party in 1934, for example, bore little relation to *union* politics, but much to civil politics.[34]

Perhaps the one really new element in the ideology expressed by the Amalgamation Party was its tendency to look toward the national government for aid. Previously the ITU, one of the strongest unions in the country, had scorned government interference of any kind, sometimes with a John L. Lewis kind of militancy. It felt confidence in its power, and saw no need to bring the government into its fight with the employers. The Amalgamationists wanted to bring the civil government in as a third factor. This was understandable during the Depression, since most printers saw the problems facing the union as beyond the power of the union administration to solve. Today, however, both major parties seem to maintain the older attitude toward government. Recently, President Randolph named "reliance on self-help as against assistance from the Government" as one of five principles which he said make up the spirit of the ITU.[35]

---

34. The four points in their platform were: a farmer-labor party, unemployment and old age security, a thirty-hour week (not only in printing, but nationally) and industrial unionism, to begin in the printing industry.

35. This was a speech at the ITU's One Hundredth Anniversary Dinner on May 4, 1952, as reported in the *New York Times*, May 5, 1952, p. 30.

(5) The Taft-Hartley issue, with its related issues of strike policies and Unitypo. These issues reflect the same difference between the parties as manifested before: the Independents' greater willingness to compromise, the Progressives' greater willingness to strike or initiate other militant action.

(6) The CIO-AFL issue. It is clear that the Progressives were sympathetic to the CIO, while the Independents wanted to maintain affiliation with the AFL.

All these issues show that more or less the same ideological division has persisted in the ITU since the union was formed. It has been this continuing ideological division and not the irregularly occurring interest issues which has most nearly characterized the union's political system through the years. What have been the sources of this cleavage, and what have been their contributions to democratic politics? These questions will be dealt with in the succeeding chapters.

Before going on, it is important to note the significance of the fact that just about all the questions which activate the ideological commitments of the members of the ITU are questions of "foreign policy"— questions arising from the relation of the ITU to its environment. Almost all of the crucial political issues have involved the relations between the ITU and the employers. As we have noted earlier, there are few sources of internal conflict among different interest groups within the ITU. In unions which are more stratified internally or include members of different occupations, there is an obvious basis for sharp internal conflict. Such conflicts cannot be a source of ideological struggle between the more militant and more conservative members of the union. They also could not be the basis of a sustained democratic political life, for those interest groups which were in a minority could never hope to have their policies adopted.

The political problems facing an industrial union have been well described by Sayles and Strauss. They note that the negotiations over wage scales may be affected by differences in the real interests of union members:

> The industrial union, like most other organizations, is comprised of a complexity of groups with competing interests. Thus the worker in the plant is not only a company employee and a union member. He is also a member of countless other special interest groups: he may be a mill operator, on the night shift, with low seniority, paid on an "incentive rate," and so forth. The members who work in each of these groups may have bargaining objectives which conflict with those of other union "brothers."
>
> Without intending to minimize the unity and the common purpose that exists on the local level, we want to emphasize the other side of the picture: the difficult adjustments that must be made *internally* within the union during

the course of its *external* negotiations with management. What may appear to management as a common union policy is often the resultant of numerous compromises among divergent interest groups within the rank and file.[36]

It is likely that industrial unions must be dictatorial if they are to survive. The dictator is necessary to arbitrate interest conflicts which can not be settled by simply counting which interest group has more members. As we noted earlier in this chapter, the minority crafts in the late-nineteenth-century ITU seceded because they felt that they could not get the ITU to fight their battles. As a general proposition, we may assert that one of the necessary conditions for a sustained democratic political system in an occupational group is that it be so homogeneous that only ideology and not the more potent spur of self-interest divides its members. It is an important property of the ITU's political system that in those "foreign policy" areas where the most important questions are raised, the self-interest of the members is rarely involved, and relatively altruistic ideological commitments dominate political conflict.

---

36. Sayles and Strauss, *The Local Union*, p. 43.

CHAPTER *15*

Sources of Diversity
among the Members

EVERY STUDY OF ELECTION BEHAVIOR indicates that class or socio-economic position is the major variable which differentiates supporters of left and of right parties.[1] Religious or ethnic affiliation, regional interests, and rural-urban cleavages, all affect voting behavior; but the stratification variables are almost everywhere of the greatest importance.

Indeed, this close relationship between voting choice and socio-economic position is so common that one recent analyst of western Canadian agrarian movements has argued that a two-party system is impossible in the western wheat provinces of Canada because the farmers are all in the same socio-economic position, and hence have no basis for dividing internally.[2] As was pointed out earlier, a similar argument is made by Communists in defending the one-party system in the Soviet Union as democratic.

And yet in the ITU, which from a socio-economic point of view is as homogeneous as any group of that size could be, men have no difficulty in finding issues on which to disagree. Indeed, they disagree on more than union issues. For example, the political preferences and voting

1. See S. M. Lipset, Paul Lazarsfeld, *et al.*: "The Psychology of Voting: An Analysis of Political Behavior," in Gardner Lindsey (ed.), *Handbook of Social Psychology*, for documentation of this point and references to literature in this field.

2. See C. B. MacPherson: *Democracy in Alberta*, Toronto, University of Toronto Press, 1954. Actually the voting data for Alberta and Saskatchewan confound this thesis. See S. M. Lipset: "Democracy in Alberta," *The Canadian Forum*, 34:175-77 and 196-98 (November and December 1954) for a critical evaluation of this analysis.

behavior of our sample in the last few general elections indicate considerable heterogeneity.

Table 22—Vote Choices of Members of Big Six in Different U.S. and New York Elections, Compared with New York City Vote

	Printers, %	New York City Total Vote, %
President 1948[a]		
Truman	72	51
Dewey	24	35
Wallace	4	14
Governor 1950[b]		
Lynch	36	50
Dewey	61	43
McManus	3	7
Preferences for President in May-June 1952, Before the Nominating Conventions, %[c]		
Republican Candidates	54	
Eisenhower	27	
Taft	15	
Warren	8	
MacArthur	2	
Other Republicans	2	
Democratic Candidates	40	
Harriman	11	
Truman	10	
Stevenson	7	
Kefauver	8	
Other Democrats	4	
Other party	2	
Undecided	5	
President 1952[d]		
Stevenson (Dem.)	56	54
Eisenhower (Rep.)	42	44
Hallinan (ALP-Prog.)	2	2
New York Senator[e]		
Cashmore (Dem.)	37	43
Ives (Rep.)	43	43
Counts (Lib.)	17	12
Lamont (ALP)	3	2

NOTE: The vote for 1948 and 1950 was obtained from the original interviews in December and January, 1951-52; the 1952 vote was obtained from a questionnaire sent out the day after the election. The 3% in each election who did not vote were eliminated from the sample to obtain comparable figures. N's for printers are: a, 204; b, 309; c, 317; d, 204; e, 183.

The voting behavior of the New York printers parallels closely the pattern of voting of the complexly stratified population of New York City. The only exception to this tendency, the election of 1948, occurred in a year in which the ITU was engaged in a major series of strikes against provisions of the Taft-Hartley Act, and in which the Union had as its principal objective the repeal of that act. ITU members in that election were under great pressure to vote as union members, rather than in terms of other factors in their background.

Election results such as the above might be expected in a stratified community, but not among members of a single occupational group, all of whom have very much the same skill, income, and status. This propensity of printers to divide politically between the middle-class party (Republicans) and the working-class party (Democrats) is probably related to their marginal positions between the working-class and the middle-class. Some may be responding to union pressures, while others are more basically oriented towards middle-class values and sentiments. The factors underlying the divisions among printers between the national parties will not be analyzed in this volume, but are the subject of a further separate investigation.[3]

Since the ideological lines of division between the Democratic and Republican Parties parallel those differentiating the Progressive Party from the Independent Party, some correlation between support for the national and the union parties should occur. And as the data of Figure 50 make evident, a relationship does exist.

There does exist a relationship between voting Republican and Independent, and Democratic and Progressive, but it is not a very close one. No one in the union either openly recognizes or tries to take advantage of the varying national political predispositions of the men. Republicans do not vote Independent because they regard it as a more Republican-oriented party. In fact, most Independent leaders, like most Progressive leaders, are Democrats. The common factor which seems to lead people into the Independent and Republican Parties is that both parties are the more conservative alternative in a choice situation, and conservatively inclined men tend to make the conservative choice in both situations.

The union leaders are almost as careful to keep national political differences out of union politics as they are to avoid any mention of religious affiliation. And the fact that both parties have prominent leaders who are affiliated with different national parties, and with some minor parties, definitely prevents the introduction of national political matters into union controversies.[4] For example, James Lynch, long ITU

---

3. In the course of this study, printers were asked, at three periods in the course of the 1952 national election, which candidate they supported. This panel study is being analyzed by Gene Norman Levine as part of a Ph.D. dissertation at Columbia University.

4. The debate between the two union parties over how to deal with the Taft-Hartley Act did not parallel the debate between Republicans and Democrats over the passage of that act. Both union parties were clearly opposed to the act, differing only over the strategy and tactics the union should use in dealing with it or evading it.

Figure 50—Relationship between Voting in National Elections and in
Union Elections

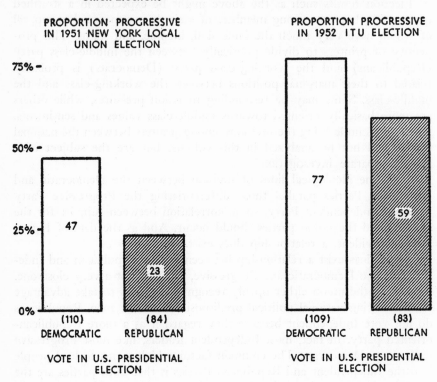

PROPORTION PROGRESSIVE
IN 1951 NEW YORK LOCAL
UNION ELECTION

PROPORTION PROGRESSIVE
IN 1952 ITU ELECTION

VOTE IN U.S. PRESIDENTIAL
ELECTION

VOTE IN U.S. PRESIDENTIAL
ELECTION

president and Wahneta leader, was a Republican. One of his closest aides,
Max Hayes, was a lifelong Socialist leader who was elected for many
years as ITU delegate to AFL conventions on the Wahneta ticket. At
AFL conventions, Hayes led the Socialist faction which fought the conservative Gompers wing. Frank Morrison, AFL secretary-treasurer, and
Gompers' closest aide in the AFL, was a Progressive in ITU politics.
"Jimmy" Simpson, one of the leading Socialists in the Canadian labor
movement, and the first Socialist mayor of Toronto, ran on the Conservative Party ticket for ITU first vice-president in 1930. Charles
Howard, Progressive leader of the ITU from 1922 to 1938, was a lifelong Republican. His closest co-worker, Woodruff Randolph, now ITU
president, is a former Socialist and is probably a liberal Democrat today.

The same pattern exists today among the New York parties. The
Progressive president of Big Six, Frank Barrett, is a Republican. The
head of the Progressive Club during the period in which we interviewed

union leaders was for MacArthur for United States President. The vice-president of the club, on the other hand, went to Moscow in 1952 as an unofficial delegate to a Communist trade-union conference. A number of other leaders of the New York Progressives are supporters of the American Labor Party, while still others back the vigorously anti-Communist New York Liberal Party, which broke from the ALP charging that it is controlled by the Communist Party. One of the leaders of the New York Independent Party is a Socialist; others back the Liberal Party; others the Republican. On the whole, however, the majority of the leaders of both parties in New York are Democrats.

Even if there were no parties within the union, the members would probably still divide between the two national parties. This suggests that the division between the two union parties rests in part on the fact that the union contains large numbers of men oriented in conservative and liberal directions. The fact that the members of the ITU continually divide almost equally, whenever faced with such choices as between arbitration or aggressive bargaining, AFL or CIO, Democrat or Republican, reflects this basic ideological cleavage. It is unlikely that there are many other unions that are so equally divided in the basic ideological predispositions of their members. What lies behind these basic predispositions?

§ Dispositions of the Men

THE ANALYSIS OF POLITICAL ISSUES in Chapter 14 indicated that the principal content of the continuing cleavage in the union was ideological, and was based on the different values that men brought with them to the union rather than on any objective differences in their positions within the union. From the time of the early split between the ali-moners and the industrialists, party differences in the ITU have expressed different "philosophies of unionism," or ideologies, which seems to stem from backgrounds and experiences independent of union politics themselves. From the analysis of issues, it is evident that the primary difference in disposition which the ideological issues in the union express is the difference between liberal or radical and conservative orientations, in the usual meaning of these terms. The supporters of the two parties should be expected to differ greatly with respect to these sets of values. As Figure 51 indicates, this is true for the men in the sample; the correlation between a liberalism-conservatism scale constructed from interview questions[5] and voting in the 1951 and 1952 union elections is

---

5. The construction of the scale is discussed in Appendix I.

quite high. (The reason for the lower correlation in 1952 will be discussed later.)

Figure 51—Vote of Liberals and Conservatives for Progressive Candidate, Per Cent

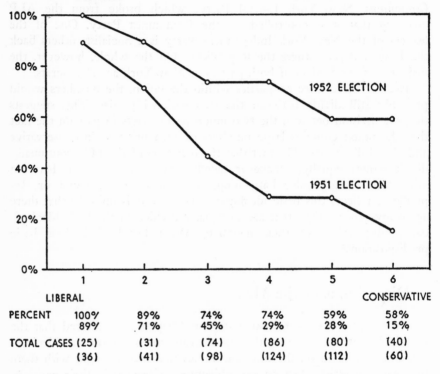

	LIBERAL					CONSERVATIVE
PERCENT	100%	89%	74%	74%	59%	58%
	89%	71%	45%	29%	28%	15%
TOTAL CASES	(25)	(31)	(74)	(86)	(80)	(40)
	(36)	(41)	(98)	(124)	(112)	(60)

The significance of this liberal-conservative split is further evidenced by the fact that no other attitude questions or scale in the questionnaire and no element of background such as religion, education, age, or father's occupation correlated so highly with voting. These background factors seem to operate *through* their effect on this stable set of values, not *apart from* it.[6]

This same relationship is evident among the party leaders interviewed, as Table 23 (including only numbers, not percentages) indicates:

---

6. This is not nearly so true in civil politics, where religion or father's occupation means many more things than in the ITU. To be a Catholic ordinarily means to live near Catholics, work with them and associate with them. Also, there is an historic identification of Catholics with the Democratic Party. Since men define this situation as real, it is real in its consequences; independently of their influence on values, such identifications engender an attachment to the party.

Table 23—Liberal-Conservative Values of Progressive and Independent Party Leaders

	Progressive Leaders	Independent Leaders
Liberal	14	5
Moderate	2	2
Conservative	3	5

But what about the men who respond to other issues—those based on interests of the various kinds we have examined, a candidate's personality, one of the "consensus" issues? For some men their own liberal or conservative attitude and the parties' positions on ideological issues are not important influences on their vote. This suggests a second disposition for investigation, the importance or relevance of the man's ideology in influencing his behavior.[7] This disposition, which we have called *ideological sensitivity*, determines the degree to which the man's liberal or conservative attitude is brought into play in union politics, as well as in other areas of his life. This disposition might also be thought of as the *saliency* of the liberal or conservative attitude.

This second measure, constructed from responses to questions of why one voted as one did, or what differences one saw between the parties,[8] separates those who mentioned any differences in ideology between the parties or any policy issues from those who mentioned other, nonpolicy differences between the parties. Thus it separates the men who see union politics in terms of *policy* from those who see union politics in nonpolicy terms. In doing this, it becomes a measure of *the degree to which one uses* his liberalism or conservatism in voting.

7. This is conceptually similar to Guttman's "intensity component" in scale analysis, though the mechanics of our index construction have no relation to his. See Samuel Stouffer *et al.: Measurement and Prediction,* Princeton, N. J., Princeton University Press, 1950, Chaps. 5 and 6; and Paul F. Lazarsfeld (ed.): *Mathematical Thinking in the Social Sciences,* Glencoe, Ill., Free Press, 1954, Chap. 5.

8. More precisely, the index was constructed from answers to questions 29, 32, and 38 (*a* and *b*). Answers to these open-ended questions were scored positive if (1) specific policy issues were mentioned, or if (2) the general liberal or conservative positions of the parties were mentioned. All other answers (e.g., personality of the candidates, "record in office," etc.) were scored zero. The respondent's index score was the sum of the positive scores on the four questions (see Appendix I for details). We will not defend this index as constituting a "scale" of exactly what we want to measure. Our justification of this procedure is simple: These questions came closer to measuring the relevance of the individual's liberal or conservative perspective than any other of our data. They constituted a kind of projective test, which he could answer in any way he saw fit. Answering in terms of something about the perspective of the parties meant that this perspective was highly salient or relevant to him. Although the questions were limited to union politics, they need not have been so in order to measure the concept we were concerned with. Later we show that even with this limitation, the index measures a general attribute which is manifested in a man's orientations in civil politics as well as in union politics.

Parenthetically it may be noted that if ITU politics were as complex as United States civil politics, it would be necessary to examine many dispositions in addition to liberal-conservatism and ideological sensitivity. Numerous values, and various attachments and antagonisms to groups and institutions, would further complicate analysis. The problem would be especially difficult since each national party is identified not nearly so much with a consistent ideology as with various groups, and these often produce within a party conflicting ideologies through conflicting interests. Besides this, historical attachments through the family or ethnic group play an important part in civil politics. The ITU, on the other hand, has a political system simple and consistent enough to allow us to consider only the single dispositional area: the liberal or conservative value position, together with its relevance to the man's behavior, i.e., his ideological sensitivity. All other dispositions (except those arising from material interest or direct social influence on the vote) are subsidiary enough to be considered unexplained deviations.

The two dispositional differences, liberalism or conservatism, and relevance or saliency, produce logically four types of men (Table 24).

Table 24—Types of Political Attitude

Relevance of attitude (ideological sensitivity)	Attitude position	
	Liberal	Conservative
High	I	II
Low	III	IV

Men of Types I and II differ in their liberal-conservative attitudes, and use their attitudes in politics. Men of Types III and IV are essentially alike, for although one group is liberal and the other conservative, their attitudes are not relevant to their political decisions. This means that the men who differ in these two ways should show three distinct kinds of political behavior. First (Type I) is the liberal who sees liberal-conservative differences between the parties and who sticks with the liberal group; second (Type II) is the conservative who similarly sees these differences, and sides with the conservative group; third (Type III or IV) is the man who, regardless of whether he is liberal or conservative, bases his vote on something other than his attitude, not using his liberalism or conservatism as a basis for his choice.[9]

The difference between these three basic types of men can be

9. It should be noted that we are not attempting to explain the man's vote completely in terms of these dispositions; the vote has many sources, social as well as psychological, as will be evident in the next few chapters. The historical accident that places one man in the *Herald Tribune* and another in the *Post*, or in a small shop rather than a large one, has important consequences in shaping the man's vote.

illustrated by a quotation from one of the Independent leaders we interviewed. This man was strongly ideologically oriented to union politics; his orientation to union politics was shaped by clashes with a few Communist or fellow-travelling Progressives in his shop. He was more liberal than most Independents, but reacted strongly aganst the values of some of the Progressives. After he discussed the differences in ideology and behavior between the active Independents and the active Progressives, we asked him about the differences between the ordinary followers of the parties in the union. Were the Progressive followers quite different from the Independent followers? He replied, "They don't differ much from ours. They vote on friendship, they argue back and forth on the record [of the candidates]. The rank-and-file members don't really *know*. We send our circulars to them."

This active Independent divides the union into three groups according to the bases on which they make voting decisions, just as we have. The difference he sees between the active party members and the followers is the difference between men who use their ideology in union politics and those who do not, as outlined above. To "vote on friendship," and "argue back and forth on the record" are typical nonideological bases for voting. The active man quoted above contrasts these, as we do, with the bases on which the active Independents and active Progressives vote. It is important to note one point, however, which this quote obscures: the ideological voters need not be politically active; it is enough that they see the party differences along liberal-conservative lines, and react to the parties on the basis of this difference. As later analysis will show, there are many men who see union politics in these terms but who take no active part in union politics.

As might be expected, men of Type I and Type II tend to support a party, that is, they support the same party locally and internationally, while men of Types III and IV tend to either split their support or support neither party (see Figure 52). Also, most of the 80% of Type I men who support a party favor the Progressives, while most of the 73% of the Type II men who support a party favor the Independents. For the few Type III and IV men who support a party, there is much less difference: their liberalism or conservatism is much less likely to be the basis of their party support. Figure 53 confirms this, showing the sharpest difference between the ideologically sensitive men.[10]

---

10. There is a generally greater support for the Progressives here than for the Independents, which skews the results somewhat. This is due to the high amount of support given to the Progressives who were in office internationally. They overshadowed the international Independents, who were somewhat in eclipse until the next election campaign.

Figure 52—Party Support among Men Differing in Ideological Sensitivity and in Liberal-Conservative Attitude

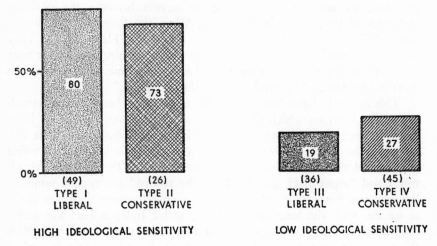

PERCENT FAVORING A PARTY

NOTE: The middle groups in each scale are not included here. It is the polar types that we are considering at present.

§ Sources of Diversity

THE SOURCES OF these dispositional differences which are so important to union politics lie quite outside the union and even the occupation itself, and are located in the cultural heritage and other deeply embedded experiences in these printers' lives.

THE PARTY LEADERS:
CRAFT ORIENTATION VS. UNION ORIENTATION

THE DIFFERING PERSPECTIVES of the party leaders are manifested almost as much in their attitudes toward the mechanics of union politics itself as in attitudes toward the policy content of union politics. The parties' differences in policy have been dampened and modified by the constraints of office: despite differences in liberal or conservative values, the continuing necessity for dealing with the employer makes the professed policy differences few. But the differing perspectives of the party

Figure 53—Of Those Who Favor One Party or the Other, Percentage
         Favoring Progressives

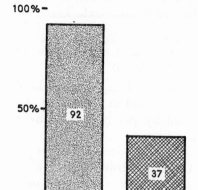

100%—

50%—

0%—

| 92 | 37 | | 86 | 58 |

(39)   (19)   (7)   (12)
TYPE I   TYPE II   TYPE III   TYPE IV

HIGH IDEOLOGICAL SENSITIVITY   LOW IDEOLOGICAL SENSITIVITY

leaders, which are somewhat masked by the constraints of office, show up most clearly in the way they approach union politics.

The Independents are often incensed by the intensity and seriousness of the Progressives' political efforts, as well as by their policies. One leader said:

> They [the Progs] come in there to the meeting as a group, and they act in there as a group. Our group goes in for good times and that sort of thing, having a drink with the boys and so on. But they're more intent on winning a point in the union regardless of how they attain it. . . . Another thing I object to—not all the Progs do it—I've served on scale committees, and when you are on a scale committee you must forget your party. There are many things done in negotiations that are pledged secret on both sides. I believe one should hold to that pledge. . . . Some of the Progs leave the negotiation sessions like cross-country runners, with a dime clutched in their hands to call Prog headquarters.

Another had a similar viewpoint:

> This group that I call the Commies are all there [at union meetings] always, and they vote in a mass. Our men are too busy working in their gardens, they don't seem to take a strong enough interest.

The more traditional, conservative approach to union politics by the Independents is likewise evidenced by the bases on which they came together to form political groups. When asked about the first union political meeting he attended, one Independent leader, who had been part of the nucleus of the group since its formation, said:

I guess it was the advocates of the five-day week in the *World*. In 1929 we started to hold gatherings against Rouse [the local president]. There was just a small group of us at that time. I guess we came together mostly by friendship. But it was more than that, because some of us had been associated through our [printer] families, and we all had the same general background. . . . When you all grow up together you just naturally stay together.

Other Independent leaders interviewed told of being "pushed into" politics by their friends in printers' clubs. As noted in Chapter 11, for many of these leaders politics was preceded by purely social activity in printers' clubs of one sort or another.

The approach to union politics taken by the Progressive leaders has much less of this "sociability" aspect. One Progressive leader, when asked about the Independents, said, "They carry on a campaign on a personal basis, on personal leadership, while Progs have a platform, strict enforcement of contract, and represent the interests of the working printer." Another said, "We of the Progs like to feel we're more intelligent and a more thinking type. For example, our people don't hang around beer gardens and such." This man was referring to a fact mentioned by several of the Progressive leaders. The Independents hold their weekly meetings in a tavern near union headquarters, making their meeting a social gathering as well as a political club meeting,[11] Characteristically, the Progressives meet under more austere circumstances, in a midtown hotel, with sociability taking a decided back seat to the business of politics.

These quotes suggest that the militant and conservative perspectives held by these two groups of men are deeply ingrained parts of their personalities. Even when there is no difference in policy, each objects to the approach taken to union politics by the other party. It seems likely, then, that such fundamentally different orientations must spring from rather basic differences in background of the two groups.

Perhaps the most obvious place to look for such differences is in religion. The New York union has nearly equal numbers of Protestants, Catholics, and Jews (in our sample, 169 Catholics, 135 Protestants, and 123 Jews). Even though there are no interest-group divisions on the basis of religion in the union, the cultural differences inherent in Catholic, Protestant, and Jewish backgrounds might easily lead to different perspectives about how the union should be run, and thus to differences

---

11. In this report, they are similar to their Wahneta predecessors, who were both a union party and a social lodge.

in party affiliations. But the leaders of the two parties are not very different in religious affiliation (Table 25).

Table 25—Religious Preferences of Party Leaders

Religion Preference	Progressive Leaders	Independent Leaders	Total Sample
Catholic	10	9	169
Protestant	5	3	135
Jewish	6	3	123
Total	**21**	**15**	**427**

NOTE: For different tabulations of leader's characteristics the numbers will usually differ, for data were not obtained in every area for each leader. Thus twenty-one Progressives and fifteen Independents are listed in this table, although the next tabulation indicates nineteen and fifteen respectively.

However, there are other respects in which the backgrounds of the Progressive leaders differ from those of the Independents. The backgrounds of these leaders may be classified as high-status or low-status, on the basis of (1) the father's occupation at the time the respondent was growing up, and (2) the financial hardship of the family during this period.

Table 26—Status Background of Party Leaders

Leaders' Background	Progressive Leaders	Independent Leaders
High-status	6	12
Low-status	13	3
Total	**19**	**15**

Table 26 hows that many more Independent leaders than Progressive leaders are from a high-status background; further examination shows that this pattern holds for the leaders in each religious group.

The distinguishing characteristic of the Independents' high-status backgrounds is a traditional printing family, or a family of craft-union activity. Of the fifteen party leaders, twelve are from such families. Eight of those are from printer families, while the other four of the twelve had a father or brother active in some other union. Of course, these eight printing families differed in the degree to which they were printing families. While some leaders' families had been families of printers for "as far back as I know of," others of the leaders had only an older brother or father in printing. The four men who were not from printing families but from union activist families had fathers who were skilled in some trade, such as a plumbing contractor or an electrician, all of them active in the union of their craft. The union activity for these men's families was not simply union membership, but strong union activity, which seems from the interviews to have pervaded the family atmosphere, just as in the traditional printing families the norms of printing played this role.

The general characteristics of the Independent leaders' backgrounds may be illustrated by excerpts from some of their interviews. One man said:

I took up printing in school. My stepmother and all her sisters had been printers and I heard the conversation at home so much that it was just the natural thing to do. Hearing it at home so much made it so that I really didn't know anything else.

Another said:

My father had been a printer, and my brother was a printer, so it was natural that the trade would be printing. . . . I've been interested in unionism all my life. When I was seven my brother would give me a handful of stickers early in the morning and tell me to go out and stick all of them up. On them it said, "Boycott the Sun." He was working for the *Sun* and they were on strike. Finally we beat them.

Perhaps the most intense printing background of any of the leaders we interviewed is described thus:

My parents were in it, and I was a printer's devil when I was twelve or thirteen, running around at three or four in the morning. My grandfather was a printer and my father was a printer, both in Dublin. They were printers at least two generations back of my father, and maybe before that. . . . They came over from Ireland in 1881. They were the first ones to carry their cases into the *World.* They lived down on Pike Street then and would walk to work. My sister operated a newspaper for a while, called the *Brooklyn Weekly News.* My mother knew more about printing than printers did, since we were a printing family, and she knew all the printers and their shops and their wives. My father died when I was six. There were nine of us. The family knew I was going to be a printer even though I didn't. . . . My mother decided I wasn't going to accomplish anything by going to school any longer. She gave me a letter to the benefit clerk at the union—she knew everybody down at the union—so he sent me out to a shop and I began as a printer's devil.

Of course, not all the Independent leaders had printing backgrounds. One of the leaders had this to say about his background:

My father was a very active trade-unionist in the painters' union. He was secretary of the union here in New York. That was when you had to keep it in your hat; it was dangerous to be active in a union then. . . . It never seemed to be that way much in printing, but in his trade it was a dangerous thing to do.

In all of these fifteen interviews with Independent leaders, only three indicated that there was a real struggle for existence in their childhood period. These leaders, then, present a picture of fairly secure, fairly high-status, skilled-labor families, imbued with craft-union norms, or most characteristically, printing norms.

The picture is startlingly different for the Progressive leaders. Only one had a father in printing, and one more a brother. Another had a brother who was active in another union. These are the only three out of the nineteen with printing or unionist backgrounds, compared to twelve out of fifteen among the Independents. Several others had friends or relatives outside the immediate family who were printers or active unionists, but only these three had such backgrounds in their own family.

The great majority of Progressive leaders have been upwardly mobile. Some had an immigrant father who gave up his craft or trade and struggled at some menial job to support the family. Other backgrounds are farm, unskilled factory worker, and coal miner. One Progressive leader, who had grown up in London, told a tale of poverty in describing his background.

> I was a kid in London and went to work at eleven selling papers at the railroad station. . . . One Monday morning I went to the book store—the office—and someone told me that a man on the platform wanted to see me. When I went there, he asked me, "Are you the boy that works here?" He invited me to a boy's party. He was interested in group welfare. After a few of them, he asked me whether I wanted to be a printer. He asked me what I wanted to be. I said, "A cooper; my father is one." He pressed me. Finally I said, "Well, see my mother." He did, and she was so impressed she said Okay. . . . I lived in a suburb of London. As I didn't look like a gutter-snipe to that group-welfare man, he thought he could help me. . . .
>
> I can give you an idea of the tragedy that could happen to a boy in those days. I worked from Monday morning to Wednesday night, including Monday and Tuesday nights, without halt, and the rest went to school. During my apprenticeship, apprentices died before they could become journeymen.

Another said:

> I was born in Europe. We were very poor and lived in dire poverty after coming to Boston. As Jews we were kicked around. My sympathies, therefore, have always been with the underdog. The union enabled me to speak freely about my opinion without fear of losing my job.

One Progressive leader, the one who was brought into printing by his brother, also had a difficult time as a child:

> My father was a bootblack, a porter. He did hard labor all his life. He's retired now. He was no labor-union member; he can't read or write. . . . I had to go to work for financial reasons—there was a family of five children. There are a lot of things you don't like to do you have to. Ours was a poor family.

At least thirteen of the nineteen Progressive leaders have backgrounds of one of these types: low-status immigrant, or native with low status, or financial hardships. (Most of the fathers of the Independent leaders were immigrants also, but they were often able to continue their trade —usually printing—after immigration.) In any case, for at least these thirteen Progressive leaders, the son's job as a printer is much higher in status and pay than the father's job. His whole position in society reflects a great increase in status and security over his origins.

These very different backgrounds of the two groups of leaders seem to be responsible in great measure for the quite different ways in which the Progressives and Independents view the aims and purposes of the union. In keeping with their printing and craft-union backgrounds, the Independents seem most concerned about "conserving our sound, craft unionism," while the Progressives are most restless, with an image of "militant, progressive unionism." The Independents, long identified with printing and unions, seem to want to *continue* the union in its traditional ways and to continue printing as a craft with high status. The Progressives, on the other hand, having themselves had to struggle in order to rise above their lower status, view the job of the union as a continuance of struggle, of fighting for *gains* in security and self-determination. Their concern for the "craft" of printing seems not nearly so strong as their concern for the strength of the union as a bargaining agent.[12]

How do these backgrounds produce such different perspectives? We can do little more than speculate. However, in speculation we may ask regarding one group whether it was the *transition*, that is the mobility itself, which produced the more militant orientation, or the *position* which their families were in. Would the low-status-background men have been as liberal if they had remained low-status? Would the printing-background men have remained as conservative if they had been reduced in status?

These questions cannot be answered, for all our men are in the same occupation. However, if it were solely the transition in status, inde-

---

12. Even *within* each party, this difference holds: the leaders with low-status backgrounds have the most liberal attitudes, while those with high-status (mostly printing) backgrounds have the most conservative attitudes, as the table below shows:

Table—Relationship between Liberalism, and Background Status of Leaders of the Two Parties

	Liberal	Moderate	Conservative
Progressive Leaders:			
Low-status Background	11	0	3
High-status Background	3	2	2
Independent Leaders:			
Low-status Background	2	0	0
High-status Backgroond	3	2	5

pendent of the direction of mobility, then men who have come to the union from backgrounds *higher* than that of printing should be more liberal, just as are those who come from a lower-status background. This should be testable; but among the leaders it is hard to distinguish more than one or two who were clearly downwardly mobile in becoming printers. Even in the total sample of union members, there are not enough men like this, and moreover, whatever downward mobility there may have been is not clear enough to allow an empirical test of this proposition. There are indications, however, from the few cases to be found in the sample, that the mobility itself—apart from direction—does play a part; men from status backgrounds both lower and higher tend to be more liberal than men with printing origins.

One final remark must be made about the perspectives of the two parties' leaders. Both groups have been considered ideologically sensitive, men of Type I and Type II (to use the typology outlined earlier in the chapter). But from the interviews it seems obvious that on the average, the Progressive leaders are ideologically more highly sensitive than are the Independent leaders. Their different orientations to union politics, as indicated by the passages from these interviews quoted in earlier pages, show this. The fact that almost all the union activities of Progressive leaders are strictly political, while those of the Independent leaders are often social, suggests this. And while the Independent group "goes in for good times and that sort of thing," some of the Progressives received their political upbringing in the Amalgamation Party, probably the most ideologically oriented of all ITU political parties. As will be seen later in looking at the determinants of ideological sensitivity, this kind of sensitivity probably stems from the same sources as does liberalism.[13]

THE RANK AND FILE: DETERMINANTS OF
LIBERALISM AND CONSERVATISM

UNFORTUNATELY, THE INFORMATION about the family backgrounds of the rank-and-file printers in the sample is not as good as the data on the leaders. Very often the father held several occupations throughout his lifetime, of widely differing status and pay. Immigrants in particular often had to change their occupations radically upon coming to this country. In most cases, too, the respondent gave his father's highest oc-

---

13. It is interesting to note that the orientations of these New York leaders reflect the same ideological difference which has characterized the international party split throughout the years. The issues discussed in Chap. 14 show that the differences between the two parties strikingly parallel the present orientations of New York party leaders.

cupation, which may have been irrelevant to the family's status at the time the man interviewed was growing up. For all these reasons or others, the father's occupation as obtained in the interview does not show a consistent relation to liberal and conservative attitudes.

However, other indicators of family background do show clearly the importance of this factor as a determinant of liberalism and conservatism. Among the men in the sample, as contrasted to the leaders, religion is the strongest indicator of this difference. Figure 54 shows the attitudes of Protestants, Catholics, and Jews in our sample. We

Figure 54—Percentage "Liberal" on Liberal-Conservative Attitude Scale among Protestants, Catholics, and Jews

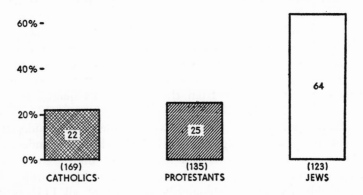

see that Jews are by far most liberal, while Catholics and Protestants are about alike on the average.[14]

This relationship of liberalism-conservatism to religion is a consistent one, and one which is not accounted for by any other background factors measured. However, as the discussion of the leaders' backgrounds indicates, other factors are quite important. One indicator of these other factors is the birthplace of the respondent and his father; that is, whether he is first generation, second generation, or from a family which has been in this country more than two generations. In examining this, as all subsequent factors, religious affiliation has been held constant, since it bears such a strong relation to liberal and con-

---

14. If the scale were more finely divided, as in the original data, it would show that there are more Protestants at both extremes, liberal and conservative, while the Catholics are grouped more closely. This is understandable, for Protestants are more diverse than Catholics or Jews, being in some ways a residual category from the other two. While there is one Catholic Church, and one Jewish cultural heritage (most Jews in our sample are from eastern Europe) there are many varieties of Protestantism.

servative attitudes. Figure 55 shows the relationship between time of arrival in this country and liberalism, for Protestants, Catholics, and Jews.

Figure 55—Relationship between Recency of Immigation and Liberalism for each Religious Group

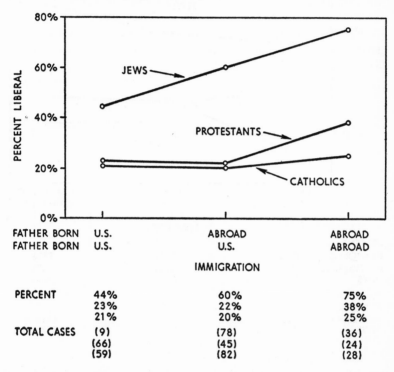

	FATHER BORN	U.S.	ABROAD	ABROAD
	FATHER BORN	U.S.	U.S.	ABROAD
			IMMIGRATION	
PERCENT		44%	60%	75%
		23%	22%	38%
		21%	20%	25%
TOTAL CASES		(9)	(78)	(36)
		(66)	(45)	(24)
		(59)	(82)	(28)

In general, the shorter the time in this country, the more liberal these men are. This is in accord with the findings about these leaders' backgrounds: immigrant status and its economic hardships produces more liberal men, while the influence of life in the United States tends to be a conservative one.

Another factor which seems to operate independently of both religion and length of time in this country is education. Figure 56 shows that for each religious group, higher education means in general more liberal attitudes.

If length of time in this country is held constant, the spread between the attitudes of the elementary-school and high-school groups would tend to *increase*, for the length of time in this country is correlated with education, and the two factors—length of time in this country and edu-

Figure 56—Relationship between Education and Liberalism for Each Religious Group

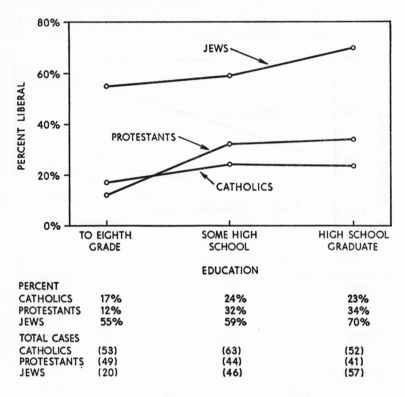

PERCENT			
CATHOLICS	17%	24%	23%
PROTESTANTS	12%	32%	34%
JEWS	55%	59%	70%
TOTAL CASES			
CATHOLICS	(53)	(63)	(52)
PROTESTANTS	(49)	(44)	(41)
JEWS	(20)	(46)	(57)

cation—have contradictory effects on attitudes: while residence in this country is a conservative influence, education (which tends to be greater the longer the time in this country) is a liberalizing influence.

Another factor in these men's backgrounds which seems to affect liberalism-conservatism is age. Of course, not all the factors so far found to be important can be held constant, but on examining again each religious group, the relations between age and liberalism turn out to be as shown in Figure 57.

For each religion, the age groups which are most conservative comprise men between forty and sixty years of age. It is hard to assess just why they should be more conservative than both the younger and the older men. These men were in their twenties, or younger, in the 1920's and began their careers at a time of prosperity. On the other hand, the depression struck them perhaps more than any other age group. Whatever the cause, the younger and the older men are more liberal than the men forty to sixty years old in each religious group.

As was pointed out, there is a correlation between voting for the Republican Party and voting Independent, and between voting for the Democrats or a minority left party and voting Progressive. It might be suggested that it is commitment to the Democrats or Republicans rather than liberalism-conservatism which determines a man's stand in union politics. In fact, however, this is not the case. The scale of liberalism-conservatism is more closely related to the way men vote in union elections than is their civil political preference (compare Figure 51 and Figure 58).

Figure 57—Relationship between age and Liberalism for Each Religious Group

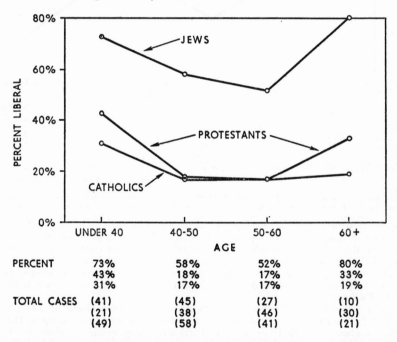

PERCENT	73%	58%	52%	80%
	43%	18%	17%	33%
	31%	17%	17%	19%
TOTAL CASES	(41)	(45)	(27)	(10)
	(21)	(38)	(46)	(30)
	(49)	(58)	(41)	(21)

But while civil political allegiance has less effect on union voting than does liberalism-conservatism, it nevertheless is related to the way printers vote in union elections, as we see from Figure 58. And it may be posited that allegiance to one of the national parties is one factor which determines whether a man is a liberal or a conservative.[15]

---

15. To present the relationship in this fashion may appear to contradict the obvious and common-sense notion that in national as in union politics, liberalism-

Figure 58—Civil Political Allegiance, and Voting for Progressive Party,
Per Cent

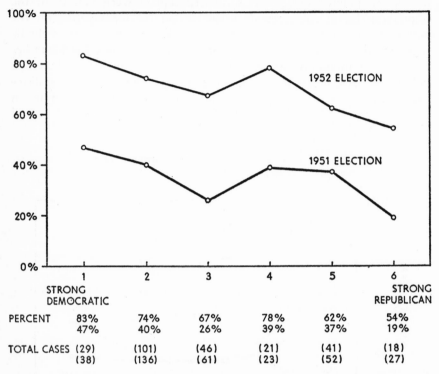

	1 STRONG DEMOCRATIC	2	3	4	5	6 STRONG REPUBLICAN
PERCENT	83% 47%	74% 40%	67% 26%	78% 39%	62% 37%	54% 19%
TOTAL CASES	(29) (38)	(101) (136)	(46) (61)	(21) (23)	(41) (52)	(18) (27)

NOTE: The scale of civil political allegiance is based on the respondent's professed party affiliation, and his votes in the 1948 Presidential election and the 1950 election for Governor in New York.

conservatism determines a man's party allegiance. The fact is, however, that allegiance to an American national party, like church affiliation, is more a matter of social influence than ideological choice. From two-thirds to three-quarters of Americans vote as their fathers did. A recent study of the 1948 United States elections indicated that family voting tradition was more important than socio-economic position or religious affiliation in determining men's political allegiances. (See Berelson et al., Voting.)

On a national level the Democratic Party is clearly more liberal or leftist than the Republican Party. We would assume, therefore, that men brought up in Democratic families and with Democratic political allegiances would be more likely to absorb or develop a liberal ideology. Thus, if our assumptions are valid, civil political background would operate like religious background to make for liberalism or conservatism among printers, and would be one of the independent factors which make for diversity within the union. This hypothesis, as such, is untestable using our data, since we cannot establish the time sequence between party affiliation and ideological convictions. We can demonstrate, however, that civil party allegiance is correlated with ideology even when we hold constant all the other measurable factors in the backgrounds of printers which make for liberalism or conservatism. Holding constant time of immigration, religious group, and education, Democrats in our sample are more liberal than Republicans.

Thus it may be argued—though we cannot prove it—that civil political allegiance affects union politics indirectly, by way of its effect on ideology. And the fact that men of diverse political backgrounds become printers is one of the elements which makes for ideological diversity within the union.[16]

In summary, the following background factors make for liberalism or conservatism among the ITU members (all are independent: that is, they remain even if the other factors are held constant).

RELIGION: Jews are far more liberal than either Protestants or Catholics; Protestants are about as liberal as Catholics, but are more diverse than either Catholics or Jews.

IMMIGRATION: The longer one's family has been in this country, the greater the chances are that one is conservative; first generation Americans are the most liberal.

EDUCATION: The more highly educated one is, the greater the chances that one is liberal.

AGE: The men below forty and above sixty are more liberal than the men from forty to sixty.

CIVIL POLITICS: Democrats are more liberal than Republicans.

It is this underlying ideological difference between the liberal and conservative printers which ultimately provides the foundation for a *continuing* opposition. And it is this continuing opposition, as contrasted with factionalism, which seems quite necessary for a functioning democratic system. If the differences between the union parties received no support from a similar difference in attitudes among the men, they could hardly continue. Issues which do not connect with this difference in outlook meet with no response among the members. One Independent leader said, when asked why the Independents do not push the issue of Communism among the Progressives more, "We as a party can't publicize it. We have in the past, but it doesn't seem to penetrate the minds of the members. We don't want to lose friends by pushing an unresponsive issue. We have banged away at the issue and it backfired." If all issues were like this, if no ideological issue were responded to by

---

16. We shall not go into the factors differentiating printers in their civil political allegiance, since this is the subject of another study and would take much more space than this chapter. Evidence, however, that the civil political allegiances of printers are a product of familial background, may be found in the strong correlation between religious background and party allegiance. Republican printers are much more likely to be Protestants than Catholics or Jews. We suggest that this is related to the fact that the cleavage between the Republicans and Democrats has traditionally been correlated with religious affiliation. It is significant to note, however, that Protestants do not have a greater tendency to be Independents in union politics than do Catholics.

their members, the parties would have a hard time maintaining themselves. Of course, the parties could fight about consensus issues and other issues having no relation to ideology. But it is the ideological issues that give the parties their distinctiveness and vitality and enable them to enlist the allegiance of large numbers of members.

All these determinants of liberalism and conservatism predate the members' union experiences. These indeed account for a great part of the ideological differences among the men. It is an indication of the strength and persistence of such attitudes that they can be so largely accounted for by factors rooted so far in the past of these men, most of whom are thirty or forty years away from their childhood. But to what extent does experience within the union and within the trade affect ones ideological outlook? Chapters 8 and 9 indicated the important effects of a man's shop on his relationship to other printers, to the union, and to his boss, and it might be expected that these different types of relationships should have lasting effects on a man's ideology. The data do show some such influence.

For all three religious groups, there seems to be a tendency toward increasing liberalism with increasing size of shop. However, the tendency is not great, and it is only in the context of what has already been indicated about the different characteristics of large and small shops that it is meaningful.

There are many other kinds of occupational experience which must have had some effect on these men's basic ideological perspective, but of these no record exists. Probably most important are the men's experiences with their employers. Among the leaders interviewed, one of the most common factors leading them to become active in union politics was a fight in the shop over a violation by the employer of some point in the contract. Experience in strikes, in organizing shops with antagonistic or friendly employers, should of course have a considerable influence on ideological outlook.

Union politics itself certainly has an effect on the individual's ideology. As one Independent leader (who had first joined the Wahnetas—the forerunners of the present Independents—in 1912) said, "My leanings were toward the conservative element in the union in opposition to the radical element. I always figured the conservative element could give the union a better deal than the radical element . . . and then naturally when you're allied with one party you get to thinking along that line."

§ Variations in Sensitivity to Ideology

THERE IS A GOOD DEAL of evidence to suggest that many of the same factors which make for liberalism make for ideological sensitivity. In the first place, the two factors are rather highly correlated in our sample. A liberal is a good deal more likely to be high in ideological sensitivity than is a conservative, as Table 27 shows.

Table 27—Relationship between Liberalism and Ideological Sensitivity

	Liberal	Moderate	Conservative
High in ideological sensitivity, %	48	28	29
N	(154)	(127)	(163)

If a man is liberal on our scale, the chances are about even that he will also be high on the ideological-sensitivity index; while if he is moderate or conservative, the chances are hardly more than one out of four that he will be high in ideological sensitivity.

What is the reason for this correlation? It seems likely that the social processes which produce liberalism also produce ideological sensitivity. That is, the hardship and deprivation which brought about the liberalism or radicalism of some of the leaders must have acted in part through making them aware of or sensitive to what they felt were injustices in the social system. This awareness or sensitivity is identical with the ideological sensitivity with which we are concerned here. To have conservative positions, on the other hand, is to have positions which generally agree with those held by most of the value-generating and opinion-molding agencies of the society. In other words, it is easier to hold conservative attitudes without these issues ever having been important or relevant.[17] One might go even further and say that if these questions on various social issues were not relevant or salient to the respondent when he was asked his opinion, he would more likely have answered conservatively, since the conservative, more socially accepted answer is "easier" to give when one is pressed for an answer.

Since liberalism and ideological sensitivity are associated, a correla-

17. This latter principle has been emphasized by several sociologists who have studied the relation between social mobility and beliefs or values. They have stressed the necessity of vertical mobility and "horizontal" or geographic mobility for the development of a positive ideology, or one in conflict with the *status quo*. P. Sorokin in his *Social Mobility* (New York, Harper & Brothers, 1927) discusses the effect of vertical mobility on ideology; while Karl Mannheim suggests that *both* vertical and horizontal mobility are necessary for development of a strong ideology (see his *Ideology and Utopia*, New York, Harcourt, Brace and Company, Inc., 1936).

tion between ideological sensitivity and the background factors which are related to liberalism-conservatism should exist. Indeed, Jews are ideologically more sensitive, just as they are more liberal, than either Catholics or Protestants. Similarly, those who are immigrants themselves or whose fathers are immigrants are ideologically more sensitive than those of native birth or whose fathers are of native birth. But in neither of these cases is the relation very great.[18] However, the other two variables which were found to be related to liberalism—age and education—are not consistently related to ideological sensitivity.

The generally low relationship of ideological sensitivity to background factors suggests that the index of ideological sensitivity (which, it will be recalled, was constructed on the basis of questions about union politics) measures something related specifically to union politics and not any generalized ideological sensitivity. One question from the interview is reassuring on this point, however. Figure 59 shows that interest in United States civil politics as well as union politics is highly correlated with ideological-sensitivity index. Interest in United States civil politics shows even a slightly higher correlation with the index of ideological sensitivity than does interest in union politics.

As mentioned above, however, it seems that ideological relevance or sensitivity is not as permanent a thing as is the liberal or conservative attitude itself. As the correlation with civil political interest suggests, involvement in civil politics may bring about ideological sensitivity. And events in the larger social and economic environment probably have their effect in stimulating or dampening a man's tendency to see things in terms of ideology.

Within the union also, there are many factors which have their effect. Activity in a party, however it initially came about, is likely to make one begin to see politics in terms of policy issues. Most of the men who are high on the ideological-sensitivity scale, whether liberal or conservative, identify themselves as supporting a party, as is shown

---

18. Distance from an immigrant background, it appears, dampens the importance or saliency of ideology and tends to make the people in our sample conservative. This raises the question whether living in this country dampens the ideological sensitivity of liberals and conservatives alike, or only of liberals. The table below suggests that living in this country reduces the ideological sensitivity of liberals alone, and not of conservatives or moderates, and if anything *increases* the ideological sensitivity of conservatives:

Table—Recency of Immigration, and Ideological Sensitivity in Liberals, Moderates, and Conservatives

	LIBERAL Generation			MODERATE Generation			CONSERVATIVE Generation		
	1st	2nd	3rd+	1st	2nd	3rd+	1st	2nd	3rd+
Percentage ideologically sensitive	55	49	39	26	28	28	17	34	27
N	(44)	(77)	(33)	(23)	(65)	(37)	(23)	(77)	(63)

by Figure 52 above. Certainly this party identification has had its effect on these men in fostering their sensitivity to policy issues, in making the perspectives of the parties more important to them. The high ideological sensitivity of both sets of party leaders shows this in the extreme. While these men brought part of their ideological sensitivity with them to party activity, some of it was surely fostered through continued interaction with one another and through opposition to the other party.

There is one other point about ideological sensitivity which is of great importance for the union. This is the effect of the clubs on the conservatives. As is shown in Chapter 7, a very high proportion of the ideologically sensitive conservatives in the sample are club members. While liberals almost "naturally" have some degree of ideological sensitivity, it seems that interaction within the shops, the party, and especially the clubs is very important in fostering and maintaining ideological sensitivity among conservatives. Many conservatives would not come directly to politics, but are interested in the social activities of the union. Once in the clubs, they become a captive audience in the sense discussed earlier, and are awakened to the importance of political issues.

The fact that the extreme conservatives *are* sometimes aroused to see union politics in terms of policy issues is indicated in Figure 60,

Figure 59—Relationship between Ideological Sensitivity and
Interest in Union and Civil Politics

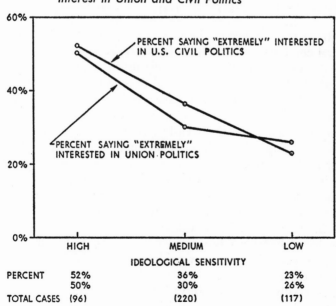

	HIGH	MEDIUM	LOW
		IDEOLOGICAL SENSITIVITY	
PERCENT	52%	36%	23%
	50%	30%	26%
TOTAL CASES	(96)	(220)	(117)

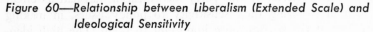

Figure 60—Relationship between Liberalism (Extended Scale) and Ideological Sensitivity

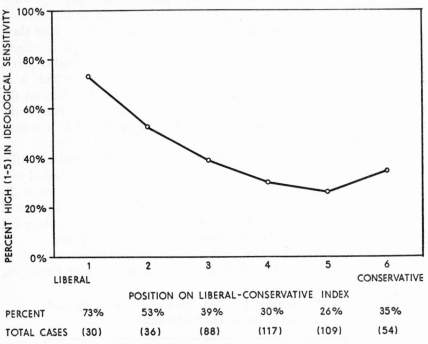

PERCENT	73%	53%	39%	30%	26%	35%
TOTAL CASES	(30)	(36)	(88)	(117)	(109)	(54)

which shows the number of the ideologically sensitive for each point in the liberal-conservative scale. This figure is the same as Table 27, except that the liberal-conservative scale is expanded to show all six positions. As the graph shows, there is a general decline in the proportion of men high in ideological sensitivity as conservatism increases, except for the most conservative position, which shows an increase. This can be interpreted as an example of the well-known U-curve of intensity; that is, intensity of feeling on an attitude continuum is greatest at the extremes and least in the center.

But it may also be true that the interaction processes mentioned above account for the greater sensitivity among the extreme conservatives. The club activities, the shop relationships, and party affiliations tend to increase sensitivity at the extremes. Perhaps if the local Independent Party had been organized prior to 1949, the increase at the conservative end of the scale would be sharper. As it is, it is certain that the interaction in these three social contexts has an effect on sensitivity, especially for the conservatives.

Ideological sensitivity is a crucial concept for the understanding of the ITU party system. Much of the work of the parties is concerned with getting the men to vote, not on some shifting basis such as the personality of the candidate, but on the basis of their "convictions," their "principles." In terms of the typology of Table 23 much of the activity of the Independents is directed toward moving conservatives up from Type IV to Type II, from ideological insensitivity to sensitivity, while much of the activity of the Progressives is directed similarly toward moving liberals from Type III to Type I. The reasons for this are obvious from Figures 52 and 53, which show the much greater support given their parties by the ideologically sensitive men than by the ideologically insensitive. It is primarily because of those ideologically sensitive men that a stable nucleus of opposition is maintained when a party has been out of power for a long time. In the following chapters it will become evident that it is the ideologically sensitive men who support their party when it loses, while those who are insensitive to policy issues are the shifters whose support swings the election in one direction or the other.

CHAPTER *16*

Individual Predispositions
and Social Environments
in Voting

IT IS TRUE, as Figure 51 in the preceding chapter indicates, that a liberal or conservative set of values is an important determinant of the way a printer votes. But is this to say that these predispositions are the sole or even the primary factors producing a vote for the Progressives or the Independents? Hardly. In U.S. voting, the historical accident which places one boy's parents in Vermont and another's in South Carolina has important consequences for the boy's vote when he comes of voting age. Similarly, the historical accident which places one printer in the *New York Times* composing room and another in the composing room of the *New Era* in Hopkinsville, Kentucky, has important consequences for these printers' ITU votes. In short, the *social context* within which a man finds himself in the union will exert a powerful, if often unrecognized, influence on his vote.

Now the aggregate consequences of these variations in social context are considerably greater than might be at first supposed. A good part of the thesis of this book, as a matter of fact, is to the effect that certain social contexts facilitate support of an opposition, while others do not. In the chapter following this one, for example, the effect of a man's being in a small local (i.e., 100 or fewer printers) or a large local (i.e., 1000 or more printers) on his tendency to support the opposition is found to be very great: if he is within a small local he is much less likely to support the opposition. The social context of a small local is apparently not conducive to support of a new and unknown opposition when opposed by a familiar incumbent. The implications of this are obvious—if the ITU were composed *entirely* of small locals, the prognosis for an opposition party would be poor indeed.

But now what if we look within such a local as Big Six in New York? What are the important variations in social context as they affect a man's vote? Perhaps the simplest point which can be made—and yet a point which is important—is that men tend to vote the same way that others around them vote. Whether the social context under consideration is the man's *shop*, his *friends*, his *chapel chairman*, or some other aspect of his occupational environment, this context modifies the relation between the man's liberal or conservative beliefs and his vote. That is to say, when this social environment is in *agreement* with these values, it reinforces their relation to his vote; when it is in *conflict* with the values, it weakens or destroys their relation to his vote.[1] For the three aspects of a printer's social context mentioned above, his shop, his friends, and his chapel chairman, Tables 28, 29, and 30 show this modifying effect.[2] Of these three elements in the printer's environment, his friends' votes show the highest relation to his own vote, the shop vote shows the second highest relation, and the

Table 28—Voting in Accord with Predisposition in Various Shop Contexts (1951)

	Man's Attitude and Shop Agree	Man's Attitude Liberal or Conservative, Shop Neutral	Man's Attitude and Shop in Conflict
Percentage voting in accord with predisposition	80	75	48
N	(93)	(228)	(65)

1. See S. Asch: "Effects of Group Pressure in the Modification and Distortion of Judgments," in H. Guetzkow (ed.), *Groups, Leadership, and Men*, Pittsburgh, Carnegie Press, 1951, p. 177-90. He had naive subjects make judgments in the face of groups which openly disagreed with the judgments their senses told them to make. Asch shows that with only a single confederate in a group of eight, most of the effect of the group in distorting the subject's judgment disappears. Of course, in a voting situation, where there is no objectively correct or incorrect answer, more social support for one's disposition will ordinarily be needed to withstand the group's influence. See also T. Newcomb: *Personality and Social Change*, New York, The Dryden Press, Inc., 1943; and M. Sherif: *The Psychology of Social Norms*, New York, Harper & Brothers, 1936.

2. We distinguish in what follows between a "liberal attitude" (1-3 on the scale) predisposing a man toward the Progressives, a "neutral attitude" (4 on the scale) predisposing him toward neither party, and a "conservative attitude" (5 and 6 on the scale) predisposing him toward the Independents. Similarly, we call the shop sentiment "Progressive" if more than 62% of the members voted for the Progressive candidate, "Independent" if more than 62% voted for the Independent candidate, and "neutral" if the vote was between these two extremes.

Table 29—Voting in Accord with Predisposition when Chairman's Vote Varies (1951)

	Man's Attitude and Chairman's Vote Agree	Man's Attitude and Chairman's Vote in Conflict
Vote in accord with predisposition	75%	67%
N	(114)	(123)

Table 30—Voting in Accord with Predisposition as Friends' Politics Vary (1951)

	FRIENDS' POLITICS FOR FIRST-NAMED FRIEND		
	Agreement	Unknown	Conflict
Percentage voting in accord with predisposition	93	65	40
N	(102)	(123)	(70)
	FOR THE SECOND-NAMED FRIEND		
Percentage voting in accord with predisposition	97	64	45
N	(100)	(146)	(49)

chairman's vote shows the least relation. This does not mean, of course, that his friends' political beliefs were most effective of these three elements in modifying his own intentions, for it is impossible to separate out the political homogeneity due to *selection* of friends and that due to *influence* by the friend. Nevertheless, these data do show that despite their liberal or conservative beliefs, printers tend to be politically homogeneous first with their friends, then with their shops, and finally with their chapel chairman.

The difference between the *large* shop (above 30 men) and the *small* shop (below 30 men) is important here. In the small shops, a man's vote was considerably more likely to be homogeneous (a) with that of the shop as a whole, and (b) with that of the chapel chairman.[3] This accords with the results of Chapter 9, where we found that in large shops men could form politically homogeneous subgroups and insulate themselves from the dominant political climate in the shop, while such insulation was impossible in the smaller shops.

Despite such insulation, however, the large shops definitely have a political character, and this character does act as an influence upon the votes of men within them. This is best illustrated by examining the differing political atmospheres of the chapels in the New York daily newspapers, and the relation between these atmospheres and the voting behavior of liberals and conservatives within them. These shops are the

---

3. The difference between small and large shops is between ten and twenty per cent in the conflict situation. That is, when the shop sentiment or the chairman's vote conflicted with a man's liberal-conservative predisposition, he was between 10% and 20% less likely to vote in accord with his predisposition if he was in a small shop than if he was in a large one.

largest in New York and among the largest in the country, ranging from 200 to about 600 in size. This places them considerably above the majority of ITU *locals* in size, for over half of the locals have fewer than 100 members.

§ The New York Newspapers

EACH OF THESE NEWSPAPER SHOPS has its characteristic political atmosphere, different from others both in the degree of political activity and the direction of political sentiment.[4] The *Herald Tribune* is the strongest Progressive shop, giving the Progressives consistently from 70 to 80 per cent of its vote. This is perhaps the only shop without a sizeable and active enough minority to put up a good fight in chapel elections. The *World-Telegram* is the next most highly Progressive, a shop where political battles are fought and politics is important. The *Daily News* leans slightly toward the Progressives. The *Times* is rather evenly split while the *Journal-American* and *Mirror* are perhaps slightly pro-Independent.[5] The *Post* is the one strong and consistent Independent paper.

All these judgments are made on the basis of the past voting records of the shops, together with voting data from our interviews and qualitative knowledge gained from interviewing the men in the shops and questioning them about their shops. These different sources of data all place the newspapers in about the same order.

It is interesting, then, to see how liberals and conservatives in our sample respond to the widely differing atmospheres in these shops. The table below shows the steadily decreasing tendency of liberals to vote with their predisposition, together with the increasing tendency of conservatives to vote with theirs, with the shift from the Progressive extreme, the *Herald-Tribune*, to the Independent extreme, the *Post*.[6]

One way of stating these percentages (if the numbers of cases were large enough so that such statements could be reasonably made) to show the strong contrast between the shops is thus:

---

4. It is interesting, but probably only coincidental, that in general the newspapers with the most conservative editorial policy have composing rooms with the most liberal political atmosphere, and vice versa.

5. Because of common ownership and the history of the two newspapers, the *Journal-American* and *Mirror* form a single chapel, and are considered together in the analysis.

6. These chapels' votes (from voting records in the 1951 and 1952 elections were:

	H.-Tribune	World-Tel.	Daily News	Times	Journal-American	Post
1951 (Prog)	72%	58%	55%	52%	47%	34%
1952	80	62	65	62	59	46

Table 31—Voting of Liberals and Conservatives in New York City Newspaper Chapels

	H.-Tribune	World-Tel.	Daily News	Times	Journal-American	Post
Liberals, (% Prog. Vote)	100%	86%	75%	71%	83%	50%
Conservatives, (% Ind. Vote)	57	50	73	100	80	89
N	(8)	(7)	(8)	(17)	(12)	(4)
N	(7)	(6)	(15)	(7)	(16)	(9)

Given that a man is liberal (1-3 on our scale) and in the *Herald-Tribune*, the probability is 1.0 that he would vote for the Progressive candidate. in agreement with his predispositions. Given that he is a conservative in the same shop, the probability is only .57 that he would vote for the Independents, the party of his predispositions.

And at the other extreme:

Given that a man is a liberal and in the *Post*, the probability is only .5 that he would vote for the Progressives, the party of his predispositions. Given that he is a conservative and in this shop, however, the probability is .89 that he would vote with his predispositions, for the Independents.

These comparisons, then, add up to one basic generalization: the quite different voting patterns of the various large shops are not due to their having "different kinds of men" in them, that is, almost all liberals in the *Herald-Tribune* and almost all conservatives in the *Post*. It is rather the case that the *same kinds of men act differently* in the various shops, due to different atmospheres created by the most active and most ideologically sensitive men in the shop.

But if the political atmospheres of even these largest chapels are so important in influencing the voting behavior of the men within them, what about the effect of the political atmosphere in the union as a whole? That such atmospheres do exist and have some effect is incontrovertible. But what is the effect, and how is it manifested?

At first glance, this study is in an unfortunate position to examine such atmospheres, for the sample is limited to a *single* local, the New York local. Thus it is not possible to test the different varieties of political atmosphere which occur in different locals. However, a fortunate circumstance does allow a test, for the study covered two elections, the 1951 local election and the 1952 international one. In the first of these, New York went Independent; in the second, it went Progressive. Thus in the *same* local at two successive elections there existed contrasting political atmospheres: Independent in the 1951 election and Progressive in the 1952 election.

§ Climate of Opinion in the Union as a Whole

By considering the climate of opinion of the union as a whole, men may be characterized not by the two factors discussed above (predisposition and shop sentiment) but by three. The two contexts of shop atmosphere and union climate of opinion may be thought of as concentric spheres surrounding the individual, somewhat as shown in Fig-

Figure 61—Concentric Spheres of Political Influences around a Union Member

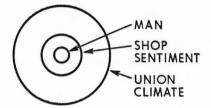

MAN
SHOP SENTIMENT
UNION CLIMATE

ure 61.[7] Four combinations of the three factors may be distinguished (Figure 62), considering only one direction for the union climate. Thus

Figure 62—Combinations of Political Influence around a Union Member

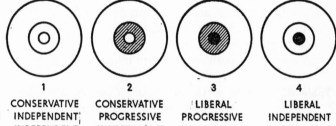

	1	2	3	4
PREDISPOSITION:	CONSERVATIVE	CONSERVATIVE	LIBERAL	LIBERAL
SHOP SENTIMENT:	INDEPENDENT	PROGRESSIVE	PROGRESSIVE	INDEPENDENT
UNION CLIMATE:	INDEPENDENT	INDEPENDENT	INDEPENDENT	INDEPENDENT

in the election of 1951 when the Independents won, a man in Situation 1 above has all influences acting in agreement. Such a man should be most likely to vote in accord with his predisposition. The other extreme is Situation 4, where the man, predisposed toward the Progressives, has both

---

7. To be precise, we should differentiate between the large shops, within which a man can form a deviant subgroup, and the small shops where this is not possible. This would give three concentric social contexts rather than two: the friendships on the job, the shop sentiment as a whole, and the union climate. But to do this would complicate matters a great deal and would reduce the sizes of our categories so as to make analysis next to impossible. The delineation of discrete spheres rather than a continuous gradation is itself artificial, but it is the best we can do with present methods of analysis.

social contexts against him. This man should be least likely to vote in accord with his predisposition. Situations 2 and 3 should be somewhere intermediate between the extreme of complete reinforcement and the complete lack of social support. Table 32 shows how men in these four situations

Table 32—Effects of Union Climate of Opinion, Shop Sentiment, and Man's Own Predisposition on Vote (1951)

	SITUATION 1: Conservative in Independent Shop	SITUATION 2: Conservative in Progressive Shop	SITUATION 3: Liberal in Progressive Shop	SITUATION 4: Liberal in Independent Shop
Percentage voting in accord with predisposition	87	55	68	38
N	(55)	(33)	(38)	(34)

actually voted. This table confirms our predictions. Those voting most completely with their predispositions are the conservatives in Independent shops, and those voting least with their predispositions are liberals in Independent shops. In comparing the other two, it appears that the shop sentiment is stronger than the union climate of opinion. The men receiving social support from shop, but not from the union, vote 68% with their predispositions; while those receiving support from the union, but not the shop, vote only 55% with their predispositions. This is understandable when we consider that the Independents won by a majority of only 52% and the incumbent was a Progressive, so the union climate of opinion could not have been very strongly Independent. However, even if the majority had been larger, it seems likely that the shop sentiment, closer to the man, would be more effective in influencing his vote, just as his own predisposition is in turn more effective than the shop sentiment.

Table 33—Effects of Union Climate Opinion, Shop Sentiment, and Man's Own Predisposition on Vote (1952)

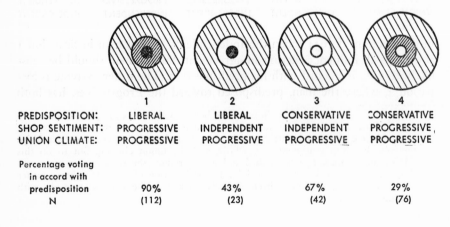

	1	2	3	4
PREDISPOSITION:	LIBERAL	LIBERAL	CONSERVATIVE	CONSERVATIVE
SHOP SENTIMENT:	PROGRESSIVE	INDEPENDENT	INDEPENDENT	PROGRESSIVE
UNION CLIMATE:	PROGRESSIVE	PROGRESSIVE	PROGRESSIVE	PROGRESSIVE
Percentage voting in accord with predisposition	90%	43%	67%	29%
N	(112)	(23)	(42)	(76)

In the 1952 international election the union climate was Progressive, and strongly so. The Progressive candidate, Woodruff Randolph, was the incumbent president, and the New York union gave him 61% of its votes. The equivalent situations to the four considered in the 1951 election and the corresponding voting behavior are shown in Table 33.

Here again the doubly reinforced predisposition in Situation 1 is most strongly adhered to, while the one without any social support, Situation 4, is least adhered to. And again, comparing Situations 2 and 3, the shop sentiment seems to be more effective as an influence than does the union climate as a whole, though the latter was much more one-sided than it was in the 1951 election.

The question arises, however, just *who* among the printers "go along" with a climate of opinion, and *why* do they do so? The answer to this question is particularly important, for a continuing democracy depends upon a stable core of supporters for each party who will resist the currents of the moment, and will stick with their party—or at least with their predispositions—whatever the climate of opinion might be.

Part of the answer to these questions lies in studying the role of *communication* within Big Six, part of it lies in studying the differences between different kinds of men. The first of these questions we will take up here; the second will be considered later in the chapter.

§ Communication and the Climate of Opinion

IN PREVIOUS CHAPTERS, we showed how crucial it is for the strength of an opposition that the channels of communication be kept open. The existence of these open channels, and the knowledge of candidates and issues disseminated through them, is a key feature differentiating large and small locals, as the analysis of Chapter 17 indicates. But even *within* a large local, there is a large difference in voting behavior between those who take advantage of this access to information and those who are still not reached. This latter group of men, not tied in to the occupational community nor willing to go out and get political information, shows its isolation by a lack of knowledge about union political issues. Without this knowledge, these men should be less able to evaluate the party's position and vote on the basis of the party's correspondence with their liberal or conservative attitude. In other words, we would expect these men who are without political information for themselves to be swayed by the general climate of opinion and responsive to shifts in this climate, with their liberal or conservative attitude not "geared in" to their vote decision.

In 1951, when the union climate of opinion was in favor of the Independents, knowledge about the issues and parties *should not* have made much difference for those men predisposed toward the Independents, but *should* have made a good deal of difference in holding men with such knowledge who were predisposed toward the Progressives from deserting to the other side. Since the climate of opinion favored the Independents, knowledge was not needed to *go along* with the prevailing climate; knowledge was needed by the liberals in order to *go against* the prevailing climate. Figure 63 shows, for three levels of knowledge about issues and parties, the proportion of Independent-predisposed men and the proportion of Progressive-predisposed men who voted in accord with their predispo-

Figure 63—Relationship between Knowledge of Issues and Voting in Accordance with Predisposition, 1951 Election

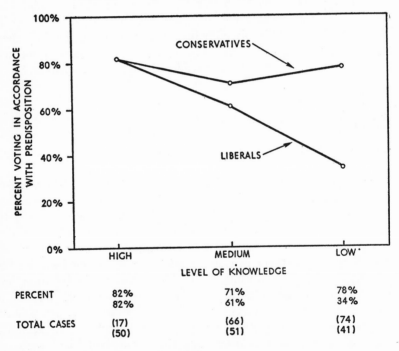

	HIGH	MEDIUM	LOW
PERCENT	82%	71%	78%
	82%	61%	34%
TOTAL CASES	(17)	(66)	(74)
	(50)	(51)	(41)

NOTE: For knowledge index, see Appendix I.

sitions. It indicates clearly the greater effect of knowledge on the behavior of the Progressive-predisposed men, the liberals, in this election. The

difference in the proportion of liberals with high and low levels of knowledge who voted for the Progressive candidate is 48%, compared with a
difference of only 4% for the corresponding groups of conservatives.
Thus, as suggested above, a knowledge of issues was almost a prerequisite
for the liberals to *go against* the climate, while it was not important in
going along with a climate which agreed with one's predisposition.

In 1952 just the reverse should have occurred, since the climate in
that election favored the Progressives. Knowledge was now important
for the conservatives, in holding them to their predisposition. It was
no longer as important to the liberals, who had only to go along with
a climate of opinion which favored their candidate. And this is just
what the data indicate, as Figure 64 shows. This time the difference in

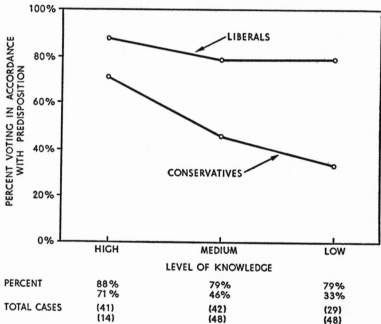

Figure 64—*Relationship between Knowledge of Issues and Voting in
Accordance with Predisposition, 1952 Election*

	HIGH	MEDIUM	LOW
PERCENT	88%	79%	79%
	71%	46%	33%
TOTAL CASES	(41)	(42)	(29)
	(14)	(48)	(48)

vote between those with high and low levels of knowledge is 38% for the
conservatives, and only 9% for the liberals.

This defection of men without knowledge of the issues extends the
previous analysis of concentric spheres of influence climates by showing
just which men are affected by these climates and which remain relatively unaffected. It also re-emphasizes the importance for democratic

politics of independent channels of communication, which are necessary to disseminate information from both points of view and thus to create knowledge as well as the interest which leads to knowledge. One of the effective implements of a totalitarian regime which maintains the forms of democracy is to *create* a favorable climate of opinion through control of all communication media.[8]

§ Communication and the Party System

THE CLIMATE OF OPINION has been treated thus far as a given and unchanging element affecting an election. Actually, of course, the climate of opinion is created in the months preceding an election; and it is interesting to discover that some months before an international election the situation in Big Six and many other ITU locals resembles that in a one-party union or one-party state. The opposition party is quiescent, and regardless of the outcome of the forthcoming election, most of the members favor the incumbents.

In December 1951 and January 1952, when the members of the New York local were first interviewed, the union approximated a one-party situation. International elections are held every two years in the even years. The actual election campaign begins in February, when nominations are made. From February to May the members are subject to propaganda and personal campaigning and have the opportunity to attend union and party meetings which discuss the election. In the twenty months between an election and the beginning of the next campaign, however, the New York membership rarely hears international issues discussed in a partisan context, unless a party-sponsored referendum takes place. They are, however, continually exposed to a barrage of propaganda and information from the incumbent international administration, in this case the Progressive Party.

The activities of the international opposition, on the other hand, are largely conducted by the local sections of the party. And since New York is historically a Progressive local in international elections, the local conservative party has since 1920 attempted to dissociate itself

---

8. At this point can be added another confirmation. After the 1951 election, those who ended up voting Progressive more often mentioned as reasons for their vote, differences between the parties, than did those who voted Independent. In 1952, those who voted Independent mentioned issues more often. This shows that one did not need an issue if voting with the climate, but did need one if voting against it. Also, the types of issues mentioned show the effect of shop atmosphere in changing *bases* of decision. See James S. Coleman: *Political Cleavage Within the International Typographical Union*. Ph.D. dissertation, Columbia University, 1955, Chap. 6.

from the international Independents as much as possible. Consequently, the local Independents do very little campaigning for their international party, except during the election campaign itself.

Thus, between May 1950 and February 1952 (a period of relative political quiet in the ITU) the members of the New York local were exposed to a considerable body of international propaganda from only one party, the incumbent Progressives.

It may be hypothesized on the basis of this situation that the incumbents' strength is greatest between elections, when the union's political state of affairs in the ITU approximates that of a one-party system, with the ordinary member receiving continuing communications from one side and almost none from the other (Figure 65).

Figure 65—Pressure from Incumbent and Opposition, through the Election Cycle

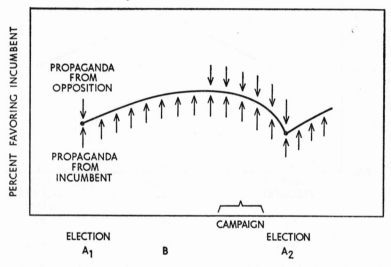

The pressure from below, from the incumbent, is maintained between campaigns; it is the removal of opposition pressure that allows the swing towards a one-party system. Its reapplication during the campaign period pushes the system back to a two-party one for the election.[9]

---

9. One major difficulty in making any definitive statement concerning shift within Big Six is that there is a 10% discrepancy between the reported voting behavior of the respondents who answered the questionnaire and the actual vote of the local. That is, in June 71% of the respondents wrote that they had voted for Randolph, the Progressive candidate, while actually only 61% of the voters did so. This discrepancy may be a result of the well-known tendency of people to

What do the interview data tell us about this? The men were interviewed just before the campaign began, in January 1952; this corresponds to Point B in the time cycle of the diagram in Figure 65. Also we know the vote for New York as a whole in 1950 and 1952, from which the sample was drawn at random. These data correspond to Points A₁ and A₂ in the diagram.

On the basis of these data, we can establish the points A_1, B, A_2 in the diagram (Figure 66) of an actual situation, corresponding to the hypothetical situation above.

Figure 66—Union Members Favoring Progressives at Three Points in the Election Cycle

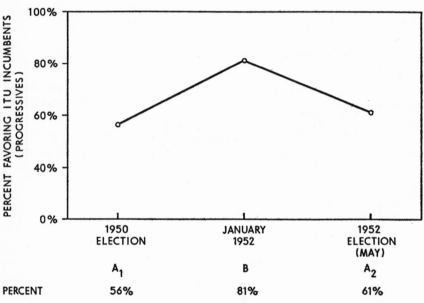

The shape of the empirical graph corresponds roughly to the hypothetical one, showing the proportion of Progressive supporters to be greatest between election campaigns. A sizable number of printers who had voted Independent in 1950 and went back to voting Independent in 1952 reported that they would vote for the incumbent Progressives when questioned before the 1952 campaign was actually under way. The significance of this finding is increased when we consider the fact that the Independent vote in the local actually declined from 1950 to 1952.

---

report that they voted for the winner in an election even though they actually supported the loser. See Mosteller *et al.: Social Science Research Council, Bulletin 60,* 1949, Chap. 10.

By simply interpreting the election statistics, we would assume that a number of men shifted from the Independents to the Progressives. While this occurred considering the two-year period as a whole, these results conceal the fact that the effect of the campaign was to increase the voting support of the Independents. Without the campaign, New York would have voted much more for the Progressive Party than it actually did.[10] During the campaign, almost all the shift was from the incumbents to the opposition, as the graph implies. Thirty-five men who were for Randolph when interviewed in January reported in June that they voted for Sparkman (the Independent candidate), while only seven shifted in the opposite direction. To put it even more dramatically, 39% of the men who actually voted for Sparkman in May were for Randolph before the campaign started, whereas only 3% of Randolph's votes represented gains from his opponent. Of those who shifted parties, 86% changed from the party which had a large majority in the local to the weaker group.

This is true only for *international* elections, for it is only in relation to international political issues that opposition party activity declines in off-year periods. Opposition party leaders continue their activities in local politics between elections. As was pointed out earlier, they attend all membership meetings, exploit issues, and so forth; and our questionnaire responses show no such curve in relation to local politics. That is, the shift between the two parties locally over a one-year period did not favor either party.[11]

These differences between the shifts in vote preference for local and international office are significant because they permit us to actually examine within the ITU two different types of political situations: in the one, two more or less equal groups with roughly equal political resources compete for support; in the other, one party has control over much of the flow of political information and propaganda reaching the membership for an extended period. These two situations correspond

10. It is interesting to note that in United States national politics while the Democrats were in office, public opinion polls indicated that the incumbent Democrats *lost* support in between national elections as compared with the opposition Republicans, and then tended to regain votes during election campaigns. This pattern is just the opposite of the ITU example. It suggests that in the context of a continually functioning two-party system, in which both parties may reach the public, the opposition is able to capitalize on transient dissatisfactions. Or even more likely, the Republicans have that near monopoly over the means of the communication in the United States that the administration has in the ITU; and consequently, in a campaign, the Democratics will win those who have fallen away under year-round Republican communication pressure.

11. Of the men who had voted for Victory (the winner) 5% had shifted away from him a year later, and 6% of the losing candidate's supporters had shifted toward him.

to the difference between the ITU and most other trade-unions. The fact that individuals whose background and ideological commitments predispose them to oppose the Progressive administration nevertheless become supporters of it when presented with the administration side of the case alone, again points up the role of an organized party system in perpetuating opposition. Voters with opposition sentiments will not become opposition voters unless they are presented with a realistic alternative. The ability of one-party states and one-party unions to secure 90% or more of the vote in one-candidate elections may not simply be a result of the fact that the electorate is intimidated, or that the votes are counted by the administration. Given complete monopoly of communication and information, a monopoly far more complete than that held by the Progressives in New York in 1950-1951, it is not surprising that the overwhelming majority of citizens or members actually vote for the only candidate on the ballot.[12]

The differences between the reactions of the members to local and international union politics suggest an important reason why in most trade unions opposition is found much more often in the locals than in the internationals. The monopoly which an incumbent administration has over the channels of intraunion communication is lessened considerably in most union locals. There, a small group of individuals with relatively few resources may reach entire memberships with their propaganda. In the ITU, the continued activity and interest in local union affairs which is generated by the occupational community, interpersonal relations in the shops, and attendance at union meetings would probably result in recurrent revivals of opposition groups even if the parties were to dissolve. Such events did occur a number of times in the late nineteenth and early twentieth century before the present party system was institutionalized. On the international level, however, the existence of international parties, which in turn are based on strong local parties, is more important for the continuation of opposition.

Finally, the analysis should be qualified by pointing out that the New York situation, where the Progressives always win internationally, is somewhat special. Some of the other large locals are almost evenly divided between the two parties on the international level, while others evidence a propensity to vote for the Independent Party. And in the latter cases, we would not expect to find the between-election increase

---

12. Evidence in this direction may also be found in the votes of the unattached members of the ITU, mentioned on page 374. These men, who belong to the ITU but work in areas where there are too few members to form a local, are cut off from the give-and-take of the party system, being exposed only to the *Typographical Journal*. They have consistently given the incumbent International president a far higher vote than he has received from the union as a whole.

in support for the incumbent Progressives that occurs in New York. For example, in the San Francisco local, which is now dominated by the Independents, the Independent leaders spend most of their political energies in attacking the international Progressives. Thus, the local paper of that union month in and month out criticizes the Progressive administration. Members of this local, therefore, are exposed to two-party propaganda on international issues even between election campaigns.

§ The 1952 Campaign

THE ROLE OF the communication process can perhaps be best seen through an analysis of the way in which attitudes toward the most important issue of the 1952 international campaign affected the vote decision of New York ITU members.

Since 1947 much of the political debate between the two parties has revolved about union policies toward the Taft-Hartley Act. While both parties oppose the act, the Progressives have favored an aggressive attack on it and have opposed the union's officers' signing the non-Communist affidavit required by that law. Evidence of the saliency of this issue for the members of the ITU lies in the fact that on an open-end question on the postelection questionnaire, more men mentioned this issue than any other as the most important one of the campaign. The effect of opinion about Taft-Hartley on voting can be examined through two questions which were asked of all men in the interview: first, whether they thought the Taft-Hartley law "basically a good law," "a good law with some bad features," or "basically a bad law"; and second, whether they favored or opposed the signing of the Taft-Hartley non-Communist affidavit.

As expected, supporters of the two parties differed in their sentiments according to the party position on this issue. However, a large fraction of those favoring each party opposed the position of their own party on the Taft-Hartley issue. As the campaign developed, men shifted from one party to the other, and it is clear that some of these defections were related to opinions on the Taft-Hartley issue.

Of the men who favored Randolph in January, the greatest defections were among those who favored the Taft-Hartley law, or who favored signing the non-Communist affidavit, while just the reverse was true for those who favored Sparkman in January. But we cannot ascribe this "effect" on the vote completely to opinions on Taft-Hartley, for it may have been opinions on other matters, themselves correlated with Taft-Hartley opinions, which were effective. Nevertheless, these changes do indicate that a conflict between party position and vote intention resulted in some men changing their vote.[13]

The fact remains, however, that a large proportion of the New York printers voted for the party which opposed their own opinion on the Taft-Hartley issue. About three-fifths of the men who voted for Randolph in 1952 were opposed to his refusal to sign the non-Communist oath required by the Taft-Hartley Act, while 48% of his supporters actually believed that the Taft-Hartley law was not a wholly bad law. There are a variety of reasons why men might have disagreed with the Progressive Party position and still supported the party in the elections. Clearly in a two-party situation, in union as in national politics, voters often disagree with the party which they back.

Much of the apparent contradiction between attitudes and vote intention is largely explained by the *perception* of the position of the party. For of the 135 men who supported Randolph but favored signing the non-Communist oath, only 23, or 17%, actually knew that the Pro-

Figure 67—Relationship between Opinion on Taft-Hartley Issues and Change in Vote Decision from January to May 1952

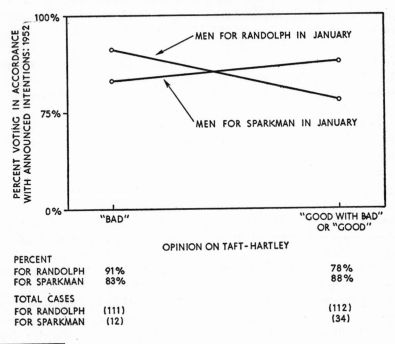

PERCENT		
FOR RANDOLPH	91%	78%
FOR SPARKMAN	83%	88%
TOTAL CASES		
FOR RANDOLPH	(111)	(112)
FOR SPARKMAN	(12)	(34)

---

13. Cf. Lazarsfeld *et al.*, *The People's Choice*, Chaps. 10 and 11.

*Figure 68—Perception of Randolph Supporters of the Progressive Party's
Position on the Taft-Hartley Non-Communist Affidavit*

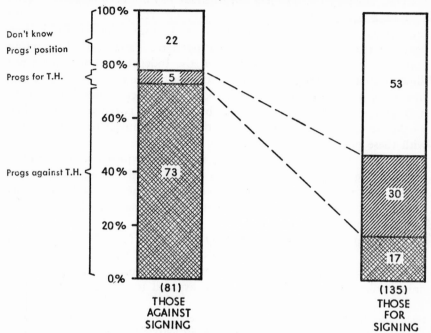

gressive Party was opposed to signing the Taft-Hartley non-Communist affidavit.

The data in Figure 68 suggest that many of the men who held views contradictory to those of their party were able to maintain this seemingly unstable position by failing to *perceive* the contradiction. If the Independents had gained the votes of all the men who disagreed with the Progressive position, the data indicate that they would have gained more than enough votes to secure a majority in New York. In other words there was a large proportion of men who objectively agreed with the Independents, but whose agreement was not exploited by the Independents.

The question arises, What led so many men to fail to know the position of the incumbent party on an issue which had divided the union since 1947? At least part of the failure to perceive the party position accurately was undoubtedly a consequence of psychological motivation. Various studies have demonstrated that men are more likely to answer "Don't know," or to misperceive facts about questions which are distasteful to them. As Krech and Crutchfield put it: "Because perception is functionally selective, new data physically available to an individual but contradictory to his beliefs and attitudes *may not even be perceived.*"[14]

However, did these men refuse to accept recognized facts or were they never really faced with them? If it is mainly the former, if men have such a strong loyalty to the Progressive Party that they refuse unpleasant facts about the party, then the Independents would have a difficult time changing votes. But if the distortion is socially based, the Independents have only to fill that social gap: to communicate to every man in every shop the differences between the two parties and then let the men choose in accordance with their agreement or disagreement with these positions.

In New York we would expect the social explanation to be true, for many printers are never reached by the locally weak Independent Party. And the Progressive Party, recognizing the unpopularity of its position on the Taft-Hartley affidavit, tends to soft-pedal its stand in its own campaign literature.[15]

This hypothesis may be tested by examining (1) whether the men who fail to perceive accurately are isolated from the union's networks of communication, and (2) to what extent their interest and activity in union politics would lead them to be exposed to political propaganda.

Table 34—"*Social Location*" *of Progressive Voters Who Perceived the Progressive Party Position on the Taft-Hartley Act Correctly or Incorrectly*

Social Location	PERCEPTION OF PROGRESSIVES' POSITION	
	Correctly Perceived That Progressives Were Against Signing Taft-Hartley Affidavit	Incorrectly Perceived That Progressives Were for Signing Taft-Hartley Affidavit or Don't Know
Percentage in shops below 30	27 (113)	47 (118)
Percentage not active in formal organization	72 (105)	92 (116)
Percentage low on social-relations index	37 (108)	51 (115)

---

14. David Krech and Richard S. Crutchfield: *Theory and Problems of Social Psychology*, New York, McGraw-Hill Book Company, Inc., 1948, p. 190; emphasis theirs. See also S. M. Lipset: "Opinion Formation in a Crisis Situation," *Public Opinion Quarterly*, 17:39-43 (1953).

15. In response to the unpopularity of its position, the Progressive Party has secured the passage of an ITU law requiring all officers to file a non-Communist affidavit with the union. These affidavits, however, are not filed with the government. Many members believe that the union affidavit is the Taft-Hartley affidavit. Thus the Progressives can maintain their position and still try to keep the support of members who want a non-Communist affidavit.

Table 32 shows the difference between those Randolph voters who knew the party position and those who misperceived it.

The large shops, the clubs, and informal social relations are three arenas in which a man can be reached by political campaigning. Many of the misperceiving men are outside these arenas. They are in small shops, not members of clubs, and not in informal social relations with other printers. This is strong evidence that much of the misperceiving is due to the *social* rather than the psychological process.

This evidence is reinforced by data concerning other, more directly political dispositions and behaviors of these men. Many more of these men talk "little" or "never" about union politics, the great majority are inactive in union politics, and many are low in ideological sensitivity.

Table 35—Political Dispositions, and Perception of Progressives' Position

Political Disposition	Correctly Perceive That Progressives Are Against Signing Taft-Hartley Affidavit	Incorrectly Perceive That Progressives Are for Signing Taft-Hartley Affidavit, or Don't Know
Talk politics "little" or "never"	38%	65%
Not active in union politics	50%	76%
Low in ideological sensitivity	14%	32%
N	(113)	(120)

These data all point to a failure on the part of the Independents to communicate the issue to these men. This is a good example of how a pre-existing cleavage in values or attitudes *could have been* but was not geared in to union politics. It re-emphasizes the importance of the occupational community, of the shop community, and of all factors in printing which make printers interested and active enough to find out the party's positions. It again shows that more than a cleavage of values is necessary to maintain an ideologically based voting cleavage in union politics. What is necessary as well is widespread access to political information of all kinds, so that the values can be *used* in the vote decision. This access seems to be made up of two elements: (1) freedom of communication by opposition sources, and (2) enough involvement of the man in union or occupational activities so that he is accessible to and interested in political information. Many unions have one or the other of these two elements, but the ITU seems almost unique in having both for many men on the most important issues.

§ Voting Decisions and Ideological Sensitivity

THE ANALYSIS UP TO THIS POINT has shown the importance of a man's social environment in influencing his vote, in pulling him away from his liberal or conservative predisposition. But where are the stable and continuing roots of the system? Who are the men, in the conflict situations delineated above and in the small and isolated locals, who go their own way, voting their own minds, sentiments, and dispositions despite the pressures on them to do otherwise? Who are the men who, instead of being influenced by their situation, influence others around them?

The Independents, who have now been out of international office since 1944, have a hard core of somewhere between 30% and 40% of the union members, below which their vote never goes. The Pro-

Figure 69—*Voting in Accordance with Predisposition by Men Differing in Ideological Sensitivity, 1951 Election*

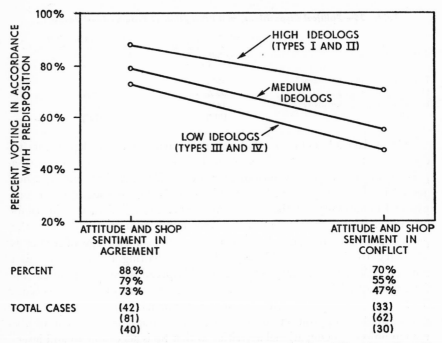

	ATTITUDE AND SHOP SENTIMENT IN AGREEMENT	ATTITUDE AND SHOP SENTIMENT IN CONFLICT
PERCENT	88% 79% 73%	70% 55% 47%
TOTAL CASES	(42) (81) (40)	(33) (62) (30)

NOTE: To increase the numbers in each category, the shops are divided at 50%, with no "neutral" category as before.

gressives, when they were out of office, similarly had a hard core of more than 40% of the union's vote. Just who are the men of these hard cores, and what role do they play in union politics?

To answer these questions it is necessary to return to a consideration of *ideological sensitivity*. The men of the hard core are those for whom policy issues are important, for whom ideological disputes are the basis of cleavage in union politics. In terms of the typology introduced in Chapter 15, they are men of Types I and II in contrast to the low ideologues, Types III and IV.

When there is agreement between a man's predisposition and the shop's vote, those high in ideological sensitivity—the high ideologues—will show a greater tendency to vote in this doubly reinforced direction than medium or low ideologues. On the other hand, when their attitude is in conflict with the shop's political atmosphere, the high ideologues adhere to their predispositions, while the low ideologues largely succumb to the predominant sentiments in the shop. These two important effects are shown in both the 1951 and 1952 elections (see Figures 69 and 70).

In examining the relation between the man's vote and his chairman's vote, we find a similar situation. The high ideologue's vote tends to stay true to his predisposition, while the low ideologue's vote goes along with the chairman's more often than not. Figures 71 and 72 show this. The important generalization that may be derived from these figures is that the high ideologues behave more in accord with their own predis-

Figure 70—Voting in Accordance with Predisposition by Men Differing in Ideological Sensitivity, 1952 Election

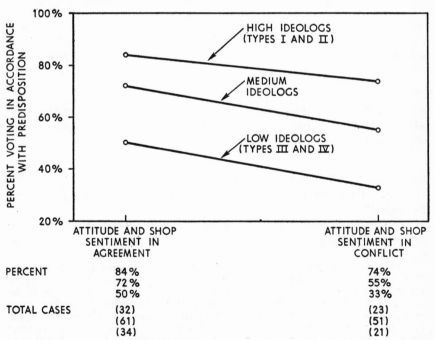

	ATTITUDE AND SHOP SENTIMENT IN AGREEMENT	ATTITUDE AND SHOP SENTIMENT IN CONFLICT
PERCENT	84%	74%
	72%	55%
	50%	33%
TOTAL CASES	(32)	(23)
	(61)	(51)
	(34)	(21)

NOTE: The N's are smaller than for the 1951 election because these data were from the mail questionnaires, some of which were not returned.

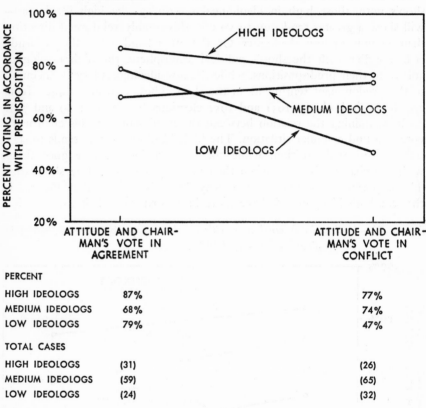

Figure 71—Voting in Accordance with Predisposition among Men Differing in Ideological Sensitivity when Chairman's Vote Intention Varies, 1951 Election

PERCENT		
HIGH IDEOLOGS	87%	77%
MEDIUM IDEOLOGS	68%	74%
LOW IDEOLOGS	79%	47%
TOTAL CASES		
HIGH IDEOLOGS	(31)	(26)
MEDIUM IDEOLOGS	(59)	(65)
LOW IDEOLOGS	(24)	(32)

positions and are *less* affected by the opposing pressure of their social contexts. They more often influence others and are less influenced by them.[16]

The political significance of what we call ideological sensitivity is that the ideologically sensitive men (types I and II) are politically

---

16. Recent experiments in social psychology show this same general tendency. One social psychologist has derived the following generalization from his experiments: "The amount of change in opinion . . . will decrease with increase in the degree to which the opinions and attitudes involved are anchored in other group memberships or serve important need-satisfying functions for the person."—Leon Festinger, in *Psychological Review*, 57:277 (1950). In our case it is by definition the high ideologues whose attitude is "anchored in other group memberships or serve important need-satisfying functions."

Figure 72—Voting in Accordance with Predisposition among Men Differing in Ideological Sensitivity when Chairman's Vote Intention Varies, 1952 Election

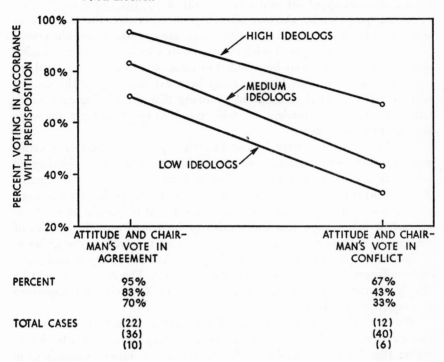

	ATTITUDE AND CHAIR-MAN'S VOTE IN AGREEMENT	ATTITUDE AND CHAIR-MAN'S VOTE IN CONFLICT
PERCENT	95%	67%
	83%	43%
	70%	33%
TOTAL CASES	(22)	(12)
	(36)	(40)
	(10)	(6)

stable, giving continuing support to one party, while it is men of types III and IV who shift, throwing the election to one side or the other. In the two elections examined, such a shift occurred, so that this can be shown concretely. Table 36 gives the percentages of men of each

Table 36—Stability of Voting in Different Ideological Types, 1951 and 1952 Elections

Ideological Sensitivity	Liberal	Conservative
High	I	II
	76%	67%
	(37)	(18)
Low	III	IV
	32%	23%
	(22)	(31)

type who voted in *both* elections for the party of their predispositions. For the liberals, on the left, the percentage who voted for the Progressives in both 1951 and 1952 is tabulated; for the conservatives on the right, the percentage of men who voted for the Independents in both years is given. The table shows the much greater stability in vote among men of types I and II (liberal and conservative high ideologues) than among men of types III and IV. Unswayed by the momentary issues of the campaign or by the incumbent's greater prestige, the existence of these men insures that the minority party always has a sizeable vote.[17]

If the ITU is compared with other unions which have no continuing opposition, it might well be asked: Do these unions not have ideologically sensitive men also? Has anything been explained about the sources of the ITU's political cleavage by showing that the ideologically sensitive men provide its nucleus of stable core? Why should not the same be true in other unions?

The answer lies partly in the fact that printing probably recruits more ideologically sensitive men than other manual trades (ideological sensitivity is correlated with education, and printers are better educated). The second part of the answer lies in the social and political framework of the union. It is not enough that men be ideologically sensitive in general; it is necessary that this sensitivity be *geared into* the politics of the union. If these men were not interested or involved in the union as an important part of their lives, their ideological sensitivity would make little difference to their voting in union politics. The election would be simply another slip of paper to mark with an X, having no important consequences for their lives as a whole.

Previous chapters have indicated the degree to which printers are interested and involved in their occupations; they have shown by implication the difference between printing and many other occupations in this regard. It is this activity and involvement which gears a man's ideological disposition into union politics. It seems likely that in many other occupations the ideologically sensitive men would concentrate their political activities and interests elsewhere, in some sphere which was an important part of their lives.

Printing and its union do play an important enough part in these potentially active men's lives to bring them into its political life. It is this fact, together with the difference in behavior of these men in union politics, that makes their existence an important element in the continuance of ITU politics.

---

17. Rudolph Heberle shows the importance of an ideological commitment in Germany in the 1930s: Stratified farm areas which had generated a worker's ideology among farm laborers kept these men from turning to Nazism. On the other hand, an unstratified middle-class farming area in which no firm ideologies had been developed swung quickly to Hitler with little regard for the implications of his program. See R. Heberle: "The Ecology of Political Parties," *American Sociological Review*, 9:401-14 (1944).

One other element besides the character of the union and the occupation should be mentioned for its effect in keeping these men involved in union politics. This is the party system itself. Without this the values of these men could find no expression; they would tend to look elsewhere for their political activity. With a democratic political system in the union, they can expend their energy there. Here again is an instance where the prior existence of a party system is a factor contributing to its own maintenance.

CHAPTER 17

Local Unions and Political Opposition in the ITU

IN THIS CHAPTER our field of vision, which since Chapter 14 has been limited to the New York local of the ITU, again expands to cover the entire union. Concentration on the New York local, necessitated by limited research funds, has nevertheless enabled us to tell most of the story of ITU democracy. It contains, after all, 10% of the national membership of the international union, and has had a strong local party system since the 1880's.

But we must now complete the story on the international level. Democratic party systems do exist in a number of union locals in other international unions (although none of them have had as long or continuous a history as those in New York and other printers' locals). There is, however, no other major union which has an institutionalized party system on the international level. It is important, therefore, to attempt to locate these factors on the international level which sustain party conflict in the ITU.

This analysis is based on the same theoretical orientation that has guided the discussion of the politics of the New York local. Our interest has been in finding in the New York local those social organizations which mediate between the individual and the union, functioning to increase political participation and to provide channels of communication and sources of autonomous power and prestige. Within the New

York local the occupational community and the shop organizations have played this role. Within the ITU as a whole, the locals themselves perform this function and are the sources of opposition strength. The crucial element in this analysis will be the size of the locals, for it is the size of a local which largely determines the amount of autonomy it possesses and the nature and amount of politically relevant communication to which its members are exposed.

§ The Nature and Sources of Local Autonomy

LARGE LOCALS in the ITU have always been semi-autonomous bodies, carrying on their collective bargaining, grievance procedures, and internal disputes of all sorts with relatively little interference from the international. Separate wage agreements exist in each local, working hours are locally determined, and in almost every area of union authority there is a broad range of autonomy for the locals. The one area in which they have little latitude is in calling strikes; because of the international strike fund, which pays men up to 60% of their wages when on strike, international approval is needed for a local to call a strike if the men are to receive strike benefits. This restriction of autonomy certainly has effects, but it is the only important restriction of autonomy in all the areas of behavior of large locals in the union.

The sources of this autonomy are several. The union mirrors the industry it serves, as we have noted before, and the industry is decentralized. Newspaper and print-shop ownership, with the exception of a few newspaper chains, does not extend beyond the local, so that negotiations can be carried out with one set of owners completely on a local level. Even the newspaper chains negotiate for each city's newspaper individually, in conjunction with the other newspapers in that local jurisdiction.

Another reason scales need not be negotiated on an international or regional basis is that most printing is noncompetitive between locals. There is little competition between newspapers of one city and those of another despite the strong newspaper competition within a city. Although commercial shops do face some intercity competition, most of their work is for firms within their city or for local, state, or national governmental offices located in their city.

Many customers of printing houses, such as editors of weekly papers or magazines, or advertising agencies, prefer to be physically near to their printer so as to be able to discuss technical problems of design with him or to correct or change copy quickly. There is little tendency for most of this work to gravitate to a town where prices, and thus wages, are low. This means that a local in New Jersey across the river from New York City can have a lower wage scale than New York without attracting much business from New York. In fact, the wage scales are and have always been lower in New Jersey shops than in New York without attracting more than a small portion of New York's printing business.

The nature of the industry is therefore one reason for local autonomy. A second is the union's two-party system. The international officers simply are not secure enough to institute measures depriving locals of their power of self-determination. Their margin of votes in elections is too small for them to risk incurring the wrath of the locals, particularly the large ones. The autonomy of the locals at a given time, presenting a potential for opposition to incumbent international officers, thus acts to prevent measures restricting their future autonomy. Because of this, it is probably fortunate for the ITU's political system that the union began as a federation of autonomous locals, rather than by spreading out from a central source.

This autonomy of course varies with the local's size. Small locals are ordinarily weak and usually allow the international representative to do much of their wage bargaining for them. Since they often have no full-time officers, they must look to the international office for many of the services that local officers provide in large locals. Not only collective bargaining but also the organization of non-union shops, the handling of grievances, and many of the incidental functions of local officers are carried out for small locals by the international. As a matter of fact, many of these locals are only a single shop; most of the union's locals, in fact, are no larger than a fair-sized commercial print shop in New York. Table 37 shows this, presenting the size distribution of locals

Table 37—Number of Locals in Each of Five Size Categories

Size of Locals by Number of Printers	Number of Local Unions of Each Size	Cumulative Proportion of Locals	
1- 15	193	24%	(24%)
16- 25	146	42%	(18%)
26- 50	171	63%	(21%)
50-100	111	76%	(14%)
100+	192	100%	(24%)

throughout the international in 1951. As Table 37 indicates, when we speak of the small locals, referring to locals smaller than fifty or a hundred men, we are discussing the great majority of the locals in the international (though a much smaller proportion of the members).

In sum, these small locals are weak and dependent on the international, while the large locals have a high degree of autonomy and considerable power of self-determination.

§ Communication in International Politics

IN AN EARLIER CHAPTER the communications functions of the occupational community and of on-the-job social relations on the local level were analyzed. As then noted, the latent political functions of these purely social relations are of major importance. Disseminating political knowledge and building up interest and involvement in political matters are among the primary political functions served by these shops and local leisure-time organizations.

On the international level, however, there are few comparable patterns. The sheer fact of geographic distance between locals precludes any strong and continuous social relations among their members. While men in a given shop in New York may have numerous associations with men outside the shop in union meetings, in clubs, and even in a neighboring bar, men in a given local can hardly have such relations with those in a local fifty miles away.

There are, however, several formal associations of printers which operate on the international level and act as a skeletal national occupational community. A printers' baseball league holds an international tournament each year, to which locals from all over the country send teams to compete for the international championship. One of the New York party leaders interviewed provides a good example of the way these baseball leagues act to increase political participation. As a young printer, in a New Jersey local, this man had been very much interested in baseball, avidly following the printers' league as well as the major leagues. Each year he would travel to the baseball tournament, which is always held near the convention and at approximately the same time. At some point he began to attend the convention as well as the tournament, paying his way as the delegate from his local. Before long he became interested in politics, joined the Wahnetas, and started his political career. Today he is very active politically, though his interest in baseball has disappeared.

Besides the baseball league, there is an international printer's golf tournament. It too is held once a year, with men from all over the country participating. Its latent political function in establishing communications on the international level may be illustrated by an example similar to the one cited above. In 1946 the secretary-treasurer of the golf association, who was not then active politically, was nominated for international office. His only important previous international activity had been as secretary-treasurer of the golf association. The Independents felt that this position alone had spread his name sufficiently throughout the international to establish him as a likely candidate for office.

These examples illustrate two different communications functions of the international occupational community. The baseball tournament served to communicate *to* the first man ideas about union politics and to generate political interest in him. It propelled him into an active political role. In the case of the golf-association officer, this probably occurred as well; but more important, his position served the function of communicating his name *to others*, of giving him prestige throughout the international. We have already noted this double role of the occupational community locally; on the one hand, those active in the community grow more politically knowledgeable and involved, becoming political participants; on the other, leaders of the large clubs have prestige throughout the local and are sought after by the parties.

The two organizations cited above are the only leisure-time groups on the international level, and they meet only once a year. Regional and state conferences of printers' unions are, however, held two to four times a year. These conferences have no authority, but serve primarily as meeting places where local leaders discuss common problems, establish apprentice-training schools, and exchange information. Despite these relatively noncontroversial activities, those who attend the conferences spend much of their time discussing union politics. One leader, active in international politics, reported that he got his start in union politics in one of these conferences. As a member of a small Westchester local he attended the Empire State Conferences (for printers' unions in New York State), was picked up by one of the parties, and has been active ever since.

On a local level the shops and the occupational community play a complementary role with respect to communication. Social relations on the job spread information within the confines of the shop, while the leisure-time relations provide the interconnections between the shops, breaking down the barriers between them. Diagrammatically, the communications network might be shown as in Figure 73, where the circles of various sizes represent shops of various sizes and the lines represent ties provided by the leisure-time occupational community. The complementary nature of the job relations and off-the-job relations is evident here: the shops have circumscribed boundaries, and it is relations off the job which break down these boundaries with respect to communication. Participation in the occupational community is not, of course, so important in producing political awareness and knowledge for men working in large shops as for those in small ones. In a large shop a man is in contact with others within his shop who are themselves active beyond the boundaries of the shop, even if he is not. Looking at it slightly differently, there are more connections from large shops to others than from small shops to others, as is suggested in Figure 73. Thus for a man to be "connected up" to the network of communication, he need not go beyond his shop, if it is a large one; while a man in a very small shop ordinarily has no one within his shop through whom he can establish this connection, and he must go outside the shop to plug into the network of communications.

The structure of communications on the international level is similar. The locals have sharply defined boundaries, and the international occu-

Figure 73—Communications Network of the Occupation within a Local

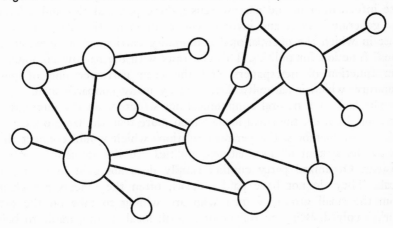

Figure 74—Gaps in Communications Network of the Occupation Internationally

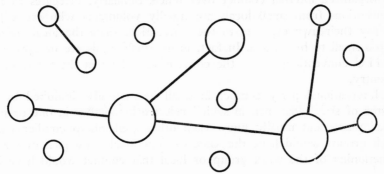

pational community establishes a few connections between these. But internationally, these connections are attenuated; for many locals, they hardly exist (see Figure 74). The small number of leisure-time organizations operating between locals, and the geographic isolation of these locals from one another make for frequent gaps in the lines of communication among locals. These gaps are more serious for the opposition party than for the administration party; the latter have the *Typographical Journal*, as well as other communications media. Party literature, disseminated from a large local like New York, might be expected to establish communication links to small locals; but some locals are not even on the mailing lists for party literature, and many others pay little attention to such partisan literature. But even if independent newspapers existed, the communication role that they could play would be a narrow one, in contrast to the broad "communications" functions which informal social relations fulfill. Social relations not only act to communicate information in the narrow sense; these personal ties and relations also generate interest and involvement in union politics. It is this broad sense in which the occupational community carries out a "communications" function for politics. This contrasts with the narrow communication function of newspapers, and the even narrower one of party literature, which is naturally distrusted by many nonparty men.

The lack of a natural communications structure on the international level should affect the small locals much more than the large ones. With only a few members, the personal relations which would connect them up to the system of international politics are less numerous or nonexistent. Organized party conflict simply does not exist in most small locals. They do not have paid officials; often the officers are chosen from the small group of men who are willing to take on the extra work involved. Being an officer of a small local is comparable to being the chapel chairman of a small shop. It carries with it few rewards, either of status, increased income, or opportunity. There is consequently no organized internal conflict over office. Similarly, delegates to ITU conventions from small locals are usually volunteers who are willing to pay their own expenses to the convention, since the local treasury is too small to bear them. In fact, many small locals are unrepresented at ITU conventions unless the convention is held in their part of the country.

International party conflict in small locals is also inhibited by the factor of size. Most men in such locals work together in one or more small plants and usually know each other well. Sharp conflict within such groups would have the same dysfunctional consequences for the functioning of the work group or local that conflict would have in a small shop in New York. Members of such locals report that the men usually avoid serious controversy about ITU politics.

Almost all of the large locals, on the other hand, have regular party groups which contest most local positions, as well as annual elections for delegates to the ITU conventions. The local affiliates of the international opposition party, whether controlling the local or in opposition, exploit the errors of the international administration and keep the political battle lines open for others within their local.

On the basis of this analysis, the differences in political behavior between men in large and in small locals should be much greater than the differences between large- and small-shop men within a local. No comparable data on the behavior of individual members of different-sized locals in the international exist, so this comparison cannot be made. But voting data do show that important differences exist between the large-local man and the small-local man in voting, as will be evident shortly. The reason, as has been indicated, is that the few channels of communications that do link up the small locals are strongly weighted in favor of the incumbents. The official *Typographical Journal* always carries political propaganda for the incumbents. It is edited by the international secretary-treasurer, the officers' reports in each issue of the *Journal* will naturally express their own partisan views, and if all four officers are of one party, as they often are, it gives the incumbents a communications medium unmatched by any the opposition has at its disposal. To be sure, the *Typographical Journal* gives more space to the opposition point of view than any other union journal. It prints statements by all candidates just before the international election, and full transcripts of the annual conventions which often contains partisan debates; but this is little, relative to the space the incumbents' point of view receives.

Perhaps more important than the *Journal* are the international representatives or organizers, who are almost always active partisans of the party in international office. The accusation is often made by the opposition, and by and large it seems to be true, that the international organizers spend part of their time organizing for their party. The information they spread, the political activity they stir up, the local political clubs they help form, all favor the incumbent party. Again the opposition has no effective political weapon to counter this. Here, as with the *Typographical Journal*, the opposition is at a distinct disadvantage compared to the incumbents.

§ The Consequences of Weakness and Isolation

THE WEAKNESS OF the small locals and their dependence on the administration make it in their interest to support the incumbents. The international organizer, the secretary-treasurer, and the president himself can favor them or neglect them, can fight their battles or lie down on wage negotiations. One of the leaders interviewed, a former international organizer, told of a particularly "ungrateful" small local which had voted against his party after he had negotiated a good contract for them. If this man's party had remained in office, he probably would not have worked so hard for this local again. It is not unreasonable to infer that most men in small locals realize this, and unlike this "ungrateful" local, take it into consideration in their vote.

Thus it is clear that there is a basis here for the operation of self-interest for each of the men in these small locals. If they do not vote for the incumbents, and the incumbents are re-elected, the representative who served them well before may work less hard for them in the future.[1]

We should perhaps reiterate here that in inferring the operation of this interest principle, we are not presenting these subjective motivations as facts. We are pointing to an objectively possible reason for small locals to support the administration on the basis of self-interest, with no direct knowledge of whether this is subjectively felt or not.

The operation of this pattern is dependent on the ability of the administration to differentially reward men, not on the basis of their different objectively determined positions, but on the basis of their *own behavior*. If, because of the laws or the norms of the organization, the administration cannot cull out the sheep from the goats in this way, then it could not apply these differential rewards.[2] In the union this

---

1. It may be noted here parenthetically that the two-party system, with its attendant insecurity for the incumbents, makes an international representative much less likely to disregard a recalcitrant local's needs. Since his party needs every vote it can get, he may work even harder after a local has voted against his party, in the hope of converting it. But it is still likely that the small locals see their interests bound up with their votes for the incumbents.

2. The Independents have recently been favoring the institution of regional scales, which would mean an economic and political structure mediating between the small locals and the international. This would undoubtedly strengthen the small locals, by organizing them into units which could act with more power vis-à-vis the employer and organize attitudes and opinions in ITU politics. The move would certainly strengthen the democracy of the union as well, as the evidence to come will show. It would, of course, weaken the tenure of the incumbent, and because of this it may never be instituted by the Independents when they gain office.

means that if there were no small locals, or if these locals were grouped under regional organizations which had a single wage contract and were in other ways administered as a unit, the pattern examined could not operate.

§ The Large Locals

THE OFFICERS OF THE LARGE LOCALS are in quite a different position. They can actively oppose an ITU administration, if they belong to the opposition party or are not members of any international party. On a number of occasions, in fact, leaders of large locals who belonged to the same international party as the ITU officers broke with their international party because of resentment against the actions of the officers.

These breaks were not only made possible by the autonomy of the large locals; the local officers seem to have been forced by their own election needs to make such breaks. The international leaders sometimes become scapegoats in a local union for poor wage negotiations or their failure to support strikes, and the local affiliate of the international incumbent party may be forced to disavow its international leaders. A common tactic of officers of large locals who belong to the opposition party is to try to make the international officers responsible for any difficulties facing the local. Specifically, they denounce the international officers either for not vigorously supporting the local in its collective-bargaining negotiations, or for developing international policies or tactics which make it difficult for the local to gain its objectives.

A basic source of tension between the members of any large local and the ITU administration is strike policy, since the sanction of the international officers is required to call a strike. The ITU is often asked to send in a representative to help in difficult negotiations, and to advise the international council concerning strike policy in that local. Each local is naturally concerned with its own contract negotiations, and wants all the support possible that the international can give, including approval of the use of the strike weapon if necessary. The international officers, on the other hand, are faced with the need to take an over-all union perspective. If they approve strikes for all major locals, the union may face a situation in which its resources are strained by too many strikes. International administrations, therefore, must discourage many strikes, and often urge local leaders and members to accept the best settlement possible.

But this pattern of behavior on the part of the international administration often enables the opposition party to make political capital, whether it controls the local or not. And partly for this reason, as time passes the international opposition party tends to made headway in the larger locals. Often this results in the opposition gaining a majority in the local; but on a few significant occasions it has also made for local officers breaking with their international party.

By members of small locals, then, the international is usually seen in the role of necessary supporter, while members of larger locals often see the international in the role of a conservative inhibitor.[3] On the international level, the large locals play the role of powerful secondary associations, which are relatively independent of the central authority and prevent a one-party system in the international.

§ Local Voting Patterns

EVIDENCE THAT THESE PROCESSES actually do operate as the above discussion suggests is presented in Table 38. The locals are separated

Table 38—Relationship between Votes for Incumbent and Size of Local

Size of Locals	Average above 50% for Incumbent, 1902-1954, %	N over the 52-Year Span
1,000+	1.7	7,837 to 23,798
500-1,000	3.8	1,705 to 10,982
100- 500	5.6	7,920 to 18,931
100—	7.8	8,156 to 19,652
Unattached*	15.2	144 to 395

* Unattached vote is based on only 19 elections, 1918-1954. Previous to 1918 there was no separate tabulation for the unattached. Other figures are based on 24 elections.

into four size groups: 1,000 members or more, 500-1,000, 100-500, and fewer than 100.[4] The average percentage of votes above 50% given the incumbent ITU president by each group over the past fifty-two years, from 1902 to 1954, is shown in the table.

The relationship between the size of a local and voting for the incumbent candidate for president is clear-cut. The smaller a local, the

---

3. There is one interesting exception to this generalization. Between 1947 and 1951, the anti-Taft-Hartley policy of the Progressive administration precipitated a large number of strikes. Some of these, as in Chicago and Miami, lasted for years, and a number were lost. In this situation, local Independent officials or opposition groups attacked the Progressives for causing unnecessary strikes and made considerable headway in a number of large locals.

4. These sizes are based on number of votes cast for president—the only method we had of determining the locals' sizes. The actual sizes would be perhaps as much as 25% greater than this, since only about 80% of the union membership votes in any election.

larger the vote which it gives to incumbents.[5] If the opposition party had to rely on the votes of the members of the small locals, there would probably be no turnover of officers in the ITU. On the other hand, if every local had more than a thousand members, the history of the ITU would probably show even more turnover in office than has actually occurred.[6]

The "unattached" group in Table 38 is particularly interesting. This group is composed of men who are not members of organized locals, and who work in communities in which there are not enough ITU members to form a local. Consequently, these printers are the most isolated members of the ITU. Their only contact with the union is through the *Journal,* or through correspondence sent out by the International office. The opposition party has no means of reaching them. Reading only one side of the case, these men end up voting for the incumbent regardless of whether he is an Independent or a Progressive.

The voting pattern of these locals is perhaps more strikingly shown by comparing each year's vote over this fifty-year period for the largest locals and the smallest local. In the graph of Figure 75 is shown the vote of the largest locals (over 1,000 votes) compared to the vote of the smallest locals (under 100 votes) tabulated as percentage in favor of

---

5. It might be questioned whether there is a general tendency for locals of a given size to align with one party, producing the relationship shown in Table 38. For example, if the large locals were voting always for the Progressives, and if the Progressives were more often in opposition, the result of Table 38 would be explained by this party loyalty rather than by our interpretations. But the table below shows that there is no general relation between size and party support. This table shows that, over the same period, the smallest locals, which as a group have favored the Independents more than the Progressives, gave the Progressives as *incumbents* even more votes than did the large locals, which tend to favor the Progressives.

Table—Relationship between Votes for Incumbent of Both Parties and Size of Local

Size of Locals	Average Percentage above 50% for Incumbent Progressives	Average Percentage above 50% for Incumbent Independents or Administration Party
1000+	4.9	−2.2
500-1000	2.5	5.3
100-500	7.8	3.0
100—	6.5	9.4
Unattached	15.5	14.5

6. It is worth noting here that the constitution of the Printing Pressmen's Union, the second largest in the printing trades, which has been controlled by one oligarchic group since 1908, deliberately restricts the voting power of the large locals. In this union each local has a fixed number of electoral votes, and the candidate who carries a local receives its votes, much as in a United States Presidential election. No local, however, regardless of size, has more than six electoral votes, while every small local has at least one vote. Thus six locals of ten members each may balance out a majority of thousands in a large city local. On at least one occasion, and probably in others, the incumbent president of the pressmen received less than 40% of the popular vote and was still re-elected.

Figure 75—Voting for the Incumbent ITU President: Large Locals (over 1,000)
and Small Locals (under 1,000)

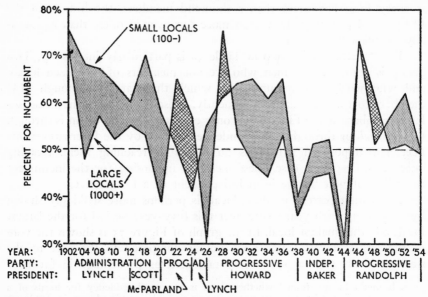

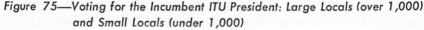

PERCENT FOR INCUMBENT

	1902	'04	'08	'10	'12	'18	'20	'22	'24	'26	'28	'30	'32	'34	'36	'38	'40	'42	'44	'46	'48	'50	'52	'54
SM. LOCALS	75	68	67	64	60	70	58	50	41	55	61	64	65	61	65	40	51	52	31	73	51	57	62	50
LGE. LOCALS	71	48	57	52	55	53	39	65	57	31	75	53	47	44	53	36	44	45	27	73	61	50	51	49
TOTAL VOTE	71	61	61	58	56	64	49	64	48	48	64	59	55	57	58	39	52	52	33	70	58	55	57	50

the incumbent. The graph shows that in only 3 elections out of a total
of 24 (1924, 1938, and 1944) did the smallest locals fail to give the incumbent president a majority of their vote.[7] The large locals, on the
other hand, gave the incumbent less than 50% of their vote in 9 of
these 24 elections. The locals having 500 to 1,000 men, and those with
100 to 500 men, not shown on the graph, gave the incumbent less than
a majority in 7 and 5 elections respectively. The differences are even
more striking than the graph indicates. The three exceptions to the rule
that small locals support the incumbents, the elections of 1924, 1938,
and 1944, actually help to confirm the hypothesis concerning the effect

7. The large-local vote is tabulated by adding the votes of all the locals with
1,000 members for a given year, then finding the percentage of this total which
went for the incumbent. A similar procedure was followed for the small locals.
The vote records were obtained from the *Typographical Journal*, July issue of
each election year (every even-numbered year, except 1914, 1916, and 1906, when
there were no opponents in the presidential race). The periods of Independent and
Progressive presidencies are shown at the bottom of the graph.

of communications and dependence on the International of the vote of small locals. Before each of these elections, the opposition party had had regular monthly access to the *Typographical Journal* by controlling one or more of the vice-presidencies or the secretary-treasurer's position.[8] In 1924 the opposition candidate was James Lynch, who had been President of the ITU from 1900 to 1912, when he voluntarily resigned to take a position as New York State Labor Commissioner. In 1938 the opposition presidential nominee was Claude Baker, then first vice-president of the ITU, who had held that office since 1932. Baker, though elected originally as a Progressive, broke with his party after being re-elected in 1936. The Progressive opposition candidate in 1944 was Woodruff Randolph, secretary-treasurer of the ITU from 1928 to 1944. Thus in these three elections the crucial variables of communication and international prestige were almost evenly balanced between the parties. In addition, the fact that the major international offices were divided between the parties meant that before each of these elections each party had a share of the power of the incumbents.[9]

§ Changes in Support through Time

SINCE THE TIME that the two-party system formally began in 1912, five distinct political eras can be distinguished in the ITU. The conservative Administration Party was dominant until 1920; from 1920 to 1928 the union was divided almost evenly between the two parties; from 1928 to 1938, the Progressive Party was victorious in all international elections; the next six years, 1938-1944, witnessed Independent control of the presidency and the Executive Council; and from that time to the present the Progressive Party has ruled in the ITU. How did these shifts occur?

In all cases the pattern was similar. The large locals were gradually or quickly alienated from the incumbent administration. The opposition party, first the Progressives and later the Independents, became the advocates of local autonomy, which concretely meant the defense of the rights of the large locals against the ITU. Sections of the opposition

---

8. The nine rejections of the incumbent by the large locals do not follow this pattern; their first vote against the incumbent, in 1920, marked the first real shift between parties in the union's history, from the Wahneta-Administration Party to the Progressives. The two other important changes in administration (1938 and 1944) were preceded by votes against the incumbents on the part of the large locals, although the small locals joined in to finally bring about the change.

9. In two of these elections, 1924 and 1944, the *Typographical Journal* was controlled by the opposition through its hold on the post of secretary-treasurer.

party won control of many of the larger locals and attacked administration policies. The small locals, on the other hand, originally opposed the change of administration, but the longer the tenure of an administration the more support it secured from the small locals. Thus we have the curious result that once an ITU party takes office, it loses the support of the locals which elected it and gains the support of the strongholds of the previous administration.

Specifically, between 1920 and 1928, while the Progressives were still the historic opposition party and failing to win complete control of the union from the Wahnetas, the large locals gave them heavy majorities. In 1928 the Progressives won control of all major ITU posts and of the international convention for the first time in ITU history; and as Figure 76 shows, this was the last year that the large locals gave them a significant majority until they were again a minority party in 1940. From 1930 until 1938, when they were defeated, the Progressives received only 47% of the vote in the large locals, compared to an average of 65% of the vote from 1920 to 1928, the period in which the Progressives were fighting for complete control of the union.

Figure 76—Voting for Progressives, 1920-1938: Large and Small Locals

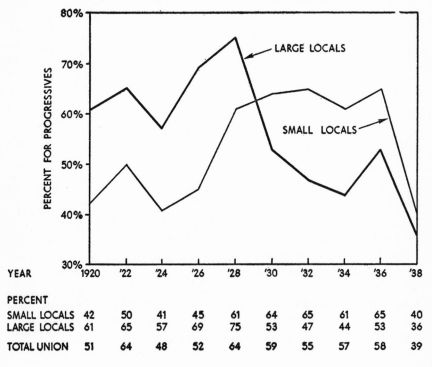

PERCENT										
	1920	'22	'24	'26	'28	'30	'32	'34	'36	'38
SMALL LOCALS	42	50	41	45	61	64	65	61	65	40
LARGE LOCALS	61	65	57	69	75	53	47	44	53	36
TOTAL UNION	51	64	48	52	64	59	55	57	58	39

The small locals behaved in an almost completely opposite manner. They voted Administration until 1928; but once the Progressives won office the small locals gave the Progressives over 60% of the vote in every election until 1938, when the Independent Party candidate for President was the incumbent first vice-president. The graph of Figure 76 gives the vote of the largest and smallest locals for the Progressives from 1920 to 1938.

Following the Independent victory in 1938, the large locals returned in 1940 and 1942 to voting for the now opposition Progressive Party. The small locals, however, continued to vote for the incumbent Independents. In 1944 both small and large locals joined together to vote for the Progressives, whose presidential candidate was a man who had been secretary-treasurer of the ITU and editor of the *Typographical Journal* from 1928 to 1944.

The new Progressive administration elected in 1944 was able temporarily to break the cycle of large-local opposition and small-local support to the incumbents. In 1946 they were re-elected with an overwhelming majority of over 70% of the vote. Both small and large locals joined together to give them this vote of confidence. This result is probably related to the end of the war, with the succeeding large wage increases which all ITU members obtained as result of the end of wartime government restrictions. In 1948, however, the small-local vote for the Progressive administration dropped to close to the 50% mark, while the large locals gave them 60%. The results of this election seemingly challenge our assumptions about the political constraints on different-sized locals.

The 1948 exception to the rule that small locals support the incumbents, however, seems to be the result of an interesting variation in the customary relations between the international and the locals. The Progressives, as a result of their vigorous opposition to the Taft-Hartley Act, actively encouraged strikes in this period. No large local could complain that the international was hampering its efforts to secure better conditions through militant action. On the other hand, small locals, which rarely if ever take part in a strike and usually have cordial relations with their employers, were forced by the anti-Taft-Hartley policy of the ITU to attempt to force their employers to agree to maintain union laws even if such laws violated the Taft-Hartley law, and to obtain informal agreements rather than contracts from these employers. These new international policies conflicted with the traditions and interests of the small locals. For the first time in the history of the union, the small locals as a group had a major interest conflict with the international. They were being forced into militant actions which were not required by their local situations, and for which they were not prepared. It is not surprising, therefore, that the vote in the small locals for the Progressives dropped by 22%. The fact that in spite of these conflicts they still gave the Progressives a majority of 51% might actually be considered evidence of the power of the Progressives' control of communications and administration, rather than of its weakness.

The loss of vote which Randolph suffered in 1954 at the hands of both the large and small locals seems to indicate a break in the pattern. While the small locals gave him a small majority, his vote among them dropped by almost 12%. Without more precise knowledge of this election campaign, which occurred after we stopped close observation of the union, we can say little to account for this seeming deviation. The one interpretation which seems plausible is that the year before the election was characterized by a number of referenda in which the Progressives attempted to increase their power over the distribution of union funds and the Independents introduced proposals to restrict administration power. On these policy issues the Independents were successful, leading many union observers to believe that the Progressive administration was about to be defeated. Traditionally the small locals have been even more predisposed to protect union funds and keep down increases than the large locals, since in general the smaller a local in the ITU, the lower its salary scale and the less likely it is to benefit directly from ITU defense funds, since it is rarely in a position to strike. While these ex post facto interpretations seem plausible as an explanation of why the small locals deviated from their traditional pattern, it is necessary to recognize that this is one case which does not conform to our generalization, and may reflect some change in the relationship of the smaller locals to the international about which we are unaware. In any case the 1954 campaign may be cited as another example of an election in which the administration was rebuffed by a majority of the large locals.

These voting patterns point directly to the processes discussed above: semi-autonomous and well-organized groups such as the large locals are able to oppose an incumbent administration, while small locals, dependent on the administration both for communication about union affairs and for services, are similar to the individual of the mass society who has no real alternative to supporting the administration. Thus as the administration becomes more entrenched, these isolated units acquiesce more and more; any alternatives they once knew are progressively removed from the range of action. And this is the case even when the large locals organize the opposition as they do in the ITU, presenting the small locals with possibility of voting for an opponent. If it were not for the active opposition party, supported by the large locals, there would be no such opportunity.

This study of the voting records of locals of various sizes emphasizes the great importance of social structure in allowing men and groups of differing interests and dispositions to organize into a strong opposition. The latent and cumulative discontent generated by the incumbent's necessity to initiate policy, while the opposition need not be constrained by the realities of office, is a potential force in favor of the opposition. But as the examples of the small locals show, although these are potential forces in favor of the opposition, in an atomized society they cannot be activated in favor of the opposition.

It is necessary to recognize that shifts in administration in the ITU are not simply a function of a political cycle. Specific historical situations create problems for ITU officers, just as they do for national governments. The administration must offer responsible solutions to these problems. The opposition, however, since it need not *act*, can espouse utopian policies without being limited by the need of carrying them out. It can find fault, pointing out the weaknesses of the administration's policies, but the weaknesses of its own policies never become evident since they are not subject to the test of action. These processes are part of the self-defeating mechanisms of office in a democracy, for they derive directly from the constraints and responsibility of office itself. They do not occur, of course, independently of the situation faced by an administration: in a period of expanding prosperity, there may be little cumulative discontent with the administration on which the opposition can grow.

Specifically, with one exception, each shift in ITU administration occurred during a period of crisis for which the incumbents were not responsible. The one possible exception to this generalization was the first one in 1920. But even in this case the deciding issues may have been an outgrowth of the inflation generated by World War I. The Administration Party refused to permit a number of large locals, especially New York, to engage in strikes, and lost their support. The Progressives, in power during the Great Depression, were faced with a demand from the large number of unemployed, largely located in the big locals, to share the available work and to permit increased taxation of the employed for unemployment relief. To give in to this demand would have alienated the majority group of employed printers. The opposition Independents could not become the spokesmen of the unemployed since that would have lost votes for them also, but they could imply, as they did, that conditions would be better if they were elected.[10] During World War II, the conservative Independents were placed in the same position as their Administration Party predecessors in World War I. They had to administer the union in a period of rapid inflation in which strikes were impossible. The opposition Progressives, as we have seen, capitalized on the situation by again advocating strikes. Thus in 1920, in 1938, and in 1944, administrations were defeated after periods of externally generated discontent.

§ Case Studies of Locals

UNDERNEATH THE PATTERN of shift toward or away from the incumbents by different-sized locals is, however, the continuity of voting patterns within many locals, both large and small. As in national politics, each ITU party can rely on a large group of locals to give it a majority regardless of whether they are in office or in opposition. And underlying the consistency of locals is the permanent Progressive or Independent orientation of many men.

The existence of a large group of partisan locals is probably as important to the continuation of the two-party system in the union as is the propensity of many ITU members to quickly shift against the administration which they helped to elect. A political party which does not have the loyal, almost uncritical, support of a basic minority of the voters and political units might be eliminated by a drastic reversal. A failure to retain control of a minority of locals would mean that the minority party would have no representation at the annual international conventions, and so could not use this opportunity to present an opposition case. Even more important, perhaps, is the fact that they would lose the opportunity to develop leaders who had actual experience in office, and who when running for international posts could point to actual accomplishments while in local office. Opposition control of locals also gives the out party the opportunity to implement alternative policies on the local level. For example, during international campaigns the opposition will often point to the collective-bargaining accomplishments of locals under their control. During the Taft-Hartley strike period of 1947-1949, few Independent-controlled locals were involved in strikes, and Independents were able to argue that their locals had been as successful in protecting the laws of the ITU as the more militant Progressive locals.

---

10. In fact, as was indicated in Chap. 3, the Communists were able to make headway among the unemployed in this period.

It is difficult, however, to locate the factors which are responsible for diversity between different large locals. To do so would have required intensive case histories of a number of these locals, and our resources simply did not permit such studies. Some hypotheses may be suggested, however. They are drawn from discussions with various union leaders and our study of ITU history.

1. A given historic event will alienate the voters of certain locals from one or the other party. Thus, some locals were centers of Wahneta excesses before World War I, and in the reaction against these the conservative faction almost disappeared in these locals. The action of a given international administration in opposing the strike of a local may also have permanent effects in eliminating the strength of its local supporters. The 1919 New York "vacationist" strike was such an event in the history of New York. This case will be discussed in more detail in the next section.

2. The collective-bargaining pattern of a local will affect its party allegiance. Thus, the San Francisco and Oakland locals of the ITU supported the Progressives from the beginning of the party down to the thirties, while Los Angeles has been a Wahneta and later an Independent stronghold. One interpretation of these differences suggests that Los Angeles supported the Wahnetas because Los Angeles was a strongly antiunion or open-shop community and unions could not wage successful strikes there. Consequently, its ITU local supported a policy of cooperating with the employers. The San Francisco Bay area, on the other hand, was an early trade-union stronghold, and had a tradition of labor militancy in a number of occupations. Thus the Progressives were unable for many years to secure support from the supposedly more cowed Los Angeles printers, while the more militant northern Californians backed the Progressives overwhelmingly.

3. Union leaders suggest, as a third set of factors, party organization and personal influence. With the exception of New York, no ITU local has more than 5,000 members; locals are consequently small political units as compared with congressional or state legislative districts. In any given local, one party may become dominant for a long period of time because of an outstanding leader or an efficient party organization. A party may also lose support in a local because of a clearly bad regime or a split in the party. The shift in San Francisco's allegiance from the Progressives to the Independents in the late thirties is an illustration of this pattern.

The predominance of one party in a given large local often sets into motion a set of reinforcing factors which perpetuate it in power. The fact that the dominant party is almost certain to win future local elections means that ambitious and capable men will be more likely to join that party. The out party, in turn, becomes the recipient of the support of the crackpots. As a weak party, the opposition usually is not able to communicate as easily and as often with the membership. Lacking experienced former local officers, its criticisms of local policy are often less sophisticated.

As in national civic politics, however, the continuation of a two-party system on the international level does prevent the emergence of a complete one-party monopoly in local politics. In most locals there are some men who identify with the international parties for ideological reasons. These men will continue to back their local party even when it is a hopeless minority. The fortunes of the ITU party either help or hurt its local affiliates, and over time a weak local party may develop strength as a result of international developments. Thus the give-and-take of international party politics is a major factor in sustaining weak local parties and allows for the possibility that such hopeless groups will gain support. Below we give three case histories of major shifts in the voting patterns of large locals.

§ New York and the 1919 Strike

PERHAPS THE MOST IMPORTANT single case in ITU history of a large local's opposition to the administration came after the 1919 "vacationist" strike in New York. The Administration Party failed to support this 1919 walkout of New York printers and incurred their strong antagonism.

Below are listed the votes of the New York union from 1900, when the first Administration Party candidate won a presidential election, until 1928, the Administration Party's last campaign. These data document the effect of the 1919 conflict with the international president, Scott. Only once before this incident had New York given the Administration less than 50% of its votes, and in 1918 it had given Scott (who was from New York) 59% of its votes.

After the 1919 incident, New York's vote for the Administration Party dropped to the lowest it has ever been, and remained low until the Administration Party ceased to exist. In 1920 Scott lost the presidency with 49% of the total international vote. If New York had not turned decisively against him, or if it had given him even half its vote, he would have won the election. In the elections of 1924 and 1926, New York even cast its vote against James Lynch, whom it had supported from 1900 until 1912, after which he had voluntarily stepped down from office.[11]

---

11. In one election during this period New York failed to support Lynch. This was 1904 when it gave him 49% of its vote.

In 1926 New York's vote was again decisive against the Administration candidate, this time removing Lynch from office. With 50% of New York's vote, Lynch would have won.

These statistics show how important the 1919 affair was for the political behavior of the New York union, as well as for union politics as a whole. Without this, the Administration Party might have continued in power through the twenties and perhaps beyond that. As it was, the party was finished in 1928. This is one of the few incidents in the union's history in which the international administration acted directly against a powerful unit within the union, and probably the only one which provoked such a strong reaction. The effectiveness of New York's reaction has probably served as a deterrent to international administrations which followed this one.

The printers of New York went out on a wildcat strike for a five-day week in 1919, and Scott, the international president, refused to back them up. He attempted to put an end to the strike by appealing to the strikers over the heads of the local officers who had previously supported

Figure 77—New York's Vote for the Administration Party, 1900-1929

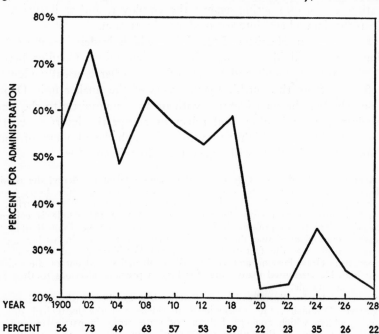

YEAR	1900	'02	'04	'08	'10	'12	'18	'20	'22	'24	'26	'28
PERCENT	56	73	49	63	57	53	59	22	23	35	26	22

him.[12] The strikers sided with their local leaders against Scott. They might have agreed with the administration and given up the strike, going against their local leaders; Scott's appeal to them shows that he considered this a possibility. Why did they identify with the local rather than the international? We cannot say with assurance, not having any data on the motivations of the men, but we can suggest what things were probably important. They had *acted together* in two ways by going out on strike. First, they had made a collective decision, through their elected (local) officers and through their union meetings, to go out on strike. While men undoubtedly differed as individuals over the decision to strike, once having made the decision through democratic processes, it was a decision of the group. When the international president, who had been elected not only by them but by 50,000 other printers outside New York, stepped in, it must have been viewed as an interference from the *outside*. Their refusal to respond may have been in part at least a reaffirmation of unity. The second way in which they had acted together, which probably reinforced their feelings of unity and of identification as a group, was in actually going out on strike. It is commonly known that strikes build a strong union by increasing the members' involvement and identification with their union. This general principle undoubtedly held in this case, increasing these printers' identification as a group acting against the employer, and as it turned out, against the incumbent international administration.

One of the mechanisms determining which leaders, local or international, men will identify with is suggested above. Conflict between leaders of the large unit and leaders of the smaller is usually viewed as interference from the outside by members of the smaller unit. Depending on whether the men identify with or are antagonistic to the leaders of their smaller unit, they will reject or accept the interference from the outside. The more highly they identify with their leaders, of course, the more strongly they will reject this "interference."[13]

---

12. However, he did not take the kind of action taken by Berry, the president of the pressmen, who went out with the printers in this same strike. Berry brought strikebreakers into New York against his own pressmen and broke the strike.

13. This identification with the part as over against the whole is evident in much of United States politics. It is said that Representative John Rankin from Mississippi once claimed that the only thing that defeated him in his last race for Congress (1948) was the fact that people from Washington and the nationwide commentators Drew Pearson and Walter Winchell had stayed out of the campaign against him. He attributed many votes for him in previous elections to their interference from outside.

This example also illustrates how a *disagreement* can be transformed into active *antagonism*. Originally, the international president and the local had disagreed about a problem which concerned them both: the strike in particular, and more generally, the nature of the union's foreign policy vis-à-vis the employer. But with

§ The Government Printing Office

THERE HAVE REEN OTHER INCIDENTS in the union's history similar to the New York incident in their effect on a local's vote. A recent one was the Washington local's sudden shift against Randolph (the Progressive incumbent) in 1948. In 1947 the Taft-Hartley Act was passed and Randolph declared the union's policy of directly fighting it. This set off a series of strikes so costly that a 4½% assessment on each man's pay was voted to support the strikes.

Figure 78—Washington (D.C.) Local's Vote for ITU President, 1944-1954

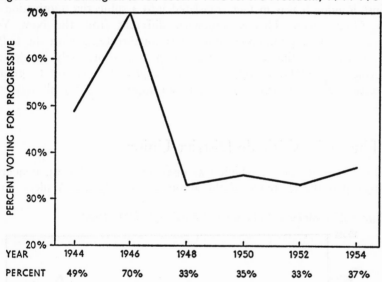

YEAR	1944	1946	1948	1950	1952	1954
PERCENT	49%	70%	33%	35%	33%	37%

NOTE: In the election of 1944 there were three parties. Randolph received 64% of the two-party vote.

The union as a whole went along with Randolph's policy, voting the heavy assessment and re-electing Randolph. Everyone paid heavily into the defense fund, but some printers could be certain that they would never receive any direct returns from the fund. Printers employed in

the action of Scott directly against the New York leaders, this disagreement over an issue was translated into direct antagonism against Scott and the whole Administration Party. Furthermore, the antagonism continued as long as the party was in existence, long after the issue was past history. This process of translating disagreement over a problem into direct antagonism which needs no problem or issue to keep it alive seems a very general one, responsible for much political fervor. It seems also to be a major mechanism through which cleavages become intensified and stabilized.

the Government Printing Offices in Washington are unable by law to strike and are prevented from using the usual collective-bargaining practices. They paid for the militant policy, but could not directly benefit from it. In 1948 the Washington membership, over half of whom work in the Government Printing Offices, turned decisively against the Progressives. Randolph's vote in Washington dropped 47% in one election and has remained low ever since. It is likely that part of the 1948 loss occurred because his opponent was a Washington man; but if this were the primary reason for the shift, the vote would not have remained low in 1950, 1952, and 1954, when there was no Washington man running and the militant tactics were still partially in force.

This evidence suggests that the objective interest basis for voting against Randolph was in fact translated into a subjective motivation for these G.P.O. men. This is somewhat different from the New York 1919 case, in that Randolph's action was not directed against the G.P.O. men; it was an action covering the union as a whole, only incidentally affecting the G.P.O. Nevertheless, Washington had reason to go into opposition, and the prior existence of an opposition party allowed it to do so.

§ The Mailers' Trade District Union

THE MAILERS' ISSUE, which was discussed in Chapter 14, concerned in large part the existence of the autonomous body, the Mailers' Trade

Figure 79—Mailers' Vote for ITU President, 1902-1954

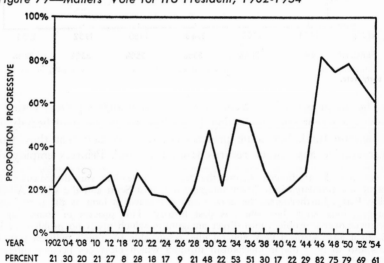

YEAR	1902	'04	'08	'10	'12	'18	'20	'22	'24	'26	'28	'30	'32	'34	'36	'38	'40	'42	'44	'46	'48	'50	'52	'54
PERCENT	21	30	20	21	27	8	28	18	17	9	21	48	22	53	51	30	17	22	29	82	75	79	69	61

District Union. Progressive ITU presidents, both Howard and Randolph, attempted to dissolve this body between 1928 and 1944, when Randolph finally succeeded. The difference in the mailers' votes before and after the demise of this intermediary organization presents a graphic example of the political effect of independent secondary institutions. The mailers had always been pro-Independent (or Administration) and always gave the Progressives a smaller vote than they received among the printers—until the Trade District Union was abolished in 1944. The chart above shows their votes for the Progressives from 1902 to 1954: The figures speak for themselves. Disorganized, the mailers have lost their potential as a support for political opposition in the ITU.

§ A Pair of Locals: Oakland and San Francisco

THE SAN FRANCISCO and Oakland locals, lying just across San Francisco Bay, have been Progressive locals since the party began. From 1912 (when the Progressives first organized) to 1938, San Francisco gave the Progressives a majority of its votes in every election, failing only three times out of eleven to give them over 60% of its vote. Oakland's voting history was similar. Since 1912 it has voted Progressive in every election except one, in 1918. In most elections the Progressives received 70% or more of the vote in these two locals.

In 1932 the Progressive president of the San Francisco local, Claude Baker, became first vice-president of the ITU. Baker soon began to differ with Charles Howard, president of the ITU, and tended to support more aggressive tactics in dealing with the problem of unemployment. In both 1936 and 1938 groups of local Progressives, including the New York and San Francisco Progressive Clubs, attempted to organize support for Baker as the Progressive candidate for ITU president replacing Howard. These efforts never came to an open conflict, and both Howard and Baker were renominated and elected as president and first vice-president of the ITU. In 1937, however, Baker openly broke with Howard and the Progressive Party and accepted the Independent Party nomination for international president. Baker took with him into the Independent Party a number of the San Francisco leaders of the Progressive Party. In the 1938 election the Progressive vote for president dropped from 68% to 35% of the vote, while across the Bay in Oakland, where no split had occurred among the Progressives, they still retained the support of the majority of the membership.

The San Francisco Progressives have never recovered from the split of 1938. Following Baker's defeat as ITU president in 1944, he returned to his home local and eventually became president of the union. San

Francisco has become a major stronghold of the Independents, publishing a local monthly paper which is practically an Independent Party campaign organ. It devotes much of its space to attacking the Progressive International administration. Since 1948, this local has given the Independents around 60% of the vote at each election. Thus through the switch of the leader of the local party, a thousand-man local broke with a twenty-five-year-old allegiance to the Progressive Party.

The Oakland local, on the other hand, has remained loyal to the Progressive Party. It continues to re-elect local Progressive administrations, and to give the international Progressive ticket an overwhelming majority.

Conclusions

CHAPTER 18

Why Democracy in the ITU?

IN SPITE OF THE DETAILED NATURE of our analysis the reader may still legitimately raise the question: Why democracy in the ITU? Is it really a necessary consequence of the structural factors which have been examined? Is it not possible that even if a union possesses all the attributes that the ITU has, it will not develop nor sustain a democratic political system? To what extent could matters have developed differently in the ITU if certain events had occurred differently, or if at some crucial periods in its existence ruthless and powerful men had been at the helm of the union and had been willing to risk destruction of the union rather than lose power? In a real sense, these questions cannot be answered, for in the context of the study of a single case it is impossible to isolate completely all the potentially reelvant factors and then specify which factors, either individually or in combination, account for the differences in internal political organization between the ITU and most other unions. We know, for example, that the particular pattern of ITU politics is not repeated in other printer unions in Europe, although there is evidence which suggests that as a group they are more democratic and less centralized than unions in other occupations.

§ Historical Analysis

THE SOCIOLOGICAL ANALYSIS with which most of the book is concerned is an analysis of the factors which contribute to the continuation of the democratic political system at the present time. But it is important to recognize that this analysis gives only a static picture, a description which shows the processes at work within the going system, but not the processes which enabled the system to reach more or less stable equilibrium. At any point in time, the political system of an organization or a society has a certain degree of stability. That is, it has a certain probability of continuing in its present form, and a certain probability of changing. The political system of the ITU is always being supported by some factors and undermined by others. By thus viewing the system as being in an equilibrium which at any point in time has a certain stability, but which could have moved in different directions if some of the factors in the situation had occurred differently, we can see the need to deal with historical materials. It remains for the historical analysis of events which were unique to the ITU to indicate which factors favored the emergence and stability of ITU democracy at different points in time, and to specify the crucial junction points at which new elements entered the situation.

In this way we see that the existence of democracy in the ITU is largely the result of the convergence of a set of events, each of which contributes to or detracts from the continuing stability of the system. If some one event in the early history had turned the other way, then present-day democracy in the union would have been less likely. The existence of democracy at present may be likened to a series of successive outcomes of casting dice, dice which are with each favorable throw more heavily loaded toward a favorable outcome on the next throw.[1] Democracy in the ITU was thus no necessary consequence of a particular set of static factors, but rather was favored from the beginning by numerous factors and even more strongly favored as time went on and numerous events added to the system's stability.

The answer to our original question, Why democracy in the ITU? can be found only by combining the structural and historical analyses to determine the system's stability at each point in time. Thus, in conclusion we would like to examine again some of the crucial turning points in the union's early history.

Many of the factors which contribute to ITU's democracy were present when the union was organized. The printers' strong identification with the craft of printing, probably more pronounced then than now, meant that they were more likely to be involved in the affairs of their organization than workers in other occupations. This same identification, together with other factors such as the high status and irregular work hours of printing, also fostered a strong occupational community. This occupational community, in turn, stimulated the desire

---

1. See Max Weber: *The Methodology of the Social Sciences*, Glencoe, Ill., Free Press, 1949, pp. 182-85, for a similar discussion, including this "dice-throwing" analogy.

of printers to participate in their union. The borderline or marginal status of printing between the middle class and the working class insured the value cleavage which provided the content of politics and evenly split the union into "radical" and moderate camps. Perhaps most important of all at this period was the fact that a large proportion of the printing trades was organized before the creation of a strong international union with a large treasury and paid full-time officials. Thus, the various large city locals of the ITU had a long history of complete autonomy and resisted efforts to create a centralized international structure.

The significance of this factor in the history of the union may be seen by comparing the implications of two ideal-type patterns through which organizations are created. One is organization from the top down, where the group which originally starts the association organizes other individuals and branches into a larger structure. In such a situation we may expect the existence from the start of a formal bureaucratic structure with the new subordinate officials and groups deriving their authority from the summits of the organization. On the other hand, a large national organization may come into existence as a federation through the combination of a number of existing groups. In such a federation the creation of a one-party bureaucratic hierarchy requires the reduction of once independent locals or groups of leaders to subordinate power and status position.

While the ITU illustrates the second pattern, which obviously has greater potential for internal conflict and politics, the International Printing Pressmen and Assistants' Union, the other large printing trades union, exemplifies the first pattern. There, George Berry became president of the union while it was a small, weak organization, and organized the bulk of the trade into a highly centralized and dictatorial organization.[2] Thus the way in which the ITU came into existence and the late development of full-time international officers was not only a factor making for early democracy in the union, but also helped insure that the next throw of the dice would be loaded in favor of democracy and decentralization.[3]

---

2. See Carolyn A. Taylor: *The Emergence and Stabilization of Oligarchy in the International Printing Pressmen and Assistants Union of North America.* M.A. thesis, Columbia University, Department of Sociology, 1952.

3. A somewhat similar variation in organizational history accounts in large part for the differences in the political history of the United Automobile Workers and the United Steel Workers, two unions formed about the same time and affected by similar structural conditions. The Steel Workers was originally formed by the Steel Workers Organizing Committee under Philip Murray. With few exceptions, almost every local of this union was created *after* the initial power structure was established. From its inception there have been no serious factional dis-

A second important event affecting ITU politics was the formation of the secret societies which over the years endeavored to control both union offices and foremen's jobs. These societies, which were the first major challenges to the democracy of the printers' locals, contributed important elements to the union's democratic system. The autonomy of the locals, referred to above, helped prevent the secret societies from completely dominating the union, for the existence of local administrations opposed to the dominant secret society gave the ordinary printers a nucleus of organization and helped to expose the activities of the society. Also important is the fact that the intense identification of printers with their craft meant that the norms of brotherhood engendered by this identification made membership in an exclusive clique illlegitimate in the eyes of many secret-society members as soon as the society lost its early legitimate function of protecting the union.

Thus the stability of ITU democracy was tested and found strong even before the institutionalization of the party system. The struggle over the secret societies, however, added another element which served to preserve the union. Large numbers of printers had a deep personal interest in the fight, since it affected their personal security of employment and opportunity to get work. At least two major cliques or factions developed in most locals, the adherents and the opponents of the secret societies, and these cleavages resulted in deep personal conflicts. The struggle, consequently, could not simply be solved by the victory of one group in an election and the subsequent disappearance of the defeated faction, a frequent development in other unions where the factionalism has not deeply involved the interests or values of the large majority of the members. In the ITU the opposing factions had their roots in a basic cleavage among the members themselves, a cleavage which outlived the tenure in office of a given group and provided the basis for continuing opposition.

---

putes in the union which have given the members the right to choose among rival candidates for office. Any local center of disturbance was eliminated by Murray. On the other hand, the United Automobile Workers was formed out of an amalgamation of a number of existing automobile unions, and a number of its other local units were organized independently of national control and with relatively little aid from the national body. The subsequent bitter factional fights in the union have in part been a consequence of the attempt of various national administrations to set up a single bureaucratic hierarchy. Most of the factional leaders in the UAW were leaders in the early organizational period of the union, and the different factions have largely been coalitions of the groups headed by these different leaders jointly resisting efforts to subordinate them to the national organization. In spite of the fact that the structural conditions in a large industrial union like the UAW are not favorable to internal democracy and large-scale rank-and-file participation, it has taken close to two decades to approach a one-party structure, and the process is still not completed.

Again, it is difficult to state why such secret societies developed only within the ITU; but one guess is that the factors making for an occupational community helped to sustain the secret societies. These groups (and their opponents as well) were not just power-politics groups, but social clubs which fulfilled many of the same functions as other clubs in the printers' community. The fact, however, that secret political societies were formed cannot be explained by the tendency of printers to mingle with fellow craftsmen, but rather must be seen as a fortuitous reaction to a crisis in the union's relation with employers. Had the union not required such instruments of defense in the 1870's, there was no necessary reason for the emergence of these groups nor for the subsequent development of bitter struggles to abolish them.

The struggle over the secret societies also facilitated the democratization of the ITU's political structure through providing a rationale (*a*) for making the election of international officers a popular election, replacing the then existing system of election-by-convention, which is more easily controllable by the administration even in the ITU; (*b*) for reserving the decision on many matters to popular referendum; and (*c*) for providing an easy method of rank-and-file initiation of referenda. These measures in turn enabled the ITU membership to hold down the salaries of their officers, since increases could only be secured with the approval of the membership in referenda, approval which usually was not given. The fact that the fight against the secret societies was defined as a struggle against domination by visible organized minority cliques, and not simply as a fight against an incumbent administration, helped give the membership a sophisticated awareness of structural dangers to democracy. Thus were instituted important legal elements which support the stability of ITU democracy today.

Again, the pressmen may be used as a comparative case. Although that union underwent a factional struggle early in its history which resulted in the overthrow of the incumbent administration in 1907, factionalism was not institutionalized and perpetuated. The Pressmen's Union had a typical factional fight organized around a specific issue— the conservative collective-bargaining policy followed by the union. Once the old administration was defeated, factionalism practically vanished, since it did not take on the deep intralocal and personal character of the early ITU fights. The new president, George Berry, was able to use his victory to change the constitution in ways which solidified the power of the administration.

These two important points in the early history of the ITU are part of a pattern of "favorable dice throws." Another example, the permanent institutionalization of a rigid priority system in the ITU, was a result of the desire by the members to restrict one of the sources of power of the secret societies and was made possible largely by the existence of the referendum. Without the secret societies and the referendum, the ITU might never have developed a rigid priority system, and one of the factors which safeguard the members' activity in politics against the administration would never have developed. The pressmen, for example, have never adopted a priority system, and its absence has been one of the major resources of the oligarchic rulers of that union.

One additional turning point in the ITU's history deserves mention because it involves the first coming to power of the opposition party. The institutionalization of the practice of gracefully giving up office to an opposition without attempting to use illegitimate means to retain office is one of the most important aspects of a democratic society, which those living in such a society take for granted, while citizens of many states and members of many trade-unions know that it is not a simple and regular event. In many unions, administrations on the verge of defeat have resorted to various means, such as the expulsion of the opposition or its leaders, in order to retain power. It is not inconceivable that the Wahneta administration of 1919-1920 might have done the same thing. One factor, however, which served to prevent this from happening was the fact that the Progressives captured only one of the executive offices, the presidency, in the election, while the Administration Party retained its hold over the rest of the major offices and the Executive Council. Given its long-term rule of the union, it is clear that it expected to regain the presidency and retain control of the union once the temporary crisis occasioned by the 1919 New York strike was over. But the union remained more or less evenly divided between the two parties from 1920 to 1928. During these years each party could well hope that the next election would give it complete power. Thus, democratic practices continued through this critical period. Comparison may again be made with the Pressmen's Union, where evidence would suggest that George Berry was on the verge of defeat in the 1920's. He averted such a result by expelling opposition locals and leaders.

The 1920 election was important for the continuation of ITU democracy for another reason. As we pointed out earlier, Marsden Scott, the Wahneta president of the ITU, attempted to break the "vacationist" strike of the New York union. Had this not led to a defeat for Scott, primarily because the New York local voted overwhelmingly against him, the autonomy of the large locals would have been seriously impaired. The international officers would have felt free to manipulate the large locals at will. As it was, this event marked the first major victory of the Progressives, and served as a warning to future international officers not to treat lightly the wishes of large locals. This occurrence also may serve as another illustration of the way in which previous events help load the dice in one direction. The 1919 strike was a joint action of the New York pressmen and typographer locals against the orders of their internationals. When the IPP local disobeyed, Berry expelled the entire New York membership and brought in strikebreakers from outside the city. Scott limited his actions to calling publicly upon the men in Big Six to ignore their local leaders and return to work. Perhaps one reason why Berry and Scott acted differently was that the political consequences of their actions were predictably different. The pressmen's constitution, drawn up by Berry before he faced internal opposition, provided for elections through an electoral-college system in which large locals such as New York have a maximum of six votes while every small local has at least one electoral vote. Thus six locals with less than two hundred members among them, which supported Berry, could balance out the vote of the entire New York membership against him. In the ITU, however, every member votes individually. Scott, therefore, had to try to retain some support in New York if he hoped to be re-elected, and this fact may have operated to restrain his strikebreaking activities. The fact that the ITU decided in 1896 to elect officers by referendum may have been a crucial element in preserving its democracy in 1919-1920.

Without discussing other events chronologically, it is worth mentioning in this context the way in which the existence of an institutionalized party system operates to preserve and extend democratic institutions. At various points in ITU history the constitution has been amended at the initiative of the opposition or by a party just returned to office, in ways designed to weaken the power of the incumbents. The right of all candidates to print statements in the *Typographical Journal*, various elaborate controls over the spending of union monies, the creation of independent auditors elected in staggered six-year terms, and other similar legislation are examples of the ways in which ITU democracy has become incorporated in the law and mores.

These examples of different historical events which have strengthened the base for ITU democracy should serve to illustrate the point that social structure—using the term in this case to refer to the social system comprising the occupation, the industry, and union—defines the probabilities that given historical events can result in an enduring institutional pattern such as a two-party system. Social structure thus constitutes a *potential* for democracy, a potential which, however, may be realized only under certain historical circumstances. This potential can exist without bearing fruit if the initiating events do not occur, or if other abortive events happen. The history of the Pressmen's Union is perhaps a case in point. More often in American unions, one can find a pattern of events which might have initiated a party system had it not occurred in an organization whose social structure offered barren ground for democratic institutions. The United Automobile Workers is perhaps a case in point here.

§ Implications for Organizational Democracy

OBSERVERS HAVE CALLED the ITU an anachronism, much like some of the small Swiss cantons which still preserve the direct citizen-assembly control of government, and there is much truth in that view. The major trends in our society are all toward further rationalization of industry, the further concentration and centralization of economic units, and the increasing division of labor, with the substitution of automatic machine operations for skilled craftsmen. Technological developments in the printing industry point in the same direction, with the introduction of new mechanical processes which require little more than the skills of the typist. Although the union is resisting efforts on the part of the employers to divide composing work into two skill levels, many union leaders and members are privately pessimistic about their ability to maintain the centuries-old principle of printers that every worker who sets type should have the same training and be regarded as of equal skill level. The threats to the union posed by new mechanical devices, plus the growing importance of international union policies which meet the need to protect past rights challenged by government legislation, seem to be gradually resulting in a decline of the autonomy of the larger locals. Identification with the craft, and the isolation of printers from interaction with people in higher or lower status levels than themselves also appears to be lessening with changes in the American status structure, and the evidence would seem to indicate that the occupational community of the late forties and early fifties, while still strong, is weaker than it was before World War II. The ITU is still one of the most powerful unions in America and may for some time absorb or cushion the impact of technological developments on the status, income, and skill definition of printing. But major changes in the structure of the industry such as are occurring could conceivably destroy the political system of the union by changing the social system in which it is rooted.

There are mitigating factors, however. The decline of democracy in the ITU is a prediction for the long run, and as John Maynard Keynes has said, in the long run we are all dead. In the meantime, those political institutions which were institutionalized as a consequence of the social conditions making for democracy may prolong for a considerable period the democracy which exists. The normative and legal safeguards to the stability of democracy which developed throughout the union's history can act to preserve democracy long after some of the factors which gave rise to them have vanished. Perhaps the most important democratic defense mechanism which has been institutionalized in the ITU is the two-party system itself. The sheer existence of a two-party system provides one of the principal opportunities and stimulations for participation in politics by the members of an organization or community. If one compares a party conflict to contests between different athletic organizations, one can see how this process operates in areas other than politics. In a city which has two baseball clubs, or two high school football teams, many individuals who have no great interest in sports are exposed to pressures to identify with one or the other team by the fans of each one. Such identification once made and reinforced by personal relations with committed fans seems to lead many people to become strongly interested in who wins a given sports contest. Political identification, while more complicated, nevertheless takes on some of the aspects of team identification. Political parties, once in existence, attempt to activate the apathetic in order to keep alive and win power. This process undoubtedly leads more people to become interested and involved in the affairs of the community or organization than when no political conflict exists.[4]

As long as some men feel strongly about union issues and others are desirous of securing or retaining the status derivative from the role of union political leader, the party organizations will be maintained in the ITU, since they are the institutionalized mechanisms through which such men can express themselves.

In a one-party structure, on the other hand, politically interested or ambitious men have only one outlet for their activity, and that is involvement in the activities sponsored by the administration. In the absence of a democratic political arena in which men may learn the skills of politics outside the administration, union officers are usually faced with a paucity of skilled and capable prospective subordinate officials, and are usually willing and even anxious to coopt capable union

---

4. Various election studies show that the closer the contest in a given electoral unit, the higher the rate of voting participation. See Herbert Tingsten, *Political Behaviour;* D. E. Butler: *The British General Election of 1951,* London, The Macmillan Co., Ltd., 1951; H. F. Gosnell: *Why Europe Votes,* Chicago, University of Chicago Press, 1930; and V. O. Key, *Southern Politics.*

activists into the administrative structure. In such one-party unions, apathy on the part of the membership is functional to the stability of the incumbent machine. The less the members know or desire to know about policy, the more secure the leaders are. The single-party organization in a trade union consequently acts to dampen participation, while in the ITU, membership interest and activity are the lifeblood of the party.[5]

This brief comparison of some of the ways in which one-party and two-party systems, once institutionalized, operate to perpetuate the existing system demonstrates again the link between the historical and the sociological levels of analysis. The historical analysis explains how the system, in this case two-party democracy, came into existence, while the sociological analysis accounts for the ways in which structural factors, either those existing in the situation or those created by specific historical developments, operate to maintain it. The latter factors, those which are created by a unique series of events, may over the years turn out to be even more important in explaining why the system continues. An example drawn from economic history may help to illustrate the general significance of this methodological point.

Max Weber, in his classic studies of the relations between economic behavior and cultural values, attempted to demonstrate that the emergence of a unique cultural ethos in certain Protestant sects provided the effective set of economic values which made possible the development of a rational capitalist economic system.[6] Ascetic Protestantism,

---

5. There is one important exception to the generalization that leaders of one-party unions or dictatorships will not attempt to stimulate membership participation. In totalitarian states and in Communist-controlled labor unions, extreme efforts are made to secure the participation of citizens or members. The totalitarian leader is concerned with having his followers attend meetings, read political or union literature, listen to broadcasts, and engage in other similar activities, since this means that he can reach them with his point of view and attempt to indoctrinate them. If the members or citizens are not "politically" active, they are also removed from the influence of the controlling power. As a general hypothesis, one might suggest that the greater the changes in the structure of the society that a governing group is attempting to introduce, or the greater the changes in the traditional functions of unions that a union leadership is attempting to effect, the more likely a leadership is to desire and even require a high level of participation by citizens or members. The radical changes that accompany social revolution, or on a smaller scale, the transformation of a trade union into a political weapon, put severe strains on group loyalties and create the potential for strong membership hostility toward the leadership. A high level of controlled and manipulated rank-and-file participation is perhaps the only effective way, given the leadership's purposes, of draining off or redirecting the discontent which violent changes in traditional patterns and relationships engender.

6. See Max Weber: *The Protestant Ethic and the Spirit of Capitalism*, New York, Charles Scribner's Sons, 1930; *The Religion of China*, Glencoe, Ill., Free Press, 1950; and *Ancient Judaism*, Glencoe, Ill., Free Press, 1952; also see Talcott

especially Calvinism, so defined the situation for its followers as to require their concentration on the maximization of economic wealth so
as to assure themselves that they were predestined to go to heaven. The
specific Protestant *religious* ethos has disappeared, however, in many
countries in which the economic "spirit of capitalism" still exists. The
religious system is no longer necessary in the United States, for example,
to support the economic ethos of a going industrial society. Any attempt
today to explain the continued existence of a secular "Protestant ethic,"
must locate the relationship between that ethic and the functional requirements of a going capitalist economic system. Such an analysis
might point to the fact that in a capitalist social system the dominant
roles through which social status is secured are best achieved or maintained by men acting in accordance with the "spirit of capitalism."
Here we have an interdependent system in which status achievement
requires adhering to certain values, and adhering to these values facilitates status achievement. Such a functional analysis, however, will not
explain why this system is best developed in countries with an ascetic
Protestant background rather than in Catholic or non-Christian countries. To deal with this problem, it would be necessary to go back to
an analysis of the conditions under which the new system first came
into existence.

§ Conclusions

THE CONCLUSIONS DERIVED from theoretical analyses of the possibilities for democracy inherent in the structure of large-scale voluntary
organizations, from empirical descriptive analysis of what actually goes
on in most trade unions and other voluntary organizations, and from
specifying the conditions which are related to democracy in the most
democratic large voluntary association, the International Typographical
Union, suggest that the functional requirements for democracy cannot
be met most of the time in most unions or other voluntary groups.

To recapitulate the major points in this analysis:

1. The structure of large-scale organization inherently requires the
development of bureaucratic patterns of behavior. The conditions making for the institutionalization of bureaucracy and those making for
democratic turnover in office are largely incompatible. While bureauc-

---

Parsons: *The Structure of Social Action*, Glencoe, Ill., Free Press, 1949, for a discussion of Weber's method. Weber's conclusions have been challenged by many
economic historians. In citing this example, however, we are not interested in
who is right in this controversy, but rather in the method of analysis.

racy reduces the area which is political—the area subject to discussion and choice among the members—it also gives an incumbent administration great power and advantage over the rank and file or even an organized opposition. This advantage takes such forms as control over financial resources and internal communications, a large, permanently organized political machine, a claim to legitimacy, and a near monopoly over political skills.

2. The normal position of the trade-union member in modern urban society makes it likely that few individuals will ordinarily be actively interested in the affairs of the union. Leisure-time activities are centered around home and neighborhood rather than around one's vocation. The absence of membership participation facilitates the existence of one-party oligarchy.

3. While the power inherent in bureaucratic social organization and lack of membership participation would be enough to account for the absence of democracy in trade unions, various pressures on trade-union leaders act as further forces making them seek means of reducing democracy in their unions. In the trade-union movement, democracy—the possibility that an official can be defeated for re-election—means that the leader must be willing to move from a position of high status, power, and income to a much lower one if he is still to remain within the union. The institutionalization of such movement from high to low status would require the union leader to accept as probable a future sharp decline in his position in society. Given the great emphasis placed by the social structure on achieving and maintaining high status, it is clear that the norms of democracy in trade unions and those of achievement in the larger society are often in sharp conflict. This may help account for the fact that democracy is found mostly in unions in high-status occupations or in small local organizations in which the status differentiation between leaders and followers is very small. Where the status gap is large, the leader is under strain from his position to institutionalize dictatorial mechanisms which will reduce the possibility that he may lose his office.[7]

Our analysis of the factors related to democracy in the ITU has pointed to conditions under which democracy may be institutionalized in large-scale private governments. Basically, however, it does not offer

---

7. Instead of suggesting that power corrupts in all situations, this analysis suggests that such corruption is a consequence of specific social structures, where *conformity to one norm necessarily involves violation of another norm.* Cf. R. K. Merton: *Social Theory and Social Structure,* Glencoe, Ill., Free Press, 1949, Chap. 4, "Social Structure and Anomie."

many positive action suggestions for those who would seek consciously to manipulate the structure of such organizations so as to make the institutionalization of democratic procedures within them more probable. We have shown that there is much more variation in the internal organization of associations than the notion of an iron law of oligarchy would imply, but nevertheless, the implications of our analysis for democratic organizational politics are almost as pessimistic as those postulated by Robert Michels.

It may be, however, that like Michels, we are too hard on trade unions and voluntary associations. Perhaps viewing such organizations in other perspectives may justify more optimistic conclusions. Before closing therefore, we should like to examine some of the alternative conceptions of the democratic potential inherent in trade-unions.

One school of thought, the Marxist, has for obvious reasons been much concerned with the problem of oligarchy in labor organizations. Those Marxists who have written on the problem have tended to agree with Michels that trade unions are oligarchic, but have suggested that some of the factors making for oligarchy are inherent in the capitalist system of social relations, and that under a new social structure of socialism or communism, some of the factors making for oligarchy will be reduced, while those making for democracy will increase. Perhaps the most sophisticated presentation of this approach can be found in a book by Nikolai Bukharin, one of the major pre-Stalinist theoreticians of Communism. Bukharin recognized the problem and even acknowledged that after the working class comes to power, "There will inevitably result a *tendency* to 'degeneration,' i.e., the excretion of a leading stratum."[8]

The answer to the problem posed by a "stratum of leaders" who would seek to control the institutions of a socialist society is, according to Bukharin, that "what constitutes an eternal category in Michels' presentation, namely, the 'incompetence of the masses' will disappear, for this incompetence is by no means an attribute of every social system; it likewise is a product of the economic and technical conditions, expressing themselves in the general cultural being and in the educational conditions. We may state that in the society of the future there will be a colossal overproduction of organizers, which will nullify the *stability* of the ruling groups."[9] Thus, interestingly, Bukharin posits that one of the conditions which will develop under Socialism is similar to one which we have suggested already exists in the ITU, namely, a

8. Nikolai Bukharin, *Historical Materialism*, pp. 310-11.
9. *Loc. cit.* (Bukharin's emphasis).

large group of men who are educated and skilled in the ways of politics, a group which is too large to be encompassed in the governing apparatus and which constitutes the base for an organized opposition to the dominant faction. On a theoretical level, however, Bukharin could not recognize that control over a "leading stratum" required an organized opposition group, a second party, since Marxian dogma prescribed that parties could only reflect class antagonism and within the working class there could be no such antagonism.[10]

We would be foolhardy to reject the possibility that major changes in the social structure will increase the potential for democracy within the labor movement. In fact, a number of the changes which are an outgrowth of the efforts for a more socialist or equalitarian society do point in the direction of reducing the factors making for oligarchy within the labor movement. Perhaps the most important of these are the efforts in Great Britain and the Scandinavian countries to reduce the income and presumably consequent status differentiation attached to various levels of skill. In addition, as trade unions assume the power to affect major national political questions such as foreign policy, national wage policy, local planning, and many others, the battles traditionally fought at the ballot box in democratic countries are increasingly becoming questions of controversy within British trade unions. Aneurin Bevan, for example, has recently threatened to work directly within the trade unions to challenge their leadership on issues which are far removed from collective-bargaining policies. Consequently the crucial way in which the emergence of Socialism improves the conditions for democracy within labor unions is by legitimating internal controversies within labor organizations that are conducted on ideological lines and involve more than the bread-and-butter questions of "business unionism." By stating that a union should be concerned with matters beyond collective bargaining, socialist union leaders are unwittingly encouraging the possibility of political factionalism within their organization.

Conversely, it should be noted that business unionism, as a set of ideas justifying the narrowest definitions of a union's role in society, also helps to legitimate one-party oligarchy, for it implies that union leadership is simply the administration of an organization with defined,

---

10. Friends of Bukharin have reported that following his defeat by Stalin, he did recognize the need for a second party in the Soviet Union. It is interesting to note that even in 1923 when he first wrote this book, Bukharin, although a leading member of the ruling group in Russia, could write that the question of whether there would be a socialist democracy or the dictatorship of the leading stratum was not a settled question. "The outcome will depend on which tendencies turn out to be the strongest."—*Ibid.*, p. 311.

undebatable goals: the maximization of the member's income and general welfare. The more narrowly an organization defines its functions as fulfilling limited and specific needs, the narrower the range there is for controversy.[11] No one has attempted either a qualitative or quantitative analysis of the relationship between diffuse political or specific business-union ideologies and the presence or absence of political conflict within trade unions. The general proposition may be suggested, however, that the more diffuse the ideology of a trade union, the greater the likelihood of internal factionalism. Consequently, the more directly unions are involved in politics and the more important their political decisions are to power in the total society, the more likely that national political ideologies and movements will affect the internal politics of labor. This pattern might have developed in a more clear-cut fashion than it has if a part of the left wing of the labor movement had not been captured by a totalitarian political movement, the Communist Party. Before the emergence of the Communist Party, many European labor unions and socialist parties were divided between left and right wings, which battled for influence and power according to the rules of democracy, much as do supporters of Aneurin Bevan and Hugh Gaitskell in the present-day British Labour Party. The Communists, by refusing to play the

---

11. It should also be noted that limiting the functions of an organization helps to reduce the likelihood that a member will feel the need to participate in and influence the policies of the organization. People may belong to many organizations, such as the American Automobile Association, a local consumer's cooperative, a medical plan, a bowling congress, a national stamp club, and many others, without feeling any obligation to participate actively in the internal operations of the group and without feeling coerced by the fact that decisions are made without their having been consulted. In large measure, each of the various voluntary associations to which people may belong is judged on the basis of the ability to satisfy a limited need of its individual members. On the other hand, the more diffuse the functions of a group or organization, the more likely an individual is to find sources of disagreement with and desire to participate actively in its operation.

Applying the above analysis to trade unions, the union which simply operates as a business union may be placed in the category of specific, one-function organizations. Outside of the shop organization where there is normally the largest participation by workers, the single major task of the business union, collective bargaining, does not take place oftener than once a year, and in many unions only once every two or three years. The day-to-day administration of union affairs need not concern the average member any more than do the day-to-day activities that go into running a veterans' group or a medical plan. It is of course true that a union deals with the individual in his occupational role, and we might expect it to call forth more of his interest and concern than other voluntary organizations to which the individual relates through his less important roles. Nevertheless, the generalization should hold within the labor movement; the more specific the functions of the union, the less involvement of members; and the more diffuse its relations to the members, the more involvement. The latter situation may be a by-product either of an occupational community, as in the case of the ITU, or of a political ideology which widens the definition of the role of the union as occurs in many European countries.

democratic game, help to break down or prevent the institutionalization of internal democratic procedures within the more political European labor movement. It is, however, possible that a democratic socialist society, somehow blessed with the absence of the Communists, will have more democratic trade unions than now exist.

A second school of thought, found most generally among supporters of existing trends in the labor movement, challenges the definition of democracy used by Michels and would presumably reject the one used in this book. These observers argue that trade unions are democratic in the sense that they represent the interests of their members in a struggle with the employers, regardless of whether internal opposition can exist within them. As V. L. Allen has put it:

It has been argued by some that a voluntary society must provide for membership participation and install the checks and brakes on authority in the manner undertaken by the State in order to achieve and maintain democracy. This contention is misleading, for a voluntary society is not a State within a State; nor does it operate on the same scale or undertake the same functions. Its end and its means are different from those of the State. The government operates the supreme coercive power within a State and the necessity of preventing the use of that power contrary to the interests of the community is of immense over-riding importance in a political democracy. . . . None of this holds for voluntary societies, which by definition, cannot impose punitive measures on their members and which have no means of enforcing their regulations other than by persuasion and sound common sense. There is not in a voluntary society "the organized force which is the distinctive mark of the state (and which) so alters the nature of the political problems as to make any analogy between democracy in politics and in non-political societies only misleading."

It is the voluntary nature of organizations within a State which is essential for the preservation of democracy within those organizations. . . .

It is contended here, however, that trade union organization is not based on theoretical concepts prior to it, that is on some concept of democracy, but on the end it serves. In other words, the end of trade-union activity is to protect and improve the general living standards of its members and not to provide workers with an exercise in self-government.[12]

It is the general assumption of exponents of this school that trade unions, even when oligarchic and dictatorial, are representative of their members' interests in the general socio-economic struggle in the same sense that political parties, although not directly controlled by the social groups which give them electoral support, nevertheless represent these social groups in the government. Presumably unions or political parties which ceased to represent their constituents or members would lose

12. V. L. Allen: *Power in Trade Unions*, London, Longmans, Green and Company, Ltd., 1954, pp. 10-11, 15. The quotation is from A. D. Lindsay, *The Essentials of Democracy*, p. 49.

their allegiance. In the most general sense of the term "represent," this assumption is probably valid. One can show that even the most dictatorial trade-union leaders must be somewhat responsive to the economic needs of their members. A union oligarchy which does not defend the economic interests of the rank and file may find its membership disappearing either into another union or into nonmembership in any union, as John L. Lewis did in the twenties and early thirties. Lewis, then a trade-union as well as a political conservative, almost lost the United Mine Workers. Only after adopting the militant tactics for which he is now famous was he able to rebuild the union. A trade union which is not an economic defense organization has no function and will not long remain on the scene.

To recognize this fact does not involve declaring that a trade union is necessarily representative of its members' interests, or must be considered a democratic organization. Control over the organizational machinery enables the officialdom of a union to define the choices available to the organization and its members. Without a sophisticated organized opposition, the members have no way of discovering for themselves what is possible. A union may, for example, present a contract as containing substantial gains by engaging in statistical double talk, as the United Steel Workers did recently. The failure of the printing pressmen to win a priority system cannot be presented as the will of the membership in that completely dictatorial union. The divergencies in the national political action of the Amalgamated Clothing Workers and the International Ladies Garment Workers are clearly a product of the political ambitions and viewpoints of Sidney Hillman and David Dubinsky, not of the membership of the two unions. Communist-led unions have on occasion engaged in prolonged strikes which were unjustifiable by any collective-bargaining criteria, while other conservative unions have attempted to avoid strikes under almost all conditions. Some union leaders have engaged in programs to rationalize their industry, even though this meant a great decline in the total number of man-hours of work available to their members, while others have fought efforts to institute labor-saving devices. The West Coast longshoremen have instituted a rigid sharing of the work according to a numerical list, while the East Coast longshoremen have retained the shape-up system of hiring, which permits hiring bosses to discriminate among the men.[13] In the face of these differences, it would be hard to assert that unions represent their members' interests when the members have little control over policy formation.

---

13. This system was legally abolished in 1954 by the states of New Jersey and New York, after the union refused to abolish it.

The lack of internal democracy also tends to reinforce a factor which makes for both oligarchy and unrepresentativeness: the widening of the salary and status gap between the members and leaders. Without the presence of opposition groups, most American union leaders have raised their salaries far above those of the members. The history of the United Automobile Workers is a good example of this phenomenon. While major factional groups existed in the union, national officers, including the president, received less than $10,000 a year. Once Reuther consolidated his power, the salaries of officers gradually increased. Perhaps even more important than salaries, however, is the union officers' opportunity to receive perquisites in the form of expense accounts, union-purchased automobiles, vacation expenses, and the like, which do not appear in the records. In recent years, union welfare funds have provided a new source of extra income for some union leaders, their families or friends, through new pay rolls and insurance commissions. In the ITU or any union with an organized opposition, such financial manipulations would be impossible, since the opposition would make them an election issue.

As union leaders secure higher financial rewards from their jobs, their sense of identification with the men and the urgency of their problems must inevitably suffer. Hence lack of opposition makes for unrepresentative action both in the form of union policies which the membership probably would not approve if they had the power to affect them, and also by diminishing the leaders' sense of importance of members' economic problems.

The principal premise, in the argument that oligarchic unions may be regarded as democratic, rests, as Allen makes clear, on the assumption that trade unions are voluntary associations which members may leave much as they may quit a stamp club when they object to what it is doing. This assumption clearly does not apply to most American trade unions, although it may be applicable to many British and European labor organizations. Under the closed shop, and more recently the union shop, men cannot legally quit their union without losing their jobs. Where the union has power, even the legal right to resign from the union and keep one's job is relatively meaningless, since the union can effectively blacklist a man either by having the cooperation of the employer who seeks to keep on good terms with the union leadership, or through sanctions imposed by men who remain in the union. The development of union welfare funds has proved to be a new restriction on the rights of workers to choose their union. Recently, a minority group in the United Textile Workers, CIO, attempted to secede from that union and join the AFL textile union. A number of locals which were sympathetic with the secession move found that their welfare funds were tied up with the international union and that they would lose them if they left the CIO.[14]

The fact, therefore, that unions must to some extent represent their members' interests in the market must not be allowed to conceal the fact that union leaders possess great power to do things which would never be approved if a democratic choice were available. As Howe and Widdick have pointed out:

> There is one decisive proof of democracy in a union (or any other institution): oppositionists have the right to organize freely into "parties," to set up factional machines, to circulate publicity and to propagandize among the members. . . . The presence of an opposition . . . is the best way of insuring that a union's democratic structure will be preserved. . . . To defend the right of factions to exist is not at all to applaud this or that faction. But this is the overhead (well worth paying) of democracy: groups one considers detrimental to the union's interest will be formed. The alternative is dictatorship.[15]

The emphasis in this book on the undemocratic character of most labor unions is not designed to negate the general proposition of the political pluralists that trade unions, like many other internally oligarchic organizations, serve to sustain political democracy in the larger society.[16] As many political observers have made clear, many internally dictatorial organizations operate to protect the interests of their members by checking the encroachments of other groups. Democracy in large measure rests on the fact that no one group is able to secure such a basis of power and command over the total allegiance of a majority of the population that it can effectively suppress or deny the claims of groups it opposes. The labor movement in particular has played a major role in fostering the institutions of political democracy in the larger society and in fostering the ideology of equalitarianism. Workers today can live and act with much less fear of the consequences of their acts than was generally true even three decades ago. There are few, although unfortunately some, unions which have as much potential power over the lives of their members as employers once held over their workers. In large measure, the chance that the collectivist society which is developing in most countries will be democratic rests on the possibility that trade unions, although supporters of socialist objectives, will maintain their independence of the state, and will act to protect

---

14. It should be noted that Allen makes an exception in his argument about union democracy for unions which have compulsory membership.

15. Howe and Widdick, *The UAW and Walter Reuther*, pp. 262-63.

16. Cf. Franz L. Neumann: "Approaches to the Study of Political Power," *Political Science Quarterly*, 65:161-80 (June 1950).

their members and the citizenry in general against the tremendous state power inherent in a collectivist society. The behavior of the trade unions of the British Commonwealth and Scandinavian countries furnishes real evidence that trade unions, regardless of their internal structure, will continue to play the role of defenders of democracy and equalitarianism under collectivism.

Nevertheless, the extension of democracy in an industrial society requires the extension of control by men over those institutions they depend on. To the sympathetic student of the labor movement, the ITU stands as a model of the trade union in a democratic society. In the ITU he sees the image of the democratic processes he prizes in the national body politic, in the organization through which printers exercise some control over the conditions of their livelihood. Although the events and conditions which have given rise to and sustained democracy in the ITU are unique and are rarely found in trade unions or other voluntary large social organizations generally, it would be foolhardy to predict that democratic processes cannot develop elsewhere. The specific factors which underlie ITU democracy are not likely to be duplicated elsewhere; but the very great variety of factors present in the situation suggests that democratic processes may develop under quite different conditions and take quite different forms.

If it is not to serve as a model, the ITU may well serve as a touchstone against which the internal political processes of other unions and of other voluntary groups, such as the American Legion or the American Medical Association, may be appraised and criticized. As Robert K. Merton has said in another connection:

In the world laboratory of the sociologist, as in the more secluded laboratories of the physicist and chemist, it is the successful experiment which is decisive and not the thousand-and-one failures which preceded it. More is learned from the single success than from multiple failures. A single success proves it can be done. Thereafter, it is necessary only to learn what made it work. This, at least, is what I take to be the sociological sense of those revealing words of Thomas Love Peacock: "Whatever is, is possible."[17]

The ITU and its democratic political system *is*; to know what makes and has made it what it is may help make possible the development of organizational democracy elsewhere. Democracy, whether in national society or in private organizations, is not achieved by acts of will alone; but men's wills, through action, can shape institutions and events in directions that reduce or increase the chances for the development and survival of democracy. For men of good will, there is much to learn in the history, institutions, and arguments of American printers.

---

17. Robert K. Merton: *Social Theory and Social Research*, Glencoe, Ill., Free Press, 1949, pp. 194-95.

§ A Concluding Theoretical Note

THE CENTRAL PROBLEM of this book has been to account for the unique two-party system through which the ITU is governed. But the nature of the problem, and of the data collected in the course of the inquiry, have been such as to lead us to discuss many questions seemingly peripheral to the central problem. It may be useful, therefore, to sketch the main outlines of the analysis.

One way to do this is to recall the questions raised in the very first chapter, together with some of the ideas regarding democracy in private organizations that led us to raise those questions in the context of a study of the ITU. The major theorist of politics in private organizations is Robert Michels; our debt to him has been apparent throughout this book. Michels' conclusion that large organization is incompatible with democracy is predicated on the belief that the nature and requirements of large-scale organization are such as to give to the men who control the organizational machinery at any given time a near monopoly over all the resources through which power is gained and exercised in private organizations: monopolies, for example, over the effective channels of communications to the membership, over the skills of leadership and the opportunities to gain those skills, over the time, money, and personnel needed to maintain a political organization. With such heavy advantages in the hands of the officials, the chances for the development of an effective organized internal opposition in most private organizations is very small.

This study has not "disproved" Michels' theory; rather, in a sense, it has given additional empirical support to his analysis of the connection between oligarchy as a political form and the overwhelming power held by the incumbent officers of most private organizations, by demonstrating that where an effective and organized opposition does exist, it does so only because the incumbent administration does not hold a monopoly over the resources of politics.

The bulk of this book, therefore, has been aimed at showing how and in what ways the nature of printing as occupation and industry tends to make more widely available than is true for most private organizations the resources of democratic politics. Where Michels studied those factors making oligarchy in large scale organizations "inevitable," this study of the most striking American exception to Michels' "iron law of oligarchy" has been aimed at identifying the factors which make for and sustain democracy in private organizations. In the course of the analysis, a number of additional variables have emerged which might enable observers to predict more accurately when and where significant deviations from oligarchic patterns might be expected to occur.

But in addition to the identification of new relevant variables, the juxtaposition of the ITU with the mass of more oligarchic trade unions allows us to suggest a number of propositions bearing on factors affecting the chances for democracy in trade unions. These propositions, while in part a product of the analysis, cannot be taken as an adequate summary of it; the social system of the ITU is a network of functionally interdependent elements, and any effort to state the relations among any two or three of these elements involves the distortions which inhere in the narrowness of the focus and the implied qualification "other things being equal." Nevertheless, stating some of the findings in the form of propositions puts the findings in a form more amenable to empirical test in other studies.

I. *Factors relating to the history and structure of the industry and union, and its relations with its environment.*

1. The greater the autonomy of its member locals, the greater the chances for democracy in a trade union.

2. Unions which come into existence through the federation of existing independent locals, as compared with unions which are organized "from the top down" by a central committee or single local, (a) are more likely to preserve the autonomy of their member locals, and (b) have internal opposition groups (the leaders of the previously independent locals) built into them. Both of these factors increase the chances for democracy in a union.

3. The less bureaucratized is a union administration, the greater the chances for democracy.

3A. The more decentralized and unconcentrated in ownership is the industry a union deals with, the less it is obliged to create a large centralized and bureaucratized administration of its own.

4. The more secure is a union in its relations with management— i.e., the less it is obliged to behave like a military organization—the greater the chances are for internal democracy. This does not rule out the possibility that democratic unions may be more militant on the average than oligarchic unions, but if they are, it is more the result of internal political pressures than of sustained external challenge from management.

5. The more homogeneous the interests of the members of a union, the greater the chances for democracy.

II. *Factors relating to the status of the occupation and to the distribution of status within the occupation.*

6. The less internally stratified an occupation, the greater the chances for democracy in its union.

7. The smaller the difference between the status of the occupation and the status of "union leader," the greater the chances for democracy.

8. The more attractive the job *in* the occupation awaiting a union leader who leaves office as compared with alternative jobs he can get outside the occupation, the more likely he is to remain within the union, strengthening the opposition and increasing the chances for democracy.

9. The less that the status of leaders in a union is dependent on their holding union office—the more status attaches to the man rather than to the union office, and the more he is able to attain status in other ways than through holding union office—the more likely leaders and activists are to support organized political opposition groups in a union.

9A. The more able a man is to retain the status of union leader on leaving union office, the more likely he is to continue to play a political role in the union, thus strengthening the opposition and increasing the chances for democracy in the union.

10. The higher the status of an occupation, the more likely its members will claim the right to participate in its union's decision-making processes; the more members who hold this value strongly, the greater the chances for democracy.

III. *Factors affecting membership interest and participation in union affairs.*

11. The greater the members' interest in their union, and the greater their voluntary participation in union affairs, the greater the chances for democracy in the union.

11A. The more that workers in the same union associate with each other off the job, informally and in various leisure time clubs and organizations, the greater is likely to be their interest and participation in the affairs of their union.

11A(1) The more that workers are cut off from association with people outside their occupation—by a "deviant work schedule," status marginality, or physical isolation—the more likely they are to associate with each other in their leisure time.

11B. The greater the chances for men to socialize with one another informally on and around the job, the more likely they are to be interested and participate in the affairs of their union.

11B(1) The more irregular are the work-loads during a normal shift, the greater the chances for workers to socialize during working hours.

11C. The more inclusive the relationships among men in the same occupation—the larger the number of roles involved in their relationships—the more likely they are to be interested and participate in the affairs of their union.

11D. The greater the number and variety of functions which a union performs for its members, the more the membership is likely to be interested and involved in union affairs.

11E. The greater the identification of workers with their occupation, the more likely they are to be interested and participate in the affairs of their union.

11F. The more interested men are in their work, the more likely they are to be interested and involved in the affairs of their union.

IV. *Factors directly affecting the distribution of political resources in the union.*

12. The more opportunities the members of a union have to learn political skills, the greater the chances for democracy in their union.

13. The greater the number of independent channels of communication to the membership available to opposition groups, the greater the chances for democracy.

14. The more leisure time and money the rank and file members have available for engaging in political activity in a union, the greater the chances for democracy in the union.

V. *Factors relating to law, legitimacy, and value systems in unions.*

15. The legitimacy of a democratic party system in a union—the sentiment that institutionalized opposition is right and proper and that political conflict ought to be carried on in accordance with certain rules of the game—develops in situations where the distribution of power in the union makes it impossible for the incumbent leadership to destroy the opposition without destroying or seriously weakening the union. However, once the norms of legitimacy have developed around a political system, they function independently to maintain the system they justify.

16. The more secure is the process of getting and holding a job against political manipulation by the incumbent officers, the greater the chances for democracy in the union.

17. The greater the protection for the rights of political opposition included in a union's code of law, the greater the chances for democracy.

VI. *Factors related to the bases of internal cleavage in a union.*

18. Political cleavages which are a result of differences in ideology are more likely to sustain permanent democratic opposition than are conflicts which reflect differences in interests.

19. The more homogeneous a union is in the income, status, and skills of its members, the more likely is political cleavage to reflect value rather than interest differences.

20. The greater the instrumental functions performed by a union, and the less its internal mediating functions, the more likely that political cleavage will reflect value differences rather than economic interest cleavages.

21. The more ambivalent the status of an occupation, the more likely are workers to differ with respect to basic social and political values. Consequently, the more "middle-class" the status of a craft organized by a labor union, the more likely that its members will divide politically on ideological grounds.

22. The greater the variation in ideologically relevant background characteristics of the members of a union, which cannot be made the basis of an interest group appeal, the greater the chances for ideological cleavage.

Students of the labor movement will be able to point to major exceptions to each proposition suggested above. Clearly, it is impossible in the case of given organizations or individuals to abstract any one variable and make it the sole or even primary determinant of a given behavior pattern. The problem of how to deal with multi-factored determinants of specific behavior patterns is a basic one in the social sciences. When dealing with individuals, analysts may partially escape this difficulty by collecting data on a large number of cases, so that they can isolate the influence of specific factors through use of quantitative techniques. The analysis of organizations is hampered, however, by the fact that comparable data are rarely collected for more than a few cases. The cost of studying intensively even one large organization like the ITU is as much as that of gathering survey data from a large sample of individuals.

It is of crucial importance, however, that students of organizational behavior address themselves to the problem of verification of hypotheses. At the present time, one may spend a great deal of time examining the large number of studies of individual trade unions or other large-scale organizations without being able to validate a single proposition about organizational behavior. The data collected in such case studies do not lend themselves to re-analysis to test hypotheses, since the researchers rarely focused their observations in terms of any set of explicit hypotheses.

A possible solution to the methodological difficulty is the analysis of *deviant cases*—in the labor movement, specifically those organizations which are characterized by a high level of democratic procedures, membership participation, or both. If one knows that a given behavior pattern, such as oligarchy, is common to almost all large unions, then the repeated study of oligarchic groups will yield few new insights in the possible variations which may affect internal political structures.[18] But the existence of a deviant case always implies that the theoretical structure—in this case, the theory subsumed in Michels' "iron law of oligarchy"—is oversimplified and suggests "the need for incorporating further variables into . . . [the] predictive scheme."[19] This book is an example of the deviant case method, the intensive study of a case which deviates from the general pattern. From a scientific point of view, the major contribution of this study is the location of new insights and propositions about the internal politics of voluntary organizations. The ultimate value of this study must rest on the extent to which it proves useful to others engaged in similar case studies by way of indicating directions and hypotheses for research. Whether all or any of the propositions advanced in this book are valid or not will only be known after a large number of comparative studies of the internal government of voluntary organizations.

18. See Joseph Goldstein, *The Government of British Trade Unions* (London: Allen and Unwin, 1952), for an excellent description of oligarchic control in a British union. This study, however, adds little except more facts to Michels' classic analysis.

19. See Patricia Kendall and Katherine M. Wolf, "The Analysis of Deviant Cases in Communications Research," in Paul F. Lazarsfeld and Frank Stanton, eds., *Communications Research 1948-1949*, pp. 153-54.

Methodological Note

THE METHODOLOGICAL ASPECTS of this study are challenging ones. Some are problems which will recur with increasing frequency in social research, and in view of this are worth discussing in some detail. Some are relatively common problems, such as scale construction and statistical tests, and these too have been deleted from the body of the study, to be included here. This note will consist of three quite different sections, each of which broadly comes under the heading of *methodology*, but contains distinctly different problems. These will be:

A. *General Problems:*—Some problems associated with developing political or organizational theory from research upon ongoing organizations or social systems.

B. *Statistical Problems:*—The use of statistical tests of significance, an explanation of why none appear in this study, and a discussion of why they are generally irrelevant for studies like this one.

C. *Specific Problems:*—Sample design, construction of indices, and similar problems to which reference is made in the body of the study.

Section A is probably of most general interest, and C of least general interest; we shall treat them in this order.

§ A. General Problems

WHEN AN EMPIRICAL ANALYSIS of a single case (in this instance, the typographical union's political system) is to be carried out, it can be of either of two general types, as follows:

(*a*) Description and explanation of the single case, to provide information concerning its present state, and the dynamics through which it continues as it does. This may be called a *particularizing* analysis.

(*b*) The development of empirical generalizations or theory through the analysis of the single case, using it not to discover anything about *it* as a system but as an empirical basis either for generalization or theory construction. This may be called a *generalizing* analysis.

The crucial element which distinguishes these two types of analysis is the way they treat general laws and particular statements about the single case. The first kind of analysis *uses* general laws or reularities in order to carry out the analysis of the particular case, much as a metallurgist utilizes his knowledge of general chemical properties in analyzing a sample of ore. That is, it uses previously-known generalizations in order to help make particular statements. The second kind of analysis is just the reverse of this: much as a biologist focuses his microscope on a living and growing fruit fly in order to make generalizations about processes of growth, the social scientist in this kind of analysis attempts to utilize the particular case in developing general statements. The particular statement and the general law trade places in these two types of analysis. In the former, the law is used to aid in making particular statements; in the second, the particular statements are used to develop the law.

Both these kinds of analysis have long and honorable traditions in the social sciences, as they have in the natural sciences;[1] perhaps the best-known case of the first in social research is Max Weber's *Protestant Ethic;* a good example of the second is Michel's *Political Parties.*[2] In the former, Weber used general, well-accepted relations between values and behavior in order to partially explain the genesis of capitalism. In the latter, Michels examined many aspects of the German Social Democratic Party over a period of time, not to make statements about that party, but to make statements about political parties in general.

The present analysis is not clearly in either of these categories; it always attempts to be in the second, though it sometimes goes no further than the first. Many statements refer to the ITU rather than to organizations in general, but at the same time there is usually implicit extension to organizations other than the ITU.

Since it is the second kind of analysis which is attempted here (though not always with success) several problems specific to this kind of analysis arise in the study.

---

1. Some men have suggested that all of social science must be a particularizing or "idiographic" science, as contrasted to the generalizing or "nomothetic" natural sciences. The most influential of these was Wilhelm Rickert; many social philosophers since his time have spent much effort in refuting him. See, for example, Ernst Cassirer: *An Essay on Man,* New York, Doubleday & Company, Inc., 1953, p. 235; and his *Substance and Function,* New York, Dover Publications, 1953, pp. 226 ff.

2. Perhaps better examples of the second type can be given if the analyses under consideration are not restricted to a single case analysis, as we have restricted them. Durkheim in *Suicide* (Glencoe, Ill., Free Press, 1951) used particular cases of suicide (or more accurately, rates of suicide) occurring in many social situations, and abstracted from those situations the properties which they held in common and which appeared to be relevant to suicide. This allowed him to make general statements about social organization and suicide, or more generally, certain kinds of deviant behavior.

MULTIPLE-LEVEL ANALYSIS: THE PROBLEM
OF UNITS AND PROPERTIES

In an analysis of the second kind, a generalizing one, several requirements arise which a particularizing analysis need not meet. An important one is the necessity of delineating *units* of analysis and characterizing the units according to certain general *concepts* or *properties*.

If, as is possible in a particularizing analysis, nothing more than a vivid picture is to be given of the system being analyzed, this problem need not arise. A faithful recording of events as they occur can fulfill the task of the particularizing analysis, much as a documentary film does, without once using general sociological concepts. But in order to make generalizations which may be applied to other organizations, general sociological concepts must be used. In the present analysis, this means characterizing several different "sizes" or "levels" of units. The man, his immediate social environment (e.g., his shop), the local, and the ITU as a whole are a minimum set of units which it is necessary to characterize. In this study the union as a whole was characterized in terms of certain structural and environmental properties: for example, the degree of stratification in the occupation, the political structure of the union, the issues which have existed at various times, the union's policies, the kind of employer attitudes toward the union.

It was necessary to characterize the New York local as well by these same kinds of variables. For example, the difference in types of policy problems at the local and international levels was documented, and this was related to an important difference in voting behavior of some men on the two levels (i.e., the predominance of wage-scale problems in local politics leads to interest voting which often unseats the incumbent).

Besides these properties of the New York union which are observable in the perspective of the union as a whole, the random sample allowed characterization of the New York union in terms of some parameters of the distribution of the men's attributes. The average age of printers, the number of men who have other printers as their best friends, and the proportion of men who work nights are examples of this. Such attributes characterize the union as a whole, even though they are based on data gathered from individual men. The interview data were used for characterizing an intermediate social unit as well, the man's direct social environment. His shop and his chapel chairman were both characterized by means of the sample data (and by the actual records of the shop's vote). Finally, the greatest amount of data characterized the man himself: his attitudes, his background, his behavior, etc.

The kinds of observations made and the properties by which the various units were characterized are indicated in Table 39, which summarizes the above discussion. In the cells of the table are listed the kinds of properties by which these units were characterized. This table suggests the complexity of the analysis, for properties in each cell must be related to those in other cells in propositions or generalizations.

Table 39—Types of Data Gathered, Types of Units Being Characterized, and Types of Resulting Properties

UNIT BEING CHARACTERIZED	KINDS OF DATA				
	TOTAL SYSTEM	INTERMEDIATE UNITS		INDIVIDUALS	
	Issues; Data on Occupation; Union Laws; Policies; Historical Data; Convention Reports	*Local's Histories and Voting Records; Issues on Local Level; Size of Locals*	*Shops' Voting Records; Shop Size*	*Interviews with Leaders*	*Interviews of the Sample of Men*
ITU as a whole	Structural, environmental, behavioral properties	By inference: communication network (structural)		Structural environmental, behavioral properties	
Locals	Behavioral properties (militancy, etc.)	Behavioral properties, size	By inference: communication network (structural)		Distributions of individual properties
Shops			Behavioral properties, and size		Distributions of individual properties
Other immediate social environment of men	The social climate, by inference from dominant issues and election outcome	The social climate, by inference from dominant issues and election outcome		Chapel chairman's attributes; friends' attributes	
Men	By inference: dominant values and interests	By inference: values, interests, and loyalties (e.g., to local over international)	By inference: values, interests, and loyalties (e.g., to shop over local)	By inference: values	Behavior, background, values, attitudes

This complexity raises a number of problems in the design of a study. Some of the most important of these, in the present study, were those related to the interview data. These data were perhaps the most important in the study. It was a primary means of characterizing at least three of the units in the analysis: (1) The population of the New York local union as a whole, in order to make statements like: "X per cent of the members have good friends among other printers off the job."[3] (2) The immediate social environment of the individual, including his shop, the clubs to which he belongs, his close circle of friends, etc. Such characterizations are used in this study primarily for locating the effect of differing social environments on the individual. (3) The man, in order to determine relations between various properties of the man: his values and his vote, his background and his values, etc.

This study is weakest in its characterization of the immediate social environment. We could have attempted explicitly to characterize shops by interviewing all or almost all the men in them, and by asking questions more specifically directed toward finding the man's relation to his shopmates and to the employer. But such concentration would have been made at the expense of other gains: interviewing more men in each shop would have meant interviewing each man less thoroughly or else covering fewer shops, thus gaining knowledge about shops at the expense of knowledge about either individuals or the union as a whole.

What this really means is that not all values can be maximized at once, and that such studies as the present one must include in their design a decision as to what units it is most important to characterize with the interview data. As suggested above, the experience of the study suggests that in a single case analysis like this, it is more important to characterize the man and his immediate social environment than to characterize the union itself, that is, the single case being analyzed.

However, this is not the end of the sampling or design problems related to the interview data. Given some decision on the problem above, it is still necessary to decide whether some manner of random sampling is best (taking into account social environments, as indicated above, by two-stage sampling), or systematic sampling determined by the social or political structure of the union. We want to locate the elements which effect these men's political decisions. But do we consider all men's decisions equally important? Are not the decisions of some active men more important in influencing the outcome of union elections than are those of the followers? And is this criterion of "importance to the outcome" the optimum criterion for our purpose? These are questions which this study only begins to answer. At the same time, they are questions whose answers are important in the design of research. One possible answer has been suggested in the analysis: to develop a pro-

---

3. Such statements are ordinarily used in comparison of the union with another, or with itself at another time. If a comparative analysis (which will be discussed later) were being carried out, this would be a more important kind of statement than it is in this single-case analysis.

visional model of the political system, conceived as a structure of interlocking decisions (e.g., union officers, party leaders, convention delegates, voters), and to accurately measure the influences on each of these decisions. This would entail a rather complex research design, one which equalizes the accuracy with which each decision point in the system is analyzed.

MULTIPLE-LEVEL ANALYSIS:
RELATIONS BETWEEN DIFFERENT UNITS

The second major problem concerning units at different levels is the problem of relating them by means of generalizations. This problem is an important one, for it is such generalizations which are the fruits of the analysis. The problem in its simplest aspects may be posed in this way: Certain properties of one unit (e.g., the total union) are determinants of behavior at another level (e.g., the individual). Yet how is it possible to really bridge the gap between the units? For example, to say that a certain political climate characterizes the union does not mean that this climate is felt by all printers alike. The climate makes itself felt more strongly by some men than others, depending upon their social and political locations.

When an analysis is not one of this multiple-level sort, then such a problem never exists: analysis relates an individual's political dispositions to his vote, or an organization's size to its bureaucratization. Both properties being related are attributes of the same unit (e.g., the individual, the organization), and there is no problem of bridging the gap between units at different levels.

We said above that relating two different levels is only the simplest case of the general problem. This certainly is so, for even if we succeed in relating properties of diverse social units to a man's vote decision, this is not at all the end of the analysis. The aim of this study is to be able to make statements about political systems as wholes, not statements about the determinants of individual vote decisions.

What we have done in focusing upon this individual vote decision has been to enter the system at a particular point and to work outward from there. The diagram of Figure 49, page 279, illustrates this well, for it shows where our attention is focused, and indicates how this leads to other parts of the system.

But is this the best strategy for analyzing a social or political system? The point at which we entered is probably a very important one in the system, but would it have been better to proceed differently? For example, having a tentative *model* of the political system, as outlined in Chapter 14, the way is pointed to certain *variables* or concepts (which are simply the properties as outlined in Table 39) and certain *processes* which seem important in the operation of the system. Only one of these processes concerns the vote decision; others concern the policy decisions of the administrative leaders, and the decision of the oppositionists or potential oppositionists. Perhaps the best mode of analysis, given that the aim is to analyze the system as a whole, would be to start with a crude model of the sort indicated in Chapter 14 and to focus upon each of the processes postulated in that model. An example of the way that such an analysis would be of aid is the following: The model indicates that óne important decision point in the system is the president's policy decisions. In particular, it suggests that to know the constraints placed by the organization upon the president is important. Thus it directs one to ask such questions as: What restrained Scott (the ITU president) from sending in strikebreakers to New York in 1919? And why was George Berry, the Pressmen president (who did send in strikebreakers for the same strike by the printing pressmen) not restrained in the same way?

If we had focused in this study on the several decision points, and on the communication processes, rather than entering the system at a particular point, the results might have been far superior to those obtained. However, this is a matter as yet unresolved, and we intend only to raise the problem: What is the most advantageous way to carry out a study of the dynamics of a social or political system?

THE PARADOX: HOW TO GENERALIZE
FROM A SINGLE CASE

Another difficult problem arises in studies of organizations or social systems rather than individuals. Often, only a single case is analyzed, as is done here. This is in strong contrast to the usual statistical procedure with studies of individual behavior, where the number of cases is relatively great. The fact that the present study includes a sample of individuals from the union, and that part of the analysis is one of individual behavior, must not be allowed to confuse this issue. Clearly in this study these individuals are not themselves the focus of the analysis; it is the union as an organization which is the center of interest. This focus upon a single case rather than the statistical study of individual behavior implies a quite different kind of analysis. Perhaps some of the differences can be suggested by an analogy.

If a chemist is developing a theory or set of laws concerning the equilibrium system existing inside a test tube containing water, sodium hydroxide, and hydrochloric acid, he may utilize many kinds of data, but all from the single system which he has before him; tests of acidity, of electrical conductivity, examination of precipitate, and general knowledge about the reactivity of sodium, hydrogen, chlorine, and hydroxyl ions. He would not need to examine a thousand replications of this little test-tube system, but would analyze the internal dynamics of the single system, using these various types of data. From these he would build up knowledge about what reactions were taking place. He would conclude, among other things, that these chemicals reacted rather rapidly to form salt and water.

However, if the same chemist were concerned with finding the chemical properties of various metals and their relative positions on a scale of activity, he would need to carry out a comparative analysis, subjecting each of the metals to similar tests and noting the differences in their reactivity.

This analogy indicates that both internal analyses and comparative analyses have a place in research, and that neither is unilaterally superior. In the present study there was a choice between the two types: an intensive analysis of this single case, or an extensive and more superficial examination of many cases. The first was chosen and the latter discarded. Can we say anything about what was gained by this choice and what lost, that is, the differences between the two models of investigation?

The outcome of both such types of analysis is the same kind of generalizations. For example, "The more highly stratified an occupation is, the more intense and rigid will be its political cleavages if its union has democratic politics." A comparative analysis seeks to develop such generalizations in the obvious manner, by comparing occupations which differ with respect either to the independent or the dependent variable and then testing whether they also differ with respect to the other variable. The "internal analysis" attempts to establish the same generalization in one of two fashions:

1. It uses variations which occur *within* the system, either (*a*) over a period of time (e.g., at one time, there was stratification between a politically important group of Mailers and the majority, typographers; at the same time, rigid cleavage between these groups occurred); or (*b*) between different parts of the system (e.g., while there is little stratification within the union as a whole, there is economic stratification between officers and men; these create issues between the membership and the administration, as indicated in Chapter 14). The internal analysis thus substitutes variations within the one system for variations between systems. This is in essence what an experimentalist does when he varies the conditions under which a particular system exists, or when he observes the evolution of an object over a period of time.

2. An internal analysis can operate in a different way. By going behind the over-all generalization to the processes through which it is presumed to exist, the internal analysis may validate the generalization by validating these processes. For example, the generalization above, relating economic stratification to the rigidity and intensity of political cleavage, can be either observed to hold true statistically or built up through more fundamental generalizations, to wit: (*a*) the economic motivation is an overriding one, which will be a very strong determinant of one's decision if economics are involved; (*b*) the policy decisions in a stratified union involved economic matters which will differentially affect persons at different economic levels. By proving that these two statements are true, one can prove, by inference, the original statement about stratifications and rigidity of cleavage. Thus internal analysis, which, in some cases, cannot directly prove a generalization, may prove it by indirection through proof of the generalizations underlying it.

An internal analysis will not ordinarily be as exhaustive of the important elements which affect a particular variable as will a comparative analysis, simply because certain things are invariant for the single system as a whole. Certain kinds of issues may never occur in this union, though they occur in others; certain aspects of the particular system are so invariant that situations common in other systems are simply absent in the ITU. These invariances can lead to overgeneralization; for example, some of Michels' generalizations from the German Social Democratic Party to organizations in general are seriously in error for certain kinds of organizations which diverge too much from the single case Michels examined.

But except for these difficulties, it seems that internal analysis has no great disadvantages with respect to comparative analysis. It may, in fact, have one important advantage: by taking simple comparative correlation out of the reach of the investigator, it focuses his attention upon the underlying processes which operate within the system. In this way the internal analysis may lead to a deeper explanation of the phenomenon and to generalization of a more fundamental kind.

But whether an internal analysis has more advantages or disadvantages with respect to a comparative analysis, it is important to realize that these two kinds of analyses of organizations both exist in social science, and a choice must be made between them in any research. The problem which begs for resolution here is the problem of spelling out the two different logics of analysis for these two methods, and of providing diagnostic indicators which will tell the relative merits of the two methods for a particular research problem.

These problems discussed above are three which seem to be of increasing importance as social research moves from description into analysis, and as it moves from focus upon individuals to a focus upon social units: voluntary organizations, the social system of communities, industrial plants, and so on. We have not attempted to give answers to the problems, but only to state them, in the hope that this will stimulate a search for the answers.

§ B. Statistical Problems

IN THIS BOOK, no statistical tests of significance have been used. This may seem unaccountable, particularly in view of the numerous quantitative comparisons which constitute much of the analysis. Can it be defended, and if so how? It can be defended, and we shall defend it at length because there seems to be no good statement of our position in print.

Statistical tests are used for a number of different purposes. One use is to indicate the precision of a descriptive statement about a population. When a random sample of a population is measured in terms of some attribute, then the sample distribution is used to make a statement about the population distribution. For example, on the basis of the ages of men in a random sample, a statement about the mean age of a population may be made. But because only a sample of the population was measured, such a statement is subject to sampling error. The statement may be made in terms of confidence intervals (e.g., "One can say [with a confidence that 95% of statements like this will be true] that the average age of printers is between 42 and 48 years") or in terms of a mean value with certain limits (e.g., "The average age of printers is 45 years, plus or minus 3 years, at the .05 level").

This, then, is one way in which statistical inference is used in survey analysis. However, such a use is confined almost entirely to descriptive studies, whose primary aim is to describe a population in terms of the attributes by which the sample is measured. If the aim of this study were to accurately describe the New York Typographical Union in terms of the proportion of members with this or that attribute, then this type of statistics would be necessary to indicate the precision of the descriptive statements. But such description is not the aim in a study like this, in which the aim is rather to establish the existence or nonexistence of relationships between attributes. For this a different kind of statistical inference is necessary.

To determine the existence of relationships in survey analysis, the usual procedure is to present contingency tables, such as are found throughout Chapters 4 to 17 of this book.[4] Sometimes such a relationship appears to be strong; in other cases it is quite weak. How does one decide whether there really *is* a relationship in the population? The usual method is through χ^2 tests of independence in contingency tables. The familiar χ^2 values presented in most published psychological work and increasingly in sociological analysis are such tests. If the χ^2 value is low, the null hypothesis (that the two variables are independent) is accepted; if it is above a certain critical value, the null hypothesis is rejected at the .05 or .01 level of confidence.[5] In the latter case, the alternative hypothesis—that a relationship does exist—is accepted.

The χ^2 test for independence is thus the test applicable to the kind of analysis carried out here, an analysis which attempts to determine the existence of relationships. But however applicable the test is in the ideal case, it is not so practically, except in special circumstances. Some factors in an analysis like the present one tend to make the test too weak, for they violate the assumptions on which the test is based. Thus a supposed relationship which is "significantly different from chance" as judged by a χ^2 test, may not be significantly different from chance at all. On the other hand, there are certain factors which tend to make usual χ^2 tests too strong; acceptance of the null hypothesis may occur even though a strong relationship does exist. Finally, there are serious questions about the relevance of such tests for analyses like this, even when they are neither too weak nor too strong. These three classes of factors will be considered in turn.[6]

---

4. If the variables are continuous, the usual method is to present an estimate of the correlation between the two variables. This is technically a different procedure, but the logic of the statement to be made here applies to such cases.

5. That is, only five times (or one time) out of a hundred will such a rejection be made when the hypothesis—that no relationship exists—is true.

6. This is not to say that no empirical analyses in social science need statistical inference. Many do, and among these are the studies which are primarily descriptive. For an excellent review of statistical problems in such studies, see William C. Cochran, Frederick Mosteller, and John W. Tukey: "Statistical Problems of the Kinsey Report," *Journal of the American Statistical Association*, 48:673-716 (1953).

1. FACTORS WHICH TEND TO MAKE SIGNIFICANCE TESTS TOO WEAK

In a posteriori analyses, the investigator can do all of the following things, any of which violates the assumptions behind the test of significance described above:

(a) He can modify in the light of the data whatever a priori hypothesis he had; if he develops an hypothesis *on the basis of* relations found in the data, then it is clearly foolish to turn around and test this hypothesis by testing the "statistical independence" of those same relations.

(b) If he is blessed with an abundance of data, some of which are substitutable for others, he can select those data which confirm his hypothesis that a relationship exists. It is easy to see how this might occur: tests of independence in contingency tables allow some such statement as "Less than five times out of a hundred would such a relationship have occurred by chance." If the investigator looks at a hundred tables, by chance alone he will find about five which show "significance at the 5% level." We have admittedly selected and discarded from many tables, just as have almost all analysts of interview material; and the rationale for such action is by no means naive. Social researchers usually begin with a plethora of hypotheses and half-formed ideas. The selection and discarding of tables is at the same time a selection and discarding from among this wealth of vague ideas. It is in this way that a consistent analysis develops from a mass of mutually contradictory or confused notions. At the same time some data must be discarded because measurement is bad. Errors of measurement tend to obscure relationships; and partly because of this, investigators often accept the table which shows a relationship and discard another bearing on the same hypothesis if it fails to show one.

(c) An added freedom is allowed the investigator in using data which must be "collapsed" in the contingency tables (such as the liberal-conservative scale or the ideological-sensitivity scale in this analysis). These scales may be collapsed at points advantageous to the hypothesis, rather than at others. If the collapsing of such scales is not done independently of the relationship being investigated, significance may be found spuriously. In both these scales we have collapsed independently of the hypothesized relations (on the basis of the numbers in each category after collapsing), but at other places we may have collapsed answer categories so as to make differences appear as large as possible.

2. FACTORS WHICH TEND TO MAKE THE TESTS TOO STRONG

On the other side of the fence, ordinary tests of significance of a single contingency table would be too strong on the following grounds.

(a) Tests of significance of a single contingency table assume isolated hypotheses, each to be confirmed or disconfirmed by the single table, and each independent of the others. But it is one of the essential characteristics of the present study that the hypotheses *are* related, and that a given table acts not to confirm a single hypothesis, but a whole network. Conversely, a given hypothesis is confirmed not by a single table, but by many. Clearly, then, what should be tested is the significance of the total set of interlocking tables (and by inference, the interlocking causal relations). This would be simple if the data for each table were independently gathered: the *product* of the probabilities that each table had occurred by chance would be the probability that the set had occurred by chance. This would mean that less restrictive restrictions could be placed on each table. For example, a set of four such interlocking tables would show a statistically significant relation at the 1% level if each were significant at about the 30% level, which is a remarkable lack of restriction.

But things are not so simple. In the present analysis, as in most like it which are reasonably complex, the data were not collected independently, but are from the same sample, and there is no tight interlocking of hypothesized relations. Though there is an attempt at such interlocking, there is still much looseness in the set of hypothesized relations. The system of relations would not collapse if one empirical result were taken away. There is some interlocking between tables, and some independence between measures used in different tables, but it is impossible to say just how much.

3. WHY THE TESTS MAY BE IRRELEVANT

Finally, it is not clear that tests such as this are even relevant to a study such as the present one, for the following reasons.

(a) This study, like many in social science, is an exploratory study, not a confirmatory one, while statistical tests of hypotheses are designed for confirmation. χ^2 tests of independence are designed to confirm and consolidate what is already believed to be true. A study like the present one is designed to find out what was not even guessed at before. That this new knowledge is not fully confirmed is no great cause for concern. Further studies upon different organizations will constitute more reliable confirmation, for they test the hypotheses in a different population, which a χ^2 test used on this data could never do. It is probably better to place one's faith in further studies to confirm hypothesized relationships than to place it in χ^2 tests. Even if all the assumptions for such tests are fulfilled, the population to which the result is to be generalized is not the population from which the sample was taken. It is a theoretical population, of all men in certain kinds of organizations. To replicate the study in another organization would confirm the result under quite different conditions, and this would seem of more value than the assurance offered by the usual χ^2 test. This is the method through which the natural sciences have made most of their remarkable advances, and there is no indication that many of these advances would have come earlier if modern statistical inference had been used instead.[7]

---

7. For example, a careful reading of W. P. D. Wightman's *The Growth of*

(b) It is useful to ask again just what is being tested by a x^2 test. This test shows whether a relationship between two measurements could have been due to chance. Often, however, these measures are simply crude indicators of the variables which it is desired to test. For example, to show that ideologically sensitive men are more active politically, we use as an indicator the amount of talk about politics reported by the men. This is only a crude indicator of political activity and might easily fail to show the relationship if one actually exists. Thus, because the variables being related hypothetically are seldom the same as the measures being related empirically, a test of independence appears irrelevant.

(c) It is important to ask whether we really want to test the existence or nonexistence of a relation. Suppose a relation is extremely weak: Is such a relation of interest? Probably not, in most cases; yet a large enough sample would find such a relation to be significantly different from chance. On the other hand, an extremely strong relationship would be found not significantly different from chance if the sample were very small.

It is probably true that we are ordinarily interested in knowing two things: whether a relation could have been produced by chance, and how strong the relation is. But probably the latter is more important to most investigators. To know this, tests of significance are not necessary; correlation coefficients or some other measures of association are.[8] Thus there seems more reason to compute the latter than the former.

(d) Finally, it is important to question whether it is the *statistical* relationship one should be concerned with testing. In the development of a science, it is causal relations which are sought after, and statistical relations are only a bad reflection of this. If two variables are both affected by a third, this can produce a statistical relation between the two where no causal relation exists at all. Thus it appears that a statistical test of the hypothesis might not be as useful as other means of testing whether a statistical relation represents a causal one. Such means are ordinarily nonstatistical, and rather of this sort: "If it is true that a variation in X causes a variation in Y (as the existence of a statistical relation between X and Y might suggest), then it should also be true that a variation in X causes a variation in Z." Through such means, followed by tests of the $X - Z$ relation, the existence of a causal relation between X and Y may be more and more confirmed, without bothering to see if the statistical relation is significantly different from chance.

There is no intention here of suggesting that statistical inference is gen-

---

Scientific Ideas (New Haven, Yale University Press, 1953), which charts the course of scientific discoveries from early times, failed to show more than one or two possible places where statistical inference might have contributed significantly to the development of any science in its early years.

8. Oftentimes $x2$-type measures have been used to measure the size of a relationship; the size of a $x2$ value in a contingency table is thus some measure of the degree of association. But it is only a crude one and would be better replaced by a measure designed for the purpose. For a review of tests of association in contingency tables, see Leo Goodman and William H. Kruskal: "Measures of Association for Cross Classifications," *Jour. Amer. Statis. Assoc.*, v. 49, 1954, pp. 732-64.

erally irrelevant in social research. It is certainly relevant for descriptive studies, to attach some measure of precision to statements made about a population on the basis of measuring a sample.

Statistical tests of hypotheses, however, seem to be of quite limited aid in building theoretical social science. As tests in certain experimental situations, to determine the effect or noneffect of an experimentally-introduced condition, they are of aid. But in testing hypotheses in field researches, they appear to be of questionable value, for the reasons given above. Since we are not really interested in statistical relationships anyway, but in causal relationships, it appears to be of much more value to test whether a statistical relationship ("significant" or not) represents a causal relation, or merely covariation between two variables. Such tests are made not by statistical tests of hypotheses, but by examining further hypotheses which would be true if the relation is a causal one, false if it is not. To devise and examine empirically such hypotheses seems a much more reasonable way of building a theoretical structure than to test the original hypothesis with a χ^2 test, however well the assumptions for such a test may be fulfilled.

§ C. Specific Problems

SAMPLE DESIGN

The primary source of data in this study was a random sample selected from the population of working New York printers (see Appendix II for interview schedule). This random sample was supplemented by sixty-six interviews with chapel chairmen, to make a total of five hundred interviews. These interviews were about an hour and a quarter to an hour and a half in length, and were conducted in the shop (sometimes during working hours, sometimes before or after) or at the printer's home. They were administered during the months of December 1951 and January 1952. Union cooperation was gained in opening the chapel roster lists for sample selection, and in presentation of the purpose of the study at a union meeting. No active participation of union or management was requested.

The sample was a two-stage stratified random sample, in which first shops were selected, then men within shops. Shops were stratified into three size groups, those from 3 to 20 men, those with 21 to 99 men, and those of 100 or more. Of the last group, all chapels were selected, of the intermediate size group a ⅓ random sample was selected, and of the one- and two-man shops, a ⅙ random sample was selected. Within the large shops, a 1/18 random sample of men was selected, within the 21-99 shops, a ⅙ random sample of men was selected, and within the 3-20 men shops a ⅓ random sample of men. For those who, through refusals, retirement, sickness, or transferral to another shop, could not be interviewed, alternates from the same shop were randomly selected and interviewed. In summary, the sample was selected as follows:

POPULATION: Active members of New York Typographical Union Number Six in shops of three or more men.

TYPE OF SAMPLE: Two-stage, first stage stratified random, second stage random.

STAGE I: Stratified by shop size, three levels:

3-20 Men	21-99 Men	100+ Men
⅙ sample of shops	⅓ sample of shops	Every shop

STAGE II: ⅓ sample of men   ⅙ sample of men   1/18 sample of men

The sample was roughly self-weighting, that is, the proportion of respondents within each shop size category approximated the proportion within the union as a whole.

A mail questionnaire was also administered to the 500 members of the sample in June 1952, shortly after the 1952 ITU presidential election. (See Appendix II, pages 448-49, for questionnaire schedule.) Three mailings elicited a 74% response (369 men of the 500, 317 of the 434-man random sample).

INDICES

The following indices used in the text were constructed from the interview questions.

1. *Liberal-Conservative Index*

ITEMS: Q. 55   Which do you think is doing more to promote labor's interests, the AFL or the CIO? (Dichotomized: "AFL" coded 0, all other responses +1)

Q. 80 (a)   I'd like your opinion of the following statements. Do you agree or disagree that immigration to the United States should be further restricted? ("Agree" coded 0. "Disagree" or "Don't know" coded +1)

Q. 80 (c)   I'd like your opinion of the following statements. Do you agree or disagree that monopoly industries should be owned by the government? ("Disagree" coded 0, "Agree" or "Don't know" coded +1)

Q. 80 (d)   I'd like your opinion of the following statements. Do you agree or disagree that the charges that there are many Communists in the government are true? ("Agree" coded 0, "Disagree" or "Don't know" coded +1)

Q. 80 (i)   I'd like your opinion of the following statements. Do you agree or disagree that with a few exceptions, most Americans have an equal opportunity to make their way in life? ("Agree" coded 0, "Disagree" or "Don't know" coded +1)

Distribution

CODE: 1. All those with score of +5   37
      2. All those with score of +4   45
      3. All those with score of +3   104
      4. All those with score of +2   133
      5. All those with score of +1   117
      6. All those with score of   o   64
                                          500

This index was ordinarily trichotomized between "Liberal" (1-3), "Moderate" (4) and "Conservative" (5,6)). Often, only the two extreme groups were used in the analysis. Whenever a category was termed "liberal" or "conservative," it included those men (1-3) or (5,6) respectively. In a few tables, the scale was used in extended form, each of the six categories separated.

2. Index of Ideological Sensitivity

This is the one index constructed of responses to open-ended questions. Since these were questions generally relating to one's approach to ITU politics, the index is a measure of saliency or sensitivity. Because of the coding of the index, it measures the saliency of ideological matters, along a liberal-conservative dimension. It is intermediate between the usual type of index constructed and a projective test, for it asks the respondent to tell what he sees in an ambiguous situation, that is, union politics.

ITEMS: Q. 29 (a) (If no shift in vote) Why did you vote for N—— in this last (local) election?

          (b) (If shift in vote) Why did you change your mind? (Responses which mentioned liberalism, conservatism, or party as basis for choice were coded +2; those which mentioned specific issues—mostly wage scale—or the nature of the campaign were coded +1; all others—mostly personality reasons—were coded o.)

   Q. 32 (a) (If no shift in vote intention) Why do you plan to vote (internationally) for him?

          (b) (If shift in vote intention) What made you change from M—— to N——? (Responses were coded as for Q. 29, except that specific issues, which were more related to ideology in the international election, were coded +2 instead of +1)

   Q. 38 (a) What do you think are the major campaign issues between the Progressives and the Independents? That is, what do you think the two parties are in disagreement about, on the *international* level? (Coded as for Q. 32)

          (b) Q. 38 (a) but ending, "on the *local* level?" (Coded as for Q. 29, except that one issues, that of Communism, was coded +2 instead of +1 as were the other, non-ideological issues)

	Distribution
CODE: 1. All those with score of +8	25
2. All those with score of +7	18
3. All those with score of +6	38
4. All those with score of +5	34
5. All those with score of +4	70
6. All those with score of +3	81
7. All those with score of +2	103
8. All those with score of +1	76
9. All those with score of 0	55
	500

This index was usually trichotomized in the analysis, with high as 1-4, medium as 5-7, and low as 8,9. In a few tables, the index was dichotomized, between high (1-5) and low (6-9).

3. Index of Knowledge of Union Political Issues

ITEMS: Q. 54 (b) Would you have any idea what positions each of the two major parties takes on the question of signing the non-Communist affidavit? (Coded +1 for correct knowledge of Progressive position and +1 for correct knowledge of Independent position)

Q. 53 (a) Have you heard anything about the ITU going into the newspaper business?

(c) (If answer is yes) Could you tell me whether the Progressive party is in favor of or against union ownership of newspapers? (Coded +1 for correct knowledge of Progressive position on newspaper ownership)

(d) (If answer is yes) How about the Independents—are they for or against union ownership of newspapers? (Coded +1 for correct knowledge of Independent position on newspaper ownership)

	Distribution
CODE: 1. All those with score of +4	55
2. All those with score of +3	55
3. All those with score of +2	87
4. All those with score of +1	108
5. All those with score of 0	195
	500

This index was ordinarily trichotomized between high (1,2), medium (3,4), and low (5) knowledge. In other cases it was dichotomized between high (1-3) and low (4,5).

4. *Index of Participation in Printers' Formal Social Organizations*

ITEMS: Q. 67 (a) Have you *ever* participated in any union clubs, benefit
societies, teams, or organizations composed mostly of
printers? What about the:
  (1) Benefit societies?
  (2) VFW Big Six Post?
  (3) Bronx or Brooklyn Typo Club?
  (4) Printers' bowling organizations?
  (5) Other printers' sports groups?
(For each mentioned)
  (b) When did you first join?
  (c) Do you still belong?
  (b) (If answer is no) When did you stop?
  (e) Do you attend meetings regularly, occasionally, or seldom?
  (f) Do you consider yourself very active, moderately active,
or quite inactive?
  (g) Have you ever held office in the group?
  (Coded for *present membership, number* of organizations, *meeting attendance,* and *activity*: coded +1 through
+5)

Q. 68 (a) Have you ever attended any printers' social affairs?
  (b) (If answer is yes) In the last five years?
  (c) Which ones?
  (Coded +½ if respondent attended any printers' social
affair within the last five years)

	Distribution
CODE: 1. All those with a score of +5 or 5½	23
2. All those with a score of +4 or 4½	28
3. All those with a score of +3 or 3½	28
4. All those with a score of +2 or 2½	30
5. All those with a score of +1 or 1½	33
6. All those with a score of +½ (attended social affairs only)	30
7. All those with a score of 0 (nonparticipant)	254
8. No answer to either question	24
	500

This index was divided between club members (1-5) and non-club-
members (6,7), or between active club members (1-3), inactive members
(4,5), those who attended social affairs (6) and nonparticipants (7).

5. Social Relations Index

ITEMS: Q. 58 (a) Now, think of all the places where you're likely to see other printers off the job. How often would you say you spend time with other printers off the job?
(1) Never?
(2) Less than once a month?
(3) Once or twice a month?
(4) Once or twice a week?
(5) Nearly every day?
(Dichotomized between "once or twice a week," coded +1, and "once or twice a month," coded 0)

Q. 57 (a) Do you ever visit any other printers at their homes or do any printers ever come to your home?
(b) (If answer is yes) Very often, occasionally, or rarely?
(Dichotomized between "occasionally," coded +1, and "rarely," coded 0)

Q. 60 (b) With whom *do* you actually spend more of your free time—other printers or those outside the trade?
(Dichotomized between "those outside of trade," coded 0, and "equally with both groups," coded +1)

Q. 64 (a) Would you think of your three closest friends—it doesn't matter whether or not they are printers. Now, just tell me their first names so we don't get them mixed up.
(b) (Asked for each friend) What is his occupation?
(Dichotomized between no printers among three best friends and at least one printer among three best friends)

		Distribution
CODE:	1. All those with score of +4	40
	2. All those with score of +3	83
	3. All those with score of +2	149
	4. All those with score of +1	131
	5. All those with score of 0	68
	6. No answer on any of four questions	29
		500

This index was either dichotomized between (1-3) and (4,5), that is, high and low in social relations; or trichotomized (1,2), (3), and (4,5), that is, high, medium, and low.

6. Index of Participation (or Activity) in Union Politics

ITEMS: Q. 41 Are you a member of either of the political parties in the union at the present time?

Q. 46 (a) Have you worked for the election of any candidate in the last two local elections?

Q. 47 (a) Have you contributed to the campaign funds of any candidate or party in the last five years?

		Distribution
CODE:	1. Positive response to all 3 questions	22
	2. Positive response to any 2 of 3 questions	66
	3. Positive response to any 1 of 3 questions	95
	4. Negative response to all 3 questions	313
	5. Failed to answer any of the 3 questions	4
		500

This index was dichotomized between 1-3 and 4; all those coded 5 were discarded. Those coded 1-3 were called active, and those coded 4 inactive.

Interview Schedule

1 In what year did you first enter the printing trade?
2 (a) Do you have a *steady* situation at the present time?
  (b) When was the last time (before *this* job) you had a situation that lasted a year or more?
  (c) (If not unemployed) When did you start working in your present shop?
3 What is (was) your primary job here (there)?
4 (a) Are you on the day, night, or lobster shift at the present time (or last job)?
  (b) When was the last time you were on the (other) shift?
  (c) In all the time you have worked in the trade, how many years have you worked on a night or lobster shift?
  (d) Which do you prefer, day or night work? Why?
5 How many different steady situations have you had since 1940?
6 (a) During the past six months, about how many days were you without any work?
  (b) In all the time you've been working, what was the longest period during which you did not have a steady situation?
7 (a) All things considered, how do you like printing as an occupation?
    Do you dislike it?
    Are you indifferent?
    Do you like it fairly well?
    Do you like it very much?
  (b) Why do you feel this way?
8 (a) Is there any occupation you would like to have other than the one you now have—either in or outside the printing trade? (If so) Which one?
9 Let's look at it another way: If you were starting all over again, what occupation would you want to get into?
10 (a) How would you rate printing as an occupation? For example:
    (1) Would you rate the *pay* as excellent, good, fair, or poor?

(2) How about *job security* in the printing trade? Would you rate it as excellent, good, fair, or poor?

(3) How about the *prestige* printing receives from people outside the trade?

11 (a) Have you ever been a foreman?

(b) Which of the following statements comes closest to your attitude about becoming a foreman?
(1) I should like to become a foreman (again).
(2) I should like to become a foreman (again) but I don't care too much one way or the other.
(3) I don't want to be a foreman (again).

(c) Would you rather be a foreman or a union officer?

12 (a) Have you ever owned your own shop?

(b) (If yes) Do you own a shop now?

(c) Would you like to own your own shop (again)?

(d) Do you think most printers would like to own their own shops?

13 (a) When did you become a member of the ITU?

(b) When did you become a member of Big Six?

14 (a) How would you rate the ITU compared with other unions? Would you say that the ITU is:
(1) The best?
(2) Better than most?
(3) About the same?
(4) Not as good as most?

(b) (If not best) Do you know any unions which are better than the ITU? Which?

(c) (Asked of all) In what way? (What do you like most about the ITU? Is there anything about the union which you think can stand improving?)

15 (a) Do you think that people like you have a lot of influence on how the union runs things, some influence, or not much influence?

(b) Why do you think that's so?

16 (a) Do you think that ITU leaders generally are more interested in gaining power for themselves, or in furthering the welfare of the union?

(b) (If both) For which most?

(c) Which do you think is better *in general*: to trust the men you elect or to have rules to keep them in line?

17 (a) Do you think that the ITU leaders are a different type of men from the general run of leaders in public affairs and politics?

(b) (If yes) In what way?

18 (a) Do you happen to know whether there is any limit to the number of consecutive terms the president of Big Six can hold office? How many?

(b) Do you think that a two term limit for the president is (would be) a good thing for Big Six?

(c) Why (not)?

19 (a) Do you happen to know whether there is any limit to the number of consecutive terms the president of the international union can hold office? How many?

   (b) Do you think that a two-term limit for the president is (would be) a good thing for the international union?

   (c) (If there is a difference between 18b and 19b) Why do you feel differently about Big Six and the international?

20 If a man would like to become a union leader, how would he go about it?

21 (a) Do you happen to know what salary the *Big Six* president gets?

   (b) What salary do you think would be about right for that job?

22 The president of the international is now getting about $250 a week. Would you vote for or against a referendum to increase his salary to about $300 a week—that is, from $13,000 to about $15,000?

23 (a) During the last year did you attend any union meetings?

   (b) (If yes) How many?

24 (a) Have you ever held any *chapel* office?

   (b) (If yes) Which?

   (c) When was the last time you held a chapel office?

   (d) Did someone run against you for that office?

   (e) How many men were there in that chapel?

   (f) (If respondent *never* held chapel office) Have you ever *run* for chapel office?

   (g) (If yes) When?

25 Would you like to be a chapel chairman (again)?

26 (a) Have you ever held any *union* office or served on a union committee?

   (b) (If yes) Which?

   (c) When was the last time you held such a position?

   (d) With party backing? Which?

   (e) (If no) Have you ever run for any *union* office?

   (f) (If yes) Which?

   (g) With party backing? Which?

27 (a) Did you vote in the last New York union election, in May?

   (b) (If yes) Would you mind telling me for whom you voted for president?

   (c) For whom did you vote for vice-president?

28 (a) Did you vote in the *1949* New York union election?

   (b) (If yes) For whom did you vote for president?

29 (a) (If no shift in vote) Why did you vote for N—— in this last election?

   (b) (If shift in vote) Why did you change your mind?

30 (a) Did you vote for president of the international union in 1950?

   (b) (If yes) For whom did you vote for president?

   (c) (If either Randolph or Sparkman is mentioned) By the way, could you tell me who the opposition candidate was?

31 If Randolph and Sparkman run again for president of the ITU in 1952, for whom do you think you would vote?

32 (a) (If no shift between Questions 30 and 31) Why do you plan to vote for him?

    (b) (If shift in voting intention) What has made you change from M—— to N——?

33 (a) Do you happen to know which party is in power now, nationally?

    (b) Do you know which party is in power now, locally?

    (c) (If "Don't know" to *both*) What are the names of the two political parties in the ITU?

       (if respondent knows neither name, skip to Question 41)

34 (a) On the whole, have most of your votes in international elections been cast for one party?

    (b) (If yes) Which?

35 (a) Which party do you favor *now, internationally?*

    (b) Why do you favor that party?

36 (a) Which party do you favor *now, locally?*

    (b) Why do you favor that party?

    (c) (If response to 35a and 36a are not the same) Can you tell me how it is that you favor the Progressives (or Independents) internationally and the Progressives (or Independents) locally?

37 When you voted for the Executive Committee in the last New York elections did all the candidates you voted for belong to one party?

38 What do you think are the major campaign issues between the Progressives and the Independents? That is, what do you think the two parties are in disagreement about:

    (a) On the *international* level?

    (b) On the *local* level?

39 Some people say that candidates without party backing tend to confuse the election issues. What do you think about that?

40 (a) Do you know personally anyone who is an *active* Progressive?

    (b) Do you know personally anyone who is an *active* Independent?

41 Are you a member of either of the political parties in the union at the present time?

42 (a) (If yes to Question 41) Of which party are you now a member?

    (b) When did you join?

    (c) Have you attended any party meetings within the last year?

    (d) (If yes) Frequently, occasionally, or seldom?

    (e) Have you ever belonged to any other political party in the Union?

    (f) (If yes) Which?

43 (a) (If no to Question 41) Have you ever in the past belonged to any political party in the ITU?

    (b) (If yes) Which one(s)?

    (c) Were you working at a different place then?

    (d) How long were you a member of the party?

    (e) When did you leave the party?

    (f) Why did you leave the party?

44 (a) Was there any period in the past in which you were more interested in union politics than you are now?

    (b) (If yes) When was that?

    (c) Why were you more interested then?

45 (a) Is there any person among the people you know (well enough to speak to) whose opinions about union affairs you most respect? Who is he?

    (b) How well do you know him—very well, fairly well, or is he only an acquaintance?

    (c) Does he work in your shop?

    (d) Does he favor either party in the union? Which?

    (e) Is he or has he ever been active in union politics?

    (f) Do you talk to him about union affairs?

    (g) (If yes) Very often, occasionally, or rarely?

    (h) Do you think he also has reliable opinions on United States *national* politics?

    (i) Do you talk to him about national politics?

    (j) (If yes) Very often, occasionally, or rarely?

46 (a) Have you worked for the election of any candidate in the last two local elections?

    (b) (If yes) To which party did he belong?

47 (a) Have you contributed to the campaign funds of any candidate or party in the last five years?

    (b) (If yes) Which?

48 Which would you say are more important, chapel meetings or union meetings?

49 (a) Do you think that chapel chairmen are influential in affecting the way their chapels vote in union elections?

    (b) Do you discuss union politics with your chapel chairman? (If respondent *is* a chapel chairman, ask: Do you discuss union politics with the men in your chapel?)

50 Do you happen to know for what party most of the members in your chapel voted in the last Big Six presidential election?

51 Do you happen to know whom your chapel chairman supported in the May election for Big Six president?

52 Do you think the union would be better off if both parties were dissolved and elections were held on a nonparty basis?

53 (a) Have you heard anything about the ITU going into the newspaper business?

    (b) (If yes) Could you tell me how many papers it owns?

    (c) Could you tell me whether the Progressive Party is in favor of or against union ownership of newspapers?

    (d) How about the Independents—are they for or against union ownership of newspapers?

54 (a) Can you tell me whether or not the ITU officers have signed the non-Communist affidavit required by the Taft-Hartley Act?

(b) Would you have any idea what positions each of the two major parties take on the question of signing the non-Communist affidavit?

(c) How do you feel about it?

55 Which do you think is doing more to promote labor's interests, the AFL or the CIO?

56 (a) Do you think that the Pressmen's Union is as good as the ITU or isn't as good?

(b) In what ways?

(c) Do you think that the prestige of the pressmen's job is as high as that of the compositors?

57 (a) Do you ever visit any other printers at their homes, or do any printers ever come to your home?

(b) (If yes) Very often, occasionally, or rarely?

58 (a) Now, think of all the places where you're likely to see other printers off the job. How often would you say you spend time with other printers off the job?

(1) Never?

(2) Less than once a month?

(3) Once or twice a month?

(4) Once or twice a week?

(5) Nearly every day?

(If "never," skip to Question 61)

(b) Are they men you work with?

(c) Where do you generally get together?

(d) Do you usually see or get together with the same group of men?

(e) (If yes) How many are there in your group?

59 (If respondent has worked both day and night shifts) Do you spend more time with other printers off the job when you work *days* or when you work *nights*?

60 Do most of the other printers you are friendly with off the job vote the same way you do in union elections?

61 When you and your friends discuss union political questions, which of these comes closest to your part in the discussion?

(1) I usually just listen.

(2) I listen a lot, but once in a while I express an opinion.

(3) I take an equal part in the conversation.

(4) I try to convince the others.

(5) Don't know.

(6) Do not discuss union political questions.

62 During union election campaigns, do you talk about union affairs with your printer friends much, little, or never?

63 Do you like your leisure time better than work?

64 (a) Would you think of your three closest friends—it doesn't matter

whether or not they are printers. Now, just tell me their first names so we don't get them mixed up.

(b) (Asked for each friend) What is his occupation?

(c) (If two printers are not mentioned) Who are the two members of ITU you're most friendly with? (First names)

65 (a) How friendly are you with A (first printer mentioned)? Is he a close friend, fairly friendly, or only an acquaintance?

(b) Has he worked in the same shop as you in the last year?

(c) Have you seen him off the job in the last two months?

(d) (If yes) Very often, occasionally, or only once or twice?

(e) Where? (Probe.)

(f) Do you happen to know for whom he voted for president in the last Big Six election?

(g) (If yes) For whom?

(h) Does he generally favor the Progressive (or Independent) Party?

(i) (If yes) How active would you say he is in support of that party—very active, fairly active, or not active?

(j) (If no to f) Do you happen to know whether he favors either party? Which?

66 (a) How friendly are you with B (second printer mentioned)? Is he a close friend, fairly friendly, or only an acquaintance?

(b) Has he worked in the same shop as you in the last year?

(c) Have you seen him off the job in the last two months?

(d) (If yes) Very often, occasionally, or only once or twice?

(e) Where? (Probe.)

(f) Do you happen to know for whom he voted for president in the last Big Six election?

(g) (If yes) for whom?

(h) Does he generally favor the Progressive (or Independent) party?

(i) (If yes) How active would you say he is in support of that party—very active, fairly active, or not active?

(j) (If no to f) Do you happen to know whether he favors either party? Which?

67 (a) Have you *ever* participated in any union clubs, benefit societies, teams, or organizations composed mostly of printers? What about the:

(1) Benefit societies?

(2) VFW Big Six Post?

(3) Bronx or Brooklyn Typo Club?

(4) Printers' bowling organizations?

(5) Other printers' sports groups?

(For each mentioned)

(b) When did you first join?

(c) Do you still belong?

(d) (If no) When did you stop?

(e) Do you attend meetings regularly, occasionally, or very seldom?

(f) Do you consider yourself very active, moderately active or quite inactive?

(g) Have you ever held office in the group?

68 (a) Have you ever attended any printers' social affairs?

(b) (If yes) In the last five years?

(c) Which ones?

69 (a) If you had your choice, would you *rather* spend your free time with other printers or with people who are not in the trade?

(b) With whom *do* you actually spend more of your free time—other printers or those outside the trade?

70 When you talk with your friends who are not printers, do you ever talk about printing or union affairs?

71 (a) Do you belong to any organizations *outside* the union—for example, clubs, lodges, veterans, sports, or church groups, whose members are mostly *not* printers?

(b) (If yes) Which?

(c) About how many meetings of such groups have you attended altogether during the last three months?

72 Outside of working hours, do you enjoy being with other people a good deal of the time, occasionally, or rarely (aside from your family, of course)?

73 Did you vote in the general election for city council president this November?

74 (a) Are you a registered member of any party? Which?

(b) (If of none) Which party do you generally support?

75 When you and your friends discuss national political questions, which of these comes closest to your part in the discussion?

(1) I usually just listen.

(2) I listen a lot, but once in a while I express my opinion.

(3) I take an equal part in the conversation.

(4) I try to convince the others.

(5) Don't know.

76 (a) Did you vote in the last election for New York State governor?

(b) (If yes) Did you vote for Dewey, Lynch, or someone else?

77 Suppose that in the 1952 elections Eisenhower and Truman were opposing candidates, for whom would you vote?

78 (a) On the whole, how interested would you say you are in United States presidential politics—extremely interested, quite interested, moderately, or not much interested?

(b) How about New York City politics—would you say you are extremely, quite, moderately, or not much interested?

(c) How about union politics?

(d) Which one are you *most* interested in?

(e) Do you get more worked up about something that happens in national politics and public affairs or about something that happens in union politics?

79 Which of these would come closest to your own feelings about the Taft-Hartley Act?
    (1) It is basically a bad law.
    (2) It is a good law but has some bad features.
    (3) It is basically a good law.

80 I'd like your opinion on the following statements. Do you agree or disagree?
    (a) Immigration to the United States should be further restricted.
    (b) The union movement should have its own third party.
    (c) Monopoly industry should be owned by the government.
    (d) The charges that there are many Communists in the government are true.
    (e) In general, the courts treat labor and business equally.
    (f) Most politicians are corrupt.
    (g) I would never cross a picket line regardless of what union was involved.
    (h) Any increase in taxes should come mostly from business.
    (i) With a few exceptions, most Americans have an equal opportunity to make their way in life.

81 (a) Do you think that most printers read the *Typographical Journal?*
    (b) Have you read it within the last two months?
    (c) (If yes) What parts of the *Journal* are you the most likely to read?

82 Have you read any newspapers within the last two days? Which?

83 (a) Have you read any magazines in the last month?
    (b) (If yes) Which?

84 (a) Have you read any books in the last month?
    (b) (If yes) Which?

85 What social class do you believe yourself to be in—the upper, middle, working, or lower class?

86 Are you:
    (1) Single?
    (2) Married?
    (3) Widowed?
    (4) Separated or divorced?

87 (If married) How well does your wife know the wives of any other men in the trade—very well, fairly well, only slightly, or not at all?

88 What was the last school you attended? What is the last grade you completed there?

89 Now there are just a few more questions and we'll be through. How old are you (last birthday)?

90 (a) How many children do you have? What is his (their) occupations (if grown)?
    (b) (If male children) What would you like (have liked) to see your son(s) do for a living?

91 (a) What was your father's principal occupation?
    (b) Do you have any relatives in the printing trade?

(c) (If yes) Who?

92 (a) In what country was your father born?

(b) In what country were you born?

93 (a) Do you attend church regularly?

(b) Would you mind telling me your religion? (If none, ask father's religion.)

To be filled in by interviewer:

Race?

Chapel?

Book-and-job or newspaper?

Home address:

Home telephone:

Respondent's name:

Interviewer's name:

MAIL QUESTIONNAIRE

1 When did you become a member of the ITU?

2 Did you happen to attend the local nomination meeting for the ITU candidate in February?

3 Did you attend one or both of the two local union meetings held in April?

4 How long does it take you to travel from your home to the union meeting hall at Stuyvesant High?

5 Did you attend the Big Six Hospitalization Ball in February of this year?

6. On the whole, how interested would you say you are in union politics—extremely interested, quite interested, moderately interested, or not much interested?

7 Do you get more worked up about something that happens in national politics or about something that happens in union politics?

8 During this past union election campaign, did you talk about union affairs with your printer friends much, little, or never?

9 What in your opinion was the most important single issue of the recent campaign for ITU office?

10 How do you feel about this issue?

11 Would you have any idea what positions each of the two major union parties takes on the question of signing the non-Communist affidavit required by the Taft-Hartley Act?

12 How do you feel about it?

13 Which of these would come closest to your own feelings about the Taft-Hartley Act?

It is basically a bad law.

It is a good law but has some bad features.

It is basically a good law.

14 Did you vote in the recent election of ITU officers in May?

15 For whom did you vote for ITU president, Randolph or Sparkman?

16 For whom did you vote for ITU secretary-treasurer, Hurd or Bante?

17 Did you vote in the election of ITU officers in 1950?

18 Do you remember for whom you voted for president in that election (1950)?
Randolph
Sparkman
Don't remember or didn't vote

19 Did you vote in the Big Six local election in May 1951?

20 Do you remember for whom you voted for Big Six president in that election?
Barrett
Victory
Don't remember or didn't vote

21 If there were an election for Big Six president right now and the same candidates were running, for whom would you vote?
Barrett
Victory
Don't know

22 With regard to the national elections to be held next November, whom do you now favor for President?

Eisenhower	Truman
Taft	Other (write in)
Warren	
Harriman	
Kefauver	
Stevenson	

23 For whom did you vote in the Presidential election of 1948?

Truman	Thomas
Dewey	Did not vote
Wallace	

Name Index

General Index

Administration Party (*see* Wahnetas), 36, 40-49, 61, 285, 286, 287-89, 292, 293, 296, 298-99, 306, 377, 379, 381, 385, 398
Age of printers, 90-92, 285, 328-29, 331
Alimoners, 33, 280, 306, 313
Amalgamated Clothing Workers, 132, 409
Amalgamation Party, 62, 207, 301-2, 306
American Federation of Labor, 7, 30, 50-51, 59, 202, 259, 290, 291, 307, 312, 313, 410
AFL and CIO fight in ITU, 50-51, 54, 290-91, 307
American Labor Party, 101, 313
American Legion, 12, 81, 412
American Medical Association, 12, 274, 412
American Newspaper Guild, 20, 30, 307
Anarchism, 8
Anti-Administration Party, 42-43, 44, 61
Apprentices, 30-34, 134-35, 323
Arbitration, 42, 43, 44, 53, 288, 306, 313
Association of Catholic Trade Unionists, 104, 221, 231
Autonomy of subgroups, 15, 79-80, 104, 254
  of locals, 18, 21, 47, 365-67, 372-74, 377, 398, 400, 414
  of shops, 181, 208
  of leaders, 213-18, 230, 255

Brotherhood (of Printers of North America, 35-38, 282-83, 284
Building trades, 132
Business unionism, 406-7

Catholic Church, 14, 79, 231, 232, 314
Caxton League, 40
Centralization, 19-20, 21, 49, 50, 146, 393, 395, 400, 414
Chapel, 64, 71-72, 78, 139, 144-97, 203, 221-27, 234, 267, 317, 339-42
Chapel chairmen, 25, 64, 101, 144-50, 176-87, 203-4, 221-27, 234
  —and voting, 339-40

Civil politics, 4, 12, 63, 74, 98, 273, 292, 294, 295, 302, 309-13, 315, 316, 329-31, 335-36, 351, 362, 386
Communism, 11, 66, 78, 132, 231, 232, 239, 248, 249, 309, 402, 405, 407, 409
Communists in ITU, 61-62, 207-8, 248, 301-3, 306, 313, 317, 319, 331, 382
Congress of Industrial Organizations, 7, 50-51, 66, 232, 290-91, 307, 313, 411
Conservative Party of the ITU, 49, 287, 289, 292, 299
Cooptation, 8, 401

Democratic Party, 4, 63, 311-14, 329-31
Deviant case analysis, x, 12-13, 418

Election of officers, 39-41, 43-47, 49, 52, 364-90,
  in New York local, 62-65, 220, 338-63
Election statistics, 46

Family life of printers, 138, 321-23
Farm Bureau, 274
Featherbedding, 22, 52
Foreign policy issues, 12, 307-8
Foremen, 23, 25, 37, 38, 39, 40, 134, 139, 143, 153, 158, 205, 284, 396
  Actor's Equity, 231
Friendship selection, 96-97, 102, 107-8, 110-11, 117-21, 124-26, 136, 156-63, 168-70, 171-75, 193-97, 250-52, 320, 340
  friends and voting behavior, 339-40

Group dynamics, xii

History and social science, 7, 393-400, 402

Ideological sensitivity, 92-102, 315-25, 333-37, 357-62
Independent Party, formation of, 49-50

(453)

BOOKS PUBLISHED BY

The Free Press

3,56